Historical Linguistics
Toward a Twenty-First Century Reintegration

Bringing the advances of theoretical linguistics to the study of language change in a systematic way, this innovative textbook demonstrates the mutual relevance of historical linguistics and contemporary linguistics. Numerous case studies throughout the book show both that theoretical linguistics can be used to solve problems where traditional approaches to historical linguistics have failed to produce satisfying results, and that the results of historical research can have an impact on theory. The book first explains the nature of human language and the sources of language change in broad terms. It then focuses on different types of language change from contemporary viewpoints, before exploring comparative reconstruction – the most spectacular success of traditional historical linguistics – and the problems inherent in trying to devise new methods for linguistic comparison. Positioned at the cutting edge of the field, the book argues that this approach can and should lead to the reintegration of historical linguistics as one of the core areas in the study of language.

DON RINGE is Kahn Term Professor in Linguistics in the Department of Linguistics at the University of Pennsylvania.

JOSEPH F. ESKA is Professor of Linguistics in the Department of English at Virginia Polytechnic Institute & State University.

Historical Linguistics
Toward a Twenty-First Century Reintegration

DON RINGE AND JOSEPH F. ESKA

CAMBRIDGE
UNIVERSITY PRESS

CAMBRIDGE UNIVERSITY PRESS
Cambridge, New York, Melbourne, Madrid, Cape Town,
Singapore, São Paulo, Delhi, Mexico City

Cambridge University Press
The Edinburgh Building, Cambridge CB2 8RU, UK

Published in the United States of America by Cambridge University Press, New York

www.cambridge.org
Information on this title: www.cambridge.org/9780521587112

First published 2013

A catalogue record for this publication is available from the British Library

Library of Congress Cataloguing in Publication data
Ringe, Donald A., 1954–
Historical linguistics : toward a twenty-first century reintegration / Don Ringe
and Joseph F. Eska.
  p. cm.
Includes bibliographical references and index.
ISBN 978-0-521-58332-9 (hardback)
1. Historical linguistics. 2. Linguistic change. 3. Language and languages – Variation.
I. Eska, Joseph F. II. Title.
P142.R56 2012
417′.7 – dc23   2012023182

ISBN 978-0-521-58332-9 Hardback
ISBN 978-0-521-58711-2 Paperback

in memory of Henry Hoenigswald

Contents

Figures

Tables

Preface

What this book tries to do

This book is intended for students with some prior training in linguistics. It attempts to integrate three scientific approaches to the analysis of language structure and language change: the Neogrammarian tradition of historical linguistics (especially in its mathematically rigorous codification by the late Henry Hoenigswald), the modern study of language change in progress pioneered by William Labov, and the generative tradition of linguistic theory inaugurated by Noam Chomsky and Morris Halle. In addition, we have tried to adduce some of the rapidly expanding scientific research on language acquisition, since it seems increasingly clear that most language changes arise as errors in native language learning.

Such a synthesis is long overdue. At least in North America, the generative paradigm has become overwhelmingly dominant and Labov's study of language change in progress is recognized as a major subfield of linguistics; a large majority of our colleagues at least recognize that both those lines of research have led to enormous progress, even if numerous details remain the subject of lively debate. If historical linguistics is to benefit from these advances and to offer new insights of its own, it must be reintegrated into the field as a whole. We hope that this book will take that process forward.

Methodological preliminaries: the nature of hypotheses

While any science must be based on careful observation, the mere accumulation of facts does not lead to scientific progress. Patterns of fact must be made the basis of hypotheses which, in order to be useful, must extrapolate significantly beyond the facts on which they are based; the predictions of those hypotheses are then tested against further facts and the hypotheses are either refined or discarded, the laws of logical inference being respected throughout the process. It is NOT necessary for a hypothesis to account for all the facts in hand at the time it was formulated; on the contrary, a complex hypothesis based on "messy" facts is much less likely to be testable than a simple hypothesis which accounts for many, but not all, of the known facts.

The last principle is more important than is sometimes realized. A simple illustration is provided by the regularity of sound change. In the 1870's a group of young linguists called the "Neogrammarians" realized that the *observed* regularity of sound change in a given dialect is statistically overwhelming; that led them to the hypothesis that there is a *process* of "sound change" that is *exceptionless*, and that apparent exceptions are the results of other, independent processes that have very different effects. Numerous linguists objected to the hypothesis that "sound change is regular," arguing that it was on the wrong track unless all apparent exceptions could be convincingly explained. But it became clear long ago that the regularity of sound change is a very good scientific hypothesis: large classes of known exceptions had been convincingly explained by 1900, work on sound change in progress and dialect contact has explained many more, and the residue of irregularities that are still puzzling can largely be ascribed to the fact that detailed information about speech communities of the past is almost always too poor to enable even a guess at any unusual linguistic events that might have occurred. Rejecting the hypothesis that there is a process of regular sound change isn't merely hypercautious or outdated; it's dead wrong, because it reveals a fundamental confusion about how science makes progress (see already Bloomfield 1933: 355–64).

We emphasize this because it seems clear to us that the same confusion persists to such a degree that it can be considered endemic in historical linguistics. We hope that this book, by taking theory seriously without losing sight of data, can help to correct the problem.

Authorship

Joseph Eska was responsible for the first draft of Chapter 9; Don Ringe was responsible for the first draft of the other chapters. However, we have both repeatedly read and commented on all the chapters; Eska's contributions to the first eight chapters have been especially significant.

Acknowledgments

We are grateful to Anthony Kroch for extended discussions that have greatly improved this book. We would also like to thank Eugene Buckley, George Cardona, Anna Morpurgo Davies, Ariel Diertani, Micha Elsner, David Embick, Aaron Freeman, Josef Fruehwald, Jonathan Gress-Wright, Matt Husband, Polly Jacobsen, William Labov, Yong-cheol Lee, Alexander Lehrman, Arthur Margolin, Jim Morgan, Aaron Rubin, Geoffrey Russom, Jon Stevens, Meredith Tamminga, Ann Taylor, Greg Ward, Jonathan D. Wright, and Charles Yang for help and feedback of many kinds. Thanks are also due to the students in Ringe's graduate courses in historical linguistics from 2005 to 2011, to the participants in a minicourse at Brown University in May of 2010, and to four anonymous reviewers. We owe a special debt of gratitude to Andrew Winnard, our commissioning editor, who encouraged us with great patience for many years. All errors and infelicities are, of course, our own.

Introduction

Special challenges of historical linguistics

"Historical linguistics" is the study of language change and its consequences. Simply because it is the study of change, it involves a number of difficulties with which other linguists do not have to cope, at least not to the same degree. We outline the chief difficulties here not merely to warn the incautious student about what (s)he is getting into, but also and especially to say how historical linguists deal with them and how their strategies for doing so define and shape the field.

Most obviously, we can describe a change from state A to state B only after we have described the beginning and ending states adequately; thus any historical linguist has to have at least a fair acquaintance with language structure and how to analyze it. In this book we have presupposed an elementary knowledge of phonetics, of the principle of phonemic contrast, and of generative phonology and syntax because we cannot even discuss sound change, phonological change, and syntactic change without using the basic concepts of synchronic linguistics. We assume throughout that some version of the generative paradigm is the standard model of linguistic description because that reflects our professional experience.

A further set of interlinked difficulties is imposed on us by the trajectories of language changes. Most significant changes take several generations to complete; thus any study of language change necessarily involves study of the past. Of course changes still in progress can actually be observed (as the work of William Labov and other sociolinguists has demonstrated), but most of the linguistic changes that we know anything about occurred entirely in the past, and past changes have to be inferred from their consequences as recorded in documents. We are often not able to infer much about the origins and progress of a specific change. In addition, reliance on written records limits the data at our disposal in at least the following further ways.

First of all, until the invention of electronic recording equipment, all records of language had to be written records. Even if an orthography records all the phonemic contrasts and much phonetic detail (as the Sanskrit system does, for example), it cannot record every aspect of speech that is of potential interest to the linguist, and of course nearly all orthographic systems are less adequate, often much less adequate. Thus the first challenge faced by a historical linguist using written records is to try to work out the linguistic structures partially expressed and partially concealed by the orthography, and exactly what must be done will differ markedly from one orthographic system to another. Strictly speaking that task is "salvage linguistics," not historical linguistics proper. It seems fair to say that this limitation has been overcome to a great extent by the work of earlier generations of linguists, and in this book we usually rely on their solid conclusions without further comment. Interested students can find further information in the Appendix.

A second, and much more serious, limitation is imposed by the amount of text that survives in any given language of the past. For instance, the York-Toronto-Helsinki Parsed Corpus of Old English Prose[†] contains one and a half million words of text – nearly all extant Old English prose documents – and one might suppose that that is enough to exemplify all the syntactic constructions of the language abundantly. But at least one construction is rare enough that it occurs fewer than two dozen times in the entire corpus (Speyer 2008), and there could be other, rarer ones that have not yet been noticed; if there are, it might not be possible to distinguish them from errors. The surviving corpus of Gothic is so much smaller – about 67,000 words – that we are not even able to construct complete paradigms of some of the attested lexemes, in spite of the great regularity of the language's inflectional morphology and the aid offered by several closely related languages that are better attested.

A third limitation has to do with the kinds of documents that were written and have survived to the present. Though graffiti occasionally survive even from the ancient Mediterranean world, as does at least one archive of private letters (not edited for publication, as Cicero's were), most surviving documents are in some sense "official." Most fall within a narrow, relatively elevated range of styles; much of the variation that must have been present in speech is suppressed (though more at some times and places than at others). The range of subjects is also usually restricted; for instance, most texts in the Tocharian languages deal with Buddhist philosophy and religion.

For a linguist used to working on languages still spoken, a final limitation of written documents is perhaps the most frustrating of all: there is *no negative evidence*. We have no native speakers of Classical Latin or Gothic to ask whether sentences exemplifying some particular construction are grammatical. If we find numerous examples in the relevant corpus, that amounts to being told that the construction is grammatical, but there is no real equivalent of being told that it isn't. If we find no examples of a suspect construction in the multimillion-word surviving corpus of Classical Latin, we can be reasonably sure that Caesar would have rejected it, but in the case of a language as poorly attested as Gothic many questions may remain permanently unanswerable.

[†] www-users.york.ac.uk/~lang22/YcoeHome1.htm

Meeting the challenges: the uniformitarian principle

The data of the past are so much poorer than those of the present that we can use them scientifically only by appeal to the *uniformitarian principle* (UP), as in other historical sciences. The UP holds that the processes that we see operating around us in the present must be assumed to have operated in the same ways at any given time in the past, unless we can demonstrate a discontinuity in their causes between that past time and the present (see Osthoff and Brugmann 1878, Labov 1972: 101). As it applies to linguistics, the UP can be stated as follows:

> Unless we can demonstrate a relevant alteration in the conditions of language use or language acquisition between some time in the past and the present, we must assume that the same types, range, and distribution of language structures existed and the same types of linguistic change processes operated at that past time as in the present.

Since people have undoubtedly been learning human language in the first few years of life and talking mostly to their family, friends, and acquaintances for tens of thousands of years, we can safely assume that the UP holds for as far back as we can extrapolate into prehistory (see below). Note that mass literacy and the mass media have not changed any of these fundamental conditions; that is the most basic reason why dialect diversification continues unabated, just as it always has. Widespread mobility of populations does increase language and dialect contact, but that is not a particularly modern phenomenon, as military gravestones from all over the Roman Empire testify.

Thus we can assume that all languages of the past exhibited phonemic contrasts between sounds, regardless of what their writing systems were like; that no syntactic construction of a past language violated the known constraints on natural language syntax; and so on. We can also assume that Classical Latin, for example, exhibited extensive dialect variation – geographical in the countryside, social in the city of Rome – of the sort we see everywhere around us today, even though we can see very little of it in the surviving corpus of Latin; and we can assume further that Latin sound changes worked their way through the speech community in the way familiar from Labov's research on sound change in progress.

However, there is something important we can learn from the records of the past that we cannot learn from observation of the present: we can see how language changes work out in the long term – over generations, centuries, and millennia. By far the most useful thing we learn concerns spontaneous changes in pronunciation, or "sound changes." It turns out that in any given line of linguistic "descent," defined as the process by which each new generation learns a dialect natively from older speakers with no significant breaks in transmission or interference from other dialects, *sound change is overwhelmingly regular*. This is a statistical observation, not a hypothesis; any working historical phonologist can demonstrate it. The reasons for this startling fact, and its consequences, will be discussed more fully in Chapters 3, 5, and 10.

We can logically extend the UP to apply as follows: just as we must use what we know about the present to interpret the poorer data of the past, so we must use what we know about the present and the documented past to extrapolate into prehistory, for which we have no linguistic data at all. If sound change is regular in the historical record, it must have been regular in prehistory too. But because sound change is regular it can be modeled mathematically, and in some circumstances we can use the mathematics of sound change to reconstruct the situation before particular changes occurred, in effect "undoing" the changes. That allows us to extrapolate into prehistory by the methods discussed in detail in Chapter 10. Conversely, the replacement of inherited words undermines this type of reconstruction by steadily subtracting items that show the consequences of regular sound change, thus imposing a practical limit on how far into prehistory we can extrapolate.

That is the most spectacular consequence of the UP, but plenty of other interesting consequences will be found in this book. The UP defines and delimits scientific historical linguistics, simply because the poverty of the historical record leaves us no choice, but it also allows us to recover a surprisingly large amount of information about the linguistic past.

Selection of illustrative examples

Though it is true that the same types of "natural" linguistic change occur again and again in widely separated languages, the range of attested changes is very wide, and no single language provides examples of more than a fraction of them. We have therefore illustrated our discussion with data from a fairly large and diverse range of languages.

However, understanding the more complex structural changes requires in-depth knowledge of the languages being analyzed, and we have therefore used most often data from those languages we know best. Since both the authors were trained as Indo-Europeanists, those happen to be the earlier stages of Germanic and Celtic languages, Classical Latin, Ancient Greek, and the Tocharian languages. Since most students and instructors are not likely to be familiar with all, or perhaps any, of those languages, we have tried to explain the data well enough to make our examples intelligible to the uninitiated.

Transcription

Issues of transcription are more salient and more problematic in historical linguistics than in any other subfield. Most of the available data on languages of the past were collected and codified by linguists who did not use the International Phonetic Alphabet (IPA); some specialist communities, such as Algonkianists and Indo-Europeanists, continue to use alternative systems of transcription which have been established for many decades. In addition, almost every human language that has been described has a "practical orthography" which is not identical with the IPA (nor, in many cases, with anything else). In order to be able to make use of those data, a linguist must be able to handle multiple systems of transcription; there is no feasible alternative. If the reader is not yet able to do that, the time to begin is now.

For the reasons just outlined we have adopted the following policy. Isolated forms which are adduced to illustrate phonological points in a discussion will usually be written in the IPA. If the issue is not phonological, or if the point at issue is clear from conventional spellings, the language's practical orthography will be used. Forms from languages that recur fairly often in the text will also be written in the transcription which is standard for that language; the phonetic values of the symbols will be explained in the notes. We outline here several systems of transcription that a student should be familiar with simply because they are widespread.

Algonkianists, like most other specialists in Native American languages, use orthographies that record surface contrasts. *č* is [tʃ] and *š* is [ʃ]; long vowels are represented either with a following colon (or raised dot) or by doubling the vowel; the latter is possible only in languages in which sequences of identical vowels do not contrast with long vowels. The palatal semivowel is written *y*.

Indo-Europeanists have a distinctive system of representation for Proto-Indo-European (PIE) forms, the phonetics of which cannot always be inferred with certainty. Three sets of dorsal consonants are reconstructed. The set furthest forward in the mouth, traditionally called "palatals" (though they were probably further back than that), are written as *$\hat{k}$, *$\hat{g}$, *$\hat{g}^h$ (or *$\acute{k}$, *$\acute{g}$, *$\acute{g}^h$); a "velar" set, further back, are written *k, *g, *g^h, and there is also a "labiovelar" set *k^w, *g^w, *g^{wh} (with lip-rounding, but otherwise identical with the velars). Three obstruent consonants, probably fricatives, are written *h_1, *h_2, *h_3; they are collectively called "laryngeals" (though the second and third, at least, were probably velar or postvelar), and there is no consensus about how they were pronounced. Syllabic sonorants are written with a circle beneath (*m̥, *n̥, *l̥, *r̥); the palatal semivowel is written *y, and vowel length is indicated by a macron (¯). Pitch accent is marked with an acute (´). For further details see e.g. Ringe 2006: 6–22.

The pronunciation of Classical Latin is recoverable in great detail; see Sturtevant 1940 and Allen 1978 for extensive discussion. The conventional spelling of Latin represents the phonemic contrasts of the language well. Note that long vowels are marked with a macron, *c* is always /k/, *v* is /w/, *qu* is /kw/ (or /k^w/; the evidence is equivocal), and *g* is always /g/ (phonetically [ŋ] before a nasal consonant).

Standardized spelling of the medieval languages of western Europe tends to follow that of Latin (marking long vowels with a macron, for example). In Old English (OE) *y* has its IPA value, *þ* and *ð* spell dental fricatives, and /k/ is normally spelled *c*. In linguistic discussions of OE *ċ* indicates a voiceless palatal stop (which had become [ʧ] by about 900 CE), and *ġ* indicates a voiced palatal fricative. In linguistic discussions of Middle English (ME) the lower mid long vowels, which have no symbols of their own in the manuscripts, are often spelled *ę̄* and *ǭ* in order to reproduce the manuscript spellings as closely as possible. The spelling of Old Norse is similar to that of Old English, except that long vowels are marked with an acute accent; *ǫ* is [ɔ].

Oscan, the ancient Italic language of the Samnites, was written in three alphabets. In representing Oscan forms the Greek alphabet is not transliterated; the Latin alphabet is transliterated in italics; the native alphabet is transliterated in boldface. The difference in the typeface of transcriptions is necessary because the spelling conventions of the different alphabets were different (!). For instance, intevocalic /s/, which was phonetically voiced in Oscan, is spelled s in the native alphabet but *z* in the Latin alphabet; the native alphabet did have a character **z**, but it was used to write the sequence [ts].

Except in Chapter 9, we have cited Ancient Greek forms both in the standard Greek alphabet and in a standardized transcription (based on the Attic dialect of the fifth century BCE; see Allen 1987). We hope that this will make it easier for interested students to learn traditional Greek orthography – a useful skill for pursuing further reading, since specialists do not usually transliterate Greek.

Finally, shaftless arrows (>) indicate regular sound changes; arrows with shafts (→) indicate historical changes of other kinds, as well as derivational processes. Morpheme-by-morpheme glosses employ the Leipzig Glossing Rules.[†]

[†] www.eva.mpg.de/lingua/resources/glossing-rules.php

1   The nature of human language and language variation

This chapter is, in effect, background reading; it presents our views about the nature of human language in the hope of making our perspective on language change more easily intelligible. We have not presented a survey of views on any of the subjects covered here because it is not our purpose to "teach the controversy" about the origin of signed languages, for example, or the extent to which apes can be taught to use human language. In each case we have presented the view that we believe is correct (or is most likely to prove correct in the long run). It will be seen that our perspective falls squarely within the generative tradition.

Students with considerable background in the cognitive basis of human language, as well as students whose primary concern is historical linguistics narrowly defined, may prefer to skip this chapter or postpone reading it until later.

Language is species-specific

"Language," as linguists understand the term, is a property of the human species, both unique to humans and universal among them. That seems obvious, but because it has important consequences it merits at least a brief discussion.

All normal individuals of *Homo sapiens* (the only extant species of humans) learn and use at least one language with a full set of linguistic structures and an adequate lexicon. In fact, most humans with sensory or cognitive impairment also learn and use human language. Though deaf humans find it difficult to learn spoken languages because they lack access to acoustic information, deaf communities have evolved dozens of "signed" languages – that is, languages communicated by gestures of the hands and face rather than gestures of the vocal tract – and every one that has been studied exhibits the same types of structures as spoken human languages (see e.g. Bellugi 1988 with references). That shows that human language is not dependent on vocalization, and that its organization resides in the brain; it is exactly what we should expect, given that most deaf humans are cognitively normal. But even humans with moderate cognitive impairment usually learn and use human language, and for the most part their language is normal. Apparently it is next to impossible to keep human beings from talking.

By contrast, the communication systems learned and used by all other species, though often complex, obviously differ in major ways from "language" as used by human beings. Of course no one denies that members of some other species can learn to manipulate meaningful symbols designed by human beings; experiments with chimpanzees and bonobos ("pygmy chimps"), in particular, have shown that they have some capacity for symbol use. But that is not what linguists mean by learning and using language. The differences between how the language use of young children develops and how the symbol use of young chimpanzees develops are demonstrated most forcefully by the work of Laura Petitto, who has studied both extensively and in detail. Most obviously, the signed "language" of chimpanzees, like all natural animal communication systems that have been studied, lacks syntactic structures that are universal among human languages (Seidenberg and Petitto 1979, Terrace *et al.* 1980). Since an autonomous syntax capable of generating an unbounded repertoire of recursive structures is the core of any language, this amounts to a fundamental difference between human language and all non-human communication systems (Pinker 1994: 334). It might be argued that the difference is basically quantitative rather than qualitative: apes can't learn syntax simply because they're not intelligent enough. But even if that is true, the quantitative difference is so large that in practice it amounts to a qualitative difference, in much the same way that the organization of a cell is qualitatively different from that of a crystal because of its vastly greater complexity. These observations are obviously true; every discussion of the subject ought to begin with an admission that they are true, and for our purposes the discussion might as well end there. (See further Pinker 1994: 332–69 with references.)

The uniqueness of human language demands an explanation, and the most plausible working hypothesis is that there is some sort of species-specific biological basis for human language. That should be no surprise: species-specific systems of communication are common in the animal kingdom; well-studied examples include birdsong, bee-dancing, and the vocalizations of whales. But those systems differ dramatically in almost every way imaginable, and it is worth asking whether any of them resemble human language in interesting ways. Surprisingly, the vocalizations of some species of birds provide one of the best parallels to crucial aspects of human language.

A biological parallel: birdsong

Bird vocalizations are species-specific (Becker 1982: 214), and most sounds made by birds not belonging to the large order Passeriformes appear to be innate – that is, genetically "hard-wired" in the individual. For example, members of particular species of doves (order Columbiformes) appear to acquire their species-specific calls even if raised by doves of other species, or if deafened early in life; the same seems to be true of chickens (order Galliformes) (see

Kroodsma 1982: 2–3 with references). Even the responses to species-specific sounds are at least partly innate in some species, though it is sometimes possible to "imprint" an individual early in life to respond to the vocalizations of other species (Becker 1982: 242–3).

But in most passerine bird species that have been well studied, and especially in the suborder Oscines ("songbirds," by far the largest suborder), production depends at least partly on learning (Kroodsma 1982: 11; see the tables in Kroodsma 1982: 8–9 and Mundinger 1982: 164–76, and note the cautions of Kroodsma 1982: 7, 10). It is not clear that the simpler calls of songbirds are learned rather than innate (Kroodsma 1982: 3–5), but the extended "songs" by which many species communicate can be shown to be learned. A range of rather different learning behaviors is attested. For example, some species do not develop normal songs without learning, but can learn only the song of their own species (or learn such songs preferentially), and can learn even from tape recordings; individuals of other species learn only from the birds which raised them, and these typically acquire the species-specific songs and the appropriate responses together (Becker 1982: 243–4). It is also clear that some species routinely learn songs native to other species (see Baylis 1982 for discussion).

A very widespread pattern of behavior betrays both learned and innate characteristics. Male North American song sparrows (*Melospiza melodia*), for example, produce abnormal songs if reared in isolation, which shows that at least some components of their normal song must be learned; but the abnormal songs that isolated birds produce show at least five salient similarities to normal song (Kroodsma 1977, especially pp. 397–8). Most importantly, it is not only human researchers who perceive the similarities between normal and abnormal songs; wild song sparrows respond to the abnormal songs in the same ways that they respond to normal songs, which shows that they recognize the abnormal songs as "acceptable" songs of their own species in spite of their peculiarity. That is especially striking because the abnormalities in question are pronounced; they are identifiable at a glance in spectrographic recordings, and a large contingent of experienced "birders" recognized them as abnormal in an overwhelming majority of instances. Such a pattern is common among songbird species. Male brown-headed cowbirds (*Molothrus ater*), for example, sing abnormal songs if reared in isolation, but normal females respond to those songs (with greater frequency than to normal songs, in fact). Females reared in isolation respond both to normal male songs and to abnormal male songs (again, more often to the abnormal songs; see King and West 1977). Literally the only hypothesis that will account for this pattern of facts – repeated in species after species – is that the crucial components of the songs are innate, while other components are learned. At least the innate components of such a system serve a clear functional purpose in cowbirds, which are nest-parasites (like the European cuckoo) and so are usually raised by "parents" of other species; but the system as a whole is not so obviously adaptive, especially for the vast majority of species. Since the learned components of bird-songs are apparently not crucial to the system, one might expect that they would vary within a single species, and often they do: the songs of many species show geographic variation that can be described as "dialect" variation (see Mundinger 1982 for an interesting discussion which, among other things, considers at length the appropriateness of the linguistic concept of dialect as applied to birdsong). In other words, there is a wide range of "correct" songs among even the normal songs of many species.

The similarities between this type of birdsong and human language are clear. Children learn the language of whatever community they begin to grow up in, and a normal child will ultimately learn it more or less perfectly if the process is not disrupted; if the child uses two or more languages regularly, all will be learned without confusion. (That is so in all cases that have been studied; early exposure to multiple languages simply does not lead to "mixed" languages.) Clearly there is no single "correct" result in the learning of human language. But it would be very surprising if the species-specific nature of human language did not impose biological constraints on how a human language can be structured. Further, those constraints might be of at least two types: general limitations on human brains, vocal organs, hearing, etc. will necessarily impose limits on language, but there might also be constraints that are highly specific to language structure.

One of the most important results of modern linguistics is the discovery of universal grammatical constraints on human language. In the following section we will argue that some of these constraints, at least, are specific to human language, not merely consequences of more general human cognitive limitations.

Universal Grammar

Exactly how do languages differ? To the general public the most obvious difference is that they use different sets of *words*, the largely arbitrary strings of partly arbitrary speech sounds (or gestures, in signed languages) that signify particular concepts, which are themselves partly arbitrary. Linguists are more likely to focus on differences in syntactic structure, which is also partly arbitrary. The repeated qualifications in these statements are not hypercautious. Hardly anything about human language is *completely* arbitrary; there are very substantial constraints on speech sounds and gestures, and non-negligible constraints on how they can be combined and on what they can mean. Some of those constraints are unarguably biological.

That much is agreed on by virtually all researchers who study human language. There is considerable disagreement, however, on whether any of the constraints on human language are also specific to the ability to learn and use language. Many linguists propose that there is such a thing as "Universal Grammar," a set of constraints specific to language that govern the structures of all possible human-language grammars. The other alternative is that all the constraints on language are automatic consequences of broader and less specific constraints on human cognition, perception, physiology, and anatomy. Both alternatives are, of course, hypotheses; neither has been proved conclusively, and both must be held accountable to all the relevant facts about human language. While the choice between them obviously will not be decided once and for all here, we can make some suggestions by confronting these hypotheses with a range of linguistic facts.

The most obvious constraints on spoken (as opposed to signed) languages are imposed by the configuration of the human vocal apparatus. They are unarguably biological, since the human oral and nasal passages have evolved distinctive shapes, and we know that they are not specifically linguistic both because the vocal apparatus has other functions and because different anatomical constraints apply to spoken and to signed languages. Some other constraints are less obvious; for example, all spoken human languages have consonants produced by constricting a steady stream of breath pushed outward from the lungs – the "pulmonic egressive airstream mechanism" – but only a minority also have consonants produced by modifying a stream of air set in motion by other means (such as ejectives, implosives, and clicks; Ladefoged and Maddieson 1996: 77–90, 246–80), and it appears that all vowels are made with the pulmonic egressive mechanism. But these purely phonetic constraints are not very interesting.

Much more puzzling, at first glance, is a universal fact about the organization of speech sounds. Speech gestures are made in a particular order, but they overlap extensively; for instance, in the English word *stack* /stæk/ the tongue is already preparing to articulate the final /k/ as the vowel /æ/ is beginning to be produced, so that if the word is recorded and played back one cannot cut off the /k/, making it inaudible, without also cutting off so much of the vowel that it cannot be recognized. (This was demonstrated to one of the authors by Charles Hoequist *c*. 1980.) In fact the vowel can be said to be coextensive with the entire syllable, since it also dramatically influences the pronunciation and acoustic signal of the /t/, which are demonstrably different from those of the /t/ in *stick* /stɪk/, for example. (This is an important focus of Articulatory Phonology, which explicitly states that the vocalic tier is coextensive with the entire syllable; see e.g. Browman and Goldstein 1992: 164–5.) But in spite of this "smearing" of speech sounds across one another, speech is always *perceived* as a *sequence* of consonants and vowels, or "segments," each of which appears to be composed of several simultaneous phonetic "features" which reflect the underlying gestures. Native speakers of English perceive /stæk/ as a sequence of four segments and are normally unaware that the segments overlap extensively. Even speakers of other languages will perceive the word as a sequence of segments; some will have trouble parsing initial /st/, others will hear the initial /s/ as a syllable /əs/, and many will find the vowel /æ/ unfamiliar, but all will be convinced that they are hearing some sequence of consonants and vowels. Gestures that are perceived as simultaneous to a sequence of segments do also occur; the tones of tone languages (such as Chinese and Vietnamese) are an example, each syllable bearing a tone that is not precisely localized in the sequence of segments. But the range of types of such "suprasegmental" gestures seems to be very narrowly restricted. (In signed languages the situation is somewhat different, though the difference is one of degree rather than kind: simultaneous gestures are more extensively used

[Perlmutter 1991: 69], evidently because the use of two hands and the face in talking provides many more opportunities for simultaneous gestures. That fact alone might lead us to suspect that all linguistic sequencing constraints are at bottom biological, though much more research into human perception will be needed to prove it.)

Any account of the segmentalization of human speech must begin with an explanation of how we perceive a sequence of discrete units in what is demonstrably an unsegmented stretch of sound waves. Though no hypothesis seems to be so well articulated yet that it can meet all objections (see Klatt 1989, especially pp. 216–18), the most promising approach seems to be the "motor theory" of Alvin Liberman and his co-workers (see e.g. Liberman and Mattingly 1985). The motor theory proposes that speech sounds are perceived by a specialized cognitive module peculiar to speech which "prevents listeners from hearing the signal as an ordinary sound, but enables them to use the systematic, yet special, relation between signal and gesture to perceive the gesture" (ibid. p. 6). In practical terms (and simplifying somewhat), when we hear a speech sound we immediately perceive the gestures that produced it, including the "targets" that the gestures are aimed at. The targets clearly are serial; in /stæk/, for instance, the speaker intended to produce a fricative /s/ terminated by the closure of the /t/, which in turn was to be released into a vowel subsequently terminated by the closure of the /k/. Thus in perceiving the gestures and their targets we naturally perceive a series of sounds. There is some experimental evidence that supports this hypothesis:

> Thus, place information for a given consonant is carried by a rising transition in one vowel context and a falling transition in another[†] . . . In isolation, these transitions sound like two different glissandi or chirps, which is just what everything we know about auditory perception leads us to expect . . . ; they do not sound alike, and, just as important, neither sounds like speech. How is it, then, that, in context, they nevertheless yield the same consonant?   (Liberman and Mattingly 1985: 4, citations omitted)

The link between speech production and speech perception is explicitly held to be biologically based; it is suggested that the ability to coarticulate speech sounds at speed and the ability to perceive the gestures in the resulting stream of sound evolved together (ibid. pp. 6–7). The discovery that human newborns can perceive the differences between consonants of languages other than their own (ibid. p. 24, Yang 2006: 43, both with references) lends considerable plausibility to this hypothesis. In fact the main alternative hypothesis – that invariant cues of consonants and vowels can be detected in the acoustic signal if the criteria used are sophisticated enough – leads to the same larger conclusion, since "infants at least as young as one month old can not only discriminate speech sounds but

---

[†] The authors are speaking of formant transitions (Liberman and Mattingly 1985: 10). See e.g. Ladefoged 1962 or Johnson 2003 for discussion; an illustration of Liberman and Mattingly's point can be found at Johnson 2003: 143 (the interaction of coronal stops and vowels).

they do so in a manner similar to adults," and the ability to find the invariant cues "could not have been acquired through experience and interaction with the linguistic environment" and so must be innate (Blumstein and Stevens 1979: 1015).

But though it seems very likely that phonological segmentation is not only a biologically based perceptual constraint but also peculiar to speech, it appears to make use of the much more widely found and broadly applicable faculty of *categorical perception*. It can be shown that many species of animals perceive continuous phenomena as series of discrete entities (see e.g. Yang 2006: 44–6 with references). That some other species can even be trained to distinguish between human consonants is not very impressive; after all, human newborns do much better with no training at all, and we have already seen that intensive training of apes to use human language signs didn't prove much. But the fact that numerous species perceive sounds or sights relevant to them categorically, and that humans perceive color categorically too, strongly suggests that the underpinnings of speech segmentation were in place long before human language evolved.

Even more puzzling is the fact that human languages organize phonological segments into larger structures; that is, spoken human languages organize the consonants and vowels of an utterance into *syllables*. In the middle of the twentieth century a great deal of effort was expended in an attempt to find a "phonetic basis" for syllabification, but no consensus could be reached (Ladefoged 1975: 218–22, Daniloff *et al.* 1980: 303–5). For instance, it is reasonable to suggest that the nucleus of each syllable is a "sonority peak," a sound more sonorous (i.e. inherently louder) than the sounds immediately flanking it; that would account for the fact that it is usually (though not always) fairly easy to determine how many syllables a given word in a given language has. But it is not always obvious how to assign the segments between the peaks to syllables, so that finding syllable boundaries is often problematic; in some languages it appears that a single consonant between two vowels can be syllabified either with the preceding or with the following vowel, and the acoustic cues differentiating those two options are complex and not straightforward (see e.g. Malmberg 1955). Still worse, in some languages a sound more sonorous than the flanking sounds can fail to constitute a syllable; the /s/ of English *next* /nɛkst/ is a case in point. Nor is it always the case that the peak clearly falls within the most sonorous sound of a sequence. For instance, though /ɪ/ is always a syllable peak when it immediately precedes /l/ in English (e.g. in *stillness*, *milk*, etc.), in Lithuanian there is a contrast between the stressed syllable of *vìlnos* 'wool', in which the peak unarguably falls within the vowel, and *vil̃kas* 'wolf', in which the syllable peak apparently falls within the /l/ even though the preceding high vocoid is not perceived as a semivowel. (In this case, too, the acoustic cues that encode the contrast are not straightforward.) Attempts to link syllables to physiological events, such as the "chest pulse" theory of R. H. Stetson (Stetson 1951: 1–3), have proved to be inconsistent with actual observations of natural speech.

Nevertheless, most colleagues who study the sound structure of human language have no doubt that syllables are real and universal (see e.g. Blevins 1995), so they must reflect a universal constraint on spoken language, which is very likely to be (ultimately) biological; but the nature of that constraint is not yet clear.[1] Further investigation only deepens the mystery. Every language constrains the structure of its syllables in stringent ways, but though the constraints differ dramatically from language to language, there are also pervasive parallels. For instance, in many languages word-initial clusters of three consonants simply cannot occur; they are "unpronounceable." In English they do occur but are tightly constrained: the first must be /s/, while the third must be /r/, /l/, /w/, or /j/ (as in *stream, splay, square*, and *skew*). In the Salish languages (spoken mostly in Washington state and British Columbia) the constraints are somewhat laxer, allowing /s/ to be followed by two obstruents; well-formed St'at'imcets (Lillooet) words, for example, include *stp'úməltxʷ* 'buckskin-colored horse', *stsʼqʷúlakaʔ* 'thumb', and so on (van Eijk 1997: 53). But otherwise the English and St'at'imcets clusters behave similarly. In particular, the English clusters in question are fully syllabified and fall entirely within the onset of their syllables; so do the St'at'imcets clusters, to judge from the language's stress system (ibid. pp. 14–17). That is not self-evident or trivial, as the following discussion (especially the discussion of Nuxalk) will show. Modern work in phonology strongly suggests that the internal structure of syllables is universal: each is divided into an *onset*, which includes everything that precedes the main vowel (or other syllabic *nucleus*), and a *rime*, which includes the rest of the syllable; the rime is in turn divided into the nucleus, the most sonorous part of the syllable, and a *coda* (which can be zero; see e.g. Blevins 1995 for a discussion of syllable structure and of the importance of the syllable in phonological analysis). (Sonorant consonants can be syllable nuclei in some languages; in most varieties of English that is the case in the second syllables of *bottle, button*, and *bottom*, and in many also in the second syllable of *butter*.) The basic division into onset and rime was discovered some fourteen centuries ago by the poet Lù Fǎyán and his friends, who used it to organize the pronunciation and rhyming dictionary known as *Qièyùn* (see e.g. Ramsey 1987: 116–20 with references); "Western" linguistic science did not catch up until the second half of the twentieth century. The Chinese rhyme tables do not distinguish the nucleus from the coda, so the ancient Chinese analysis is not as developed as modern analyses. Nevertheless the similarity of the ancient and modern analyses is difficult to explain if it does not reflect some aspect of universal grammar.

Of course it is reasonable to test an apparently universal property of spoken human language against extreme examples, and the relevant extreme in this case is provided by another Salish language, Nuxalk (Bella Coola). Nuxalk permits indefinitely long clusters of obstruents, especially at word boundaries, e.g.:

(1)   tasʔastxʷɬts stsslxaɬs waʔaɬwlaɬs
        'when I was inside, the rain started to really pour'
                    (Nater 1984: 5; note that /ɬ/ is an obstruent, and that both /l/'s are syllabic
                    sonorants in this sentence.)

Moreover, and much more surprisingly, Nuxalk permits words and even sentences that contain no vowel or syllabic sonorant, even phonetically, e.g.:

(2)   stp 'freckle'
            t'kʷ 'to bleed'
            ɬtˢʷt 'to go through a narrow passage'
            k'xɬtˢxʷ sɬtˢʷtɬtˢ 'you had seen that I had gone through the passage'
                        (Nater 1984: 5, who observes that the sentences are "somewhat contrived.")

Currently there are two competing hypotheses regarding how Nuxalk utterances are syllabified (Bagemihl 1991, 1998 vs. Cook 1994), based on the behavior of segments in the application of phonological rules; surprisingly, they agree that Nuxalk has "normal" syllables and that many obstruents remain unsyllabified, though they disagree about how such a failure to be syllabified is possible. It appears that syllables are linguistically universal, though in extreme cases syllabification is not. (In at least one language, the Berber language Tashlhiyt, even voiceless stops can be syllable nuclei; see Ridouane 2008 for discussion, including detailed phonetic and phonological evidence.)

There is some experimental evidence that very young prelinguistic children pay attention to syllables (see e.g. Bertoncini and Mehler 1981, Yang 2006: 53–4 with references). Since they are clearly not producing utterances and have had little exposure to human language, it is reasonable to hypothesize both that syllabification plays a role in language processing and that it reflects a biologically based constraint on human language. Moreover, this constraint – however it works exactly – is a good candidate for a purely linguistic constraint, both because it is difficult to imagine an analogue in any other area of human perception and because the basic concepts underlying the syllable depend on the articulation of human speech – a property of language that does not recur in other animal communication systems.

Constraints on the meanings of words appear to be social and pragmatic: concepts not useful in human society or discourse are not represented lexically. However, constraints on the constructions into which lexemes enter are less immediately obvious and much more interesting. Verbs and the determiner phrases that they are construed with are particularly worth examining because they exhibit fairly elaborate phrase structures that are tightly constrained. Here is an extended example.

Consider the English verbs *give*, *hand*, *present*, and *donate*, which to a large extent can be used to describe the same set of real-world events. One would expect that verbs so nearly synonymous would occur in all the same syntactic constructions, but that is not what we find. Note the following sets of sentences, in which ungrammatical examples are marked with an asterisk:

(3)   John gave the books to his brother.
            John gave his brother the books.
            *John gave his brother with the books. [uninterpretable]

(4)   John handed the revolver to the guard.
           John handed the guard the revolver.
           *John handed the guard with the revolver. [uninterpretable]

(5)   John presented a petition to the king.
           (*)John presented the king a petition.
           John presented the king with a petition.

(6)   John donated a painting to the museum.
           *John donated the museum a painting.
           *John donated the museum with a painting.

(The second example under (5) is grammatical for some speakers of English but not for others; one of the authors finds it completely ungrammatical, while the other finds it completely unobjectionable.) There is a minimal degree of parallelism: all these verbs can be used in the construction "verb X to Y," where X is an object and Y is a person or a personified entity (such as a charitable foundation); but some can be used in additional constructions while others (like *donate*) cannot, and even those that can appear in more than one construction do not all appear in the same set. It is reasonable to ask why that should be so.

Looking at the histories of these words does not help much. *Give*, though its shape in modern English is etymologically Norse, represents in its usage an inherited verb which already appeared in both of its modern constructions in early Middle English (though not in Old English; see Mitchell 1985: 512–13). *Present* first appears at the end of the thirteenth century (in the meaning 'bring [someone] into the presence of [another]') and was clearly borrowed from Old French *presenter*; already in the fourteenth century it appears in the meaning under discussion here. For some centuries it is attested in *all three* of the constructions listed, as well as in a construction in which the thing given was not expressed (so that 'present you' could mean 'give you something'); around the end of the eighteenth century it settled into its current, more restricted usage in some dialects of English. But that is not the oddest thing about *present*; much stranger is the fact that the construction with *with* appears right from the start of its attestation in English – despite the fact that neither Old French *presenter* nor Medieval Latin *praesentare* ever appears in any similar construction (see the *Oxford English Dictionary* [*OED*] s.v.). *Hand* in the meaning 'give by hand' is quoted first from 1650 in the prepositional construction; the construction with no preposition can be quoted from 1777 (see the *OED* s.v. *present*). Finally, *donate* is a very recent creation; it was backformed from the much older noun *donation* in the mid nineteenth century in the USA. We might suggest that its recent coinage is responsible for the tight restriction on the constructions in which it can be used; but then why does the history of *present* show such a different pattern, with a maximal range of constructions as soon as the word itself appears?

Even more remarkably, roughly the same types of construction appear in Latin with the corresponding verbs *dare*, *dōnāre*, and *mūnerārī*, all of which can be translated as 'give' or 'present', and *trādere* 'hand (over)', even though there is *no direct historical connection* between any of the English verbs and the Latin ones that translate them. (There is no Latin verb that exactly translates *donate*.) Of course in Latin the details are a little different. For one thing, Latin makes much less use of prepositions, because nouns have *case endings* that mark their function in the sentence; for instance, the dative case marks indirect objects (such as the object of *give* which in English is marked with the preposition *to*), the ablative case marks (among other things) the instrument by means of which something is done (typically marked in English by the preposition *with*), the accusative case marks the direct objects of verbs, and so on. The interesting facts, though, have to do with how verbs and structures combine. Note the following sets of examples:

(7)   a. Caesar-ī   lanc-em   da-mus.
           Caesar-DAT   platter-ACC   give-1PL
           'We're giving Caesar a platter.'

        b. *Caesar-em   lanc-e   da-mus.
           Caesar-ACC   platter-ABL   give-1PL [uninterpretable]

(8)   a. Mihī   ist-ud   trāde-∅.
           me-DAT   that-ACC   hand-2SG.IMP
           'Hand me that (thing you have)!'[†]

        b. *Mē   ist-ō   trāde-∅.
           me-ACC   that-ABL   hand-2SG.IMP
           [Ungrammatical in the meaning of the preceding example; can only
           mean: 'Betray me by means of that (thing of yours)!']

(9)   a. Caesar-ī   lanc-em   dōnā-mus.
           Caesar-DAT   platter-ACC   give-1PL
           'We're giving C. a platter.' / 'We're presenting a platter to C.'

        b. Caesar-em   lanc-e   dōnā-mus.
           Caesar-ACC   platter-ABL   give-1PL
           'We're presenting Caesar with a platter.'

(10)   a. Nātūra-∅   ali-ud   ali-ī   mūnerā-tur.
           nature-NOM   other-ACC   other-DAT   give-3SG
           'Nature gives one (talent) to one (person), another to another.'

        b. Mātr-em   h-ō-c   mūner-e-r.
           mother-ACC   this-ABL-this   present-SBJV-1SG
           'Let me give (my) mother this (present).'

The correspondence between English and Latin structures is only partial, but there is a remarkable amount of overlap; in both, for example, 'hand' behaves like the most basic verb 'give', and the pairs of structures that can be used with

---

[†] The demonstrative *iste* implies ownership by or proximity to the person addressed; that is what the parenthetical parts of the translations attempt to convey.

verbs translatable as 'present' are exactly parallel, if we abstract away from the Latin use of case endings rather than prepositions – and in the case of English *present* the pattern appeared in the fourteenth century, so any kind of common inheritance is excluded.

But maybe this is still no surprise; after all, both English and Latin are Indo-European languages, and though their prehistories were largely separate, speakers of English have been learning Latin and borrowing Latin words for well over a thousand years. It's at least imaginable that structures were somehow transferred too, even though there isn't any evidence for that in the historical record (and it's actually very unlikely; see further Chapter 4). What about languages which we cannot show to have any historical connection with European languages before the modern period – say, the Bantu languages of sub-Saharan Africa? Amazingly, the same patterns reappear – different in detail, of course, but obviously parallel. Here are some relevant sentences in Chichewa, a Bantu language spoken in Malawi. (See Baker 1988a: 14, 187 with fn. 24 [pp. 460–1], 280–1, 1988b: 353 fn. 1; we illustrate dialect "B" of Baker's description. Note that APPL glosses the applicative suffix, on which see further below; Roman numerals indicate concord class markers, assigned to the classes in the order given by Bentley and Kulemeka 2001: 11, without distinguishing the subclasses of the first class.)

(11)   a. M-bidzi   zi-na-pats-a   m-sampha kwa n-khandwe.
             v.PL-zebra v.PL-PST-give-IND II.SG-trap   to   v.SG-fox
             'The zebras gave the trap to the fox.'

         b. M-bidzi   zi-na-patsa   n-khandwe m-sampha.
             v.PL-zebra v.PL-PST-give-IND v.SG-fox   II.SG-trap
             'The zebras gave the fox the trap.'

         c. *M-bidzi   zi-na-pats-ir-a   n-khandwe m-sampha.
             v.PL-zebra v.PL-PST-give-APPL-IND v.SG-fox   II.SG-trap
             [intended: 'The zebras gave the fox the trap.']

(12)   a. M-bidzi   zi-na-perek-a   m-piringidzo kwa m-tsikana.
             v.PL-zebra v.PL-PST-hand-IND II.SG-crowbar to   I.SG-girl
             'The zebras handed the crowbar to the girl.'

         b. *M-bidzi   zi-na-perek-a   m-tsikana m-piringidzo.
             v.PL-zebra v.PL-PST-hand-IND I.SG-girl   II.SG-crowbar
             [intended: 'The zebras handed the girl the crowbar.']

         c. M-bidzi   zi-na-perek-er-a   m-tsikana m-piringidzo.
             v.PL-zebra v.PL-PST-hand-APPL-IND I.SG-girl   II.SG-crowbar
             'The zebras handed the girl the crowbar.'

In some ways these Chichewa constructions are actually much more like English than those of Latin are. The most salient difference is that most verbs must be suffixed with the "applicative" morpheme *-ir-* ~ *-er-* in the non-prepositional construction – though *-pats-* 'give', the unmarked verb of this class, is not so suffixed; note also that while English and Latin treat 'hand' like 'give', in contrast to more specialized verbs of giving, Chichewa "draws the line" between 'give' and everything else. Otherwise the similarity of Chichewa to English is striking: we find a preposition *kwa* meaning 'to', there is no case-marking on nouns, and the normal order of objects shifts between the two constructions. And the similarity runs deeper than that. In Chichewa, as in English, 'fox' is a genuine direct object in (11b), as is 'girl' in (12c); that can be demonstrated by further tests. For example, in the following sentence 'hunters' recapitulates the direct object marked by the prefix -*wa*- on the verb:

(13)   Ndi-ku-fun-a   kuti mu-wa-pats-e   m-phatso a-lenje.
         1SG-PRS-want-IND that 2SG-3PL-give-SBJV II.SG-gift I.PL-hunter
         'I want you to give them a gift, the hunters.' (Bresnan and Mchombo
         1987: 751)

Note that the direct object is the recipient, not the gift. (See Bresnan and Mchombo's discussion for evidence that -*wa*- is an incorporated object pronoun, not an agreement marker.) And 'girl' can appear as the subject of a passive made to the derived applicative verb -*perek-er*-:

(14)   M-tsikana a-na-perek-er-edw-a   m-piringidzo ndi m-bidzi.
         I.SG-girl 3SG-PST-hand-APPL-PASS-IND II.SG-crowbar by V.PL-zebra
         'The girl was handed the crowbar by the zebras.' (Baker 1988a: 14)

The parallel of the last example with the corresponding English sentence is especially striking. Latin has no similar construction.

Clearly we are in the presence of properties which are *potentially* universal in human language – that is, *options* of which any human language can avail itself, though not all of them will appear in every language. Not only is it normal for some verbs to appear in multiple constructions, but the same narrow range of constructions for verbs meaning approximately 'give' appears (with minor variations) in language after language. This is not an isolated fact, restricted to particular languages or particular semantic areas; on the contrary, many sets of verbs in thousands of human languages exhibit this property.

The constraints on the syntactic structures of verbs are strongly reminiscent of the constraints on the organization of speech sounds. In both cases there is plenty of variation from language to language, but the variation falls within a surprisingly narrow range. It also seems clear that these constraints are not practical or social, but somehow internal to the human mind, and therefore somehow the result of human biology. Moreover, it is not obvious how they could be language-specific consequences of more general cognitive constraints; at least until human cognition is much better understood, the best working hypothesis is that constraints so detailed, and without discoverable relevance to anything nonlinguistic, are part of a well-defined mental "module" dedicated to producing and processing language. We seem to be looking at a piece of "Universal Grammar."

It is not surprising that evidence that might support the universal grammar hypothesis begins to present itself the moment we start to look at the *structure* of human language, rather than the properties of individual sounds or words, because linguistic structure is unlike anything else in human cognitive experience. In the following section we will discuss in greater detail the leading theory of Universal Grammar.

The Principles and Parameters model

Patterns of comparative grammatical facts like those just discussed have led generative linguists to a general hypothesis: the structure of language is governed by general *principles*, for each of which specific *parameters* are set to one of a few possible alternative settings (Chomsky 1981; a good overview is Cook and Newson 1996). This effectively extends the class of universals to phenomena in which a language must "choose" one of a limited number of options rather than being required to exhibit a single universal property (David Embick, p.c.).

Simple illustrations of parameters and their settings in familiar languages come readily to mind. A language may have case markers on its nouns, like Latin, or it may dispense with them, like English; in other words, the case-marking parameter for nouns can be set to "+" or "−". (It's more complicated than that, of course, but that is a reasonable description on an informal level.) A further, purely functional difference between English and Latin then seems to follow automatically. Because the functions of nouns in a clause can be "read off" the case markers, a speaker of Latin can *scramble* the order of words in a sentence, for emphasis or for stylistic reasons, without changing the basic statements being made; in all circumstances in which *lancem Caesarī damus* is true, for example, *Caesarī damus lancem* (and the other four permutations of these three words) will also be true. English, which does not mark all the nouns in a clause so explicitly, has to have a more rigid word order; so does Chichewa. (In fact scrambling is independently parameterized; some languages, like German and Icelandic, scramble much less than Latin, while others, like Ancient Greek, are even less constrained.) But word order in Latin isn't exactly "free"; there is a *basic* or "natural" word order (used by default whenever there isn't any reason to do anything else), in which the subject appears first in the clause and the verb appears last – after the other nouns (such as the direct object), prepositional phrases, and the like. English and Chichewa put the subject first too, but in those languages the verb precedes the other nouns. In other words, Chichewa and English are VO ("verb then object") languages, whereas Latin is OV – and that is clearly the result of different parameter settings in these three languages.[2]

The same pattern of contrasting parameter settings appears in other areas of morphosyntax as well. Moreover, in many areas of the grammar we find actual gaps in the distribution of possible alternatives, apparently reflecting genuine constraints of Universal Grammar. Thus we expect to find, and do find, languages in which prepositions follow their objects, so that they are "postpositions"; once in a while we find a "circumposition," like German *um, . . . willen* 'for the sake of'; we even find languages with only one preposition, like Tzotzil, or with none at all, like Dyirbal. But we never find a language in which the default word order inserts prepositions into the middle of their objects, or one in which a preposition can have two objects, like some verbs (so that one can say "between a rock a hard place," parallel to *teach John music*, instead of *between a rock* AND *a hard place*, parallel to *see lions and bears*). We find languages (such as English) in which every verb normally has to have an overt subject (even if the subject is semantically meaningless, as in *It's raining*), and languages in which the subject often need not be expressed, in some cases because the verb contains a subject-agreement marker (as in Spanish), but in others when the subject is simply inferable from the context (as in Chinese); but we do not find (and do not expect to find) languages in which the subject is obligatorily unexpressed. Strangest of all, in languages which have auxiliary verbs (symbolized by "T," with the main verb symbolized by "V" and the subject by "S"), we find the basic orders STVO (as in Modern English), SOVT (as in Latin), and STOV (as in late Old English), but never SVOT, so far as we know.[3]

It should be noted that only linguistic *structure* can usefully be thought of as parameterized. Every human language also includes thousands of idiosyncratic facts, namely the specific shapes of its words and affixes, and in many cases also odd and unsystematic quirks of its inflectional morphology. It clearly makes no sense to think of these latter units in parametric terms. This is essentially the familiar division between rule-governed linguistic material and material that must be listed, a dichotomy that every theory of grammar must account for in one way or another.

It is the Principles and Parameters pattern of evidence – considerable morphological and syntactic variation within tight constraints – that is most reminiscent of those types of birdsong which are partly learned and partly innate; and it is reasonable to hypothesize that those aspects of morphosyntactic constructions shared by all human languages that have been investigated are in some sense "crucial" and somehow reflect innate properties, just as innate parts of passerine songs are crucial, while other properties are learned. The place to look for hard evidence to support this hypothesis is in first-language acquisition, just as the innate and learned components of passerine song have been teased apart by investigating song acquisition. Of course we cannot perform with human children the same kinds of experiments as with birds; but we can analyze the experiments which nature performs, so to speak.

Learning from inadequate evidence

In recent decades psychologists have struggled to understand the ability of very young children to discover the meanings of the words they hear around them while they are learning their first language. The naïve view that they deduce the meanings of individual words from the immediate contexts in which they are used becomes less and less plausible the more data one examines. The difficulties include, but are not limited to, the following (see Gleitman 1990: 5–23 with references).

(a)   The coocurrence of real-world situations and the words that refer to them is at best only fair; for example, one extensive study of the inter-action between children from 1 to 2 years old and their mothers found that in more than a third of the instances in which a mother used the basic verb 'open' nothing was being opened in the child's perceptual field. Since children do learn that verb at an early age, anyone who believes that children learn meanings by "word-to-world" matching has to conclude that their hypotheses about verb meanings are not especially rigorous: they can tolerate a high rate of counterexamples.

(b)   But if children's hypotheses about the meanings of words are *not* tightly constrained, the number of possibilities that the child must consider for the meaning of each word becomes vast. This is an instance of the infamous "Scandal of Induction" (see Yang 2006: 11–12 with references): how does a human being trying to figure out the nature of experience – such as, in this case, a human child trying to figure out the meanings of words used by others – choose the right answer from a virtually limitless range of possibilities? Considered in that light, the fact that children do learn the meanings of thousands of words in a remarkably short time becomes extremely difficult to explain.

(c)   To make matters worse, many sets of verbs, such as 'buy' and 'sell', or 'win' and 'beat', describe the same real-world events from different points of view. If children are matching individual words to aspects of the real-world situation, how do they learn to use such verbs correctly?

(d)   Worse still, there are quite a few basic words, learned early in life, whose referents simply are not observable; *know*, *think*, and *remember* are examples that come immediately to mind. That children learn the meanings of such words by observation defies even common sense – and amply justifies the charge that the old assumption of word-to-world matching is nothing but "empiricist speculation" that has been "a barrier to empirical inquiry" (Gleitman 1990: 20).

(e)   Finally, and most disconcertingly, *blind* children have been shown to acquire basic perceptual vocabulary almost as early and as quickly, and in much the same way, as seeing children (Landau and Gleitman 1985: 22–50, 98–119).

These observations demand an explanation.

The only possible explanation is that children deduce the meanings of words not only from their real-world contexts, but also from their linguistic contexts; in other words, they learn the meanings of words in part from their constructions (Gleitman 1990: 23–7). Landau and Gleitman have managed to demonstrate this experimentally, and their results are worth recapitulating briefly.

'See' and 'look' mean somewhat different things to blind and to seeing children. If you tell a seeing child to look at something, the child will assume that the object is in view; a blind child responds to the same command with the assumption that the object is within reach, since blind children see objects by exploring them with their hands. But an extensive record of interactions between a blind 3-year-old and her mother shows a poor correlation between the mother's use of *look* and *see* and the availability of objects within the child's reach; such objects were available in only 72 percent of the instances when *look* was used, and in only 39 percent of the instances when *see* was used (Landau and Gleitman 1985: 213–14; Gleitman 1990: 9). However, when the syntactic environments of the verbs are taken into account, the picture changes radically; for example, it turns out that when *look* is used in syntactic isolation or with a locational argument (*at DP*, or an adverb indicating place), there is almost always an object within the child's reach, whereas when *look* occurs in other constructions (*look like DP*, *look AP*, *look how TP*) there is hardly ever an object within the child's reach (Landau and Gleitman 1985: 108–17, Gleitman 1990: 24–7). It seems clear that the child is not making word-to-world mappings, but sentence-to-world mappings.

Now the significance of universal cross-linguistic similarities in syntax comes into focus. If a child learning any human language can count on finding words of a particular meaning in structures of a particular type (or in one of a restricted range of types), the range of hypotheses the child needs to entertain about the meanings of words and structures is greatly reduced – and learning a human language in a short childhood becomes feasible. Moreover, there is plenty of evidence that children pay attention to syntactic structure in learning their first language. As is well known, they overgeneralize structural patterns to produce sentences which adults do not. The literature on child language acquisition is full of examples; Pinker 1989: 18–26 lists dozens, including the following from five different children (whose ages in years and months are given in brackets):

(15)   Then put her some more. [2.4]
        Don't say me that. [3.3]
        Button me the rest. [3.4]
        Ross is gonna break into the TV and is gonna spend us money. [4.0]
        You finished me lots of rings. [4.11]

Clearly all these children are generalizing "dative shift" patterns: they have extended the patterns of occurrence of English *give* (see above) and of verbs like *buy* (*buy a car for John* = *buy John a car*) to similar verbs which, in adult speech, do not show the full range of structures that *give* and *buy* do. (Of course this also shows that children do not learn to speak by imitation, but by constructing rules – a point established so overwhelmingly by the research of recent decades that we take it for granted.)

But can we really say that the expectation of particular syntactic patterns on the part of the language learner is *innate?* We might ask what else it could possibly be in view of everything that has been said above. Bear in mind that children learn their first language from scratch; we cannot argue that the suitability of particular structures to particular verbs is "obvious," because that's part of what they have to learn – unless, of course, the patterns are based on something innate, and are obvious because we're hard-wired to think so! But in addition there is actual evidence that supports the innateness hypothesis – this time from the deaf community.

The signed languages used in deaf communities bear no relation to the languages of the surrounding hearing communities; for example, American Sign Language (ASL) is not related to English (though it is related to French Sign Language). (For a concise informal introduction to signed languages see Perlmutter 1991.) Some deaf children – the lucky ones – learn signed languages from birth; but some of them learn from adults who acquired those languages late in life and very imperfectly. Astonishingly, this appears to make little difference. Jenny Singleton and Elissa Newport studied a deaf child acquiring ASL from his parents, both of whom learned ASL as teenagers non-natively and very imperfectly (Singleton and Newport 2004: 377). Though their child Simon had only their faulty ASL from which to work (because he was otherwise raised in the non-deaf community), he learned the language much more systematically than they had, extrapolating from their relatively clumsy use of verb inflections, for example, to acquire much of the sophisticated ASL system. Singleton and Newport summarize their extensive statistics as follows:

> Simon surpasses his late-learner parents, and performs as well as the comparison group of eight children who received native ASL input on all but two of the seven morphological domains tested. Only on the two handshape categories does Simon's output appear to suffer as a result of his impoverished input; yet, even here, Simon appears to be in the process of surpassing his input. Simon does not incorporate the irregularities present in his parents' signing; instead, he extracts the moderately frequent forms in his input, and boosts these frequencies in his own usage. Furthermore, he appears to be developing a morphological system with features organized in a contrastive fashion, even in a subportion of the language in which his ability to surpass his input was at first not evident.   (Singleton and Newport 2004: 398–9)

The most straightforward explanation for this outcome is that humans have an innate predisposition to learn the structures of human language.

Moreover, while the case just discussed is unique in the literature (so far), it is not isolated. Corroborating evidence comes from the deaf community of Nicaragua, in which a signed pidgin language, originating around 1980 when the advent of public education for the deaf suddenly brought numerous deaf individuals into a single community, is being "creolized" by young children now learning it natively (ibid. pp. 375–6 with references). Though that situation is not amenable to experimental control, there is ample evidence that native learners are expanding and regularizing the pidgin, transforming it into a normal human language with a full range of linguistic structures.[4]

Consequences of the model

The study of innate constraints on human language is a relatively new field, and much work remains to be done, but it is already clear that the hypothesis is plausible and has led to substantial progress. Some fundamental consequences of the innateness hypothesis are especially helpful in thinking about language change.

On the most basic level, the general constraints on human language must constrain the *outputs* of historical changes: they prevent impossible structures from arising in the course of change. As usual, this is easy to see on the phonetic level; for example, no matter what changes in pronunciation a language undergoes, the results will never include a consonant that the human vocal apparatus cannot produce. In morphosyntax the consequences are perhaps equally clear. For instance, it is possible for the number of arguments (obligatory noun phrases) required by a given verb to change over time; an intransitive (one-argument) verb might become transitive (two-argument), and so on. But we do not expect any natural language change to produce a verb requiring *four* arguments, since no such verbs are known from any human language. Conversely, when we reconstruct protolanguages (see Chapter 10) we must not reconstruct impossible structures if we hope to approximate what a language of the unobservable past was really like.

The Principles and Parameters model makes an especially useful prediction about linguistic changes: changes that involve altering the value of one parameter should be relatively natural and easy, other things being equal. The syntactic changes that have been studied so far seem to bear that prediction out; typical changes involve a shift from OV to VO word order, or the loss of the "verb-second" (V2) construction.

An inverse argument applies when we look for evidence that two or more languages have shared some part of their histories, either through "descent" from a single earlier language or through contact. The history of any human entity or object involves contingent events, which need not have occurred (so far as we can tell) but actually did; to prove shared linguistic history one must therefore demonstrate that the languages in question experienced *the same* contingent events (in the same order, if the relative chronology of events is reconstructable) during some definable period of their development (see Chapter 11). Universally available parameter settings obviously do not qualify. Thus the "raw material" for proving linguistic relationships, subgrouping the members of language families, and reconstructing protolanguages consists in those highly idiosyncratic aspects of language that are *not* governed by the Principles and Parameters model, namely the specific phonological shapes of words and affixes and the more unusual quirks of languages' inflectional morphology. In that sense "linguistic archaeology" depends on just those aspects of human language that are otherwise of least interest to a linguist.

But by far the most important consequence of the principles-and-parameters model, from the point of view of a historical linguist, is what it tells us about language acquisition, because it turns out that acquisition is the most important focal point of language change. We therefore devote the next chapter entirely to the consequences of first-language acquisition.

Notes

1 Some recent work suggests that syllables are not as important for the definition of phono-tactic constraints as is commonly supposed (Blevins 2003 with references); however, the reality of syllables is not denied (ibid. p. 375). If it is true that the syllabification of a given language is actually derived from other phonological properties (Blevins 2004: 232–5), it does not follow that syllabification *in general* is not a part of universal grammar – after all, it could be a parameterized universal – but it does follow that syllabification cannot be phonetic.

2 In discussing the relative position of object and verb we are talking about *underlying* constituent order. Whether one posits a fixed order of syntactic constituents in underlying structure is a theoretical decision; some other models that are effectively equivalent to ours, such as arc pair grammar, specify constituent order at a different point in the derivation (see Aissen 1987 for an extended exemplification). If an underlying order is posited, it must be the order that permits the most economical and explanatory description of the syntax as a whole, and in that sense the orders of object and verb that we give for these languages are uncontroversial. Thus we reject the approach of Pinkster 1990: 163–88, which attempts to dispense with a default order of major constituents, though in most other respects Pinkster's analysis is readily convertible into a Principles and Parameters approach.

In most cases the underlying order of constituents that gives the best description of the syntax as a whole is the default surface order – the order used if there is no positive reason to do anything else. That is the case for the languages we cite in this chapter; though Latin surface constituent order is highly variable, the high proportion of verb-final clauses in the deliberately straightforward prose of Julius Caesar shows that the default order was verb-final. There are exceptions to this generalization, however; for instance, for German and some other "verb-second" languages the default constituent order of subordinate clauses is the optimal underlying order.

3 The Latin construction exemplified by *quā dē causā*, literally 'which for reason' (meaning 'for which reason') is not a counterexample to the generalization that prepositions are not inserted into objects by default. The crucial detail is that the preposition must follow *exactly one* coherent constituent of its object; in other words, it is still ordered with respect to the *boundaries* of the object, not merely inserted into the middle. Thus one can say *hōc in oppidō permagnō* 'in this very large town', with 'in' immediately after 'this'; but ?*hōc oppidō in permagnō* seems odd (in prose; extreme permutations of word order can occur in verse). Since it is also possible to put the preposition to the left of the object, the most economical description of this pattern is to recognize the latter order as underlying and to posit a rule moving the leftmost constituent of the object to the left of the preposition.

The point of the example *see lions and bears* is that *see* takes only one object, but that object, like all noun phrases, can be expanded indefinitely by conjoining with *and*. Languages (such as Hittite) that can drop the conjunction corresponding to *and* could appear to be counterexamples to the generalization that adpositions take only one object, but we predict that they will be only apparent counterexamples – that is, that the apparently multiple objects will turn out to be conjoined.

The omission of pronominal subjects ("null subject," formerly "*pro*-drop") is less straight-forward than it at first appears. In the case of Spanish we might suggest that the subject can be omitted because its person and number are marked on the verb; but – as many observers have noted – Chinese often omits the subject even though none of its morphosyntactic properties are ever marked on the verb. This illustrates a general point: a parameter setting which decreases the overt expression of information in a sentence does not necessarily depend on another which encodes the same information elsewhere in the sentence; if the information is inferable from context, that can be sufficient.

4 The point that the creolization of a signed pidgin argues an innate predisposition to learn language structures has of course been made from other instances of creolization; the work of Derek Bickerton is perhaps the most prominent example (see e.g. Bickerton 1977, 1981, 1995). However, Bickerton also attempts to argue that specific parameter settings – for example, the organization of the verb system by aspect rather than tense – are innate, and evidence from a broader range of creoles does not seem to support those more specific contentions. For a discussion of Bickerton's thesis from a modern generative perspective see e.g. Roeper 1995; for a range of up-to-date views on the relationship between creolization and acquisition see the papers in Wekker (ed.) 1995.

2   Language replication and language change

The universality of language change

Human language would presumably function much better as a medium of communication if it did not change over time, because dialects would not diverge and mutually unintelligible languages would not multiply (see Chapter 10). But that is not what we find; on the contrary, any language or dialect recorded for even a few centuries can be shown to have changed over the course of its recorded history, and in recent decades William Labov and his students and colleagues in sociolinguistics have uncovered evidence of change in progress in practically every speech community in which they have looked for it. Apparently language change is universal. That is all the more surprising because in modern literate societies there are institutional forces (such as schools and newspaper columnists) that militate against linguistic change – and invariably fail. One naturally wonders why, but that question is not fundamental enough; we need to ask "how" before we can ask "why." Let us begin by looking at the mechanics of change: how specific language changes originate, and what happens to them over time. (See already Paul 1960: 18–20, 24–5, 32–4 – originally written in 1880 and last revised in 1920!)

Potential sources of language change

A linguistic change has occurred when an innovation has spread and become accepted in a speech community. If we want to understand the entire course of the change, we first need to ask where the innovation came from.

The most obvious source of linguistic innovations is contact with speakers of other languages. Any speaker of English is aware that we adopt and use foreign words to talk about foreign things; fairly recent examples include *sushi*, *duma*, *ulema*, *Taliban*, and so on. Contact with other dialects of the same language leads to similar "borrowings"; for instance, a speaker of North American English is most likely to have learned the word *devolution* from British discussions of British politics. These are all examples of the borrowing of "words" – that is, of listed items, as opposed to rules or structures – from other languages or dialects.

The extent to which structure can also be borrowed from significantly different dialects or foreign languages is the subject of ongoing debate. We will examine the linguistic consequences of contact with other languages in Chapter 4 and the consequences of contact with mutually intelligible dialects in Chapter 3.

An almost equally obvious source of innovations is deliberate manipulation of one's language; the coining of new words, including brand names, is a familiar example. This resembles borrowing from foreign languages in two ways: adult native speakers are typically responsible for such changes, and while it is clear that conscious manipulation can give rise to new words, it is not clear that it can affect language structure. For instance, American advertisers' coining of *Uncola* as a description of the soft drink 7-up, with *un-* prefixed to a noun in defiance of normal derivational rules, did not lead to the widespread use of *un-* in similar functions; its only linguistic effect was to prompt Volkswagen to describe its "beetle" as *the uncar* for a short time.

A much less obvious source of innovations follows from the nature of human language (as discussed in the preceding chapter) and its transmission from generation to generation. Though the ability to learn a language is innate, each specific language must be learned. It seems likely that errors made in learning a native language might occasionally persist into adulthood and eventually spread in a speech community; presently they would cease to be regarded as errors, and a linguistic change would have occurred. In the generative tradition this has become a common hypothesis for the source of structural change (see e.g. Halle 1962: 64–5).

Finally, there is a potential source of innovations that involves both language contact and learner errors. Individuals who come to live in a community whose dominant language or dialect is not their own usually find it necessary to learn the dominant language or dialect, but if they must learn it as adults they almost always do so imperfectly – that is, they make errors which they are *chronically unable to correct*. It seems possible that, at least in exceptional circumstances, those errors might ultimately be a source of language change in the community at large.

An optimist might suppose that once we have figured out what the potential sources of innovations are, we need only go find examples. Unfortunately reality is not so accommodating.

Why the source of any particular change is elusive

There are at least two practical problems which severely limit our ability to identify the source of any particular change.

In the first place, records of the past are of almost no use in attempting to find the sources of linguistic change; they often show *what* changes occurred over a given time period, but they hardly ever provide any evidence for *how* they occurred or how they started. This is part of a larger problem. Almost all linguistic records from before the twentieth century are impoverished in a wide variety of ways:

in most cases we have limited information about the phonetics of the language; the surface contrasts of the phonology are sometimes imperfectly recorded; rare inflectional categories and syntactic constructions may not be adequately attested if the corpus is small; words for some concepts may fail to appear by chance. Still worse, the variation that is normal in the speech of any community is almost always poorly represented in documents of the past. From most times and places only "officially approved" dialects and styles are represented; even when that is not the case (as in the Middle English period), a large proportion of the variation is excluded from the record by sheer chance because writing in the language was sporadic, or much of what was written fails to survive, or both. Finally, no one thought normal language acquisition interesting enough to record it in any detail before the twentieth century, and without records of acquisition we of course have no record of learner errors. Under the circumstances, the odds that we might be able to pinpoint the source of a particular linguistic change of the past are almost always nil.

A simple example will illustrate the problem. In all dialects of Old English (OE; i.e. English before the Norman Conquest) the 3sg. and all the forms of the plural ended in -þ (pronounced [-θ]) in the present indicative of most verbs. In late tenth-century interlinear glosses written in the Northumbrian dialect we begin to find -s occasionally instead, and in the northern dialects of Middle English (ME) -s has become the normal ending. No language with which OE was in contact had such a verb ending, so it is difficult to see how it could have been borrowed into the language. The change does not seem to be a regular sound change (on which see Chapter 5), because word-final -þ in general was not affected; for instance, Northumbrian OE mōnaþ 'month' and ġigoþ 'youth' never appear with final -s, and their northern ME descendants mōneth and ȝouth likewise preserve the final consonant unchanged. Is it then a learner error? But what sort of error, and how could learners fail to learn such common and basic inflectional endings? The documents do not provide us with enough information to answer those questions.

Historical linguists have long known how we must try to compensate for the impoverishment of our records of the past. So long as human biology and the conditions of language acquisition and daily use have not changed (and they clearly have not for tens of millennia), we must assume that human language is a single phenomenon, exhibiting always and everywhere the same general characteristics, organization, and structures; that allows us to interpret the fragmentary records of the past in the light of our much fuller knowledge of the present, using the *uniformitarian principle* (UP) in much the same way that historical geologists and palaeontologists do (see Osthoff and Brugmann 1878, Labov 1972: 101). As it applies to linguistics, the UP can be stated as follows:

> Unless we can demonstrate a relevant alteration in the conditions of language use or language acquisition between some time in the past and the present, we must assume that the same types, range, and distribution of language structures existed and the same types of linguistic change processes operated at that past time as in the present.

(For instance, we expect all human languages of the past to have organized their sounds as contrastive phonemes; we do not expect there to have been any phonemes outside the attested modern range of speech sounds; we expect sounds that are very common cross-linguistically now to have been so in the recoverable past; and we expect sound changes of the past to have been of the same types we can observe today.) In other words, we must interpret the records of linguistic change in the past in the light of what we can discover about the linguistic changes going on around us now. The present must help us to explain the past – not the other way round. In fact we have no practical alternative: if we can't assume that ancient languages functioned and changed like modern ones, we have no way of knowing how they functioned and changed, and we're reduced to sheer speculation.

So we principally want to study the origins of current linguistic changes. But any serious attempt to do so will soon encounter the second practical problem. It is very likely that most changes begin their long careers as idiosyncracies in a single individual's speech, or perhaps in the speech of several individuals who by chance innovate in the same way; discovering the origins of the changes will mean discovering how *those individuals* came to use the linguistic peculiarity in question. But the odds that any particular individual's idiosyncracies will be observed by even the most zealous sociolinguist are, once again, virtually nil. Constraints on time and funding do not permit the sampling of more than a few score individuals' speech, and even in a speech community as small as 10,000 people that is a woefully inadequate sample if our goal is to find potential language changes. Much larger samples of variation can be culled very cheaply from the internet (as an anonymous reviewer observes), but most of the information about individual speakers that is crucial for a sociolinguistic analysis of the progress of a change is absent from internet postings. Telephone interviews, which were used in compiling Labov *et al.* 2006, are another inexpensive alternative, but neither alternative will be of much help in trying to pin down the origins of innovations that give rise to linguistic changes. More importantly, even if innovations were observed they could not be identified as future linguistic changes with any probability of success; after all, most quirks of a particular individual's speech do not survive the individual's death because they are not imitated by other speakers. We are constrained to search instead for potential language changes that are used by a very small subcommunity within which they presumably originated – and even they are overwhelmingly likely to be overlooked.

In some cases that doesn't matter: we don't care which speakers of English first began to use *sushi*, because it's obvious that the word was borrowed from Japanese and the historical and cultural circumstances in which it was borrowed are well documented. But as usual, those are the trivial cases; vocabulary items come and go without materially affecting a language's structure. The moment we look at a really interesting case we run head-on into the evidential problem. The "positive anymore" of American English is a case in point. In most dialects of English (including most dialects of American English) *anymore* is a negative polarity item, used only in negative and interrogative clauses; one can say

(1)   I don't drink so much coffee anymore.

and

(2)   Does he even show up anymore?

but not

(3)   *I used to think that show was boring, but anymore I kind of like it.

But in North America there are also "positive anymore" dialects in which the third example is grammatical. That is clearly an innovation, but it is not clear how it happened. The phenomenon did not even begin to be reported until it was fairly widespread; by that point children were learning the construction natively, and one could no longer be certain that any given individual had not learned it natively (e.g. from schoolmates at an early age). Since the word itself is native, borrowing is not in question; but how could a change in the usage of a contextually restricted item have started? It is much too late to discover the answer by direct investigation.

For these reasons we are constrained to *infer* the origins not only of all linguistic changes of the past, but also of all or most of the changes in progress that we can still observe. If our inferences are to be any better than guesswork, we need to construct them in the context of a fully detailed, realistic model of how languages continue to exist through time. As we will see, knowledge of how languages are perpetuated will allow us to make some surprisingly solid inferences about the sources of linguistic change.

The cycle of language replication

A language continues to exist only so long as it is used by a community of native speakers; thus the survival of any language depends on the replication of its native speech community. (A spoken language with no native speakers, such as medieval Latin, though not exactly "dead," is not fully alive either; in particular, its structures are influenced by the native languages of those who speak it, so that it no longer has a fully autonomous existence.) Speech communities replicate themselves one speaker at a time, by the process of native language acquisition (NLA). Several of the unique properties of NLA are crucial for our understanding of language change.

NLA is developmentally driven. Children growing up in a community of human language users – that is, all normal children – acquire the language or languages that they hear around them, without any conscious teaching (and sometimes in spite of attempts to teach them). There is ample evidence that they do not learn by simple imitation; rather, they construct subconscious grammars on the basis of the speech that they hear around them. At first their grammars are very unlike adult grammars and yield obviously anomalous outputs, but over time they gradually bring their internal grammars into conformity with the adult grammars around them until they are more or less indistinguishable from other native speakers of the language.

By contrast, millions of human beings have discovered that when they leave childhood behind they are unable to learn further languages well enough to pass as native speakers; the almost universal inability of adults to learn further languages well is a basic fact of research on second-language acquisition (see e.g. Schachter 1996: 159–61). Of course some do much better than others; a few appear to be able to learn languages perfectly as adults. But it is commonplace to find that when such second-language speakers are under stress their control of the non-native language slips, and phonetic and grammatical features of their native language begin to show through the façade of perfect competence. Examples come readily to memory. One of the authors is acquainted with a colleague born and raised in Russia who usually appears to speak American English perfectly even though it is his *fourth* language, learned when he was already an adult; but on two occasions when he was under considerable stress his ordinarily perfect English phonology was observed to deteriorate, and he began to palatalize English consonants before front vowels heavily, as though speaking Russian. A former academic adviser of the same author once observed that, though she had used English as her primary language for years, when she was tired the inanimate objects in the room began to acquire the genders of her native Italian, the bed becoming "he," the lamp "she," and so on. It seems clear that the grammar of a language learned in adulthood is actually overlaid on the grammar of one's native language.

A pattern of behavior which appears to be universal demands a universally applicable explanation. Most linguists accept the hypothesis that a native language must be acquired within a "critical period" which is developmentally defined (Lenneberg 1967: 142, 153, 178–9). Why that is so is not clear, since the physiological development which causes the "window of opportunity" to close has not been identified and the results of attempts to find neurological differences in the processing of native and non-native languages are difficult to interpret (see e.g. the discussion of Bhatia and Ritchie 1999: 579–80). But regardless of the cognitive mechanisms involved, some version of the critical period hypothesis must be correct. Experimental evidence shows that the ability of children to acquire *second* languages natively begins to decline slightly at the age of about 8 to 10, then declines much more dramatically around the age of puberty (see the careful discussion of Johnson and Newport 1989 with references). The critical period hypothesis is also strongly supported by observed differences in the recovery of patients from traumatic aphasia: patients whose brains were damaged in childhood usually recover their full capacity for language, whereas damaged adults do not (see the detailed discussion of Lenneberg 1967: 142–50).

Children who are exposed to more than one language during the NLA developmental window do not acquire "mixed" languages; though there may be some confusion to start with, the children invariably sort it out, eventually becoming native speakers of all the languages that they have occasion to use on a regular basis (Fantini 1985, Meisel 1989, Bhatia and Ritchie 1999: 574–5). At least four languages can be acquired natively by a single child; there is probably no inherent limit to how many a child can acquire, though the finite length of the critical period must impose a practical limit (see e.g. Meisel 1989 with references). One of the languages is usually "dominant," in the sense that the multilingual uses it more often, or preferentially, or in a wider range of social situations.[†] But though bi- or multilingual speakers are seldom "perfectly balanced," it would be misleading to insist that only one of their languages can be native; the evidence shows that "early bilinguals are remarkably close to two monolinguals in terms of the development of formal features and mechanisms of language acquisition (i.e., in the development of phonology and syntax . . .)" (Bhatia and Ritchie 1999: 572–3). Since native bilingualism is a type of language contact, we will consider its consequences for language change in Chapter 4.

Let us take a closer look at exactly what is learned in NLA and what aspects of language are normally learned later in life.

Children invariably acquire the inflectional system(s) of their native language(s) by about the age of 5 (though individual inflectional irregularities may not be mastered until later in childhood; see e.g. the papers in Slobin 1985). That is true even if the inflectional morphology of the language is extremely elaborate and productive, as in West Greenlandic (Fortescue and Olsen 1992: 111–13, 210–16), or exhibits pervasive lexical idiosyncracies, as in the case of Georgian (Imedadze and Tuite 1992: 56–8, 104–5). Most of the basic syntax is also acquired by that time (see e.g. Meisel 1989, who discusses the acquisition of French and German syntax by a bilingual child, and Imedadze and Tuite 1992: 56–8, 104–5), though some constructions in some languages may take a little longer; for instance, there is good experimental evidence that English-speaking and German-speaking 6-year-olds do not consistently understand passive constructions, though younger native learners of some other languages apparently do (see e.g. Mills 1985: 157, Lust 1999: 133 with references, Wexler 1999: 101–3 with references). The acquisition of phonological contrasts and automatic phonological rules, too, can extend into the earliest school years; for instance, one of the authors once encountered 5-year-old English-speaking twins who were still pronouncing word-initial [s, z, ʃ, ʒ, tʃ], and [dʒ] all as [s]. By middle childhood all these components of the grammar are in place.

Since the sorts of errors made in the early stages of NLA apparently never survive beyond the end of the developmental window (Dresher 1999: 303–4) and so cannot give rise to historical changes, we do not need to consider whether the Universal Grammar initially available in NLA is the same as it will be by the end of the process (see e.g. Wexler 1999 vs. Lust 1999); it is the latest stages

---

[†] Cutler *et al.* 1989 demonstrated that there can be fundamental cognitive effects of language dominance by showing experimentally that native English–French bilinguals parse words of the two languages somewhat differently depending on which language is dominant. The effects are extremely subtle and have no practical impact on the linguistic competence or performance of the speakers.

of NLA, when adult Universal Grammar is unarguably in place, that demand our attention. On the other hand, a question of obvious interest is the extent to which hypotheses about the language being learned constructed by the learner on the basis of inadequate evidence survive into the period when adequate evidence becomes available (Dresher 1999), and thus potentially into adult speech. As we will see in Chapter 6, some phonological reanalyses can be explained by exactly such a scenario.

Also of interest is the observed fact that native systems of phonological rules and contrasts, inflectional morphology, and basic syntax all resist modification later in life; it is famously difficult to acquire a phonological contrast from another dialect of one's own language if one has not learned it natively (see Labov 1994: 518–26), and it seems equally difficult to learn a new morphosyntactic category or basic syntactic pattern. For instance, working-class speakers of American English whose native dialect includes the past counterfactual construction exemplified by *if I would have known* experience great difficulty in learning to produce the standard construction (*if I had known*) with consistency in spite of the fact that their native construction is stigmatized. It seems that these are the components of the grammar that cannot be acquired natively after the relevant window has closed. That accounts for the "foreignisms" in the English of the non-native speakers discussed briefly above; it also accounts for the observed fact that speakers who have learned a second language imperfectly as adults fairly often use their native phonology and morphosyntax in their non-native language, but seldom the reverse (Prince and Pintzuk 2000).

Other components of the grammar, especially the basic vocabulary and other common words, are learned in NLA as well. But it continues to be easy to learn new words throughout life. Evidently for that reason, non-native lexical items can supplant native ones more or less completely in the speech of an adult. In some languages, derivational morphology and the phonological patterns peculiar to it, such as those exemplified by the English pair *divide* : *division*, also appear to be learned largely outside the developmental window of NLA.[1] Finally, some speakers (though by no means all) find it fairly easy to replace one superficial phonetic implementation rule with another in adulthood, provided that they are not required to learn a new contrast. Thus language acquisition continues throughout life, but beyond the NLA window there are significant restrictions on what components of the grammar can be acquired with complete success (so that they are produced completely automatically in the absence of conscious control).

Let us now reconsider the possible sources of linguistic change in light of the above discussion.

Learner errors as a source of language change

Consideration of the constraints on language replication leads immediately to a large-scale inference: while a lexical innovation can have entered the language of a speech community by practically any route, a *significant* innovation in the basic phonology or morphosyntax *is overwhelmingly likely to be a learner error* of some sort. That is because the odds that an adult might have *successfully* borrowed a non-native contrast, phonological rule, or basic morphosyntactic structure *into his or her native dialect* are very small; those components of the grammar are too deeply ingrained to be modified by an adult with complete success.

We will need to return to this inference in Chapter 4; discussion of alleged counterexamples, and of why we believe that they are not cogent, will be found there. For the moment the point can be illustrated by examining a few apparent counterexamples from modern English.

It is not too difficult for a monolingual native speaker of English to learn to pronounce the name *Bach* with a final velar fricative [x], even though that consonant is not systematically used in English. An idealized analysis of the contrastive sounds of that speaker's English might suggest that it included a "marginal phoneme" /x/; the speaker, if American, might even claim to possess a "minimal pair" /bɑx/ 'Bach' vs. /bɑk/ 'bock (beer)'. But more extensive investigation would almost certainly cast doubt on those claims. For instance, it would be surprising if the speaker *never* pronounced the composer's name as [bɑk]. Moreover, the speaker could hardly help being aware that the name is foreign, that it ends in a foreign consonant, and that other speakers of English frequently replace that consonant with the native /k/ even if the speaker does not. In other words, the community as a whole has not imported a new phonological contrast into their language, and probably no individual speaker has done so; those speakers who do use [x] in *Bach*, even more or less consistently, are employing a "foreignism" that has not been integrated into the structure of English. Thus the [x] of an English speaker's *Bach* is not a significant innovation by any measure.

A somewhat different type of case involves the borrowing of a different version of a syntactic rule from a closely related dialect. For instance, whereas a native speaker of American English would say:

(4)   If I had known how to fix the bicycle I would have.

the corresponding sentence in more conservative dialects of British English is:

(5)   If I had known how to fix the bicycle I would have done.
         [or, in maximally conservative dialects, *should have done*.]

This latter alternative uses the "pro-verb" *do* in the second clause instead of zeroing the verb entirely. The first alternative may now be native to some British speakers, but the second definitely is not native in the USA. One occasionally encounters Americans who have adopted the conservative British rule (usually together with some attempt at a British accent). But it is unclear whether they use that rule natively, i.e. without conscious control (see above), and self-reports are completely unreliable, not least because an American who adopts features of British English usually does so for reasons of perceived prestige. In this case, too, it is unclear how well integrated into the grammar the borrowing is.

Attempts to borrow morphosyntax from very different languages (as opposed to different dialects of one's native language) are usually even less successful, even if they are lexically mediated. Over the last few centuries there has been a concerted attempt to borrow into standard formal English Latin and Greek nouns with their Latin and Greek plurals (all in the nominative case); the following are representative:

(6)
Singular	*Plural*	*Singular*	*Plural*
datum	data	cactus	cacti
bacterium	bacteria	alumnus	alumni
medium	media	alumna	alumnae
phenomenon	phenomena	formula	formulae

For the most part this attempt has been a failure. For very many educated speakers of English, *data* is now a singular; the plurals of many others of these nouns have been regularized (*antennas, formulas*; see already Jespersen 1914: 35–7); there is massive confusion in the use of *phenomena*, the singular *phenomenon* being unknown to many speakers; for many others *alumni* is simply the name of an organization, both the singular and the corresponding feminine being unknown; *medium* and *media* have been dissociated, the former acquiring a regular plural *mediums* while the latter has become a collective noun meaning roughly 'news organizations'. Not all these developments are very recent; *forums*, for instance (for *fora*), is quotable from the 1850s. Possibly the most successful importation has been *cacti* (Greg Ward, p.c.; googling the form gives about 2.8 million hits), but even that plural has to compete with *cactuses* (for which the google test yields about 185,000 hits). Whether any of these plurals, even *cacti*, occurs in the vernacular dialects of English speakers with no college education is highly doubtful. Not all attempts at lexically mediated borrowing of morphosyntax from foreign languages are such total failures, and in Chapter 4 we will examine two cases that turned out rather differently; but under most sociolinguistic circumstances failure appears to be the rule.

In short, there is enough evidence of failure in attempts to borrow structure to justify the working hypothesis that structural changes in human language are *normally* the result of learner errors. We next need to consider how errors can evolve into real linguistic changes.

The evolution of errors into linguistic changes

We begin with a thought experiment: what would have to happen for a native-language or second-language learner error to develop into a linguistic change? A native-language learner error would have to remain uncorrected throughout the period of NLA, so that it became a stable feature of the speaker's adult speech; only then could it become part of the normal variation in a speech community and spread through the community by the well-known sociolinguistic processes that we will discuss in the following chapter. But since children normally do bring their grammars into conformity with the adult norm, the survival of a native-language learner error must be a fairly rare event, and therefore difficult to observe. A second-language learner error is already a permanent feature of an adult speaker's speech, but that is not enough to qualify it for the competition between variants in the native speech community; this speaker clearly comes from outside the native speech community, and such speakers are rarely imitated by native speakers. A non-native error will become a competing variant only after it has been learned natively by a child for whom it is not an error – that is, a child attempting to acquire her parents' non-native language, unaware that it contains features which do not conform to native-speaker norms. Such an event must also be rare; normally the children of immigrants learn the dominant language of a community primarily from native-speaker children, and the non-native dialect of their parents does not survive.

But what does "rare" mean in practice? It has to mean quite different things in the two types of cases in question.

In any major city in the world there must be at least tens of thousands of children in the NLA developmental window at any given time. If only one child in a thousand persists in a learner error until the period of NLA is past, that type of event will be too rare to be recognizable in any sociolinguistic survey, yet there will be a steady stream of new variants brought into the speech community as the children grow up. In fact it is possible to cite anecdotal evidence which at least demonstrates that native-language learner errors can survive until NLA is more or less complete. A senior colleague whose sons grew up in the Philadelphia area noticed that his elder son, at an age when he was still learning English from his parents, was saying *this day* and *this night* instead of *today* and *tonight*. The boy's parents called the difference to his attention, but he declined to change, on the grounds that one says *this morning* and *this evening*. As he began to acquire friends and playmates his parents noticed that they were copying his innovation, and for some years there was a group of small boys that used *this day* and *this night*. Our colleague's son finally abandoned his lexical innovation around the age of 8, at a time when basic vocabulary has already been acquired; he could have maintained it much longer. Someone did, since the same colleague heard *this day* used by an adult on New Jersey Public Radio some years ago. (Of course he is more likely than most listeners to have noticed that because of his experience with his son.) If the individual in question was a native speaker, it is likely that *this day* was a native-language learner error in his case too. There is not likely to be any direct connection between the two cases, but the innovation "makes sense" in terms of the structure of English and can have arisen independently many times; native-language learner errors which do give rise to linguistic changes are likely to have arisen repeatedly in the speech of numerous learners.

Though this anecdote is just an isolated datum, it reveals an important aspect of the survival of native-language learner errors: the spread of the innovation to other speakers *still in the NLA developmental window* helps to explain how an error can resist the usual process of self-correction. Most small children spend much of their time with playmates approximately their own age. They therefore learn their native language in large part from slightly older peers, learning one another's errors and reinforcing them in frequent conversation. Further potential examples are easy to find. For instance, a child of one of the authors reached the age of 6 with an unusual vowel merger in place: the syllable nuclei /ɔr/ and /ər/ of standard American English were both pronounced [ɔɹ], so that *bird* and *board*, for instance, were homonyms. The child certainly did not learn that detail of phonology from parents or teachers, since no such merger is current in the adult speech of the area, but it might have been reinforced in preschool by conversation with other children who shared the error. Astonishingly, the child's elementary school teachers did not remark on the merger; apparently all they noticed was an odd pronunciation of postvocalic /r/. The merger seemed to have been suppressed completely by age 9, but further observation showed that that was an illusion. At the age of 10 the same child spontaneously produced the word *version* as [vɔɹʒən]; several months later the correct pronunciation [vɹ˙ʒən] was recorded. Apparently this child has overlaid a mainstream but non-native contrast on her native merger, and like all such persons she slips up once in a while.

Whether the survival of native acquisition errors beyond the window of NLA will have any further consequences depends on further developments. The innovation has to be salient enough to be noticed and copied, and it has to actually be copied by a child's peers – not only in middle childhood, but into adolescence. We return to this point in Chapter 3.

Though much more work on the phenomenon is urgently needed, it is reasonably clear how native-language learner errors must survive into adulthood, and equally clear that their survival must be common enough to be a significant source of language change. What of second-language learner errors, which (as we have argued above) must be learned natively by children in order to become part of the mainstream variation in a speech community? Such learning can take place only if a child of non-native speakers does not have enough contact with native speakers to learn the native variety of the language, or if the child has some other reason to learn features of the non-native dialect. Given such a situation the learning of errors will be easy and automatic, and they might not have to run the gauntlet of negative reinforcement to which native language learner errors are always subject; but such situations do not seem to be common. We should therefore expect that second-language learner errors will ultimately give rise to linguistic changes only in exceptional circumstances, and that changes of such an origin might be less common than those of wholly native origin. We will discuss that scenario in detail in Chapter 4.

Beyond anecdotes: inferential investigation

How can we move beyond anecdotes and general observations, if it is so difficult to catch these developments "in the act"? Since it is clear that changes in basic phonology and morphosyntax must begin as learner errors, we ought to study the types of errors that learners make and the types of linguistic changes that are recorded and attempt to find correlations between them. It will be especially important to distinguish between errors characteristic of native learners and those that appear only in the imperfect speech of adult second-language learners. Among the native errors we will want to concentrate on those that persist late in the NLA window, since those are much more likely to survive than the more extreme errors characteristic of the youngest children. Such study should not be very difficult and is certainly long overdue.

The American English merger of /ɔr/ and /ər/ which was observed to persist in the speech of one child (see above) is a case in point. Conditioned mergers of vowels are a very common type of change observed in the linguistic records of the past; mergers of vowels before /r/ are known to have occurred repeatedly in English during the past half-millennium or so. The syllable nuclei of *fur, fir*, and *fern*, now all /ər/ but originally distinct, were apparently undergoing a long and complex process of merger in Shakespeare's time (see Jespersen 1909: 319–21, Kökeritz 1953: 249–54); within the past couple of centuries all the back round vowels followed by /r/ have merged in /ɔr/ in the standard English of Britain and in that of the USA, so that *for, four*, and *poor*, for example, now all rhyme (though they do not necessarily rhyme in Scotland, nor in the rural south of the USA). The child's merger of /ər/ with /ɔr/ is simply "more of the same." Its most striking characteristics – that it is an error of NLA, that it might have been reinforced by interaction with other native learners, and that it escaped the notice of most adults (and therefore stigmatization) – can have been true of all the similar earlier mergers, and that helps to explain how such extensive mergers of common syllable nuclei could have succeeded.

However, pursuit of a case-by-case approach to the problem encounters difficulties of two kinds. Surprisingly, the first problem is a dearth of solid evidence. There is plenty of evidence on the historical side: traditional historical linguists have described hundreds of linguistic changes that are observable in the historical records of individual languages or can be reconstructed with complete confidence, and though no one has made an extensive catalogue and classification of such changes, it would be comparatively easy for specialists to do so. But there is very little evidence regarding native-learner errors that persist into the latest stages of NLA, because colleagues who study NLA are interested in how the children *succeed*, not in the comparatively rare instances in which they fail. Unfortunately what we who study language change need is a comprehensive study of those failures, and until such a study is undertaken we will be constrained to work with anecdotal evidence of lapses in NLA.

The other difficulty is more fundamental: a purely descriptive research program has little potential for explanatory power. Of course we do want to know how changes of particular kinds emerge from learner errors; but we also want to know how *in general* errors become entrenched in late childhood speech (and thus become part of the normal variation in the language of a speech community), and a "bottom-up" approach is unlikely to discover the causes of that phenomenon. What we need is a well-articulated model of language acquisition, consistent with the known facts, that can suggest possible causes for linguistic changes and tell us where to look for confirmation of our hypotheses.

Part of such a model has recently been developed by Charles Yang (see especially Yang 2002). It depends crucially on the observed fact that all human languages, and therefore all languages which provide input for NLA, exhibit variation in many dimensions. Because the target grammar is always *under-determined* by any small subset of the evidence available to the learner, the learner has to consider a range of possible settings for many of the Universal Grammar parameters of the target grammar; thus potential grammars are *in competition* in the process of NLA. Some of the pieces of evidence that the learner hears might be compatible with any of the possible parameter settings, but most will be compatible with some and incompatible with others. Every time the learner hears a piece of evidence incompatible with a given parameter setting, that setting is assigned a *penalty*. The penalties are probabilistic in nature: they reflect the decrease in the probability that the setting in question will ultimately be able to account for the whole range of relevant data. As the penalities accumulate over time, the setting best able to account for the pattern of target language data gradually wins out over the other options, and the child's grammar thereby conforms to the adult norm (Yang 2002: 26–32).

Here is an example, restated from Yang 2002: 34–6 (with references). Suppose that a child is learning standard Dutch. About 64.7% of the declarative main clauses she hears will have SVO word order, about 34% will have XVSO order (where X is a topicalized constituent), and about 1.3% will have OVS order. The child must consider at least the following possible analyses for the word order of these clauses:

(a)   the clauses are "verb-second" (V2), with the verb in second position and any one constituent to the left;

(b)   the clauses are VSO, at least some with topicalization (including topicalization of S);

(c)   the clauses are SVO;

(d)   the clauses are OVS.

The SVO examples are compatible with (a), (b), and (c); the XVSO examples are compatible with (a) and (b); the OVS clauses are compatible with (a) and (d). As the penalties accrue, (d) will rapidly drop out of the competition; (c) will take longer to go. Analysis (b) will hang on until the learner realizes that *every* declarative main clause has a topic; but in the long run analysis (a), which is never penalized, will win out, and the child will have learned the Dutch V2 rule.

Yang's approach can also explain how a native learner of American English could fail to acquire the contrast between /ər/ and /ɔr/ (see above). Suppose that some of the children on the preschool playground have acquired the contrast, while others have not. Hypothesizing that the two syllable nuclei contrast in their English causes no problems when the learner is talking to a child who has acquired the contrast; the hypothesis accounts adequately for the data heard, and the child with the contrast will always be understood. But a child who has not acquired the contrast will either produce examples of the two nuclei distributed randomly over the combined phonetic space of both or will produce only one of the correct outputs, using it for both underlying nuclei. In talking to such a child it is actually a disadvantage to suppose that two different nuclei are in question, because relying on the phonetics that one hears will lead to a correct inference of what word is intended only about half the time (see Herold 1990: 91–9); the better hypothesis is that /ər/ and /ɔr/ are just two different pronunciations of the same thing. But that hypothesis works almost as well in talking to a child who *has* acquired the contrast, for two reasons. Not only is the difference between, say, *turn* and *torn*, or even *bird* and *board*, usually clear from context; in most cases one of the new homonyms created by the merger is vastly more common than the other(s), so that even without context it is usually possible to guess which word was intended.[2] So the grammar with the merger will be penalized much less often than the grammar without the merger, and over time it will win out. (A similar process leads to the "Bill Peters effect," which has been known to sociolinguists for some time [see especially Herold 1990: 182–6] and will be discussed further in the following chapter.)

The above is a superficial description of Yang's model; a more adequate description would also consider the mathematics of the grammar competition model and the predictions about long-term language change that the model makes. (An illustration of how the full model handles a phonemic merger is offered in a still unpublished paper by Charles Yang, "Population structure and language change.") But even this "quick and dirty" exposition has led to some surprising results. Linguists have tended to suppose that phonemic mergers are dysfunctional, at least to some extent, because they erode the system of contrasts that collectively distinguish utterances of different meanings. But there is so much redundancy built into human language that the structure of the learning algorithm can easily yield the opposite result: mergers are actually favored. In other words,

(a)   because the meanings of homonyms are usually disambiguated from context without difficulty, and

(b)   because the disparity in frequency between some homonyms is so great as to leave little scope for ambiguity anyway, and

(c)   because the learning algorithm heavily favors grammars compatible with all the evidence, and

(d)   because a grammar incorporating a phonemic merger can give an
           adequate account of unmerged data, given (a) and (b) above,

mergers will tend to spread rapidly among native language learners. That
explains the prevalence of phonemic mergers in the historical record at one blow,
so to speak.

There are also NLA situations in which the alternative grammars being learned
do not compete with each other. Most obviously, children natively acquiring more
than one language are acquiring two or more grammars that are not in competition,
each grammar being appropriate to one of the languages being learned. Evidently
children figure this out. Learning two well-differentiated dialects of the same
language likewise does not lead to grammar competition. Even learning a formal
register of one's native language can involve learning divergent parameter settings
that do not compete with the ones normal in colloquial speech; for instance, a
native learner of English eventually learns that in verse – even popular verse and
songs – one can use some word orders that no one uses in speech, the unstressed
auxiliary *do* in positive declarative clauses (where it is always stressed in normal
English), and so on.

But there are also cases in which grammars do compete, yet neither wins out;
in those cases the native learner acquires a grammar which exhibits variation
even though it is dialectally uniform. This is a common occurrence in some areas
of the grammar; for instance, variable phonetic implementation rules are well
attested in phonology, and in many languages there are a few verbs which are
variably inflected. It also seems clear that variably set syntactic parameters can be
acquired. In every case of long-term syntactic change that has been studied, the
change proceeds through a variable stage; for instance, a language which was OV
at the beginning of the change and VO at its completion passes through a period
of at least a couple of centuries in which both underlying orders are possible,
though their frequency gradually changes. (See Chapter 9 for an example and
discussion.) In some cases one could argue that while both parameter settings
were current in the speech community, no single individual need have internalized
both; the appearance of both settings in a single document might reflect a range
of distinctively different styles, or even alteration of a text with a single parameter
setting by a copyist whose setting was different. But there are also cases in which
the dialect and style of a text are completely uniform, the author was not working
from any prototype, and significant alteration of the word order by copyists is not
likely because other contemporary texts show the same mix of parameter settings;
the history of Herodotos, discussed in Chapter 9, is a clear example. Identification
of current native speakers of variable word order languages with a similar mix of
parameter settings would be welcome confirmation of this inference.

How can grammar competition not yield a winner? If a body of input data is
heterogeneous enough, but the learner has good reason to believe that those data
are dialectally and stylistically uniform, both the competing parameter settings
will be penalized often because neither can account for the vast majority of the

evidence – so often that, by the time NLA is complete, there is no clear winner. The child will then have acquired a grammar with a variable component (see Yang 2002: 32–4).

The fate of linguistic innovations

However they arise, new variants in the adult language of a speech community enter a competition with older variants. What happens to variants in competition in a speech community is well understood, thanks to the work of Labov and his students and co-workers. In the following chapter we examine the relationship between variation and change in speech communities.

Notes

1 There are languages whose derivational morphology is learned within the window of native acquisition. For instance, Fortescue and Olsen 1992 report that Greenlandic children begin to acquire the exuberantly productive derivational morphology of their native language at the age of 2, and that the entire system is in place by the age of 5; Allen and Crago 1989 report similar findings for Inuktitut. However, the English and Eskimoan cases are not similar: English derivational morphology is limited and serves to make words of major classes; Eskimoan derivational morphology routinely packs an entire clause into a noun or verb. In functional terms the acquisition of Eskimoan derivation thus overlaps significantly with the acquisition of English phrase structure. The transparency of Eskimoan derivational morphology is also likely to be a relevant factor, since Mithun 1989 reports that noun incorporation in Mohawk – a language with famously opaque derivational morphology in which phonological words are often whole clauses – is *not* acquired by the age of 5; see especially Allen and Crago 1989: 54–6 for more detailed discussion. This is obviously an area of acquisition that would greatly repay further study.

2 In an effort to estimate how much confusion a merger of /ər/ and /ɔr/ in North American English would be likely to produce even in the absence of context, one of the authors consulted a frequency dictionary of English compiled from texts read in American schools (Carroll *et al.* 1971) and found that pairs and sets of words of similar frequency distinguished only by that contrast are actually rare. For instance, it turns out that in the merged dialect [fɔɹ] must be either *for* or *four* well over 99% of the time, because *fur* is so much rarer and *fir* rarer still (*fore* being the rarest of all); [fɔɹst] is *first* at least 96% of the time, because *forced* is rare; [mɔɹ] can only be *more*, since *myrrh* not only is very rare but is encountered virtually only in the Christmas story; [lɔɹn] can only be *learn*, and so on. The most easily confused words are the common and basic nouns *bird*, which appeared 812 times in the corpus of 5 million words on which the dictionary was based, and *board*, which appeared 536 times.

3   Language change in the speech community

Change in the context of variation

It is clear that native-learner errors must survive in the speech of individuals until the end of the developmental window for acquisition in order to become language changes; that is the first bottleneck or filter through which they must pass, so to speak. But if they are to "succeed" as linguistic changes, learner errors must then become accepted variants in the system of linguistic variation in the adult speech community; that is the second external constraint on language change (see Weinreich *et al.* 1968: 99–102). Virtually nothing is known about that process, for the reasons discussed in the preceding chapter; we can only infer that for social reasons operating on the level of individual relationships some idiosyncrasies of speech are not only tolerated but imitated, and that for structural reasons some innovations are inherently more likely than others to succeed. In any case, a change that begins to spread has crossed an important threshold in its development, because it thereby acquires a significant identity in the speech of the community at large.

From that point forward linguistic change occurs in the context of variation unless and until an innovation becomes universal in a speech community, when it is said to have "gone to completion." During that part of its trajectory one can study the change only by studying the variation in which it participates – a type of study pioneered and still led by William Labov.

Longitudinal patterns of variation

Unfortunately, though all change is at some point variation, not all variation turns out to be long-term change; one of the first things a sociolinguist must do is try to determine whether or not particular observed phenomena are changes in progress. The most important distinction is between variation which is stable in the long run, including variation which is in dynamic equilibrium and variation which undergoes repeated short-term fluctuations in the occurrence of the variants, and variation which is undergoing a long-term statistically significant shift in the distribution of the variants; only the latter is change in progress.

A wide variety of sociolinguistic processes can produce stable variation. In clearly stratified societies different social groups may accommodate their speech to each other's usage when they interact linguistically, so that different linguistic forms present in the speech community may fluctuate in frequency of occurrence over time because of temporary changes in the overall social context, or in the frequency of different specific social contexts; the result is not necessarily long-term change. For instance, though the pronunciation of low vowels has been socially significant in French since at least the sixteenth century, exactly which pronunciations are prestigious has shifted repeatedly: fronting of /a/ seems to have been prestigious in the sixteenth century, stigmatized in the later seventeenth, prestigious again in the nineteenth, and stigmatized in the twentieth (Lennig 1978: 141–4 with references)! Currently the distinction between the vowels of *patte* /pat/ and *pâte* /pɑt/ is being lost by middle-class women and to some extent even by working-class women because the merged pronunciation is perceived as more "refined" (Lennig 1978: 144–6, 150–8). But it would be rash to assume that the merger of the two low vowels in Paris is a change that will go to completion and become irreversible *throughout the whole community*, given the fluctuations of the past. A similar situation has recently been observed in Charleston, South Carolina. More than a century ago there was a merger or near-merger of the higher tense front vowels before /r/, so that *fear* and *fair*, for instance, became homonyms; but by the middle of the twentieth century that merger was in retreat, partly because of an influx of residents from elsewhere, and all but the oldest native Charlestonians now maintain the contrast clearly (Baranowski 2006: 99–121 with references). It appears that changes of this sort can reverse themselves if social conditions change – provided that a merger does not establish itself in an overwhelming majority of sub-populations. Aside from the last proviso, we do not yet know in detail under what circumstances such fluctuations lead to irreversible linguistic change.

Another type of variation whose relation to real change is at best problematic is diachronically stable stratification by age, or "age grading," in which the use of a form is correlated with age simply because the speakers *of each generation* alter their usage as they grow older. For example, the pronunciation of /ð/ as a stop ("dese," "dem," etc., for *these, them*, etc.) in the vernacular speech of some American cities is increasingly abandoned by speakers as they age, no doubt because that pronunciation is a severely stigmatized stereotype of lower-class speech (Labov 1994: 73 n. 2, based on the data of Labov 1966 and other studies). Finally, stable variables typically correlate with socioeconomic factors and style (formal vs. colloquial, etc.) in patterns that can be fairly complex; see especially Labov 2001: 74–120 for detailed discussion.

Like age-grading, change in progress is characterized by regular differences in the usage frequencies of variants across ages, with younger speakers using innovative forms more often than older speakers. In the vowel rotations currently under way in United States cities of the East and Midwest, for instance, there is a regular negative correlation between the acoustic distance of the vowel from the standard pronunciation (the conservative norm) and the age of the speaker: the younger the speaker, the greater the distance. The fronting of general American English /ɑ/ (as in *socks*) to [æ] in Chicago, and the other changes that occur there as part of the same pattern of vowel shifting, are regularly found to be most extreme among the youngest speakers at any given time (both in terms of the frequency with which the shifted variants are used and in terms of how far the vowels are shifted from the conservative norm). *In addition*, the available "real-time" information about the shift – some twenty-three years of observations, from 1968 to 1991 – reveals that the change is progressive over time (see Labov 1994: 185–95). It is the latter finding that proves that the vowel rotations in question are actually changes in progress.

In what follows we will concentrate on verifiable examples of long-term change.

Key questions about the progress of real changes

The most extensively investigated cases of variation in usage frequencies have been phonological. Among the best known are studies of the rotations of vowels (such as Labov *et al.* 1972 and the numerous other studies cited in Labov 1994), of vowel mergers (most notably Herold 1990), and of various sandhi processes, such as the deletion of word-final /t/ and /d/ in English or the loss of word-final /s/ and nasals in the Spanish and Portuguese of the western hemisphere (see Labov 1994: 556–61 with numerous references). The deletion processes usually affect consonants and tend to be diachronically stable instances of external sandhi, while vowel rotations and mergers most often prove to be true linguistic changes.

Vowel rotations in particular appear to have characteristic linguistic and social profiles. Linguistically, they often begin with the shift of a vowel from one subsystem of vowels into another (for instance, from the system of lax vowels into the system of tense vowels, or vice versa), followed by its progressive movement through the vowel space (a two-dimensional Cartesian space defined by the first and second formants; see Labov, Yaeger, and Steiner 1972: 31–4, Labov 1994: 159–60, 165–6). Vowels belonging to the same subsystem tend to move together, maintaining their distance from one another as they move through the vowel space. These movements are gradual, taking place over periods of two generations and more, with each birth cohort slightly shifting the target positions of the vowels further in the same direction. Because the vowel space is defined by the formant frequencies of the open vocal tract used in vowel pronunciation, vowel rotations are continuous rather than categorical changes; though examples of rotations within which mergers (eventually) occurred are known from the historical record, it appears from studies of rotations in progress that mergers are not a typical result. Socially, rotations seem to arise in the vernacular language among the section of the population with the strongest and most stable ties to the local neighborhood community, but they spread more or less uniformly to all segments of the population of a given geographic region. Why these changes have a consistent direction and proceed to completion in the way that they do is an important question that needs to be answered.

Vowel mergers occur when phonetically similar but distinct vowel phonemes are no longer perceived or pronounced differently, leading to homophony. Unlike rotations, mergers are categorical: either two vowels are distinct or they are not, and once two vowels have merged, the contrast can never be reestablished in the same distribution by processes internal to the merging dialect. (That is true of all mergers, of course, not only of vowel mergers; see Chapter 5 for further discussion, as well as discussion of near-mergers.) Dialectologists have observed that when a geographic area in which two vowels have merged is adjacent to one in which the vowels remain distinct, the area of merger tends to expand at the expense of the area with the distinction. The reasons for that pattern have become clear in recent work; they were discussed in Chapter 2, and we will have occasion to return to this phenomenon below.

Two further aspects of the spread of innovations are central to the process of linguistic change. On the one hand, a new form spreads from its locus of origin to new geographic, social, and stylistic environments, while on the other hand it also increases in frequency within the speech-community environments in which it already exists. These two aspects of diffusion raise significantly different issues. The spread of an innovation to new social or stylistic environments can conveniently be thought of as borrowing (from social group to social group, or from one style into another); but increasing frequency of use within a given speech-community environment is clearly something else. Both processes can be accompanied by spread of the innovation to new *structural* – i.e. phonological, morphological, or syntactic – environments; we will note that aspect of the spread of change in our discussion below, though for the most part we focus in this chapter on linguistic environments whose definition is external to structure.

Spread of an innovation as borrowing

From the start it has been clear that innovations can be borrowed from one part of the speech community by another. In Labov's pioneering study of Martha's Vineyard, the distribution of [əɪ] and [əʊ] (the variants of /aɪ/ and /aʊ/ with raised nucleus) by age and ethnic group shows clearly that the descendants of Portuguese immigrants have borrowed this change from the longer-standing population of "Yankee" Vineyarders: whereas the speech of second-generation Portuguese-Americans on the island did not show much raising, contrasting sharply in that regard with Yankee speech of the same generation, third- and fourth-generation Portuguese-Americans have adopted the innovation (Labov

1963: 295, 301–2). In fact, the borrowers can be said to have overdone it, showing more spread of raising from /ɑɪ/ (its original locus, Labov 1963: 281–2, 293–4) to /ɑʊ/, and more raising overall (p. 302); that is, the borrowing of the change from one speech-community environment into another has been accompanied by its spread from one phonological environment into another, as well as by an increase in the frequency of use of the new form.

Similar socially motivated cases are not hard to find. Penelope Eckert and other linguists have shown that a sharp ideological and social division among Midwestern adolescents typically has large linguistic consequences. The "antiestablishment" students, who will (mostly) not be applying for university admission and are anxious to get out from under adult authority and become adults themselves as soon as possible, tend to adopt and even exaggerate linguistic innovations characteristic of vernacular speech (Eckert 1991, Habick 1991). This can provoke the establishment-oriented students into creating speech norms that exaggerate in the opposite direction – for example, fronting a vowel in the environments in which the antiestablishment crowd backs it (Eckert 1991: 228–30) – though linguistic behavior of this latter sort seems less common.

Borrowing of a change across social (including ethnic) boundaries is of course not the only type of borrowing attested. Borrowing from one geographical area to another has been known and studied for more than a century; examples of the spread of changes across the European countryside in a wavelike fashion, typically outward from cities in which the innovations appear to have originated, can be found in any of the more traditional introductions to linguistics or historical linguistics (cf. e.g. Bloomfield 1933: 328–38, Bynon 1977: 173–83, Hock 1991: 432–41, all with references to earlier classic studies). But geographical borrowing need not take place between geographically contiguous populations (Trudgill 1983: 52–87). For instance, Callary reports a raising of /æ/ in specific phonological environments in the English of Chicago and other urban centers of northern Illinois that is not shared by adjacent rural areas; interestingly, the larger the urban area in which the speaker lives, the more extreme the raising (Callary 1975). So far the best available explanation is that the change has been borrowed from Chicago English by residents of smaller cities as a means of asserting their urban identity, though more work will be needed to establish that definitively (ibid. p. 168).

In general, it seems clear that the innovations characteristic of dominant social groups are borrowed by other groups that desire acceptance by the dominant group; that is especially clear in the Martha's Vineyard study. But some strong caveats are in order. In the first place, the definition of social dominance can be extremely localized in space and time. No one would argue that the Philadelphia working class was in any sense dominant, relative to the "old money" families of the Main Line, during the period that the older upper-class speakers interviewed by Kroch were growing up and acquiring their definitive patterns of speech; yet the distinctive innovations of Philadelphia working-class speech were clearly borrowed by upper-class speakers. The explanation for this pattern seems to be that, as small children, upper-class Philadelphians of the older generation were typically raised with working-class playmates, and to some extent by working-class servants, and thus acquired the innovations characteristic of local working-class speech (Kroch 1996: 26–7). In other words, the patterns of authority and social acceptance characteristic of early childhood were decisive in this particular case, even though they were completely reversed in adulthood! Something similar appears to have happened in Charleston, where the local dialect of the white natives may have been influenced by Gullah, a creole spoken by former slaves who were employed as domestics and nannies by wealthy families (Baranowski 2006: 66–71, 234). Moreover, it is not any objective economic or political dominance that motivates the borrowing, but the *perception* that one group enjoys socially favored status. That is clear enough from Callary's study. It seems quite unlikely that residents of the smaller urban areas of northern Illinois are in daily contact with Chicagoans or have any objective need to be accepted by them; nevertheless, they seem to have adopted a striking feature of Chicago speech as a means of asserting that they, too, are urbanites. Presumably that is not only a matter of asserting an identity, but also of rejecting one: residents of Dixon, Illinois, for example, with a population of less than 20,000 at the time of Callary's study, can reasonably be suspected of saying [beɔk] for *back* as a means of proclaiming, "We are not hicks!"

A final, and rather surprising, pattern has emerged from a variety of sociolinguistic studies: many changes are implemented first and most vigorously by women, while men lag behind. To some extent this must mean that innovations are borrowed from the speech of women into that of men. Positing such a development for vowel rotations is something that must be attempted with care, because the apparent "lead" of the women could simply be an artefact of incomplete normalization: because the pitches of men's and women's voices, and thus the fundamental frequencies of their speech, are different, the hearer mentally "corrects" the harmonics (formants) of the vowels to bring them into line, and incomplete correction can appear to leave women with relatively higher second formants – thus fronter vowels (Anthony Kroch, p.c.). But not all the changes in which women are ahead are vowel rotations. In modern Cairene Arabic, palatalization of the dental stops before high front vocalics is clearly a relatively new sound change in progress (Haeri 1997: 70–3), and women lead the implementation of the change by a wide margin (ibid. pp. 68–9, 73–83). However, Cairene men – including men who wish to project an overtly masculine image – do use the palatalized variants (ibid. pp. 96–8, 100). In fact, while many interviewees agreed that there were differences between the speech of men and women, not one mentioned the much greater use of palatalized variants by women (ibid. pp. 221–2)! It is even possible to find similar sound changes which are led by men in one dialect and by women in another; for instance, the raising of the nucleus of the diphthong /aɪ/ in North American English is led by men in Philadelphia (Labov 2001: 284, 289), but the parallel raising of /aʊ/ is led by women in Ann Arbor, Michigan (Dailey-O'Cain 1997: 114–16). Still, though not all changes in progress exhibit the same pattern of gender differentiation and though the differences between male and female speech are not always large, it is fairly typical to find some difference and to find women innovating more. This is all the more surprising because in the case of innovations whose spread has "stalled out" and which have become stigmatized, women seem to play an opposite role, rejecting the stigmatized variants in favor of the conservative norms and so helping to enforce the latter (see Labov 2001: 366–7).

Recent research by Labov and his students and co-workers has begun to make sense of this pattern. Surveying the available evidence, Labov concludes that the leaders of vigorously progressing linguistic changes "are women who have achieved a respected social and economic position in the local networks. As adolescents, they aligned themselves with the social groups and symbols that resisted adult authority . . . without deviating from their upwardly mobile path within the local social structure" (Labov 2001: 409). However,

> [t]here is no evidence that attitudes, ideologies, and opinions . . . will bear directly upon linguistic changes from below . . . These attitudes may influence who a person talks to and how often they talk, and so affect the flow of linguistic influence . . . From this point of view, the use of local Philadelphia speech forms is the product of speakers' social trajectories, and we can best explain the leaders' linguistic performances by the history of their social contacts in their formative years. (ibid. pp. 409–10)

In other words, the women who are "out in front" in implementing a linguistic change apparently acquired their relatively extreme innovative pattern of speech as disaffected (but not alienated) teenagers and, upon becoming highly successful adults (by local measures of success), tend to spread that innovative pattern both because of their wide and varied contacts in the local social networks and because of their respected status – their interlocutors tend to want to speak like them. In short, it appears that women are better positioned to be agents of linguistic change because of their greater adeptness at social networking, on the average, and that vigorously independent-minded women are the actual agents of change both because they are likely to have embraced linguistic innovations when young and because they are likely to be influential in their communities as adults. The significance of innovations among young speakers will call for further discussion below.

In the very long term – the point of view taken by most historical linguists – the borrowing of innovations has important consequences. In the borrowing of phonological changes, phonemic units usually remain intact; phonological constraints on an innovation are usually borrowed unaltered, tightened or relaxed in phonologically intelligible ways, or abandoned altogether. For instance, the merger of /ɑ/ and /ɔ/ in North America is not reported to be acquiring exceptions as its spreads; as the raising of the nucleus of /aɪ/ on Martha's Vineyard became more frequent and more extreme, raising spread to the parallel back diphthong /aʊ/; and so on. In other words, borrowers of phonological innovations usually do not disrupt the *diasystem* – the system of equivalences between the discrete phonological units of different dialects within which variation occurs – evidently because the rules required to map the pronunciations of one dialect onto another are easy to learn so long as no new contrast must be learned. That is one reason why sound change, even when broadly defined, is overwhelmingly regular.

But occasionally the borrowing of a sound change is inconsistent, resulting in lexical exceptions (positive or negative). Maps illustrating traditional dialect geography offer numerous examples (see e.g. Bloomfield 1933: 328). An almost certain example in North American English involves the tensing of /æ/. That innovation seems to have begun in New York City in the first half of the nineteenth century, to judge from the fact that it was well advanced in that city by the 1890s (see Babbitt 1896: 461). The conditioning of the tensing in New York is very complex (Labov *et al.* 1972: 48–50), and the full pattern of conditioning seems to have been present already in the early twentieth century, to judge from the descriptions of Trager 1930, 1940. The pattern that Trager described was that of his own speech (Trager 1930: 399); he was born in 1906 in Newark, New Jersey, to which the New York pattern had apparently spread. (Tensing of inherited /æ/ in some phonological environments is quite widespread in the USA [Trager 1930: 399; Labov *et al.* 1972: 48], but the phonemic split is more restricted [see Trager 1940: 255; Labov *et al.* 1972].) Tensing of /æ/ seems to have spread to most of the large cities of the USA's eastern seaboard, sometimes with its conditioning almost intact; for example, the pattern among the oldest surviving natives of New Orleans closely resembles Trager's (Labov 2007: 365). However, the spread of tensing was accompanied by changes in its conditioning in some areas, and in New York itself the phonological scope of tensing has not remained static. A very complex pattern of development can be summarized briefly as follows. The basic New York rule tenses /æ/ before anterior nasals, voiced oral stops and affricates, and voiceless fricatives, provided that the conditioning consonant is followed by word-end, a morpheme boundary, or an obstruent and the word is fully stressed (Labov *et al.* 1972: 48–9; note the examples in Babbitt, 1896). However, words which are acquired relatively late, as well as words which are abbreviations of longer words, sometimes fail to exhibit tensing of /æ/; typical examples include *math* (shortened from *mathematics*), *adze* (typically learned late in childhood), *lad* and *lass* (which are purely literary words, never used in spontaneous speech; these exceptions were noted already by Trager 1940: 257 and appear to be characteristic of many dialects in which a split between lax /æ/ and tense /æː/ has occurred). Moreover, tensing has spread beyond its original phonological environment in New York, and lexical exceptions have developed as it has spread (Labov *et al.* 1972: 49–50). Failure of tensing in abbreviations might actually be rule-governed, and borrowing from literary dialects is a relatively marginal feature in educated dialects of all kinds. At least some of the other lexical exceptions that have developed in New York might reasonably be ascribed to dialect borrowing and imperfect second-dialect learning, especially since the city has never ceased to be full of immigrants from the rest of the USA and elsewhere (see immediately below); but it is no longer possible to figure out exactly what happened by looking at the eventual outcome in a single speech community. If we look at the spread of tensing across the map, however, a much clearer pattern emerges. In southern New England tensing has been restricted to the position before anterior nasals (Labov *et al.* 1972: 48); in the industrial cities around the Great Lakes /æ/ is tensed in all positions (Labov 1994: 290, 429). Both developments are radical but regular simplifications of the rule. In Philadelphia /æ/ is tensed in fewer environments than in New York, normally appearing only before anterior nasals and anterior voiceless fricatives followed by word-end in fully stressed words (see the chart in Labov 1994: 520). However, a few positive lexical exceptions developed in Philadelphia: tensed /æ:/ appears in exactly three stressed monosyllables ending in /d/, namely in *mad*, *bad*, and *glad* (but not, for example, in *sad* /sæd/ or *dad* /dæd/). There are also a few negative exceptions: the past tenses *swam*, *began*, *ran*, and *wan* (the past of *win* in the Philadelphia vernacular) all exhibit lax /æ/, though tense /æ:/ appears in *pan*, *fan*, *van*, *man*, *Dan*, *ham*, *lamb*, etc. (Labov 1994: 430–2). Exactly how these lexical exceptions arose is now unrecoverable; the events lie too far in the past. But since it is clear that tensing of /æ/ spread, and almost certain that the Philadelphia speech community borrowed the change, we can infer with some confidence that this irregularity in the sound change was a result of borrowing.

Moreover, once lexical irregularities have arisen in this fashion, they become perturbing influences potentially giving rise to further irregularities. That is because a system including lexical irregularities is far more difficult to learn than one in which the phonological pattern is exceptionlessly rule-governed; even speakers of closely related dialects are unlikely to learn the distribution of exceptions perfectly. That is why it is reasonable to ascribe the lexical irregularities in the spread of tensed /æ:/ in New York to (sub-)dialect contact (see above); a probable example was noted already by Trager 1940: 256 (*family* with /æ/ or /æ:/). There is a considerable body of sociolinguistic data showing that the tensing of /æ/ has continued to spread in the Philadelphia area and that the spread proceeds lexeme by lexeme in the environment before /mV/, /nV/, and /lV/ (Labov 1994: 432–7 with references). We might therefore expect irregularities in the long-term pattern of sound change to cluster around the development of particular phonemic oppositions. We will return to that point in Chapter 5.

Borrowing and/or native learning: the spread of mergers

We noted above that the geographic spread of mergers is a widespread and well-documented phenomenon. The dynamic which underlies this generalization has been discussed by Ruth Herold, who studied the expansion of the merger of /ɑ/ and /ɔ/ in some dialects of American English (in which the vowel of words like *caught* and *hawk*, which generally have /ɔ/ in North America, has come to be pronounced identically with the vowel of *cot* and *hock*, which generally have /ɑ/; Herold 1990: 86–106, 171–86). Herold suggests that, in border areas between dialects which exhibit the distinction between these vowels and dialects which lack it, speakers who have the distinction behave in a startling and characteristic way that actively promotes the spread of the merger. Although they must know subconsciously that the vowels which are undergoing merger are in principle distinct, because they can accurately *produce* the distinction in at least some circumstances, they claim that the two vowels "sound the same," and in their fluent speech they can allow the ranges of variation of the two vowels to overlap to a considerable degree, making it more likely that children will fail to pick up the distinction in the course of language acquisition. The failure of speakers in border areas to maintain or acknowledge a distinction in pronunciation that they are capable of making (called the "Bill Peters effect" after an informant from near Harrisburg in whose speech the phenomenon was first noticed) appears to be an adaptive reaction to the fact that the distinction has little communicative use, since so many other people in the area neither make nor recognize it. In fact, since the pronunciations of those who no longer distinguish the two vowels typically range over the whole phonetic space originally occupied by the vowels – so that, in the case studied by Herold, *hock* may sound like "hock" or "hawk," and *hawk* may equally well sound like "hock" or "hawk," unpredictably and in no discernable pattern – the attempt to maintain a difference between the vowels will actually lead to more confusion than a determination to ignore it and to rely solely on context to disambiguate (Herold 1990: 226–9; see the discussion of mergers in native language acquisition [NLA] in Chapter 2). This is highly plausible because cross-dialectal confusion of that kind has actually been demonstrated in a range of cases in North American English (Labov 1994: 324–7). Since that asymmetry is a stable factor in the contact situation, it might be supposed to maintain the pressure for merger across generations, thus accounting for its long-term spread.

But other evidence suggests that something else is going on too. Herold's real-time and apparent-time analyses of the trajectory of the merger show that in at least some towns it went to completion within about a generation (Herold 1990: 86–91, 94–9). That suggests that many speakers learned the merger in the course of NLA by the mechanism that Yang has posited (see the preceding chapter) – though the existence of speakers who can produce the distinction reliably (and thus must *not* have learned the merger in NLA) but profess not to hear any difference between the vowels shows that that cannot be the whole story. Clearly more research on this point, which is central to historical phonology, is urgently needed.

The long-term direction of change

The study of the increasing frequency of use of linguistic innovations faces a large issue which purely synchronic studies of frequency patterns do not: why does the frequency of use of alternative forms change over time, and why do changes so often go to completion, with a new form completely replacing an old one? The very existence of stable variation raises the possibility that every change could have developed into stable variation; therefore it also raises the question of why so many changes have not. One way of thinking about the spread of change, then, is that the variation found between new and old forms is not alternation but competition: the forms in variation are competing for use in the same environments and the form whose frequency is increasing is, for some reason, winning the competition.

From this perspective the crucial question in the study of the spread of new forms in language change is what advantage they have over the old forms they replace. The unanimous verdict of twentieth-century linguistics is that language change does not produce functionally improved languages; nineteenth-century notions of linguistic "superiority" have proved to be based on nothing more than Eurocentric bigotry, and observation readily shows that there is no correlation between the structure or typology of a language and the political fortunes or material or mental culture of its speakers. Consequently the question of what sort of competitive advantage an innovation can possibly have has not received a satisfactory answer.

Where can we look for indications of relative advantage of competing speech-forms? Ideally we would like to find evidence in changes currently in progress, but it is surprisingly difficult to get the information that we need to solve this problem definitively. The *social* advantage of one form or another is generally clear, and we can say (for example) that such advantages are always highly localized, since it is the viewpoint of particular speakers in particular social contexts that matters. But the same pattern of social advantage is found in cases of stable variation as in cases of real change in progress! Evidently a more detailed investigation is necessary.

The obvious place to look for an answer to this question is the behavior of those individuals who are implementing an innovation in the most extreme fashion – that is, the most vigorous leaders of the change. In sufficiently well-studied cases those individuals are normally teenagers, typically girls, from the middle of the socioeconomic hierarchy (see Labov 2001: 168–70, 190, 385–411, 438–45). Actual measurements of vowel shifts seem to show that their advance in the female population is best modeled by the logistic function (see Kroch 1989: 203–6), which is typically generated by change in the frequency of competing alternatives, and that the age group that contributes the greatest increment of the change – the steepest part of the s-curve, so to speak – is younger teenagers (Labov 2001: 449–60). They are literally the group driving the change forward, and it seems clear that each new cohort of younger teenage girls drives it a little further forward. That begins to explain why the pronunciations of vowels shift; does it also begin to offer an explanation for the increase in the frequency of an innovation?

As Labov observes, "[d]espite the fact that the community system advances over time, a girl who enters this system must quickly perceive that girls older than she is use more advanced forms of changing linguistic variables" (Labov 2001: 463). This is because of the following configuration of events. Each cohort of young children brings a new set of native acquisition errors into the speech community, and some of them are copied by peers and by younger children, thus becoming changes in progress; but individuals who are already adults at that time do not copy those errors or participate in those changes. A child a decade or more younger begins approximately with the variants of her mother, who belongs to the older generation and did not participate in the latest round of changes; thus with respect to changes already well under way she has some catching up to do. "In adopting these more advanced forms, the speaker is following the normal path of taking the behavior of older children as a model. Following the incrementation pattern, she eventually surpasses their level. This can occur only when they have become linguistic adults, with a stabilized phonology, while she is still advancing" (ibid.). The attempt to copy the speech of older children is inevitably overdone just a little, in the same way that the attempt of non-Yankees on Martha's Vineyard to copy Yankee patterns was overdone, and the slight exaggerations of each age cohort quickly add up to a perceptible pattern of directed change. The exaggerations can and apparently do occur along at least two parameters: the innovative variants of continuous variables (such as vowels) become increasingly more extreme, and the frequency of the innovative variants increases steadily. While more work is needed to establish this scenario as a definitive explanation for female-led change, the hypothesis just outlined is well supported by the available facts and is highly plausible.

This hypothesis exhibits some interesting characteristics. One is that the relevant social factors must remain stable in order for the change to go to completion, because only under those circumstances will successive cohorts of teenagers continue to behave in the same way; thus it is social *stability*, not social change, that gives rise to at least some linguistic changes. Of course it is the same stability that allows us to recognize the logistic progression of the change, since altering the "rules" of competition between the variants could lead to a quite different competition. Finally, it is very striking that the striving of young people to be accepted by their older peers – an integral part of growing up in all human societies – can be a motor of linguistic change.

It would be highly convenient if the progress of all linguistic changes within a narrowly defined speech community could be described by this single model, but that would be too good to be true. For one thing, there has been hardly any study of how the (much rarer) male-led changes proceed and what drives them. For another, it is clear that drastic social change can also produce linguistic change. Very little is known about the latter phenomenon, but we can at least describe one case that has been studied.

Change by loss of a stylistic register

Goddard 1988 describes a set of apparent phonological changes over the past hundred years in Fox, an Algonkian language, which turn out to be something rather different from what a cursory inspection suggests. The situation can be summarized as follows.

Fox was well recorded in the decades immediately following 1900, and the language appears from the records to have been very conservative phonologically (by comparison with closely related languages). By 1968, however, an extensive series of phonological changes had taken place (Goddard 1988: 193–9). Intervocalic semivowels had been lost and the resulting vowels in hiatus (the only hiatuses in the language) had been shortened; thus "Classical" Fox *e:h=a:pi-ki:wita:ya:ni* 'when I stayed' has become *e:h=a:pi-kiitaa:ni*.[†] Word-final vowels have been lost in some environments and variably lost in others. A number of "functional" morphemes, often clitics, appear in what seem to have been allegro forms originally; for example, *pwa:wi* 'not' appears as *pai* (with loss of postconsonantal *w* in addition to the changes already noted above), and the future proclitic *wi:h=* appears as *i:h=*. The oldest speakers interviewed in 1968 still knew the older forms (with a few innovations, such as *pa:wi* for *pwa:wi*), but the youngest speakers had only an imperfect command of them, often restoring the wrong intervocalic semivowel, for instance (Goddard 1988: 197–9). It would appear that a great deal of phonological change occurred rapidly in Fox in the first half of the twentieth century.

But there is also some evidence that the innovative forms already existed at the beginning of the twentieth century. Several, including *pa:wi*, *pai*, and *i:h=*, appear in material collected in 1914 from a native speaker born in 1890; a few can be found in the extensive and otherwise conservative materials recorded by William Jones, such as *šepaita* for *šepawita* 'it's lucky', and others occur in other material collected early in the twentieth century (Goddard 1988: 199–206). Most striking of all are the hypercorrect forms that occasionally appear in Jones' classic texts. He regularly writes the preverb *ma:wi* 'go and . . .' for correct *mawi* (confirmed by comparison with related languages), and he gives inanimate *ohpwa:kani* 'pipe' for the animate *ohpwa:kana* of other sources; these startling errors on the part of a scholar who was a speaker of the language can only be explained as incorrect attempts to construct formal forms on the basis of colloquial *mai* and *ohpwa:kan*, which must have been the forms Jones actually used in speaking (Goddard 1988: 200–2). In short, the stylistic diglossia typical of the oldest speakers in 1968 must have already existed before 1900. This fact is largely but not completely concealed by the decision of William Jones and others to record the most formal and conservative style of the language in their publications.

It follows that there was no rapid period of phonological change in twentieth-century Fox. What happened was quite different and much simpler: successive cohorts of native learners did not receive adequate access to the formal style of the language during the developmental window of NLA. That might have

---

[†] See the Introduction on the transcription of Algonkian languages. In the forms cited here a hyphen marks the open juncture between members of a verbal compound, and "=" is a clitic boundary.

been partly because an increasing number of young people were sent away to boarding schools for much of each year, where they were required to speak English and punished for speaking their native language (see Goddard 1988: 208 n. 7, who cautions that this is likely to have been only one factor). In any case the increasing use of English in the Fox-speaking community has contributed heavily to the obsolescence of the formal register, which is phonologically more conservative at virtually every point of difference; as a result, the more innovative colloquial style has become the only form of the language natively available to most of its speakers (Goddard 1988: 206–8). Thus the linguistic consequences of social change have triggered structural change in Fox by eliminating its more formal and conservative register from use.

It should be emphasized that this change in Fox was not an aspect of language death; in 1968, when the modern pattern of linguistic knowledge and use was reported, the language was still almost universally used in the community (Goddard 1988: 195). How common this type of externally motivated register shift might be is unknown, since no one has looked for other cases (so far as we know). In the present state of our knowledge we also do not know what other kinds of social change can lead to changes internal to a language (as opposed to the obsolescence or death of the language), though it is a fair bet that the range of phenomena which actually exist is much wider than the range which has been studied.

After variation: going to completion

Most of the changes that have been discussed in this chapter are innovative "phonetic implementation" rules, below the level of surface contrast, because the spread of that type of change through the speech community has been most thoroughly investigated. When such a change goes to completion, native learners begin to acquire it as a fixed rule of the phonology. At that point it crosses another threshold in its development, since it has become part of the computational system which must be learned in acquiring native competence in the language. Its further development is in consequence very different in character. We will deal with the fate of phonological rules in Chapter 6.

4   Language contact as a source of change

Dialect contact and language contact

We have seen that linguistic innovations spread from dialect to dialect by borrowing in contact situations. While it seems clear that the innovations are often reanalyzed, so that the borrowing is not "perfect," it appears that linguistic material of any kind can be borrowed from one dialect into a mutually intelligible dialect. This chapter will address contact between dialects that are not mutually intelligible – that is, between different languages. Of course such a distinction is merely practical: dialects of a single language can differ from each other in all and only the ways in which obviously different languages can differ, and there is no sharp boundary between "dialect differences" and "language differences" – there is a cline of intermediate cases. But the practical consequences of this practical distinction are important: borrowing of linguistic *structure* into one's native dialect from a mutually unintelligible speechform is clearly much harder than borrowing from a readily intelligible dialect, and the circumstances in which it is possible at all remain a subject of debate.

To address this problem coherently we need to make several conceptual distinctions of fundamental importance. On a purely linguistic level we distinguish between lexical material and structural material; the latter includes all morphosyntax, i.e. syntactic structure and those items dominated by "functional heads," such as Tense. On the cognitive level we distinguish between monolingual speakers, who speak only one language with any facility (though they may control a range of its dialects), and bilingual (including multilingual) speakers, since it seems likely *a priori* that they behave differently and since bilingualism can be viewed as language contact of a special kind, within the individual rather than within the community. We also need to distinguish between individuals who are *natively* bilingual and those who have learned a second language imperfectly in adulthood, after the critical period for native language acquisition has closed. Finally, we distinguish between importation of linguistic material *into* one's native dialect, which we refer to as "borrowing," and importation of material *from* one's native dialect into a second language learned imperfectly in adulthood, which we refer to as "interference." This last distinction was first clearly articulated by Thomason and Kaufman 1988: 37–45 and van Coetsem 1988: 2–3. We will use "transfer" as a cover term for borrowing and interference.

It also needs to be kept constantly in mind that linguistic borrowing or linguistic interference on the part of isolated individuals is *of no importance*; only if new linguistic material is accepted in the community at large can real change in the language of the community occur. Thus a sociolinguistic perspective on language change is just as important in dealing with contact-induced change as it is in dealing with internal change. In the long term even the behavior of small subcommunities that are not in the linguistic mainstream can fail to have any impact on the future development of a language. It is especially important for academics, who almost always overestimate the importance of their own speech and of literate speech in general, to remember this.

Transfer by monolingual speakers

Since monolingual speakers control no linguistic structure but that of their native language, we do not expect them to be able to transfer structure from one language into another successfully; they should be able to transfer only lexical items. On the other hand, since lexical items are largely arbitrary "counters" which can be inserted into the structures of very different languages (sometimes with adjustments), it should be possible for monolinguals to borrow them into their native languages. That is what we find. By far the most frequent consequence of language contact is the borrowing of lexemes, and it appears that nothing more than casual familiarity with a foreign lexeme and its referents is necessary to enable lexical borrowing. Because loanwords are normally assimilated to fit the phonological structure of the borrowing language, English words borrowed from Malay, for instance (such as *bamboo*, *caddy*, *gong*, and *ketchup*), fit into the language no less well than those borrowed from a close relative like Dutch (such as *brandy*, *catkin*, *gas*, and *wagon*). Of course languages with a significant amount of inflectional morphology must employ strategies to fit loanwords into their inflectional systems. For instance, Russian йод /jod/ 'iodine', borrowed from French *iode* (masc.) and/or German *Jod* (neut.), has been assigned masculine gender because nouns ending in non-palatalized consonants in the nominative singular are normally masculine, and it exhibits the usual case endings of masculine nouns (genitive йода /ˈjoda/, instrumental йодом /ˈjodom/, etc.); Russian регистрировать /rʲegʲistrʲiroˈvatʲ/ 'to register', borrowed from German *registrieren*, has been assigned to the productive class of verbs which normally accommodates loanwords. When inflectional accommodation is infeasible a variety of default strategies may be employed. For example, since Russian кенгуру /kʲenguˈru/ 'kangaroo' (from English) and кепи /ˈkʲepʲi/ 'cap' (from French) end in vowels which are not normally found word-finally in the nominative singular forms of nouns, they are "indeclinable," exhibiting zero endings in all caseforms. Some languages obviate inflectional difficulties in the borrowing of verbs by using a "dummy" verb of very general meaning to carry the inflectional markers, so that the foreign verb is borrowed as a phrase. For instance, there is a productive Japanese construction in which a noun – nearly always of Chinese or other foreign origin – is followed immediately by the verb *suru* 'do', which bears the inflection; this is probably a type of compounding, since the noun seems to participate in no syntactic relations (see Hinds 1986: 371–2). In much the same way Tocharian B makes compound verbs with nouns and the verb *yāmtsi* 'to make, to do', many of which take direct objects. Some of the attested examples include native nouns, e.g. *telki yāmtsi* 'to sacrifice' (*telki* '[a] sacrifice'), but in others the noun is a loanword; for instance, Buddhist Hybrid Sanskrit *codayati* '(s)he accuses' is translated as *cotit yamaṣṣäṃ* (see Adams 1999: 491–2). Evidently Tocharian B had a native construction that could be extended to accommodate borrowed verbs completely naturally.[1] The Northern Chiapas Zoque strategy for borrowing Spanish verbs is similar: the present stem of the Spanish verb is compounded with *tsǝk-* 'do', so that we find *duratsǝhku* 'it lasted' (Spanish *durar* 'to last'), *gjanatsǝhku* 'he won it' (Spanish *ganar* 'to win'), and so on.[2]

A more interesting case is borrowing from an obviously related language by speakers who are aware of some systematic differences between the two speechforms. Such speakers can attempt to "translate" the new word into their own dialect by transposing it sound for sound according to the usual correspondences – and their attempt will be reconstructable to the extent that they fail to replicate the real historical relationships between sounds, as the following example demonstrates. Dutch *dijk* 'dike' (< Middle Dutch *dijc*) and High German *Teich* 'pond, pool' (< Middle High German *tîch* 'gully with no permanent stream') are probably cognates, both apparently inherited from Proto-West Germanic *dīk (as is English *ditch*; see the discussion of Christmann 1964: 191–3). The Dutch word, specialized to denote an earthwork of crucial importance in the low countries, was also borrowed into High German, whose upland speakers were unfamiliar with large-scale hydroengineering (Kluge 1995 s.v. *Deich*). But instead of borrowing MD *dijc* straightforwardly as late MHG "*dîc*" (which would have become ModHG "*Deik*"), the speakers who borrowed the word substituted High German /x/ for the final consonant, yielding *dîch* (whence ModHG *Deich*). Those speakers obviously knew that MD /ī/ (spelled *ij*) normally corresponded to MHG /ī/ (thus MD *bijten* = MHG *bîzen* 'to bite', for example) and that postvocalic MD /k/ normally corresponded to MHG /x/ (thus MD *maken* = MHG *machen* 'to make'). Why, then, was the initial consonant not replaced with the etymologically appropriate *t* – that is, why did the speakers of MHG not realize that the MD word was the same word, etymologically, as *tîch*? The confusion arose from the fact that MD /d/ participated in *two* regular correspondences: whereas some /d/ corresponded to MHG /t/ (e.g. MD *drinken* = MHG *trinken* 'to drink'), others corresponded to MHG /d/ (e.g. MD *dinc* = MHG *dinc* 'thing'). It wasn't clear which initial consonant should occur in the "translation" of MD *dijc*. In fact speakers arrived at both possible solutions, assigning new meanings to *tîch* as well as creating a new *dîch* (Grimm and Grimm 1860 s.v. *Deich*);

in the modern language the more straightforward, but etymologically incorrect, alternative prevailed. Similar cases can be found in other languages.

Structurally interesting examples can arise when speakers borrow from a different language which they do not actually speak but about whose structure they know enough to try to imitate it. For instance, the Modern English voiced postalveolar fricative /ʒ/ originally occured only intervocalically in words that have been in the language since the Renaissance, such as *measure* and *vision*; but many speakers of English use it word-finally in more recent French loans like *garage* /gɔˈrɑʒ/ and *collage*, which entered English in the first decades of the twentieth century. Possibly the first person who used each of these words in English was bilingual in English and French, but it is the behavior of the community that matters (see above), and it is obvious that millions of monolingual speakers have also adopted these words; it therefore seems clear that word-final /ʒ/ was borrowable by monolingual speakers of English even when there were no native word-final examples of /ʒ/. Evidently lexical borrowing by monolinguals can cause marginal alterations of phonotactics. It also seems clear that allophones which are the output of native phonological rules can be borrowed as underlying phonemes in loanwords; however, the impact of that development on the phonology of the borrowing language is usually limited. Northern Chiapas Zoque provides an interesting example as follows.

In native Zoque words all stops and affricates are underlyingly voiceless, and there is a phonological rule which voices them when they are immediately preceded by nasals (Wonderly 1946: 92); thus we find *tatah* 'father' but *ndatah* 'my father' (*n-* 1sg. possessive prefix), *petpa* 'he's sweeping' but *minba* 'he's coming' (*-pa* imperfective suffix), and so on. At least a few early Spanish loanwords conform to this allophonic rule; clear examples are *akuʃa* 'needle' (Spanish *aguja* – note that the word was borrowed before the change of [ʃ] to [x] in Spanish), *mandeka* 'grease, fat' (Spanish *manteca*), and *kulandu* 'coriander' (Spanish *culantro*). More recently Spanish words containing *b*, *d*, and *g* in other positions have also been borrowed into the language, and in those words the voiced stops can only be underlying; in addition to *duratsɔk-* 'to last' and *ganatsɔk-* 'to win', cited above, we find *botas* 'boot', *buru* 'donkey', *golondrina* 'swallow', etc. Even voiceless stops after nasals are retained in recent loans; thus we find *manta* 'blanket', *kampana hɔjɔ* 'white jimsonweed' (Spanish *campana* 'bell'; Zoque *hɔjɔ* 'flower'), and so on. It might be supposed that the voicing rule has begun to be lost, but that is not the case: exceptions occur only *within* morphemes, and the rule continues to apply automatically to words of all origins whenever the inflectional morphology brings a nasal and a stop into contact. Among Spanish loans we find *paloma* 'bird' (Spanish 'dove, pigeon') but *mbaloma* 'my bird', *tʃaketa* 'jacket' but *ndʒaketa* 'my jacket', *kompromete-tsɔk-* 'to promise, to agree to do' (Spanish *comprometerse* 'to commit oneself') but *ŋgomprometetsɔhku* 'you promised', etc. Though the loanwords have clearly had an impact both on the underlying phonemic inventory of the language and on its phonotactics, the system of rules has not been touched. Some similar cases will be discussed in Chapter 6.

Whether a community of monolinguals can successfully borrow completely new underlying phonemes is a different question. The abortive case of *Bach* with /x/ in English (see Chapter 2) is probably typical. But there are certainly languages which have acquired completely new sounds through lexical borrowing; for instance, many native languages of Mexico have acquired a phoneme /f/ in Spanish loanwords (see Wonderly 1946: 93–4, Laughlin 1975: 143). It seems clear that widespread bilingualism has been a factor in those developments, though we know of no rigorous research on the lexically mediated borrowing of phonemes.

The borrowing of morphosyntactic material by monolinguals is even less easy; English provides some striking examples of its failure. We noted in Chapter 2 the sharp decline in the use of Latin and Greek plurals of nouns borrowed into English from those languages. The reason for this development is clear enough: the attempt to borrow Latin and Greek noun plurals never penetrated vernacular English to any appreciable extent, and once the artificial prop of a Classical education was removed – so that even well-educated speakers of English did not know what the plural of, say, *incubus* was supposed to be – the native formation of noun plurals won out by default. Since some knowledge of the Classical languages was crucially necessary to support the attempt to borrow foreign plurals, that was not a case of *successful* borrowing. Occasional attempts to borrow French phrase structure have been no more effective; *court martial* is a case in point. The phrase was borrowed in the mid sixteenth century as *martial court* (!) and as *court martial* (see the *Oxford English Dictionary* under *court martial* and under *martial* A.I.4); the latter form, with its adjective following the noun, is an obvious attempt to assimilate the borrowed term to its French original in phrase structure. Since only nouns take plural markers in English the plural of this phrase is supposed to be *courts martial*. But while that plural still occurs in writing, and perhaps in carefully monitored educated speech, the usual plural is *court martials*; indeed *Court-Marshalls* (sic) appears as early as 1661. The hyphen in that early spelling reveals what happened: within a century or so after *court martial* (in that order) began to be used, monolingual native speakers reanalyzed it as a compound word and formed a plural in the usual way. The use of *court-martial* as an attributive or adjective (attested from 1833) and the formation of a verb *to court-martial* (attested from 1859) presuppose the same reanalysis. It appears that the attempt to impose French syntax on this borrowed phrase never really got off the ground.

Let us turn to bilingualism in the hope of finding more interesting examples of linguistic transfer.

Bilingualism and the community

In principle every natively bilingual individual has the means at her disposal to transfer both lexemes and structure from one language to another.

However, that is not what native bilinguals usually do; normally the two languages which a native bilingual commands remain separate systems without
interpenetration beyond normal lexical borrowing. That is not surprising, since a
typical bilingual is a member of two speech communities: one language is used
with one community, the other with the other, and transfer of structures, at least,
is likely to be dysfunctional in many situations.

However, in talking with other persons bilingual in the same languages bilinguals engage in *code-switching*, shifting from one language to the other and back,
usually at major syntactic boundaries. Code-switching is not in any sense mixing
or confusing grammars; as its conventional name implies, it amounts to switching from one system to another without infringement of either. (Code-switchers
do engage in casual lexical borrowing, and it is sometimes, though not always,
possible to tell the difference between nonce borrowing and code-switching; see
e.g. Poplack *et al.* 1989, Poplack and Meechan 1995, King 2000: 86–9.) There
are extensive bilingual communities in which code-switching is a normal part of
communication, such as the Puerto Rican community in New York City (Poplack
et al. 1989: 132–4 with references). This is important, because it is in substantial
bilingual communities that we should expect transfer of linguistic *structure* to
occur (Sankoff 2002: 638 with references). Exactly how such structural transfers
occur in bilingual communities, and what their relation to code-switching might
be, are central questions in the study of linguistic transfer. Linguists have been
able to learn very little by examining the results of transfer after the fact. For
instance, it seems reasonable to infer that conjunctions and complementizers can
be borrowed because they are weakly embedded in the grammar but important
pragmatically (Matras 1998), and of course they tend to occur at the junctures
where code-switching takes place; but other structural items seldom exhibit such
obvious patterns. It is the processes in question that we must study, not simply the
results, if we are to make any further progress in understanding contact-induced
change (see already Appel and Muysken 1987: 153–4).

Unfortunately, work detailed and rigorous enough to provide convincing
answers to those questions is not much more than a decade old. Most work on
language contact in bilingual communities has been conducted on the basis of
structuralist assumptions using traditional fieldwork methods; the classic example
is Gumperz and Wilson 1971, which reports on apparent convergence between
Kannada (a Dravidian language), Marathi, and Urdu (two Indo-European
languages of the Indic branch), and the supposed grammatical simplification
which results, in Kupwar village in southern Maharashtra. That study is now
useful chiefly because its shortcomings have been pointed out by Thomason and
Kaufman 1988: 86–8 and King 2000: 44–5 (see also ibid. 45–8); they can be
summarized as follows. No account is taken of the fact that the languages are
already typologically similar, and the authors compare the village dialects with
literary standard dialects, not with other local varieties; thus there is no secure
basis for distinguishing genuine contact phenomena from preexisting structures
which happen to be similar, and the probability of internally motivated parallel

development (which we expect to be significant in typologically similar languages) is not reckoned with. Variation within each of the three linguistic communities is not even discussed, and the corpus underlying the report was apparently so small that significant variation is not likely to have been found in any case. Though most of the examples adduced are morphosyntactic, the analysis is so superficial that its correctness cannot be gauged. Finally, no serious attention is paid to the process by which structural convergence (if there is any) has occurred; it is simply assumed that borrowing rather than interference is involved. It should be obvious that studies of this kind cannot answer the questions that need to be asked.

More recent work is often still inadequate in these regards. For instance, though it is now generally accepted that the social context of linguistic transfer is crucial and that one must distinguish between borrowing and interference (Thomason and Kaufman 1988: 4), most work on language contact still does not attempt an in-depth sociolinguistic analysis of the contact situation. Many students of language contact have not attempted to find structural patterns which are typical outcomes of borrowing on the one hand or interference on the other, apparently in the belief that any such "socially based predictions" are "simplistic" and "will inevitably fail" (ibid. p. 47). Yet Sankoff 2002: 640–1, 658 points out that the cumulative evidence does not justify a rejection of structural constraints on linguistic transfer, and that there is an overwhelming statistical imbalance in what sort of linguistic material is observed to undergo transfer: it is almost all lexical. (Like this chapter, Sankoff's survey article is organized so as to contrast borrowing with interference because that distinction "holds up very well in general" [Sankoff 2002: 658].) Even very recent work on language contact has, for the most part, not moved forward enough; for instance, though the most careful researchers make a serious attempt to "weed out" similarities that are not the result of convergence and are well-informed enough to note patterns of multilingualism, exolinguistic marriage, the possibility of language obsolescence as a relevant factor, and so on, almost none come to grips with the question of how specific linguistic transfers occurred. In fact, "borrowing" is still the standard term for all types of linguistic transfer, and discussions of patterns of linguistic transfer almost always focus exclusively on *results*, without any consideration of *processes* in detail. For those reasons most existing work on language contact is not useful to us; if the transfer of linguistic material occurred in a sociolinguistic setting that no longer obtains, or if that setting still exists but has not been documented in great detail, it is usually the case that "the processes involved are less clearly determinable" (Sankoff 2002: 649) than they need to be to contribute definitively to our knowledge of *how* contact-induced change really occurs.

In order to discuss what is known and what can be rigorously inferred about the transfer of linguistic structure in bilingual communities we must therefore do two things. First, we must rely heavily on King 2000, the only study that provides substantial direct evidence about the transfer of structure. Secondly, we must look for cases in which particular inferences about past contact situations are rendered *overwhelmingly* likely (not just more likely than not) by specific linguistic or social details. The rest of this chapter is organized accordingly.

Lexically mediated structural borrowing

By far the most detailed study of structural transfer is King 2000, which analyzes the borrowing of English "function words" into the Acadian French of Prince Edward Island (PEI), Canada. Exceptionally, the demographic record of the island is complete enough to exclude the possibility that any significant number of English speakers ever switched to French (King 2000: 13–16, 18–21); thus it is clear that borrowing, not interference, is in question. By comparing the pattern of English loans in PEI French with that in other dialects of Canadian French, King is able to demonstrate that chronic intensive language contact can lead to lexical borrowing with significant morphosyntactic consequences, and that chronic intensive contact appears to be necessary for the borrowing of "function words."

King's study is the first to *demonstrate* the transfer of function words *by borrowing* rather than by interference, and for that reason its results are somewhat surprising. However, as King is careful to note in detail, the limits within which such borrowing occurs and the limits on its structural consequences are clear. The social constraints are immediately obvious. Unlike the French of Quebec, PEI French has been under great pressure from English for generations, with the result that contact with English has been intensive and prolonged. Comparing the borrowing of English *back* into PEI French and other Canadian dialects, King observes that

> a certain threshold of contact with English is necessary for *back* to be borrowed. There are no instances at all of *back* in the large computerized corpora for Estrie (the Eastern Townships of Quebec) constructed by Normand Beauchemin and his colleagues . . . nor is it found in Raymond Mougeon's Quebec City corpus . . . There is also geographical variation at least partially explicable in terms of the degree of contact with English. For instance, no instances of *back* were found in the French of Hawkesbury, the Ontario community with the least contact with English. In the urban context of Ottawa-Hull located on the Ontario/Quebec border, we find limited use of *back*: an examination of the Ottawa-Hull French corpus collected under the direction of Shana Poplack reveals *back* use in the speech of 21 of 120 informants . . . Only two tokens [of 39] came from residents of Hull, located in Quebec, and these came from Vieux-Hull, a working class neighborhood.   (King 2000: 119)

That is more or less what we should expect. The structural consequences of these borrowings require more discussion.

King begins her discussion with an in-depth analysis of the borrowing of English *back* into PEI French (King 2000: 115–33). She accepts the generative analysis of the English word as an "intransitive preposition" (ibid. pp. 129–30);

considering it a "particle" (of the sort with which English makes compound verbs) leads to much the same analysis of its fate in French. King finds not only that the loanword is firmly entrenched in the dialect, but also that it has been reanalyzed both semantically and syntactically. Semantically, *back* retains its English meaning 'returning', e.g. in the following (all examples cited are from King's discussion):

(1)   a. I' m'ont donné mon argent back.
         'They gave me my money back.'

      b. Là, je mettais la roue back ensemble.
         'There, I put the wheel back together.'

      c. Ça devait être de la misère pour eux quand qu'ils avont back venu.
         'That must have been hard on them when they came back.'

But it has also been extended to mean 'again', as numerous examples attest:

(2)   a. Tu peux aller leur dire back.
         'You can go tell 'em again.'

      b. Veux-tu back me conter ça?
         'You wanna tell me that again?'

      c. Je l'avais assez haï que je l'ai jamais back fait.
         'I hated it so much that I've never done it again.'

      d. Faut qu'on le refasse back.
         'We gotta do it again.'

Syntactically, *back* cannot be a particle (or intransitive preposition) in French, which does not have such a lexical category. In some Canadian French dialects it occurs in the same position as locative prepositional phrases (King 2000: 130).[†] In PEI French, however, it occurs in the same position as adverbs, i.e. after the tensed verb but either before or after a past participle or an infinitive (see the examples cited above); as King notes (p. 131), in the examples in which it means 'again' *back* occupies the same place as standard French *encore*. Evidently the syntactic category of *back* has been reanalyzed to fit the preexisting grammar of French; the word has been borrowed, but its syntactic category has not.

The borrowing of (transitive) prepositions from English into PEI French yields more startling surface structures that require a more interesting analysis (King 2000: 135–49). French, unlike English, does not normally allow prepositions to be "stranded" by wh-movement of their objects or promotion of an object to the subject of a passive clause; yet in PEI French one routinely finds examples like the following:

(3)   a. Quoi ce-qu'ils parlont about?
         'What are they talking about?'

      b. Ça, c'est le weekend que je me souviens de.
         'That's the weekend that I remember.'

---

† King does not suggest an analysis of these cases, which are not the focus of her discussion.

It looks like an English syntactic construction has been borrowed; but further analysis reveals a more nuanced situation.

As King points out, a superficially similar construction does occur in French dialects not in contact with English. (All the examples in this paragraph are from European French, not PEI French.) In topicalized sentences a preposition can be "orphaned," e.g. in

(4)   Cette valise, je voyage toujours avec.
        'That suitcase, I always travel with it.'

(Zribi-Hertz 1984: 46). In colloquial French such orphan prepositions can also occur in relative clauses, e.g. in

(5)   la fille que je sors avec
        'the girl that I go out with'

(King 2000: 137, see Bouchard 1982: 105). Apparently they do not occur in wh-questions, nor in infinitival relative clauses (King 2000: 13–9 with references). But in any case the zeroed element that follows the preposition is not a trace, but a null *pro* argument; that is proved by the fact that the noun phrase

(6)   la fille$_i$ $_{CP}$[que je connais très bien $_{DP}$[le gars $_{CP}$[qui sort avec *pro*$_i$]]]

('the girl whose steady boyfriend I know well') is unproblematically acceptable in colloquial French, whereas its literal translation

(7)   *the girl$_i$ $_{CP}$[that I know quite well $_{DP}$[the guy $_{CP}$[who goes out with t_i]]]

is completely unacceptable in any dialect of English, since the antecedent of its trace has been "ripped out of an island" (Bouchard 1982: 121–2).

Remarkably, PEI French agrees with English rather than with other French dialects on these points. Prepositions with null objects do occur in wh-questions; in addition to the example cited above:

(8)   Qui ce-que t'as fait le gâteau pour?
        'Who did you make the cake for?'

Moreover, the null object in wh-questions, at least, is apparently a trace (as in English), not a null *pro* (as in other dialects of French), to judge from the unacceptability of wh-movement out of complex NPs:

(9)   *Qui$_i$ ce-que tu connais le projet à t_i?
        ?*'Who$_i$ do you know the project of t_i?'

Finally, like English but unlike other dialects of French, PEI French can reanalyze at least some sequences of V + PP as $[V + P]_v$ + NP and either wh-move the NP object or promote it to be the subject of a passive clause:

(10)   a. Le ciment$_i$ a été marché dedans t_i avant d'être sec.
           'The concrete was walked in before it was dry.'

        b. Tu connais pas la femme$_i$ que je te parle de t_i.
           'You don't know the woman I'm talking to you about.'

It seems beyond dispute that English syntactic constructions have been transferred into PEI French; but we need to ask exactly how it happened. It appears that examples like the first one above containing *about* are the key: PEI French has borrowed some sixteen prepositions from English (King 2000: 224), and while some are intransitive prepositions (i.e. particles), one of the commonest, *about*, takes objects and allows itself to be "stranded" by movement which leaves a trace. The most likely analysis is that PEI French borrowed English prepositions along with their syntax, then reanalyzed the preexisting native null *pro* as a trace under the influence of the new syntactic rule. Evidence that reanalysis occurred can be found in the fact that examples of stranding which are ungrammatical, or at least odd, in English are unproblematic in PEI French(!); note the following (among others, King 2000: 146):

(11)

    a. Quoi ce-que tu as parlé hier à Jean de?
       ?'What did you speak yesterday to John about?'[†]

    b. Quoi ce-que tu as parlé hier de à Jean?
       ?*'What did you speak yesterday about to John?'

King suggests (2000: 146) that the English examples are ungrammatical because the preposition needs to be closer to the verb to allow syntactic rebracketing; it seems more likely that some sort of prosodic constraint is involved (the prosodic structures of English and French being quite different, as is well known). But in either case the point is that the grammar of PEI French is *not* "just like English" in the relevant respects. The borrowing of English prepositions has indeed led to the borrowing of a syntactic rule and the reanalysis of preexisting French structures, but the borrowed structures themselves have been reanalyzed in native French terms. King's discussion of the borrowing of compound wh-words in PEI French (ibid. pp. 151–66) leads to similar conclusions. The most important conclusion of her work is that function words can be borrowed and can mediate the borrowing of syntactic rules, but only under intense and prolonged contact – and even in those cases independent structural reanalysis in the course of, or as a result of, borrowing is perhaps to be expected.

Cases from the past: some secure inferences and their consequences

In considering other cases of linguistic transfer, none of which is so well documented, we can draw firm conclusions only if some specific information

---

[†] An anonymous reviewer notes that (s)he does not find the English example 'What did you speak yesterday to John about?' very odd; that is not surprising, since native-speaker judgments about examples that are not clearly ungrammatical often differ. However, there is still a qualitative difference between the acceptability of the PEI French examples and that of at least some of their English translations.

virtually forces an inference that has important consequences. We here adduce three such cases in detail, two of which are clearly similar to whole classes of other cases.

Our first case is the simplest, but also the least secure.[†] It is clear that numerous Hebrew elements have been transferred into Yiddish, of which the grammar is mostly High German. Though the processes by which Yiddish arose continue to generate controversy (see e.g. Jacobs 2005: 9–22, Kleiner 2006: 418–21), it is at least clear that there were no native speakers of Hebrew that learned Yiddish (or any of the Romance languages from which speakers of Yiddish might have shifted); Hebrew was a language without native speakers by the early centuries of the Common Era. It is at least *conceivable* that the Hebraisms now in Yiddish originated as interference elements in Palestinian Aramaic and survived the shift to Greek, then to Romance, then to Yiddish. But it seems naïve to suppose that the large Greek- and Latin-speaking Jewish communities of the Roman Empire and the large Yiddish-speaking communities of eastern Europe arose entirely by natural growth. Conversion *to* Judaism was a significant phenomenon in the ancient world (see e.g. Acts of the Apostles 2:11, Peters 1970: 307–8, Grant 1990: 169) and remained so in medieval Europe (see e.g. Fletcher 1997: 289–302); many of the Roman Empire's Jews must have been converts, and even in Charlemagne's Empire conversion of Christians to Judaism was common enough to be considered a problem by the ecclesiastical authorities. For these reasons we conclude that *at some point(s)* in the prehistory of Yiddish significant numbers of individuals must have borrowed Hebraisms into Romance languages or High German, even if they were borrowing Hebraisms that were already embedded in other languages as a result of interference phenomena that had occurred centuries before.

This conclusion is important because Hebrew nouns were borrowed with their Hebrew plurals; thus the Hebrew pluralizer *-im*, for example, appears as a native Yiddish pluralizer *-əm*, which has even spread modestly. The following examples are typical (Jacobs 2005: 135, 165):

(12)   *Singular*   *Plural*
          nign 'melody'   nigúnəm
          lamdn 'scholar'   lamdónəm
          talməd 'pupil'   talmídəm
          sejfər 'holy book'   sforəm
          šojmər 'guard'   šomrəm
          məkor 'source'   məkojrəm
          dóktor 'doctor'   doktójrəm (!)

In the first five examples both the singular and the plural have been borrowed from Hebrew. However, in the sixth the plural marker *-əm* has been extended to a noun that has a different plural (*məkorot*) in Hebrew, and in the last it has been extended to a noun of non-Hebrew origin; thus at least some nativization of the ending

---

[†] We are grateful to Aaron Rubin for helpful discussion of this case; it should not be assumed that he agrees with us on every point.

has clearly occurred. This is exactly the same kind of scenario as the borrowing of Latin and Greek plurals into English, except that in the Yiddish (or early Judaeo-Romance, or Hellenistic Judaeo-Greek) case the borrowing succeeded.

We need to ask why the outcomes were different. The reason can only be that for many generations half the Jewish population – the male half – had a semi-native passive command of Hebrew (since boys typically started Hebrew school at the age of 3). In fact, because of the pervasive ritual use of Hebrew in traditional Jewish life, the line between borrowing and interference is not as clear in this case as in most others (as Aaron Rubin reminds us). However, the exceptionality of structural transfer in Yiddish must not be overstated. The borrowed endings mark plural number on nouns, a category already marked in every Romance and Germanic language and in Greek; thus *no morphosyntactic category has been borrowed*, only a new marker for a preexisting category. Moreover, there has been little spread of the plural marker *-əm* beyond its original base of (masculine) Hebrew nouns. Finally, it seems impossible to recover the process by which the transfer occurred in any detail. Native bilinguals usually keep their native languages distinct (as their ability to code-switch demonstrates); why didn't they do so in this case? It might be because there was no fully native speech community of Hebrew, or because there were no convenient vernacular terms for many of the Hebrew words transferred, or for some other reason; work on this problem would certainly be welcome, but it is not clear that the answer will be recoverable.

Possible parallels to various aspects of the Yiddish case are not hard to find. Lefebvre 1984: 31–3 argues persuasively that Spanish plural nouns in *-s* were first borrowed into Cochabamba Quechua as singulars, then (when bilingualism became more extensive) reanalyzed correctly as plurals; finally the plural marker *-s* was extracted and spread to native Quechua lexemes, competing with the preexisting *-kuna*. There is also a well-known parallel case in the history of English involving derivational rather than inflectional morphology. Sometime around the year 1200 English began to borrow analyzable French words derived with the adjective-forming suffix *-able*. Since the French bases of those French words were often also borrowed (though not necessarily at the same time), English gradually acquired a small nucleus of adjectives from which the suffix *-able* could be extracted by native language learners. The earliest analyzable loanwords in *-able* cited in the *OED* seem to be the following:

(13)
    a. *merciable* 'merciful' before 1225 (*mercy* in the same texts and in the earlier *Lambeth Homilies*)[3]

    b. *perdurable* 'eternal' *c.* 1275 (*perdure* 'endure, persist' first attested in a fifteenth-century mystery play from Coventry)[4]

    c. *delitable* 'delightful' *c.* 1290 (*delite, delight* [nn. and intrans. vb.] before 1225, [trans. vb.] *c.* 1300)

    d. *defensable* 'defensive' 1297 (*defense* [nn.] 1297, [vb.] *c.* 1400)[5]

    e. *comenable, co(n)venable* 'suitable' before 1300 (*convene* 'be suitable' not before the late sixteenth century; in other meanings not before the fifteenth century)

In the fourteenth century such loans gradually become more numerous, and derivational pairs including transitive verbs begin to appear; the earliest that we have found so far is

(14)   *movable* (trans.) before 1325 (intrans. also fourteenth century; *move c.* 1275)

A suffix -*able* with passive meaning was then extracted from such pairs and used to coin new words; fourteenth-century examples with native roots include *understandable* (from Wycliffe), *unspeakable* (from the corpus attributed to Richard Rolle of Hampole), and a few others, mostly negative compounds (see Jespersen 1954: 398–9). Note that in this case, as in the Yiddish case, a "bound" morpheme was *not* borrowed directly; rather, enough analyzable words including that morpheme were borrowed to allow its subsequent extraction and spread. Unlike the Yiddish borrowing, the English one is completely unsurprising because only lexical material, not including inflectional affixes, was borrowed.

Another case in which we have some chance of figuring out what happened in the distant past involves dialects of Greek spoken in the interior of Asia Minor until the population exchanges of the 1920s.[†] (A fuller discussion of this case and the next will be offered in a paper by Don Ringe and Anthony Kroch currently in preparation.) Fieldwork by R. M. Dawkins in the early years of the twentieth century demonstrated that Turkish grammatical structures had been transferred into those dialects to varying degrees (Dawkins 1910, 1916). For instance, in some dialects use of the definite article was largely restricted to the accusative case, while in others only definite NP objects were marked with the accusative (Dawkins 1916: 46–7, 87, 94, 164); both peculiarities obviously correlate with the fact that Turkish has an inflectional marker for definite NP objects but not for indefinite ones. In two dialects Turkish verb endings had even been added to fully inflected 1pl. and 2pl. forms of deponent verbs (Dawkins 1916: 58–9, 144, 148).[††] But the process by which those and other morphosyntactic transfers occurred is clearly revealed when we consider a phonological peculiarity of the dialects. In a majority of the dialects the inherited interdental fricatives /θ/ and /ð/ have developed into other sounds; but in all the dialects except one (including most of the dialects in which /θ/ and /ð/ are largely preserved unchanged) there are randomly distributed *inconsistencies* in the reflexes of these phonemes. The dialect of the village of Araván is representative (Dawkins 1916: 75–6). The regular reflex of word-initial /θ/ was /x/, that of word-initial /ð/ was /d/, and that of both consonants intervocalically was /r/; note the following examples, each followed by its equivalent in standard Modern Greek: /xíra/ 'door' (/θíra/), /xeós/ 'God' (/θeós/), /xélo/ 'I want' (/θélo/); /károme/ 'I sit' (/káθome/), /émara/ 'I learned' (/émaθa/), /kalár/ 'basket' (/kaláθi/); /dén/ 'not' (/ðén/), /despóʧis/ 'master' (/ðespótis/), /derpándʒ/ 'scythe' (/ðrepáni/); /perí/ 'child' (/peðí/), /peɣár/ 'well' (/piɣáði/), /íra/ 'I saw'

[†] At least one of the Cappadocian subdialects still survives in northern Greece; see Janse 2009 for details.

[††] In some other respects the influence of Turkish on Anatolian Greek dialects has been overestimated; see Karatsareas 2009 for discussion of the loss of gender concord.

(/íða/). But /θ/ appears word-initially as /t/ in /tinjatós/ 'censer' (/θiniatós/) and as various back fricatives intervocalically in a variety of words: /orníx/ 'chicken' (/orníθi/), /nixér/ 'stone' (/liθári/), /kluɣára/ 'spindle' (/kloθára/), /peheró/ 'father-in-law' (/penθerós/). In a few words /d/ appears for /ð/ intervocalically, e.g. in /adelfó/ 'brother' (/aðelfós/), /dadí/ 'torch' (/ðaðí/), and /andíderos/ 'blessed (but unconsecrated) liturgical bread' (/andíðoro/); in /xedíra/ 'cupboard' (/θiríða/) and /daxʧilía/ 'ring' (/ðaxtilíða/) still other deformations have occurred. These inconsistencies must at first have been errors, and – crucially – they are errors of a kind which do not normally survive the process of native language acquisition, in which native phonemes are either learned perfectly or subjected to phonologically coherent mergers. On the other hand, they are a typical outcome of imperfect second-language learning by adults. We are forced to conclude that non-native interference phenomena somehow entered the Anatolian dialects of Greek, and the source of the interference can only have been native speakers of Turkish (so Dawkins 1910: 270, 289, retracted without explanation in Dawkins 1916: 80 n. 1).

At first that seems to make no sense in sociolinguistic terms: why should native speakers of Turkish, the overwhelming majority language of the Anatolian interior, have felt obliged to learn Greek, spoken by a small minority? Muslim speakers of Turkish would have had no reason to do so; but it turns out that a large majority of the Greek Orthodox Christians in Anatolia were also native speakers of Turkish, the so-called *Karamanlides* (Alexandris 1999: 60–2, Clogg 1999: 119). What we need to imagine, then, are circumstances in which Turkish-speaking Christians influential in the village communities where they resided might have been obliged to learn Greek. Since we know that Greek-speaking communities were still shifting to Turkish late in the nineteenth century (Dawkins 1916: 11), it is reasonable to suppose that Greek suffered a "near-death experience" in some villages – being reduced to the point at which many remaining speakers were really only semi-speakers whose native language was actually the dominant language (in this case Turkish), as is often the case with dying languages (Dorian 1981: 114) – and was then revived, probably under the influence of Greek-speaking priests, with the Turkish interference phenomena of the semi-speakers thereby entering the mainstream of the dialect. Of course we cannot be sure exactly what happened, and there are other possible scenarios; for instance, Turkish-speaking priests (with Turkish-speaking families, since Eastern Orthodox priests normally marry before ordination) must sometimes have been ordained for Greek-speaking villages, where they would of course find it necessary to learn the language (to hear confessions, for example), and it is at least conceivable that their faulty Greek might have been copied because of their social eminence and influence. But though the details are not recoverable with any certainty, this is a case in which the linguistic evidence compels us to posit *some* interference scenario.

Scandinavian influence on northern English in the early Middle Ages is a good example of a reverse case: we *know for certain* that substantial language shift occurred, and we can interpret the observed linguistic patterns in the light of that knowledge. Our reasoning is as follows.

Scandinavian names of villages and parishes are so numerous in northern England, especially in Yorkshire and the "Five Boroughs" (Lincolnshire, Nottinghamshire, Derbyshire, Leicestershire, and Northamptonshire), that they cannot be explained by supposing that English-speaking farmers renamed large numbers of existing settlements in the alien language of a new ruling class (for the place-name evidence see e.g. Ekwall 1930, 1936, and the map in Richards 2000: 44). History shows that settled rural populations don't do that; if they did, there would be Norman French names all over rural England, which is not the case. Thus we can confidently infer that significant numbers of speakers of Old Norse settled in England following the Scandinavian invasions in the second half of the ninth century. (See Morse-Gagné 2003: 24–41, 45–64 with references, who argues persuasively that attempts to minimize Scandinavian settlement are unrealistic.) But by about 1200, and probably long before, all those regions had become English-speaking. It follows that the speakers of Old Norse – at least several thousand strong, and including entire communities – shifted to Old English (OE) after the English conquest of the "Danelaw," which was complete in 954.

Late OE in the areas settled by Scandinavians is poorly attested (though see further below). But the Middle English (ME) dialects of those areas, from the beginning of their attestation, exhibit massive Norse influence. Old Norse loanwords are very numerous (Björkman 1900–2); even more significantly, we find clear signs of grammatical transfer from Norse to English in northern ME dialects. Structural material of three kinds can be attributed to Norse influence:

(a)   several Old Norse closed-class "function words" appear in northern ME, most famously the pronoun *they*, but also including *till* 'to', *fra* 'from', the complementizer *at* 'that', and the particle *at* used to introduce infinitives, like native *to*;

(b)   the interdental fricative of the OE present tense endings 3sg. *-eþ* and pl. *-aþ* has been replaced by *-s*;

(c)   the complex OE order of major constituents has been replaced by a much simpler V2 pattern resembling that of modern German (Kroch *et al.* 2000).

All these peculiarities can be explained as interference of the kind that occurs in language shift when adults are constrained to learn a second language, though the argument is different for each peculiarity, since they affect different areas of the language's structure.

Analysis of the code-switching patterns of bilinguals who learned their second language in adulthood reveals an interesting assymetry: while lexemes of either language are used in clauses which are largely in the other language, closed-class "function words" of the native language are used in clauses of the other language overwhelmingly more often than the other way around (Prince and Pintzuk 2000: 247–51). This strongly suggests that at least some speakers learn non-native closed-class items as though they were lexemes rather than structural material, and that when the non-native "closed-class lexeme" is not accessed in production the native equivalent automatically replaces it (ibid. pp. 252–6). The fact that Old Norse closed-class items appear in northern ME is thus prima facie evidence that the faulty English learned non-natively by speakers of Norse has somehow influenced those dialects.[6] The replacement of -þ by -s in verb endings (but not, for example, in mōnaþ 'month', which shows that this was not a regular sound change) reveals a different defect of late second-language learning. Word-final *-þ had been voiced to -ð in Norse in the sixth or seventh century, depending on the dialect (Noreen 1923: 162); those speakers of Norse who could not readily learn to pronounce the voiceless word-final -þ of OE would therefore have had to replace it either with voiced -ð or with voiceless -s. That they did the latter is the only plausible explanation of the appearance of -s for -þ in northern English verb paradigms that has ever been proposed in the (extensive) literature on the subject (Kroch et al. 2000: 378–80).[7] Finally, the simplification of OE major constituent order *to a pattern not found either in earlier OE or in Old Norse* is best explained as a failure of non-native learners to acquire an unusually complex syntactic pattern, defaulting to a similar but simpler pattern, though the specific reasons why this pattern (rather than some other) emerged remain somewhat problematic (see Kroch et al. 2000: 378–82).

As in the case of Anatolian Greek, we need to explain how non-native interference patterns got into the mainstream speech of local communities, and in this case we do not have any hard information about the sociolinguistic structure of those communities. We might suppose that some Norse-speaking communities were so isolated that their children had no opportunity to learn English from native-speaker playmates or elders and so were constrained to acquire their parents' imperfect English natively. But in that case how did the adults learn English? Two observations help to explain how this scenario could have worked. Morse-Gagné points out that, from what we know of medieval farming villages in Scandinavia itself, we can assume that the settlers pursued a mixed economy which included a significant amount of trade and involved seasonal movements of the population (Morse-Gagné 2003: 7–11); thus many of the adult male settlers, at least, would have had occasion to visit other settlements and could have been a vehicle for the spread of English. The second crucial point is an inspired suggestion of Thomason and Kaufman, namely that "Norsified English" spread most successfully not to English-speaking villages but to those villages where only Norse was spoken at the time (Thomason and Kaufman 1988: 285) – so that the *only* English they learned was the non-native variety, which they of course then passed on to their children as a native language! By that process the resulting dialects would have ceased to seem foreign after a generation or two; they would simply be further dialects of English, mutually intelligible with some others and so able to pass on their Norse peculiarities by ordinary dialect borrowing.

This scenario would clearly increase in plausibility if the establishment of imperfectly learned English as a native dialect happened fairly rapidly; the longer it took, the more opportunity to learn native English there should have been. In fact there is some evidence that Norsification did happen quickly (Kroch *et al.* 2000: 382–6). In the Northumbrian glosses to the *Lindisfarne Gospels*, written in the middle of the tenth century, we already find both *-s* for *-þ* in verb endings and the new, simplified V2 rule, though both peculiarities are variable. That suggests that a Norsified dialect of English was already being spoken as a native language somewhere in Northumbria less than a century after the Scandinavian settlement began.[8]

Like the case of Hebrew plurals in Yiddish, the case of Norsified English is representative of a class of known cases. Among the clearest is syntactic interference from the Celtic languages in the "Celtic Englishes," of which several examples will be adduced in Chapter 9. In those cases, too, we can be confident that what we see is the result of interference rather than borrowing, because the socioeconomic necessity for speakers of Celtic languages in the British Isles to learn English is well documented in recent centuries.

Some general conclusions

Though the number of convincingly analyzed cases at our disposal is still small, we can suggest some conclusions about contact-induced change. It seems clear that the transfer of linguistic structure occurs only in the context of intensive bilingualism. It also appears that structure is rarely borrowed directly into a native language, and that even when it is, only superficial aspects of structure – such as the specific shapes of noun plural markers – are borrowed. On the other hand, lexical borrowing clearly can mediate structural borrowing (as in PEI French), and there is some evidence that non-native linguistic interference is an important phenomenon in structural transfer.

Notes

1 The two closely related Tocharian languages, spoken along the northern arm of the Silk Road in Xinjiang until about the tenth century of the Common Era, are conventionally called A and B; their native names are not certainly recoverable. Tocharian is a subfamily of Indo-European not closely related to any other subfamily.

2 Northern Chiapas Zoque is a language of southern Mexico belonging to the Mixe-Zoque family. Zoque *ə* is a mid central unround vowel. The perfective suffix *-u* preaspirates a root-final stop or affricate; transitive third-person subjects are marked by a prefix *j-* which undergoes regular metathesis with the initial consonant of the verb root. Zoque data are from Wonderly 1946 and Engel and Allhiser de Engel 1987; not all the lexemes cited here are reported from both subdialects, but in all relevant respects the subdialects appear to be identical.

3 *Merciable* first appears in the *Ancrene Riwle* and closely related texts; though the earliest surviving manuscripts are from the 1220s, it is clear that the texts were composed earlier. The manuscript of the *Lambeth Homilies* is of similar date, but the texts are from the second half of the twelfth century, and some are copied from eleventh-century originals. See further

the notes to the *Penn-Helsinki Parsed Corpus of Middle English* (www.ling.upenn.edu/hist-corpora/PPCME2-RELEASE-3/index.htm).

4 Instead of *perdurable* itself, what is actually attested in the thirteenth century is the derived adverb *pardurableliche* (*perdurably*). Since the base adjective *perdurable* is not securely attested until Chaucer, it is possible that this early attestation of the adverb was a nonce coinage based on OF *pardurablement* (as hinted by the *OED* in its quotation of the passage s.v. *perdurably*).

5 *Defensable* is listed in the *OED* under *defensible*, a separate and much later borrowing.

6 The replacement of non-native by native closed-class items is part of a much wider pattern of interference of L1 (i.e. a native language) in the performance of L2 (i.e. a second language learned after the critical period for native acquisition has passed); see e.g. Schachter 1996: 161 with references. The asymmetry in the code-switching of closed-class items occurs temporarily even in the speech of children acquiring two languages natively, where L1 is the dominant language and L2 the other language being acquired; see Lanza 2000: 231–3 with references for exemplification and discussion.

7 Note that the replacement of non-native OE *-þ* by native Old Norse *-s* runs counter to the borrowing of preexisting allophones in new phonotactic positions discussed above. It seems clear that the abilities of non-native speakers in this area vary enormously, and that the outcome in any given case depends partly on contingent events, such as the language-learning abilities of those speakers with great enough prestige to influence the speech of the community.

8 An anonymous reviewer notes (from personal experience) that it is possible for a child exposed both to native and to non-native varieties of a language to acquire features of the non-native variety even in an environment in which the native variety is dominant. While we do not doubt that report, we suggest that the eventual success of non-native variants in spreading through the community would be much more likely if the non-native variety were dominant; that is why we suggest that exceptional sociolinguistic conditions obtained in the Norse-and-English case.

5   Sound change

Spontaneous changes in pronunciation – for which "sound change" is, unexpectedly, the technical term – are the best understood type of language change. In this chapter we discuss the basic facts of sound change, the motivation of sound changes in phonetic terms, and their effects on a language's phonological system; in the following chapter we will discuss the evolution of the phonological rules into which some sound changes develop.

The trajectory of sound changes and the regularity of sound change

Every sound change must begin as an acquisition error which survives and is copied (see Chapter 2). Since the beginnings of that process are practically impossible to observe, we must infer the sources of those errors. At least the following are probable sources of new sound changes (see Ohala 1993, 2003 for amplification and much further discussion).

(a)   The child simply fails to learn a meaningful contrast between two sounds, so that a merger of the sounds results. The widespread North American English merger of /ɑ/ and /ɔ/ mentioned in Chapter 3, and the merger of /ər/ and /ɔr/ in a child's speech mentioned in Chapter 2, are typical examples. Merger can of course result from each of the other types of error (b) through (d) listed below; we list failure to learn a contrast separately because it seems possible that in some circumstances such a failure is not motivated by any of the other factors listed.

(b)   The child misinterprets recurrent performance errors as the outputs of a variable phonological rule, which is therefore learned. This is a probable scenario because the sound changes which are attested in the historical record overlap significantly with typical performance errors. Long-range metathesis, the transposition of two sounds not adjacent in the stream of speech (as in Spanish *milagro* 'miracle' ← medieval Latin *mīrāculum*[1]), is an obvious candidate for this scenario; so is haplology, dropping one of two syllables that begin with the same onset (as in North American English *prob'ly* for *probably*; see further Chapter 6). But sound changes of other kinds might also begin this way (see Browman and Goldstein 1991: 324–5).

(c)   Because certain articulatory gestures or (more often) sequences of gestures require unusually great effort and/or precise timing, the child fails to learn to produce them, or to produce them consistently. A large proportion of sound changes could arise this way.

(d)   The child mistakes the acoustic signal of an articulation for the similar acoustic signal of a quite different articulation. A process like this must underlie the replacement of /t/ with the glottal stop in syllable codas in many varieties of English, for example; Blevins and Garrett have also suggested that certain types of metathesis involving adjacent consonants result from the misperception of acoustic cues spread out over several segments (Blevins and Garrett 1998: 508–27 with references). Ohala 1981 argues persuasively that many types of sound change involve misperception on the part of the listener.

To one degree or another the motivations for these types of errors can be said to be phonetic. Type (d) is intelligible in acoustic terms, types (b) and (c) in articulatory terms; even mergers are phonetically motivated in that it is normally a pair of phonetically similar sounds that the child fails to learn to distinguish. Since we are often unable to determine exactly what type of error gave rise to a particular sound change, it makes sense to discuss the changes in phonetic terms, rather than in terms of the type of error involved, and we will do that in a later section of this chapter.

Once an innovation begins to be copied by other native speakers, it ceases to be an acquisition error and becomes a variable sound change. No doubt most errors never get this far on the evolutionary path to sound change, and many get no further. But if an incipient variable sound change is adopted as a marker of social identity (see Chapter 3), it will both spread through the community and apply more and more frequently in the speech of successive generations until it becomes categorical rather than variable. During this period native learners acquire not only the variable rule but the statistical pattern in which it applies and the rule's fine phonetic conditioning. The rule gradually gains ground by the process discussed in Chapter 3, but it is not usually restructured or otherwise disrupted.

The most surprising aspect of this process is that, *unless some other process interferes*, a typical sound change does not develop lexical or grammatical exceptions as it progresses to completion within the speech community in which it arose. This phenomenon has been investigated most recently, and perhaps most thoroughly, by William Labov, whose argument is worth summarizing in some detail. Though lexical diffusion of sound changes – that is, the progression of a sound change by acquiring *positive* lexical exceptions, i.e. new words to which it applies – is often reported in the literature, Labov casts serious doubt on the prevalence of this phenomenon by investigating several of the apparently most secure examples in depth (Labov 1994: 424–37). He finds that one is actually a change in progress – possibly arrested before going to completion – in which detailed but regular phonetic conditioning appears to apply (ibid. pp. 444–51), some are actually cases of dialect borrowing (ibid. pp. 451–3), and still others are likely to reflect inconsistent suppression of a stigmatized sound change (ibid. pp. 453–4). The normal situation is that shifts in pronunciation are gradual, are subject to fine phonetic conditioning (ibid. pp. 455–71), and exhibit no lexical irregularities; that is confirmed by an extensive survey of sound changes in progress (ibid. pp. 443–4, 540–3, with references). Lexical diffusion of sound changes does occur, but only when sound changes are borrowed from one dialect into a closely related dialect (and lexical diffusion is not always the mechanism of spread even in those contact situations; see Labov 1994: 429–37).[2] Labov suggests that lexical irregularities are most likely to arise in the context of a contrast between discrete classes of vowels, such as the lax vs. tense contrast (ibid. pp. 526–31).

Working historical linguists with broad experience of language change are aware that the written record is fully consistent with Labov's findings. Regular sound change is the norm; in fact, the regularity of sound change is statistically overwhelming. The following crude experiment gives a good idea of the numbers involved. The first 200 words of the glossary in an Old English (OE) textbook, Moore and Knott 1955, which survive in Modern English (ModE) were compared to their contemporary reflexes.[3] The shapes of at least 88 percent of the modern words inspected can be derived from those of the OE words *entirely* by regular sound changes and known morphological changes; thus the incidence of apparent phonological irregularity is not more than 12 percent over the past thousand years as measured by listed lexemes. Moreover, words exhibiting apparent irregularities typically exhibit only one each; and since the average length of the words in question is about four phonemes, the incidence of apparent phonological irregularity is not more than about 3 percent per millennium as measured by tokens of phonemes in a wordlist. Finally, it is actually surprising that these numbers should be so low, since standard English is the result of prolonged dialect contact in London from the thirteenth to the seventeenth centuries, and borrowing between dialects is a principal cause of phonological irregularities. We should expect the incidence of apparent phonological irregularities to be *even lower* in dialects that have not been subjected to such massive dialect contact. The observed regularity of sound change is a statistically robust pattern of facts.

The following hypothesis is the best available to account for this pattern of facts. Let the regularity of sound change be defined as follows:

either all examples of sound *x* in a dialect at the time of the change become *x′*,
or, if *x* becomes *x′* only under certain conditions, those conditions can be stated
    entirely in phonological terms.

Table 5.1 *Latin stressed ē in open syllables in French*

Latin		French	
crēdere 'to believe'	>	croire	/kruar/
dēbet '(s)he owes'	>	doit	/dua/ '(s)he must'
habēre 'to have'	>	avoir	/avuar/
lēgem 'law'	>	loi	/lua/
mē 'me'	>	moi	/mua/
mēnsem 'month'	>	mois	/mua/
movēre 'to move'	>	mouvoir	/muvuar/
pēnsum 'weighed'	>	poids	/pua/ 'weight'
quiētum 'at rest'	>	coi	/kua/ 'quiet'
rēgem 'king'	>	roi	/rua/
sē 'himself'	>	soi	/sua/
sedēre 'to sit'	>	seoir	/suar/ 'to be fitting'
sērum 'late hour'	>	soir	/suar/ 'evening'
stēllam 'star'	>	étoile	/etual/
tē 'you (sg.)'	>	toi	/tua/ 'you (sg. familiar)'
tēlam 'warp, web'	>	toile	/tual/ 'cloth'
tēnsam 'stretched (fem.)'	>	toise	/tuaz/ 'fathom'
valēre 'to be well'	>	valoir	/valuar/ 'to be worth'
vēla 'sails, curtains'	>	voile	/vual/ 'veil'
vēra 'true things'	>	voire	/vuar/ 'indeed'
vidēre 'to see'	>	voir	/vuar/

The outcome of a sound change within the community in which it originated is completely regular in those terms, unless other, different processes interfere with the process of sound change before it has gone to completion. (See also the Preface.)

Exemplifications of the overwhelming regularity of sound change over millennia are easy to find; the following is typical. When no special conditions obtain, Latin *ē* /eː/ in a stressed open syllable normally appears in French, one of Latin's descendants, as the diphthong *oi* /ua/ (in which the second element is the syllable nucleus[4]); note the examples in Table 5.1 (the French words translate the Latin words except as noted).

Of course Latin /eː/ did not develop directly into French /ua/; the latter is the result of the last of a long series of changes, roughly as follows. When vowel length was lost in the western dialects of late Latin, long /eː/ merged with short /i/ (phonetically [ɪ]) in a higher mid vowel /e/ (distinct from the lower mid /ɛ/ that had developed out of Latin short /e/). In northern Gaul this new /e/ was diphthongized to /ei/ whenever it was stressed in an open syllable (as we know from eleventh-century French documents, including the *Song of Roland*). Subsequently the first element of the diphthong, which was the syllable nucleus, was rounded and backed, so that by about the thirteenth century the Parisian pronunciation was /oi/ (much like the modern English diphthong). Then the second element of the

Table 5.2 *Latin stressed ē before nasals in French*

Latin		French	
rēnem 'kidney'	>	rein	/rɛ̃/
frēnum 'bridle'	>	frein	/frɛ̃/ 'bit'
plēnum 'full (masc.)'	>	plein	/plɛ̃/
plēnam 'full (fem.)'	>	pleine	/plɛn/
vēnam 'vein'	>	veine	/vɛn/
pēnam 'punishment'	>	peine	/pɛn/ 'pain, trouble'

diphthong was lowered and became the syllable nucleus; subsequently the first, now nonsyllabic, element was raised and the second element lowered again. The entire process can be represented as follows:

(1)   e:, ɪ > e > eị̯ > ø̯ị (or əị̯) > oị̯ > oe̯ > o̯e > u̯e > u̯ɛ > u̯a.

Because every one of these sound changes was regular, confrontation of the Latin and modern French words reveals a pervasive regular pattern.

   Not all of those sound changes were unconditioned. We have already observed that the diphthongization of the vowel was conditioned by stress and by whether the vowel was syllable-final. The Old French shift of /ei/ to /oi/ was conditioned as well: it did not occur when a nasal consonant followed immediately, as the examples in Table 5.2 demonstrate. (The last item in Table 5.2 was *poenam* in Classical Latin, but its diphthong merged with *ē* in all the dialects ancestral to the surviving Romance languages.) As the modern forms show, further changes have occurred; for example, wherever the diphthong /ei/ was not backed it was subsequently monophthongized. Most importantly, vowels other than /a(:)/ in Latin final syllables were lost very early in the history of French, and the resulting word-final nasals nasalized preceding vowels and were eventually lost; but final-syllable /a(:)/ was preserved as /ə/ for centuries, so that preceding nasals were intervocalic and survived.

   So far we have been discussing only stressed Latin /e:/. Unstressed /e:/, when it survives at all, appears in modern French as /ə/; thus the infinitive *dēbēre* /de:be:re/ 'to owe', which was stressed on its penultimate syllable, became French *devoir* /dəvuar/ 'to be obliged (to)'. Similarly, the French clitic pronouns *me* /mə/, *te* /tə/, *se* /sə/ are etymologically identical with *moi, toi, soi* – that is, both sets developed regularly from Latin *mē, tē, sē* – but the clitics exhibit the regular development of unstressed /e:/. In many phonological environments the /ə/ has been lost; for instance, the descendant of Latin *sēcūrum* 'without worry' was still disyllabic *seur* /sə.yr/ in Old French, but the /ə/ has been lost in modern French *sûr* 'certain, sure' because it was followed immediately by a stressed vowel. In word-final position /e:/ had already been lost by the eleventh century; thus *hodiē* 'today' had become Old French monosyllabic *(h)ui*, the last element of Modern French *aujourd'hui*.

As the reader can see, the development of Latin /e:/ in French has been complex but completely regular, since the operation of each sound change has been conditioned only by phonological factors. That is normal; similar patterns are pervasive in every language whose historical development can be traced.

We noted in Chapter 3 that the spread of sound changes across dialect boundaries is a significant source of irregular sound change outcomes. It should follow that irregular outcomes in a given language or dialect tend to involve specific sounds, namely those affected by a sound change that spread across a dialect boundary. The historical record corroborates that inference. As we saw in Chapter 3, the phonemic split of /æ/ in the English of the northeastern USA is a major locus of irregularity, probably resulting from borrowing of the tensing rule from dialect to dialect. At a much earlier date something similar seems to have happened to the outcomes of Middle English (ME) /o:/, which became /u:/ in the fifteenth century by the Great Vowel Shift, and unshifted /u:/ before labial consonants. The usual outcome in modern English is /u:/ or /uw/ (depending on the dialect and the phonemic analysis), e.g. in *food, fool, boot, coop, stoop*, etc. But we find shortened /ʊ/ in *foot, good, hood, stood*, etc. – variably in *room* and *roof* – and shortened and unrounded /ʌ/ in *blood, flood, glove, stud* (reflecting ME /o:/) and in *dove, gum, sup*, etc. (reflecting unshifted ME /u:/). Exactly what happened is difficult to determine from the historical evidence (see Jespersen 1909: 236–8, 332–5 for brief discussion), but the high incidence of irregularities in the reflexes of these vowels (but not others) makes it very likely that spread of a sound change between dialects was involved.

We now turn to an examination of the phonetic motivations for various types of sound change.

Understanding sound change in phonetic terms

It seems inadvisable to present the student with a long catalogue of types of sound change at this point; though it is necessary to acquaint oneself with the range of actually attested sound changes, that is best done in the context of dealing with the histories of particular languages. For a classification and discussion of sound changes in phonetic terms, the student should consult Hock 1991, chapters 5 through 7; also useful is Kümmel 2007.

Instead we will consider the phonetic motivations for sound change, hoping to find explanations for the errors that become sound changes regardless of exactly how the errors are made (see above). The discussion will be easiest to follow if we structure it around an example; we choose lenition, a common and typical conditioned sound change.

Though the exact conditions on attested examples of lenition vary somewhat, prototypical lenitions are sound changes affecting consonants between vowels which result in less of an articulatory interruption between the vowels, in one

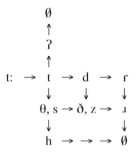

Figure 5.1 *Typical lenition paths of long /t:/*

or more ways: voiceless consonants become voiced (since vowels are usually voiced); stops become shorter (thus interrupting the sequence of vowels more briefly), or become fricatives, or lose their buccal features and are replaced by the glottal stop /ʔ/; fricatives become approximants or (if voiceless) /h/; approximants, /h/, and /ʔ/ are lost. Thus the typical leniton paths of long /t:/ (dental or alveolar) can be diagrammed as in Figure 5.1 (see Hock 1991: 83).

Romance languages provide good examples of lenition. In most of the Po valley, in Gaul, and in most of the Iberian peninsula, the Latin voiceless stops /p, t, k/ were voiced between sonorants, including vowels; thus they appear as /b, d, g/ in those positions in Old Provençal and in Brazilian Portuguese, for example. In Spanish a second lenition has also occurred, changing the new voiced stops to fricatives [β, ð, ɣ] (though the spelling has not changed). The Spanish examples in Table 5.3 are typical.

Lenition is traditionally described as a type of "assimilation," i.e. a sound change by which sounds become more like other sounds with which they are in contact in the stream of speech; but that is a description of the *result*, which may or may not shed light on what motivated the change. Given that this example of lenition must have begun either as a performance error or as an acquisition error, we want to ask why this was a "natural" error to make.

It might seem obvious that lenition is motivated by the increased ease of artic-ulation that results from it; for instance, producing a voiced consonant between voiced vowels ought to involve less articulatory effort than switching from voic-ing (for the first vowel) to voicelessness (for the consonant), then back to voicing. But there are several reasons why ease of articulation is not a useful explanation for sound changes. Most straightforwardly, it is difficult to quantify articulatory effort, and in the absence of any rigorous way of doing so we often cannot deter-mine whether one articulation requires less effort than another. For instance, does it require more or less effort to close off the oral cavity completely for a few milliseconds (a stop) than to hold an articulator close to the upper side of the cavity and force the air through the opening (a fricative)? Moreover, "ease" is not simply a matter of physics and physiology; the articulations of one's native language are easier to produce than non-native articulations because one has

Table 5.3 *Lenition of Latin voiceless stops in Spanish*

Latin		Spanish
acūtum 'sharp'	>	agudo
aperīre 'to open'	>	abrir
aquam 'water'	>	agua
capillum 'hair (of the head)'	>	cabello
capram 'she-goat'	>	cabra
equam 'mare'	>	yegua
fricāre 'to rub'	>	fregar 'to scour'
lacum 'lake'	>	lago
latus 'side'	>	lado
lupum 'wolf'	>	lobo
marītum 'husband'	>	marido
māteriam 'timber'	>	madera 'wood'
patrem 'father'	>	padre
petram 'rock'	>	piedra 'stone'
rotam 'wheel'	>	rueda
sapere 'to be wise'	>	saber 'to know'
secāre 'to cut'	>	segar 'to mow'
sēcūrum 'without worry'	>	seguro 'secure'
socerum 'father-in-law'	>	suegro

learned them natively. That might not be a factor in errors made early in the process of native acquisition, but those are not typically the errors that survive into adolescent speech. Finally, and most awkwardly for the ease-of-articulation hypothesis, some sound changes clearly involve making more articulatory effort, not less; we will see some examples in the discussion of vowel rotations later in this chapter. We could suggest that they are motivated by a desire on the part of the speaker for clarity of articulation, or by an exaggerated expressiveness, or other factors. But the result will be that we have two different explanations tailor-made to account for *diametrically opposite* developments; with them we should be able to explain everything that can occur – and a hypothesis that can account for all possibilities, rather than explaining why we observe some and not others, is untestable and therefore not scientifically useful.

Better explanations for lenition and many other sound changes have emerged from work in the theory of Articulatory Phonology (see e.g. Browman and Goldstein 1991, Studdert-Kennedy and Goldstein 2003, both with references). Articulatory Phonology analyzes the phonological shapes of forms in terms of the gestures that speakers use to produce speech sounds; consequently it is an ideal approach for understanding the phonetic motivations of many sound changes.

A salient fact about speech gestures is that they overlap temporally (Browman and Goldstein 1991: 319–23). For instance, in pronouncing the syllable [ta] a

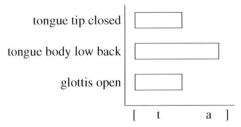

Figure 5.2 *Gestural score of the syllable [ta]*

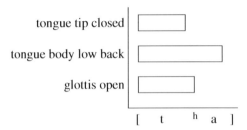

Figure 5.3 *Gestural score of the syllable [tʰa]*

speaker begins with complete closure of the mouth (at the alveolar ridge), then shifts to a maximally open oral cavity; simultaneously the speaker begins with the vocal chords in position for a voiceless consonant, then shifts into the voiced position for the vowel. In principle, the alveolar closure and voiceless gesture are coterminous, the wide-open mouth and voicing gesture are coterminous, and the two transitions (from closed to open and voiceless to voiced) are simultaneous; the timing of the gestures must be precise, since each of the resulting segments is only a fraction of a second long. The "gestural score" in Figure 5.2 illustrates what should happen.

But speakers frequently make mistakes, including mistakes in the timing of gestures. If the laryngeal gesture of voicelessness is held too long (or the closure in the mouth opened too soon), a brief stretch of voiceless vowel (that is, [h]) will appear after the consonant, as in Figure 5.3. In other words, the [t] will become aspirated [tʰ] (Browman and Goldstein 1991: 321). Thus a change of voiceless stops into voiceless aspirated stops can be explained straightforwardly as the result of a *slippage in the timing of articulatory gestures*. Other similar cases include the assimilation of nasal consonants in place of articulation to following obstruents (in which the gesture for the obstruent is begun too early); palatalization, in which a front vocalic articulation is anticipated to such an extent that it becomes coextensive with a preceding consonant; "excrescence" of consonants, e.g. the appearance of [p] in the pronunciation of English *warmth* as [wɑɹmpθ] (in which the velum is closed too soon, Browman and Goldstein 1991: 326–7); and intrusive vowels (see especially Hall 2006).

Though it might not be immediately obvious, similar slippages can account for many instances of lenition. If the gesture which should produce a closure in the mouth between two vowels is significantly delayed (while the timing of all other gestures remains constant), there may not be enough time to make the closure which the speaker intends: short stops will be produced in place of long ones, hypershort stops (taps) in place of typical ones, fricatives (in which the articulator doesn't quite reach the roof of the mouth) in place of stops, and so on (see Browman and Goldstein 1991: 325).

On the other hand, there are common types of sound change that are difficult to account for as the result of slippage in gestural timing. Among the best studied are vowel rotations in which tense vowels rise along a peripheral track while lax vowels fall along a nonperipheral track (see Labov 1994: 170–95); a stereotypical example is the pronunciation of /bæːd dɔːg/ as [bɪ·əd dʊ·əg] in some urban working-class dialects of the northeastern USA. While it is not completely impossible that those outcomes are the result of maintaining the gestures to produce tense vowels too long and those to produce lax vowels not long enough, that is not obviously correct. On the contrary, the fact that in the progress of such chain-shifts each new cohort of teenage girls pushes the changes a little further (see Chapter 3) suggests that sheer exaggeration is involved: speakers are *overshooting* the targets for tense vowels and *undershooting* the targets for lax vowels. Lenition could also result from target undershoot; Ní Chasaide 1989 offers a phonetically plausible analysis of voicing and fricativization as a single process of undershoot. Other possible examples of target overshoot include the shift of [θ] to the dental stop [t̪] (in some North Frisian dialects, for example).

Apparently we must recognize both slippage in timing and target undershoot/overshoot as phonetic causes of sound change; at least some changes can be explained either way, though others are amenable to only one of those explanations. That seems disappointing; clearly more work on phonetic change is needed. However, the work in phonetics that we have cited reflects real progress in the understanding of sound change in two different ways. In the first place, even when we cannot say for certain which type of gestural error has caused a phonetic change, we can usually be confident that some gestural error is responsible. Secondly, we are *not* working with diametrically opposed principles that can explain everything and are thus not amenable to testing; we do not have a unitary articulatory explanation for sound change, but we do have some testable hypotheses.

Acoustic motivations for sound change are very different. A straightforward example is the change of velarized [ɫ] to [w] in recent centuries in Polish. Except for the fact that both articulations involve raising the back of the tongue toward the velum, the two are not similar: one is characterized by lowering the sides of the tongue (and perhaps a midline closure at the alveolar ridge), the other by lip-rounding. But the acoustic signatures of the two are surprisingly similar (Jonasson 1972: 1127–9), and it seems clear that misperception on the part of native learners led to the replacement of the one articulation with the other. Thus this speaker error actually originated as a hearer error.

Table 5.4 *Latin /kt/, /gn/ (= [ŋn]) in Romanian*

Latin		Romanian
coctus 'cooked, ripe'	>	copt 'ripe'
dīrēctus 'straight'	>	drept 'right, straight'
facta 'deeds'	>	faptă 'deed'
frūctus 'produce'	>	frupt 'food that cannot be eaten during lent'
lac, lact- 'milk'	>	lapte
nox, noct- 'night'	>	noapte
octō 'eight'	>	opt
cognātus 'related'	>	cumnat 'brother-in-law'
dignus 'worthy'	>	demn 'dignified, worthy'
lignum '(fire)wood'	>	lemn 'wood'
pugnus 'fist'	>	pumn
signum 'sign'	>	semn

There are also acoustically motivated sound changes for which articulatory gestures can provide a partial explanation. For instance, it is certainly possible that the early Modern English change of [ɔʊx] to [ɔf] in words like *cough* occurred partly because of misperception of the velar articulation as a (fairly similar) labial; but it is also likely that lip-rounding persisted through the velar fricative (so that it was [xʷ] phonetically), and possible that that contributed to the misperception (see the discussion of Browman and Goldstein 1991: 328–9). A possibly similar case is the regular Romanian change of velars to labials when coronals follow immediately, as in Table 5.4 (note that Latin *gn* was phonetically [ŋn]).[5] Though they are somewhat similar acoustically, labials and velars are not ordinarily confused. However, when unreleased before coronals their acoustic signatures are overlaid with the signature of the following coronal, and it is reasonable to suppose that that can make them similar enough to be misperceived by some native learners.

Ohala 1981 points out that many sound changes could have involved failure on the part of a listener to "reconstruct" the articulatory gestures of the speaker (according to the motor theory of speech perception; see Chapter 1). One of Ohala's many examples is especially informative because he shows that it could give rise to errors in opposite ways. When a back round vowel is followed immediately by a dental or alveolar, the resulting modification of the vowel's formants causes the vowel to sound a bit fronted, even if it was produced in fully back position; thus [ut], for instances, sounds somewhat like [yt] (Ohala 1981: 179–80 with references). Normally the listener factors out the deformation and "reconstructs" [ut] as what the speaker intended (ibid. p. 182). Failure to reconstruct properly can lead the listener to hear [yt], and so to produce [yt] herself (ibid. p. 183). Alternatively, if the (first) speaker intentionally produces [yt], the listener can reconstruct too much and conclude that [ut] was intended;

the listener will then produce [ut] as a hypercorrection. The range of sound changes that could have involved such processes is surprisingly wide, as Ohala demonstrates.

Much work on the phonetic motivations of sound changes remains to be done, and there are some attested sound changes that will always be difficult to motivate phonetically (see Goddard 1974 for some extreme examples). But it is clear that the native-learner errors that persist long enough to give rise to sound changes are usually phonetically "reasonable" mistakes; that is why most sound changes are "natural," and why a large proportion of the phonological rules to which they give rise likewise seem natural. This has an interesting implication for the theory of phonology: the prevalence of natural phonological rules can be a simple consequence of their origins, having nothing to do with the grammar as such (see Buckley 2000, Buckley and Seidl 2005).

The phonological effects of sound change

During the period when a sound change is still in progress it is a variable rule of phonetic implementation. Once it has gone to completion, however, it can be integrated into the grammar in a number of ways.

If native-learner reanalysis is minimal, the sound change becomes a categorical phonological rule at the end of the ordered sequence of phonological rules. If more extensive reanalysis occurs, the sound change can be conflated with already existing rules or altered in other ways.

But it often happens that a new sound change doesn't interact with the existing system of rules; and even if it does, in derivationally isolated words the effects of the sound change are likely to be learned as underlying, since those words participate in no surface alternations which would lead the native learner to conclude that what she hears is phonologically derived. Such cases are naturally of little interest to the phonologist. But for the comparative reconstruction of undocumented ancestral languages, or "protolanguages," they are of the utmost importance, for the following reason. Only in derivationally isolated words can we be sure that the effects of regular sound change have not been altered by subsequent phonological or morphological changes (see Chapters 6 and 8). Thus it is only in such words that the patterns produced by regular sound change, which are the basis of comparative reconstruction, reliably survive unchanged for long periods of time.

In the following section we discuss in detail both the impact of sound changes on the basic pattern of contrasts among a language's sounds and their impact on the system of phonological rules, attempting to give a more or less complete picture of how sound changes affect phonology. Subsequent changes in the phonological rules into which sound changes typically develop will be dealt with in Chapter 6.

Patterns of sound change: contrasts and rules

A form not affected by any phonological rules is simply a memorized lexical item; it participates in the language's phonology only in that its phonological shape is subject to the constraints governing the feature content and sequencing of segments and the structure of syllables. However, such isolated words do exhibit structure of another kind: their underlying segments and metrical features participate in the system of phonological contrasts by which one utterance is distinguished from another, and statements about the overall distribution of those contrasts can be made.

Facts about the distribution of contrasts are almost certainly not part of a native speaker's grammar (a point which will repeatedly have interesting consequences). They are nevertheless of great interest to historical linguists because we are able to reconstruct protolanguages only by comparing the distributional patterns of contrasts in inherited words in two or more related languages (see Chapter 10). How sound changes alter the distribution of contrasts in a language is therefore of primary importance. The classic exposition is still Hoenigswald 1960: 86–98, which every historical linguist should internalize; here we offer a less formal summary of the most important points, with brief discussion of the consequences for systems of phonological rules.

An unconditioned sound change that affects only the phonetic realization of one or more non-alternating sounds obviously has no effect on the distribution of segments or on phonological rules; it simply substitutes one segment type for another. Typical examples include:

(2)   Proto-West Semitic *p, e.g. in *paqada 'he has paid attention to' (cf. Hebrew *pāqad*) > Arabic /f/, e.g. in *faqada* 'he has searched (in vain) for' – without merger, since there was no other source of /f/;

(3)   Proto-Polynesian *t, e.g. in *tapu 'forbidden' (cf. Tongan, Samoan, Maori *tapu*) > Hawaiian /k/, e.g. in *kapu* 'forbidden', again without merger because Proto-Polynesian *k had already become /ʔ/ in Hawaiian;

(4)   Proto-West Germanic *w, e.g. in *wīn 'wine' (cf. OE *wīn*, ModE *wine* /waɪn/) > High German /v/, e.g. in *Wein* /vaɪn/ 'wine', again without merger;

and so on. Since the output of the sound change is necessarily learned as underlying, the segment inventory of the language changes, but the *pattern of contrasts* between the segments is not altered: the new segment contrasts with every other segment in the language that can occur in the same phonotactic position, just as the old segment did; moreover, it contrasts in exactly the same sets of forms. From the point of view of contrasts, the new segment *is* the old segment, with new phonetics.

If sounds that already participate in phonological rules are affected by a change of this kind, the result is necessarily more complex. The fifteenth-century English

Table 5.5 *The English Great Vowel Shift*

	c. 1400		*c.* 1500
'bite'	biːtə	>	bəit
'beet'	beːt	>	biːt
'beat'	bɛːtə	>	beːt
'abate'	abaːtə	>	abaːt (> abɛːt)
'boat'	bɔːt	>	boːt
'boot'	boːt	>	buːt
'about'	abuːtə	>	abɔut

Great Vowel Shift (GVS) is a case in point. The GVS was a classic rotation of long or tense vowels, in which the long mid vowels rose and the long high vowels were diphthongized. The effects of the change can be illustrated with a near-minimal set of late ME words, as in Table 5.5. (The fronting of inherited /aː/ lagged significantly behind the rest of the shift and probably was not part of the same sound change. Various other changes occurred in subsequent centuries, as the reader can see by comparing the right hand column with modern forms. See also Jespersen 1909: 231–47.) Except for the fact that inherited [uː] did not shift when immediately followed by a labial consonant (see Jespersen 1909: 236–8), this was an unconditioned sound change; thus very few mergers occurred, and the preexisting system of contrasts emerged largely intact.

However, the underlying long vowels that underwent this change were already inputs to a phonological rule which shortened them before many consonant clusters and whenever they were followed by two or more syllables in the same word. For instance, late ME underlying /iː/ had been shortened to [ɪ] in the inflectional forms and derived words in the right-hand column in Table 5.6, but not in those in the left-hand column, and in the same way late ME /eː/ was shortened to [ɛ].

After the unconditioned shift of surface [iː] to [əi] and of [eː] to [iː] had gone to completion – so that the forms in the left-hand column in Table 5.6 were [həid], [ʧəild], [fəiv], etc., and [kiːp], [fiːd], [griːn], etc. – it might seem reasonable to suggest that in these sets of alternating forms, at least, native learners might still have posited underlying /iː/ and /eː/ respectively, deriving the forms in the left-hand column by a phonological rule more or less identical to the GVS and the forms in the right-hand column by the old shortening rule.

But what about words like (shifted) [əis] 'ice', [fəir] 'fire', [swəin] 'pig', [məin] 'my, mine', [diːr] 'animal', [kniː] 'knee', [hwiːl] 'wheel', [kwiːn] 'queen', [miː] 'me', [hiːr] 'here', etc., which participated in no alternations with forms exhibiting shortened [ɪ] or [ɛ]? A generative linguist might still posit /iː/ and /eː/ respectively in such words, based on the overall pattern of vowels in the language, but native language learning is not the same thing as linguistic analysis. A child learning such words in the first two or three years of life could only conclude that their [əi] was underlying /əi/ and their [iː] was underlying /iː/. We propose the following *invariant transparency hypothesis* (ITH):

Table 5.6 *Part of the shortening rule in late Middle English*

1.	[hi:də] 'hide'	[hɪddə] 'hid'
	[ki:ðə] 'make known'	[kɪddə] 'made known', [kɪθθə] 'acquaintance'
	[ʧi:ld] 'child'	[ʧɪldərən] 'children'
	[fi:və] 'five'	[fɪftə] 'fifth', [fɪfte:n] 'fifteen', [fɪfti] 'fifty'
	[wi:zə] 'wise'	[wɪzdom] 'wisdom'
	[wi:ldə] 'wild'	[wɪldərnəs] 'uncultivated land'
	[li:n] 'flax'	[lɪnse:d] 'flaxseed, linseed'
	[hwi:t] 'white'	[hwɪtsʊndei] 'Whitsunday' (the seventh Sunday after Easter)
	[kri:st] 'Christ'	[krɪstəmassə] 'Christmas'
2.	[ke:pə] 'keep'	[kɛptə] 'kept'
	[me:tə] 'meet'	[mɛttə] 'met'
	[fe:də] 'feed'	[fɛddə] 'fed'
	[de:mə] 'judge'	[dɛm(p)tə] 'judged'
	[de:p] 'deep'	[dɛpθə] 'depth'
	[θe:f] 'thief'	[θɛftə] 'theft'
	[fre:nd] 'friend'	[frɛndʃip] 'friendship'
	[ʃe:p] 'sheep'	[ʃɛp(h)ɛrdə] 'shepherd'
	[gre:nə] 'green'	[grɛnwɪʧ] 'Greenwich'

> Native learners in the developmental window for NLA do not posit abstract forms if there is no alternation to account for; instead they project surface segments, defined by the language's system of distinctive features, into underlying forms.[6]

This hypothesis may seem so obvious in the case at hand as to be trivial, but it will turn out to have important consequences in Chapter 6.

What would the native learner do upon learning enough alternating sets of forms to abduce the shortening rule? She might revise her analysis, and the result could be identical with the linguist's analysis: underlying /i:/ and /e:/ with a shortening rule and a "GVS rule," as suggested above. If the alternation between surface [əi] and [ɪ], and between surface [i:] and [ɛ], occurred in a large majority of the language's lexemes, the abstract solution would indeed be optimal. But as every linguist who has worked with English ought to know, that is not the case; there is a large "critical mass" of non-alternating lexemes. It therefore seems overwhelmingly likely that a native learner would stick with her original analysis, concluding that the underlying vowel nuclei were /əi/ and /i:/. It would then be necessary to posit very complex shortening rules changing /əi/ to /ɪ/ and /i:/ to /ɛ/ in appropriate environments. Of course different native learners could have arrived at different analyses of the same system, but the less abstract analysis (with the more complex rules) is likely to have been the majority analysis.

How long those rules remained productive is unclear; we might suggest that the appearance of *width* as a neologism in the 1620s (competing with inherited

Table 5.7 *Palatalization in two Tocharian B verb paradigms*

	Present	Preterite
/nətka-/ 'push'	act. 3sg., 3pl. nätkanaṃ	act. 3sg. ñatka, 3pl. ñitkāre
/ləma-/ 'sit'	[suppletive; subj. act. 3sg. lāmaṃ, 3pl. lamaṃ]	act. 3sg. lyama, 3pl. lymāre
/kəla-/ 'bring'	act. 3sg. källāṣṣäṃ, 3pl. källāskeṃ; med.-pass. 3sg. källāstär, 3pl. källāskentär	act. 3sg. śala, 3pl. śilāre; med.-pass. 3sg. klāte, 3pl. klānte
/tərka-/ 'let go'	act. 3sg., 3pl. tärkanaṃ; med.-pass. 3sg. tärknātär, 3pl. tärknāntär	act. 3sg. carka, 3pl. cärkāre; med.-pass. 3sg. tärkāte, 3pl. tärkānte

wideness < OE *wīdness*) shows that at least some native learners were positing some sort of rule more than a century after the sound change had gone to completion. But in the long run the rules were almost certainly lost; that is strongly suggested by the fact that a native speaker of modern English who first encounters the word *midwifery* in writing, without having learned it in childhood, cannot say with confidence whether the vowel of its second syllable is [ɑɪ] or [ɪ]. (The standard pronunciation of *midwifery*, at least in North America, is in fact ['mɪd͵wɪfəɹi]; but one also hears [ɑɪ] in the second syllable, as the *OED* duly records. The inherited pronunciation, also recorded by the *OED*, was apparently ['mɪdɪfɹi]; we have never heard it.) Of course this is the same end result as if the vowels affected by the GVS had participated in no alternations, but the developments leading to that eventual result were quite different and more involved.

If the sounds that underwent the unconditioned sound change (without merger) had been the output instead of the input of a phonological rule, a different type of reanalysis would have occurred: the new sound change would have been conflated with the old rule. The Tocharian languages provide a convenient example. A pre-Proto-Tocharian sound change palatalized consonants (except *j – written *y* in Tocharian – and, probably, *r) when a front vocalic immediately followed. At first the palatalized consonants must have simply been pronounced with the front of the tongue raised toward the roof of the mouth, much like palatalized consonants in modern Russian. However, subsequent sound changes shifted the pronunciation of several; for instance, in the attested languages palatalized *tʲ has become an affricate [t͡ʃ] or the like (written *c*), and palatalized *kʲ has become a fricative [ʃʲ] or the like (written *ś*). Thus the palatalization rule in attested Tocharian B, for example, includes the subrules /t/ → [t͡ʃ] and /k/ → [ʃʲ]. (Numerous other changes also occurred, so that the conditioning environments for the palatalization rule are morphological rather than phonological in the attested languages, but that does not affect the point at issue.) Note the Tocharian B examples in Table 5.7 (with surface forms given in conventional transliteration[7]). It can be seen that in

Table 5.8 *The loss of *w in Attic Greek*

Attic Greek		Proto-Greek	
ἔργον /érgon/ 'work'	<	*wérgon	(cf. Arkadian ϝεργον /wergon/)
ἔνδον /éndon/ 'inside'	<	*éndon	
καλός /kalós/ 'beautiful'	<	*kalwós	(cf. Boiotian neut. καλϝον /kalwon/)
ὁμαλός /homalós/ 'level'	<	*homalós	
βασιλέως /basiléɔːs/'king's'	<	*gʷasilê:wos	(cf. Mycenaean *qa-si-re-wo*)
πόλεως /póleɔːs/ 'city's'	<	*póle:jos	(loss of *j preceded loss of *w by several centuries)

the active preterite (but not in the mediopassive) the initial consonant of the root is palatalized according to the subrules stated above.

Conditioned sound changes have no effect on contrasts or on underlying forms so long as no merger results; for instance, the voicing of /θ/ and /s/ in fully voiced environments after a stressed syllable in OE had no effect on underlying forms (and was not normally represented in writing). Sound changes of this type usually become new phonological rules with minimal reanalysis.

Unconditioned loss obviously does alter the distribution of contrasts (and the language's phonotactics); this is one of the reasons why loss is conveniently thought of as "merger with zero" (Hoenigswald 1960: 91). The loss of Proto-Greek *w in the Attic dialect of Ancient Greek is a typical example. Not only was the inventory of consonants reduced by one; the number of vowel-initial words and word-internal hiatuses between vowels (both already very large) were increased, the number and incidence of consonant clusters were reduced, and so on. The examples in Table 5.8 illustrate the situation.

Conditioned loss has similar effects, but locally rather than globally; for instance, the loss of word-initial *k* before *n* in Early Modern English (rendering *knight* homonymous with *night*, for example) eliminated one word-initial consonant cluster and modestly increased the number of *n*-initial words, but the overall effect on the language was slight.

The impact of phonemic mergers on the distribution of contrasts likewise depends on the type of merger involved. The results are least interesting if the merger is unconditioned: a contrasting unit is eliminated, and the distribution of the merger product is simply the sum of the distributions of the inputs. If the inputs did not participate in any phonological rules, or if they were affected by the same rule(s) in a way that did not differentiate them, the only effect on the grammar is to reduce the number of underlying contrasts. A case in point is the pair of late ME long nonhigh front vowels /e:/ and /ɛ:/ (see above). Both were affected by the shortening rule, and the output of shortening in both cases was short /ɛ/; the following examples are typical:

(5)   a. [meːtə] 'meet', [mɛttə] 'met'; [feːdə] 'feed', [fɛddə] 'fed'
       b. [mɛːtə] 'dream', [mɛttə] 'dreamed'; [lɛːdə] 'lead', [lɛddə] 'led'

(The verb [mɛ:tə] was actually impersonal, meaning 'a dream occurred'; thus 'I dreamed' was [me: mɛttə], literally 'a dream happened to me'.) In the fifteenth century the GVS shifted these long vowels to /i:/ and /e:/ respectively; in the sixteenth century they merged in some dialects (including the one ancestral to standard ModE) as /i:/. (That is why *beet* and *beat, see* and *sea, peel* and *peal*, etc., are now pairs of homonyms.) The only result of the merger was to reduce the number of underlying long vowels – and, incidentally, to simplify the shortening rule, since there was now only one input /i:/ that yielded short [ɛ].

If one of the inputs of an unconditioned merger is input to a phonological rule while the other is not, the result is naturally more complex; Algonkian languages provide an illustrative case. Proto-Algonkian had a consonant, usually reconstructed as *θ (because it survives in that shape in Arapaho and merges with *t in Cree), that was palatalized to *š before high front vocalics (Bloomfield 1946: 87, 92). In Fox *θ merged with *n, which underwent no such alternation.[8] The result is that there are in effect two underlying *n*'s in Fox, an /n[1]/ which does not alternate and an /n[2]/ which is palatalized to š before high front vocalics. Of course the latter can be assigned a different underlying identity; we present this maximally opaque solution to emphasize that there is no other difference between them. The examples below are typical (Bloomfield 1925: 225, Goddard 1994a; we have modernized the orthography):

(6)   Morpheme-final n[1]   Morpheme-final n[2]
       /ata:hp-en[1]-/ 'pick (someone) up':   /kan[1]o:n[2]-/ 'speak to':
       e:h-ata:hpen-a:či 'he took hold of him'   *kano:n-e:wa* 'he speaks to him'
       maw-ata:hpen-i 'go pick him up!'   *kano:š-i* 'speak to him!'
       /čapo:k-en[1]-/ 'dip (someone) in water'   /awan[2]-/ 'take (someone) with one'
       čapo:ken-e:wa 'he dips him in water'   *ket-awan-a:pena* 'you and I take him with us'
       ke-čapo:ken-i 'you (sg.) dip me in water'   *ket-awaš-ipwa* 'you (pl.) take me with you'

There seems to be no tendency to eliminate this opaque alternation in Fox, possibly because non-alternating /n[1]/ and alternating /n[2]/ are both frequently encountered in the relevant environments: a large majority of relevant morphemes end in the latter, but the former occurs in the very common verb suffix /-en[1]-/ 'by hand' (Bloomfield 1925: 225).

If the merger is conditioned, so that only some allophones of a phoneme merge with some other phoneme, the result is a systematic gap in the distribution of segments and of contrasts: in the merger environment the earlier contrast between the merged sounds is no longer possible, and only the single merger product occurs in that environment. Latin "rhotacism," in which the (voiced) allophone of *s* between vowels merged with *r*, is the classic case. Note the examples of actually attested inherited *s* and *r* in a variety of phonotactic positions in Table 5.9.[9] It can be seen that after the change had gone to completion *s* did not occur between vowels, whereas the distribution of *r* had changed only in that

Table 5.9 *Inherited *s and *r in Latin*

Archaic Latin		Classical Latin	
sakros 'holy'	>	sacer	(*s* unchanged)
siēd 'let it be'	>→	siet → sit	"
deivōs 'gods (acc.)'	>	deōs	"
iovestōd 'rightly'	>	iūstō	"
iovesāt 'calls to witness'	>	iūrat	(*VsV* > *VrV*)
lasēs 'tutelary gods'	>	larēs	"
rēcei /re:gei/ 'for the king'	>	rēgī	(*r* unchanged)
satur 'satisfied, sated'	>	satur	"
vircō /wirgo:/ 'girl'	>	virgō	"
Castorei /kastorei/ 'to Castor'	>	Castorī	"
kalātōrem 'attendant (acc.)'	>	calātōrem	"

there were more intervocalic examples than previously. (Latin later acquired new intervocalic *s*'s by various processes.)

This sound change too became a phonological rule, but one whose output was identical with an underlying segment. Since Latin had a moderately complex inflectional system, there were numerous paradigms in which the rule operated, allowing native learners to recover both the rule and the underlying forms. The list of examples below could easily be expanded.

(7)   Verb suffixes and endings:
         active infinitive *-re* ~ *-se* < *-si: present *amā-re* 'to love', *habē-re* 'to have', *dīce-re* 'to say', *audī-re* 'to hear', *da-re* 'to give', *ī-re* 'to go', etc., etc.; but *es-se* 'to be' and perfect infinitive *-is-se*
         imperfect subjunctive *-rē-* ~ *-sē-* < *-sē-: to the present stems just listed, impf. subj. *amā-rē-*, *habē-rē-*, *dīce-rē-*, *audī-rē-*, *da-rē-*, *ī-rē-*, and also *fo-rē-* 'would be'; but *es-sē-* 'would be' and pluperfect subj. *-is-sē-* (cf. Oscan **fusíd** '(that) it should be', **patensíns** '(that whenever) they open (it)')

(8)   Verb stems:
         s- ~ *es-* ~ *er-* 'be (pres. stem)', e.g. in *s-unt* 'they are', *es-t* 'it is', pres. subj. *s-ī-*, impf. subj. *es-sē-*, pres. inf. *es-se*; but ipf. indic. *er-ā-*, fut. indic. *er-V-* (cf. Oscan pres. inf. *ezum*; Skt. *s-* ~ *as-*, e.g. in *ásati* 'it will be' = Lat. *erit*)
         ger-e-re 'to carry', perf. *ges-s-isse*, perf. participle *ges-tus*
         quer-ī 'to complain', perf. ptc. *ques-tus*
         ūr-e-re 'to burn (trans.)', perf. *us-s-isse*, perf. ptc. *us-tus* (cf. Skt. *óṣati* '(s)he's burning (it)')
         haur-ī-re 'to draw (water)', perf. *haus-isse* < *haus-s-, perf. ptc. *haus-tus* (cf. Old Norse *ausa*) *haer-ē-re* 'to cling', perf. *haes-isse* < *hais-s-
         quaer-e-re 'to look for; to inquire', perf. *quaesīv-isse* < *kwais-s . . . , perf. ptc. *quaesītus*

(9)   Nouns:

    a. Polysyllabic neuter s-stems with inherited ablaut. Example: *genus* ~
       gener- 'lineage', the latter alternant e.g. in gen. sg. *gener-is* (cf. Skt.
       jánas, gen. *jánas-as*)

       So also *foedus* 'treaty', *fūnus* 'funeral', *latus* 'side', *mūnus* 'gift', *onus*
       'load', *opus* 'work', *pondus* 'weight', *scelus* 'curse; crime', *sīdus* 'con-
       stellation', *ulcus* 'sore', *vellus* 'fleece', *viscus* 'internal organ', *vulnus*
       'wound', and five others.

    b. Polysyllabic neuter s-stems with levelled ablaut. Example: *corpus* ~
       corpor- 'body'.

       So also *decus* 'distinction', *facinus* 'crime', *faenus* 'interest (on a loan)',
       frīgus 'cold', *lītus* 'shore', *nemus* 'grove', *pectus* 'chest, breast', *pecus*
       'herd, flock', *penus* 'provisions', *stercus* 'dung', *tempus* 'time', *tenus*
       'snare'.

    c. Non-neuter polysyllabic s-stems: *cinis* ~ *ciner-* (masc.) 'ashes', *pulvis* ~
       pulver- (masc.) 'dust', *lepus* ~ *lepor-* (masc.) 'hare', *lepōs* ~ *lepōr-*
       (masc.) 'pleasantness', *Venus* ~ *Vener-* (fem.), name of the goddess of
       sex; *Cerēs* ~ *Cerer-* (fem.), name of the grain goddess; *tellūs* ~ *tellūr-*
       (fem.) 'earth' (poetic only), and a few others.

    d. Neuter monosyllabic s-stems. Example: *aes* ~ *aer-* 'bronze' (cf. Skt. *áyas*
       'iron').

       So also *crūs* 'leg', *iūs* 'law, rights', *ōs* 'mouth', *pus* 'pus', *rus* 'country-
       side', *tūs* 'incense'.

    e. Non-neuter monosyllabic s-stems. Example: *mūs* ~ *mūr-*, e.g. gen. sg.
       mūr-is (masc.) 'mouse' (cf. Skt. *mū́s*, gen. *mūṣ-ás*)

       So also *glīs* (masc.) 'dormouse', *flōs* (masc.) 'flower', *glōs* (fem.) 'sister-
       in-law', *mōs* (masc.) 'custom', *rōs* (masc.) 'dew'.

(10)   Other common examples: adjectives *vetus* ~ *veter-* 'old', *mās* ~ *mar-* 'male';
       herī 'yesterday' : *hesternus* 'of yesterday'.

Native learners would not have had any reason to believe that the surface *r*'s
in the lexemes listed above were underlying and the *s*'s derived, because there
were other, otherwise similar lexemes that exhibited surface *r* in all forms; for
instance, contrasting with *iūs* 'right', *iūris* 'of right' was *fūr* 'thief', *fūris* 'of
a thief', and contrasting with *latus* 'side', *latere* 'at the side' was *later* 'brick',
latere 'with a brick'. Thus rhotacism was clearly a fully functioning phonological
rule in Classical Latin. On the other hand, non-alternating intervocalic *r*'s < *s
could only be learned as underlying /r/; examples include the surface *r*'s of *cūra*
'care; administration', *caret* '(s)he lacks', *āra* 'altar', and genitive plural *-ārum*,
etc. (Cf. Paelignian *coisatens* 'they administered', Oscan **kasit** 'it is necessary',
aasaí 'on the altar', gen. pl. **-asúm**, *-azum*.)

The greatest effects on the distribution of contrastive units are caused by a
conditioned split followed by a merger or loss that obscures the conditioning
environment. Hoenigswald 1960: 93–4 calls this "secondary split," since the
split becomes contrastive only secondarily, upon the (partial) destruction of the

Table 5.10 *Secondary split of /θ/ in late Middle English*

Old English	late Middle English	Modern English
bæþ /bæθ/ [bæθ]	bath /baθ/ [baθ]	bath /bæ:θ/
baþian /baθian/ [baðian]	bathe /ba:θə/ [ba:ðə]	bathe /beið/
clāþ /klɔ:θ/ [klɔ:θ]	clo(o)th /klɔ(:)θ/ [klɔ(:)θ]	cloth /klɔθ/
ġeclāþian /jəkla:θian/ [jəkla:ðian]	clothe /klɔ:θə/ [klɔ:ðə]	clothe /kloʊð/
lāþ /la:θ/ [la:θ] 'hateful'	lo(o)th /lɔ(:)θ/ [lɔ(:)θ]	lo(a)th /lɔθ/, /loʊθ/
lāþian /la:θian/ [la:ðian] 'cause loathing' (impersonal)	lothe /lɔ:θə/ [lɔ:ðə]	loathe /loʊð/

conditioning environment. This is the usual way in which languages acquire new surface-contrastive units. The development of voiced fricative phonemes in English is a typical example. We noted above that /θ/ was voiced to [ð] in fully voiced environments after a stressed syllable in OE, but that the distribution of the voiced and voiceless allophones remained automatic. Eventually, though, parts of the environment for voicing were destroyed in some relevant words – typically by the loss of word-final /ə/ in the decades around 1400. Those developments introduced voiced [ð] into environments in which only voiceless [θ] had previously occurred; the two allophones thereby became surface-contrastive. Note the examples in Table 5.10.

Since at the time that the postconsonantal voiced environment was lost the dental fricative occurred almost exclusively in native words, this is an almost "pure" example of secondary split. In the examples given above the newly word-final [ð]'s were probably still derived from underlying /θ/ for a few generations, but the rule that derived them must now have been morphologically conditioned (roughly, "stem-final /θ/ is voiced in noun plurals and in derived verbs"). In the long run, of course, the rule was lost; it is doubtful at best that any dialect of modern English can be said to have a rule that voices underlying /θ/. That is why we represent the /ð/'s in the right-hand column in Table 5.10 as underlying.

The most striking thing about secondary split is that the effects of a phonological rule persist even after the conditioning environment, or part of it, is destroyed. Why shouldn't the rule cease operating, and the underlying segments reemerge on the surface, when the rule's trigger is lost or compromised? The answer can only be that at least some native learners learn *non-alternating* outputs of phonological rules as underlying segments *even if their occurrence is completely predictable*, in accordance with the ITH advanced above. We will return to this important point in the next chapter.

Sound change and rule ordering

If the phonology of a language is formalized as a set of (partially) ordered rules, each new sound change is normally added to the ordered sequence

Table 5.11 *Counterfeeding of rhotacism and [ss] → [s] in Classical Latin*

Underlying forms	Surface forms	Meanings
/ges-e-t, ges-s-it/	gerit, gessit	'(s)he wages, (s)he waged'
/hais-e:-t, hais-s-it/	haeret, haesit	'it clings, it clung'
/kwat-i-t, kwat-s-it/	quatit, quassit	'(s)he shakes, (s)he shook'
/ri:d-e:-t, ri:d-s-it/	rīdet, rīsit	'(s)he laughs, (s)he laughed'
/lu:d-e-t, lu:d-s-it/	lūdit, lūsit	'(s)he plays, (s)he played'
/sed-e:-se, sed-su-m/	sedēre, sessum	'to sit'
/lu:d-e-se, lu:d-su-m/	lūdere, lūsum	'to play'
/hais-e:-se, hais-su-m/	haerēre, haesum	'to cling'

of rules at its end. This is most obvious when the new rule and an already existing rule stand in counterfeeding order, so that the new rule creates a sequence of sounds which the old rule would have altered (but does not because it does not apply again). The further history of Latin rhotacism provides a well-known example. As we noted above, it is clear that rhotacism was still a phonological rule in the first century BCE, recoverable by native learners from alternations in the surface outputs of the grammar. A new rule was then added to the grammar reducing geminate *ss* to single *s* immediately following a long vowel or diphthong. The instances of *s* which were the outputs of this rule were *not* inputs to rhotacism. Typical examples of paradigms with geminate *ss* and with degeminated *s* include those in Table 5.11.

Two relevant rules apply to 'laughed', etc.: first /ts/, /ds/ → [ss] (as in 'shook'), then [ss] is reduced to [s] if anything other than a short vowel immediately precedes.[10] It can be seen that the rules are in counterfeeding order because the rule simplifying geminate [ss] was added to the grammar later than rhotacism (some centuries later, in fact). Many other similar examples can be adduced.

It is sometimes suggested that a rule can be added to the ordered sequence so as to apply *before* a preexisting rule. However, the few examples of this phenomenon that have been investigated in detail raise serious doubts about the possibility of such a development. Perhaps the best researched case is that of Dutch; the situation is as follows (see now Gress-Wright 2010; we are grateful to Jonathan Gress-Wright for helpful discussion).

We have very few Germanic documents from the low countries before the thirteenth century; adequate description must therefore begin with that period, conventionally called "Middle Dutch" (MD). By then word-final obstruents had already been devoiced and were usually written with symbols for voiceless consonants (Franck 1910: 78–80); the examples in Table 5.12 are typical. (In Table 5.12 we justify the Proto-West Germanic reconstructions by reference to outcomes in other daughter languages, as is usual in the specialist literature. In the last two examples the final consonants were phonetically fricatives [ɣ, β] in Proto-West Germanic.) The sound change of devoicing gave rise to a robust phonological

Table 5.12 *Word-final devoicing in Middle Dutch*

Middle Dutch		Proto-West Germanic
goet 'good'	<	*gōd (OE, OS *gōd*, OHG *guot*)
hant 'hand'	<	*handu (OE, OS *hand*, OHG *hant*)
wart 'it became' < *ward	<	*warþ (OE *wearþ*, OS, OHG *ward*)
dinc [dɪŋk] 'thing'	<	*þing (OE *þing*, OS *thing*, OHG *ding*)
sanc '(s)he sang'	<	*sang (OE, OHG *sang*)
dach [dax] 'day'	<	*dag (OE *dæġ*, OS *dag*, OHG *tag*)
gaf '(s)he gave'	<	*gab (OHG *gab*; in this case OS *gaf* shares the Dutch change, while OE *ġeaf* exhibits devoicing independently)

OS = Old Saxon, OHG = Old High German.

Table 5.13 *Further word-final devoicing in Modern Dutch*

Middle Dutch		Modern Dutch
ic scrive 'I write'	>	ik schrijf [ɪk sxrɛif]
grave 'count'	>	graaf [ɣraːf]
oghe 'eye'	>	oog [oːx]
brugghe 'bridge'	>	brug [brʏx]
beelde 'picture'	>	beeld [beːlt]
ic vinde 'I find'	>	ik vind [ɪk fɪnt]
ic hebbe 'I have'	>	ik heb [ɪk hɛp]

rule; compare MD *goede* (pl.), *hande* 'hands', *worden* 'they became', *dinghe* 'things', *singhen* 'to sing', *daghe* 'days', *gâven* 'they gave', which show that all the lexemes listed had underlying voiced obstruents /d, g, ɣ, v/ in root-final position. Subsequently, in the transition from MD to Modern Dutch, many word-final /ə/'s (spelled *e*) were lost. Obstruents which became word-final by that loss have also been devoiced. The examples in Table 5.13 are typical.

It has been suggested that the already existing devoicing rule applied to these forms automatically as soon as /ə/ was lost, so that the rule deleting /ə/ was effectively added to the phonology at a point before the end of the sequence of ordered rules. (See the references in Goossens 1977: 3–4, nn. 5–6 and the extensive quote from Van Marle ibid. p. 5.)

However, there is actual evidence that that is not what happened. There are three geographical regions in the Dutch-speaking area in which loss of final /ə/ ("apocope") did not occur (Goossens 1977: 7–8), and at the borders of all three are spoken village dialects in which apocope did occur, *but resulting word-final voiced obstruents had not been devoiced* at the time when those dialects were first described scientifically (ibid. pp. 8–12); in addition, there is an area along the southeastern border of the Dutch *Sprachraum* that exhibited the same peculiarity (ibid. pp. 12–13). Moreover, in at least two of these areas devoicing was spreading at the end of the nineteenth century, and voiced word-final obstruents were recessive variants (ibid. pp. 13–14). The map of the southern part of the Dutch/Flemish speech area on p. 11 of Goossens 1977 is especially eloquent: the distribution of villages with voiced word-final obstruents shows that they are relic areas around the margins of the region of apocope, and that devoicing has been spreading outward from the more central parts of that region. The only hypothesis that makes sense of this pattern is that there was a *second* regular sound change of devoicing after apocope had occurred, and that this second devoicing spread through the Dutch speech area like any other regular sound change. Evidently the first devoicing did not remain an automatic phonological rule when apocope occurred. That is a sobering result, because it follows that whenever we do not have evidence to show whether a natural sound change became a rule that applied automatically to the outputs of more recent rules we must consider the possibility that the natural change simply occurred a second time.

The limitations of phonological contrast: "functional load" and near-mergers

Since mergers decrease the inventory of contrastive segments and lead to homophony, one might suppose that from at least some points of view they are dysfunctional (though see the discussion in Chapters 2 and 3). Chain shifts such as the English GVS, in which the phonemes of a single subsystem all shift in the same direction simultaneously so that no mergers occur, might then seem to be evidence of the *avoidance* of mergers in sound change. In the middle of the twentieth century this attractive idea was elaborated by André Martinet, who organized his hypothesis around the concept of "functional load" (see especially Martinet 1955). Robert King's explanation of this concept is clear and concise:

> The term FUNCTIONAL LOAD is customarily used in linguistics to describe the extent and degree of contrast between linguistic units, usually phonemes. In its simplest expression, functional load is a measure of the number of minimal pairs which can be found for a given opposition. More generally, in phonology, it is a measure of the work which two phonemes (or a distinctive feature) do in keeping utterances apart – in other words, a gauge of the frequency with which two phonemes contrast in all possible environments.   (King 1967: 831)

Martinet conjectured that phonemic oppositions with low functional load are more likely to be destroyed by merger than those with high functional load, other things being equal. That seems plausible. Consider the GVS, in which a whole subset of English vowels shifted in lockstep with almost no mergers. That entire set of vowels had a relatively high functional load; it is not difficult to construct a six- or seven-member (near-)minimal set to illustrate the change, as we did above. The GVS looks like a convincing illustration of Martinet's thesis. Moreover, if the vowels shifted in tandem so as to avoid mergers, we might ask whether the lowest vowels began to be raised first (in which case the higher vowels must have moved to get out of the way, so to speak, and the chain shift was a "push-chain") or the highest vowels were diphthongized first (in which case each lower vowel must have moved into vacated phonetic territory, and the chain shift was a "pull-chain"). A great deal of ink has been spilled over that question.

Unfortunately Martinet never provided any hard evidence to support his conjecture. The first serious test of the relevance of functional load to sound change was published in King 1967. King tested three specific hypotheses: "that, if all else is equal, sound change is more likely to start within oppositions bearing low functional loads" (the "weak point hypothesis," ibid., pp. 834–5); "that, if all else is equal, and if (for whatever reason) there is a tendency for a phoneme x to merge with either of the two phonemes y or z, then that merger will occur for which the functional load of the merged opposition is smaller" (the "least resistance hypothesis," ibid. p. 835); and "that, if an opposition $x \neq y$ is destroyed by merger, then that phoneme will disappear in the merger for which the relative frequency of occurrence is smaller" (the "frequency hypothesis," ibid. p. 535). His tests were the phonological development of Old Icelandic to Modern Icelandic, of Old Saxon to Middle Low German, of Middle High German to Modern High German, and of Middle High German to some dialects of Yiddish (ibid. p. 836). All three hypotheses failed the tests dramatically. The weak point hypothesis failed in nearly two-thirds of the relevant cases (thirteen out of twenty-one); the other two hypotheses were supported by about half the relevant cases – the proportion expected by random chance (ibid. pp. 847–8). King concluded that Martinet's conjectures could not be proved and should be abandoned as unexplanatory. Recently Dinoj Surendran and Partha Niyogi have retested Martinet's hypothesis computationally on a recent Cantonese consonant merger using a much more sophisticated definition of functional load (Surendran and Niyogi 2006: 44–5, 55–7). They, too, found no correlation between functional load and susceptibility to merger. That confirms the consensus of opinion among rigorous historical linguists that functional load has no demonstrable effect on mergers and should be disregarded in framing hypotheses about sound change.

The failure of functional load hypotheses shows that, though phonological contrast is important, there are limits to its relevance. Another phenomenon reinforces that conclusion in a surprising way. Though the loss of contrasts through merger is normally a fairly rapid process, often going to completion in a single generation, occasionally the outcome is more complex: the phonetic realizations of phonemes can overlap to a considerable extent – in extreme cases roughly half the tokens of a particular phoneme can be ambiguous in isolation – and the situation can persist for generations. This outcome is referred to as "near-merger." The clearest and best-studied case is the system of tense front vowels in the vernacular English of Belfast (Milroy and Harris 1980). This is possible because native learners posit underlying forms not on the basis of one or a few tokens of a phonological unit, but based on the whole range of tokens that they hear; if the distribution of tokens is complex enough to penalize all simple solutions on a daily basis (see Chapter 2), a system of phonemes with overlapping phonetic realizations can be learned. (For information on a broader range of cases of near-merger, including the "Bill Peters phenomenon," see Labov *et al.* 1991.)

This is important for historical linguists in a very specific way. The historical record of a near-merger can be difficult to distinguish from that of a genuine merger, especially if the writing system is inadequate to express all the underlying contrasts. If the near-merger is reversed by later sound changes, it can appear that a genuine merger that has gone to completion has been reversed. Since the latter is impossible *within a single dialect*, such a configuration of evidence can be interpreted to signify that the apparent merger was in fact a near-merger.

Notes

1 Spanish *milagro* cannot be directly inherited from Classical Latin *mīrāculum*, because in that case regular sound changes would have given "*mirajo*"; therefore it must be a loan from medieval Latin. A similar case is *peligro* 'danger' ‹ medieval Latin *perīculum*.

2 Because lexical diffusion of sound changes seems to be the most important way in which irregularities can arise, it is important to remember that the *effects* of dialect borrowing can persist for a long time, because the introduction of variable irregularities into a dialect can give rise to subdialects distinguished by phonological irregularities, and that creates the potential for further borrowing between the nearly, but not quite, identical subdialects (see the discussion of the split of /æ/ in Chapter 3). The famous Chaozhou case discussed by Wang and Lien 1993 apparently falls into this category. They seem to be suggesting that such a situation is more or less universal; we believe that the results of modern sociolinguistics suggest otherwise.

3 In identifying OE words surviving in ModE for the experiment reported in the text, etymologically related words actually borrowed from Norse had to be excluded; the fact that most surviving OE documents are written in the West Saxon dialect (which is thus the basis of the glossary), while all the standard dialects of ModE are descended from Anglian dialects of OE, also had to be taken into account. Different experimenters might have made different decisions in detail, achieving slightly different results, but all reasonable counts will give figures in the same ballpark.

4 We analyze the initial segments of, e.g., French *hier*, *huit*, *oiseau* as high vowels /i y u/ respectively, since there is no clear evidence that prevocalic high vowels and semivowels contrast in that language, and some evidence that these segments are simply vowels (note that they do not inhibit elision or *liaison*). Latin nominals are here given in the accusative case, which is the etymological ancestor of the modern French forms. (So also in the Spanish and Romanian examples.) All Latin *ē*'s in these examples are stressed; all the French words are stressed on the last non-schwa vowel. The closed stressed syllables of some forms had all become open by the time the first relevant sound change occurred; for instance, *n* immediately before *s* had already been lost in Classical Latin (at first with nasalization of the preceding vowel).

5 Romanian *ă* is a central mid vowel. The development of 'milk' must have involved at least some paradigm restructuring. The Romanian direct case reflects the Latin nominative, accusative, or both, but in Latin both the nominative and accusative of the neuter 'milk'

were *lac*; evidently the oblique stem *lact-* was leveled into the direct forms (as also in Italian *latte*, French *lait*, Spanish *leche*, etc.).

6 We state the ITH carefully because it is difficult to define the phonological units that native learners project into underlying forms; as we will see, not all are surface-contrastive. It does appear that all are definable by the set of distinctive features that are employed to distinguish underlying phonemes. The ITH is different from Kiparsky's alternation condition (Kiparsky 1982a: 58–62); in some ways it is more constraining, since the alternation condition prohibits absolute neutralization in phonological derivation – equivalent to prohibiting the use of "concrete" distinctive features as diacritics – whereas the transparency hypothesis demands that some degree of phonetic substance be projected into underlying forms.

7 The Tocharian languages were written in an Indian alphabet. *ś* was a palatal or prepalatal sibilant fricative; *ś* and *c* were probably pronounced at the same point of articulation, given that *ś* is the only sibilant allowed to be the immediate left neighbor of *c*. (For instance, the nominative singular of Tocharian B /məstó-/ 'fist', with an ending that palatalizes the /t/, surfaces as *maśce*.) It is possible that *c* was a palatal stop, but an affricate is more likely. *ñ* was a palatal or palatalized nasal; the corresponding lateral was written *ly*.

8 Our account of the development of Proto-Algonkian *θ is simplified; what really happened is the following. There were *three* relevant underlying consonants in Proto-Algonkian, as follows:

Underlying	Before *i, *y	Elsewhere	
*/θ/	*[ʃ]	*[θ]	
*/l/	*[l]	*[l]	(or possibly */r/, = [r] in all environments)
*/n/	*[n]	*[n]	

In most Algonkian languages *θ first merged with *l as *l; the result was a system in which some */l/ were palatalized to *[ʃ] before high front vocalics, while others were not. Some languages leveled the alternation; others, including Fox, generalized it to all */l/'s. Subsequently */l/ – which now always underwent palatalization in Fox – merged with */n/, giving the situation described in the text. For further details see Bloomfield 1946: 92, Hockett 1981: 56–7, Goddard 1994b: 189–90.

9 Archaic Latin spelling of the velar stops was somewhat confused (for reasons having to do with the origin of the Roman alphabet). The voiceless velar stop /k/ was variously spelled *c*, *k*, and *q;* but the voiced stop /g/ was originally also spelled with *c* (i.e. with *gamma*, e.g. in 'king' and 'girl' in the table), and it was some time before an additional letter was devised to represent it. The final *-s* of *sakros* was lost by a different sound change not relevant to our discussion.

10 In the last three examples in Table 5.11 the first form is the usual Latin present infinitive; the second, called the "supine," is used to express purpose when governed by a verb of motion. The supine suffix was etymologically *-tu- but had been reanalyzed as /-su-/ in some verbs, e.g. *manēre*, *mānsum* 'to stay', *fīgere*, *fīxum* 'to insert', etc.

6   The evolution of phonological rules

In the preceding chapter we focused on the process of sound change and the initial integration of a completed sound change into the grammar, keeping the discussion of phonological structure to a minimum. In this chapter we investigate the further development of the rules into which sound changes typically evolve – that is, change within the structured phonological system.

These developments can be discussed only in the context of a coherent model of phonology. We adopt a generalized version of generative phonology as developed in the 1970s and 1980s, with ordered rules, autosegments, and metrical structures. We are well aware that this approach has its limitations, but so does every other model of phonology; we have chosen this model because it is exceptionally convenient for the discussion of phonological change. (We have chosen not to work with Optimality Theory because it does not seem well adapted to the description of phonological change; see especially the critique of McMahon 2000: 57–128.)

In the first section below we illustrate some of the advantages of fully articulated modern phonology in describing the effects of sound change; readers who require a fuller introduction should consult, e.g., Goldsmith 1990 or Kenstowicz 1994. We then proceed to consider the evolution of phonological rules that have already become categorical.

Sound change and formal phonology

From the point of view of a historical linguist, a major advantage of autosegmental phonology is that it decomposes the traditional sequence of segments (i.e. consonants and vowels) into parallel "tiers," each of which represents a different kind of phonological information. It is very often the case that the articulatory gestures which are so useful in understanding sound change (see the preceding chapter) translate more or less directly into operations on a specific phonological tier (see McCarthy 1988 with references; we are grateful to Eugene Buckley for helpful discussion of this section). This is especially apparent in dealing with distant assimilation between similar sounds which are separated in the string of segments by sounds of other types: the sounds participating in the change are in fact adjacent on the relevant tier because they share

Figure 6.1 *First assimilation of Old English* gædeling

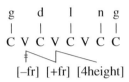

Figure 6.2 *Second assimilation of Old English* gædeling

distinctive features. In Old English (OE), for example, the inherited word *gadul-ing 'kinsman, companion' (attested in that form in Old Saxon) became *gædyling: the high vowel of the second syllable was fronted because the vowel of the last syllable was high and front; then, since the second syllable now contained a high front vowel, the vowel of the first syllable was fronted too. (Eventually the word became *gædeling* by reduction of the most unstressed vowel; see Campbell 1962: 82.) Because the "melodic" tier, which represents the articulatory and acoustic features of speech sounds, is actually composed of several tiers of feature bundles, each containing a different group of related features, it is easy to capture the fact that the assimilation of the vowels ignored the intervening consonants, which had no frontness feature. The first assimilation can be represented as in Figure 6.1 (with features not relevant to the rule omitted, and vowel height represented by an *n*-ary feature with values [1] (low) to [4] (high)), and the second as in Figure 6.2.

Of course the frontness feature must occupy a (sub-)tier of its own within the tier of vocalic features, but it does: since frontness, height, and rounding are articulatorily independent of each other, autosegmental phonology recognizes them as separate tiers. The tier analysis replicates faithfully the fact that the trajectory of the body of the tongue (which produces the vowels) is articulatorily independent of the consonants in this example, so that the vowels are actually adjacent and can easily assimilate to each other. (For a full representation of phonological tiers see e.g. the diagram in Schein and Steriade 1986: 695.)

Autosegmental phonology also gives an insightful account of the details of the Sanskrit retroflex assimilation rule. To make the analysis of Sanskrit retroflexion intelligible we must first describe the relevant subsystem of sounds in some detail – a task which is possible thanks to the extraordinary accuracy of the ancient Indian phonetic treatises (see Allen 1953). The [-cont] (i.e. stop) consonants of Sanskrit are produced at five places of articulation, phonetically bilabial, dental, retroflex, palatal, and velar; they have the following place-of-articulation features:

(1)   *Bilabial Dental Retroflex Palatal Velar*
           [−cor]   [+cor]   [+cor]   [+cor] [−cor]
           [labial] [+ant]   [−ant]   [−ant] [dorsal]
                              [retr]

All nasal stops are [+son, +vce]; the variety of laryngeal features associated with oral stops (which are [−son]) are not relevant here. The only underlying fricatives in the language (which are [−son, +cont]) are laryngeal (also not relevant) and sibilant; the sibilant fricatives have the following place features:

(2)   *Alveolar Retroflex Palatal*
           [+cor]   [| cor]   [+cor]
           [+ant]   [−ant]   [−ant]
                     [retr]

There are both syllabic and nonsyllabic l- and r-sounds, which are [+son, +cont]; the former are [+cor, +ant], the latter [+cor, −ant, retr].

    The retroflex assimilation rule can be described informally as follows. When the dental nasal *n* follows a retroflex continuant (i.e. *ṣ*, *r*, or syllabic *ṛ*) within the word and is itself immediately followed by a sonorant, it becomes retroflex *ṇ* – that is, it assimilates to the preceding retroflex continuant in place of articulation – unless another coronal intervenes. The effects can be seen by comparing two sets of deverbal neuter nouns formed with the suffix /-ana-/:[†]

(3)   a. *pácanam* 'cooking implement', *bʰójanam* 'nourishment', *yójanam* 'team
               (of draft animals)', *sádanam* 'seat', *skámbʰanam* 'supporting pillar'
           b. *káraṇam* 'deed', *kṛpáṇam* 'lamentation', *krámaṇam* 'stride', *cákṣaṇam*
               'appearance'

Examples in which retroflexion is blocked by a coronal are easy to find:

(4)   a. *nivártanam* 'return'   (blocked by /t/)
           b. *nṛsádanam* 'assembly of men' (blocked by /d/)
           c. *prarécanam* 'remainder'   (blocked by the palatal stop /c/)
           d. *vṛjánam* 'place'   (blocked by the palatal stop /j/)
           e. *dárśanam* 'sight'   (blocked by the palatal fricative /ś/)
           f. *prāṇanam* 'breathing'   (blocked by *ṇ*, ← /n/ by this rule)

But though *ṇ* blocks the assimilation from a distance, as the last example shows, it does not do so in contact; that is, *nn* is assimilated to *ṇṇ*, not half-assimilated to "*ṇn*." Note the following derivations of past participles formed with the suffix /-ná-/:

(5)   a. /tṛd-ná-/ → tṛnná- → *tṛṇṇá-* 'split'
           b. /ni-sad-ná-/ → niṣadná- → niṣanná- → *niṣaṇṇá-* 'having sat down'

(Retroflexion of the sibilant is effected by the notorious "ruki-rule," by which /s/ becomes retroflex immediately following dorsals, rhotics, and high vocalics.) Any analysis needs to account for all these details.

[†] In the standard transliteration of Sanskrit the retroflex consonants are represented by dental or alveolar symbols with a dot beneath. The voiced aspirates are breathy-voiced.

An autosegmental account of the above is the following. The [+cor] segments occupy a tier of their own (cf. Schein and Steriade 1986: 695), and the assimilation takes place on that tier. The trigger is any segment that is [+cont, retr] and the target is any coronal nasal that is immediately followed by a sonorant; the rule links the feature [retr] rightward onto any target that is adjacent on the coronal tier, and [retr] automatically brings with it [−ant] (replacing any [+ant] feature that the target may have). The rule applies vacuously to nasals that are already [retr]. It fails to apply to the palatal nasal because of a phonotactic accident: the palatal nasal occurs only immediately preceding a palatal oral stop (which exempts it, since the target must be followed by sonorant) and in the cluster *jñ* (in which the palatal stop *j* blocks the assimilation). It applies to geminate *nn* because on the coronal tier there is only one feature bundle [+nas, +son, −cont, +cor, +ant] which is linked to two C-slots on the CV-tier; this exemplifies the Obligatory Contour Principle (OCP), which states that adjacent identical units on the melodic tier are not allowed in lexical representations.

Strikingly, almost no detail of this analysis needs to be stipulated arbitrarily; nearly all points are straightforward consequences of the articulatory gestures involved in the sound change that gave rise to the rule. Coronals occupy a separate tier because the blade and tip of the tongue move more or less independently of the lips and the body of the tongue (which is manipulated in producing vocalic sounds). Retroflex continuants trigger the change because the gesture of a continuant can be prolonged, whereas the closure of a stop is released with a change in the direction of the articulatory gesture. Geminates are affected because a geminate is the result of a single gesture held for two timing units, not two separate gestures. The only point that might be difficult to motivate is the fact that only nasal stops, not also oral stops, are targets of the rule; possibly the reason for that restriction had something to do with the sociolinguistic pattern of spread of the original sound change.

Syllable structure, as described in metrical phonology, also plays a role in phonological rule systems because it plays a role in sound change. The type of rule called "compensatory lengthening" is a case in point. Various dialects of Ancient Greek provide three examples of compensatory lengthening; the most straightforward is the "second compensatory lengthening" (2CL), which operated in most of the dialects. By the (synchronic) 2CL *n* is lost before *s* and the vowel preceding the *n* is lengthened. The following examples from the Attic dialect are typical:[1]

(6)   a. /mélan-s/ 'black (nom. sg. masc.)' → *méla:s* μέλᾱς (cf. nom. pl. masc.
          mélanes μέλανες etc.)

       b. /spénd-sa-i/ 'to pour a libation' → *spénsai* → *spê:sai* σπεῖσαι (cf.
          spénde:n σπένδειν 'to be pouring a libation, to pour libations [repeat-
          edly]')

       c. /hel-ónt-si/ 'to those who have caught' (dat. pl.) → *helónsi* → *helô:si*
          ἑλοῦσι (cf. *helóntes* ἑλόντες 'those who have caught' [nom. pl.])

       d. /pánt-sa/ 'all, whole' (fem.) → *pánsa* → *pâ:sa* πᾶσα (cf. masc. nom. pl.
          pántes πάντες)[2]

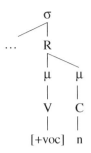

Figure 6.3 *Second compensatory lengthening in Ancient Greek*

(A few dialects lack the 2CL, and forms with *ns* on the surface are actually attested; for instance, *spensai* σπενσαι and *elonsi* ελονσι are attested in Cretan, and *pansa* πανσα is attested in Thessalian.) In each of these examples the syllable rhyme is *Vn*, occupying two moras, at some point in the derivation, as in Figure 6.3. The entire feature bundle of the vowel is then linked to the C-slot to the right (which thereby becomes a V-slot), and the *n* is delinked; the structure of the metrical tier does not change.

This rule too replicates what happened historically, but it replicates two sound changes, not just one. The vowel was probably nasalized before [n] was deleted; that was probably an automatic coarticulation, not a separate change (Ohala 1981: 181–2 with references, 186, 1993: 247–8). Failure to close the stop *n* between the open vowel and the relatively open fricative must at first have resulted in a long nasalized vowel; that was the first actual change. The second change was simply the loss of nasalization on vowels. Latin underwent a precisely similar set of sound changes, but in that case we have documentation of the intermediate stage: what we write as *mēnsa* 'table', for example, was underlyingly /mensa/ but phonetically [mẽ:sa] (see Sturtevant 1940: 153–4, Allen 1978: 28–9); nasalization of the vowel was maintained for some generations in some dialects but was eventually lost everywhere in the Latin speech area – whence, for example, Spanish *mesa* with no *n*. These examples illustrate how a whole sequence of sound changes can affect sounds in exactly the same environment, so that native learners are led to simplify the system by conflating them into a single rule.

All the phonological changes we have discussed so far are typical "bottom-up" sound changes: they clearly began as low-level variable phonetic implementation rules, went to completion in the usual way (without acquiring lexical exceptions in the process), and were integrated into the grammar as phonological rules at the end of the sequence of ordered rules. But while the great majority of sound changes fit that description, it appears that some take place at a more abstract level of phonological structure. We discuss those cases next.

Change at the level of structure: abrupt sound changes

In the mid-1980s Henry Hoenigswald made the following observation (p.c.): we need to account for the fact that while assimilation often gives rise to new feature bundle types (such as the voiced fricatives of Spanish), metathesis and dissimilation almost never do; their outputs are virtually always feature bundles already present in the language. In modern terms, they are structure-preserving in the narrowest sense. The most plausible account of this fact is the hypothesis that metathesis and dissimilation do not result from low-level phonetic implementation rules with gradient outputs, as most other new phonological rules do; apparently they occur within the system of categorical phonology, yielding categorically different outputs.

Metathesis seems at first to be the more obvious case, since the errors that give rise to it are evidently errors in the timing of phonological units which are already part of the language. The (inconsistent) metathesis of OE *græs* 'grass' to *gærs*, for example, must at first have resulted from the mistiming of two articulatory complexes already in the mental representation of native speakers, and the same is true of the metathesis that underlies Spanish *milagro* 'miracle' and *peligro* 'danger' ($\leftarrow$ medieval Latin *mīrāculum* 'prodigy, miracle' and *perīculum* 'test, danger' respectively). But metathesis of only some features in a bundle also occurs, and one might suppose that that could give rise to new bundles. That does not seem to be the case; in the examples known to us the resulting feature bundles are of already occurring types. We will describe them briefly here, since the matter is potentially of importance for the understanding of this type of sound change.

The Proto-Indo-European (PIE) word for 'wolf' is securely reconstructable as *wĺkwos (cf. Sanskrit *vŕkas*, Avestan *vəhrkō*, Old Church Slavonic *vlŭkŭ*, Lithuanian *vilkas*, Gothic *wulfs*), with a typologically unusual sequence of an initial nonsyllabic vowel followed by a syllabic lateral. In Greek *lúkos* λύκος the syllabicity features have remained in place, but the residues of the bundles have undergone metathesis. The same thing has apparently happened in Latin *lupus* 'wolf' (the *p* probably shows that this word was borrowed from some other Italic language, since *kʷ does not normally become *p* in Latin).

A converse change has affected the PIE noun-forming suffix *-wr̥, but not in the same daughter languages. In Greek this suffix developed normally to *-war; e.g. Homeric Greek *ê:dar* εἶδαρ 'food' < *édwar (cf. *édmenai* ἔδμεναι 'to eat'). In Sanskrit, however, the suffix became *-ur* by metathesis of syllabicity, the rest of the bundles remaining in place; cf. *párur* 'joint' < PIE *pér-wr̥ 'transition' (or the like; verb root *per- 'go across/through'), also the source of Proto-Greek *pérwar > Homeric *pê:rar* πεῖραρ 'end (of a rope)'. So also in Hittite, where we find, e.g. *pahhur* 'fire', dat.-loc. *pahhueni* 'in the fire' < PIE *péh₂-wr̥, *ph₂-wén-i (Melchert 1994: 55). A similar change may have occurred in the Old Irish name *Olc*, if its original meaning was 'wolf' (McCone 1985).

In the cases just sketched it is perhaps unsurprising that metathesis yielded already existing feature bundles, given how common syllabic *u* and nonsyllabic *r* and *l* are cross-linguistically. Much stranger are the metatheses that affected the word for 'tongue' in two less well-known daughters of PIE. The ancestral word can be reconstructed as *dn̥ǵʰwéh₂- (see especially Peters 1991); it developed into Old Latin *dingua*[3] and Proto-Germanic *tungō-n- by regular sound changes (plus the addition of *-n- in Germanic; see Ringe 2006: 81, 90–2, 276), but in other daughters it has been subject to a fantastic variety of changes of other kinds for unclear reasons. In Oscan we would expect its outcome to be *dangvā- by regular sound change, since *n̥ became *an* in initial syllables (Meiser 1986: 69–70), breathy-voiced stops became normal voiced stops after nasals (ibid. pp. 75–7), and the remaining changes are trivial; instead we find (acc. sg.) **fangvam**. The initial *f* of this form can only reflect a breathy-voiced consonant, and that can be accounted for only by positing metathesis as follows:

(7)   PIE *dn̥ǵʰwéh₂- > *dn̥gʰwā- → *dʰn̥gwā- > *fangvā-*

in which only the laryngeal features of the stops have switched placed in the sequence of feature bundles. A converse change may have affected this word in the prehistory of Tocharian. The attested forms and the reconstructable Proto-Tocharian form show that some sort of metathesis has occurred (see Peters 1991):

(8)   Tocharian A *käntu*, pl. *käntwā-ñ*, Tocharian B *kantwo*, dimin. *käntwā-śke* < Proto-Tocharian *kəntwá-, nom. sg. *kəntwó

One might suppose that the *d and *ǵʰ of the PIE word had simply been transposed. But PIE *d normally disappeared without a trace in Tocharian whenever a nonsyllabic immediately followed (cf. Ringe 1996b: 64–6 with references). We could suggest that the metathesis occurred only after the loss of *d before nonsyllabics, so that this *d escaped. But an alternative possibility is that only the place of articulation features underwent metathesis, leaving the laryngeal features in place (Ringe 1996b: 45–6):

(9)   PIE *dn̥ǵʰwéh₂ > *dn̥gʰwā- → *gu̯dʰwā- > Proto-Tocharian *kəntwá-

For this metathesis a parallel from the speech of young children can be cited. At about the age of 2 a daughter of one of the authors evolved a rule that if a word contained both a bilabial and a velar articulation, the bilabial must precede; laryngeal features, however, were not affected, so that *camel* (for instance) was pronounced [pʰæŋi] and *grape* was pronounced [breɪk].

In all the cases of metathesis discussed in the preceding paragraph, the metathesis of only some features in a bundle fails to yield a novel bundle. However, that might be because all three cases involve stop consonants, which tend cross-linguistically to occur in parallel series (see Blevins and Garrett 1998: 520, end of n. 8). A major desideratum of research into this obscure corner of phonological change is the identification of an example of one of two kinds: either (a) a partial-feature metathesis that does yield a novel feature bundle, or (b) such a metathesis

Table 6.1 *Latin /-li-/, /-āli-/, default realizations*

Derivational base	Derived adjective
caput 'head'	capitālis 'chief; punishable by death'
nāvis 'ship'	nāvālis 'naval'
speciēs 'appearance'	speciālis 'individual'
ūniversus 'whole'	ūniversālis 'general, universal'
faucēs 'throat'	faucāle 'scarf'
Saturnus (mythical king of Latium)	Saturnālia 'midwinter feast of Saturn'
anima 'soul'	animal 'animal'
cīvis 'citizen'	cīvīlis 'of citizens'
vir 'man'	virīlis 'manly'
currus 'chariot'	sella curūlis 'magistrate's chair'

that might be expected to yield a novel feature bundle but fails to do so. Either will be of theoretical interest.

Blevins and Garrett 1998: 512–22, 525–7 and 2004 suggest that metatheses involving inversion of consonants and vowels, and those involving the "migration" of laryngeal features from one consonant to a non-adjacent consonant, are acoustically motivated, resulting from learner reanalysis of acoustic cues whose underlying locus is misperceived because they are distributed over several segments (so already Ohala 1981: 189–91). That is possible, but it does not solve Hoenigswald's riddle; even if the motivation of metathesis is phonetic in some cases, the point is that the result is *not* a low-level phonetic rule. Blevins and Garrett argue against an abstract analysis (1998: 519–20), suggesting that "[i]f linguistic change arises in first language acquisition . . . then it is hard to see why structure preservation should have any effect." But only learner errors from late stages of acquisition, in which the adult grammar is more or less in place, survive into adult speech. Geoffrey Russom (p.c.) suggests that that is why these changes do not produce novel segments: the phonological system that has already been learned might be acting as a kind of filter to prohibit unfamiliar segments. Note also that the only violations of structure preservation that Blevins and Garrett cite involve creation of a novel *sequence* of segments, not of a novel feature bundle. Constraints on sequences of segments are notoriously hard to determine – for instance, the borrowing of *Vladimir* and coinage of *vroom* in English appear to have violated a sequencing constraint, yet they were unproblematic – and we need to consider the possibility that some such constraints are less than absolute. More work on all these problems is, of course, needed.

The outputs of dissimilation seem similarly constrained by the inventory of already existing feature bundle types. The best-known examples involve the interchange of rhotics and laterals. For instance, Latin inherited several adjective-forming suffixes ending in *-li-*, the commonest of which is *-āli-*, and in the default case the suffixes surface unaltered, as in Table 6.1. However, if the derivational

Table 6.2 *Latin /-li-/, /-āli-/ with dissimilation*

Derivational base	Derived adjective
lūna 'moon'	lūnāris 'lunar'
cōnsul 'chief magistrate'	cōnsulāris 'of consular rank'
lūmen 'light'	lūmināre 'window-shutter'
planta 'graft, plant'	plantāria 'young saplings'
calx, calc- 'heel'	calcar 'spur'
pellis 'skin, hide'	pellīris 'made of leather'

Table 6.3 *Latin /-āli-/, dissimilation blocked*

Derivational base	Derived adjective
līber 'free'	līberālis 'characteristic of a free person'
Flōra (the flower goddess)	Flōrālia 'festival of Flora'
Lupercus (a minor deity)	Lupercal 'grotto of Lupercus'

base contains an *l*, the *l* of the suffix dissimilates to *r*, as in Table 6.2. The dissimilation is blocked if an *r* intervenes between the two *l*'s, as in Table 6.3. It seems clear that in Latin there is a constraint against having two *l*'s adjacent (on the tier on which the melody of *l* resides) in derived environments; but it is striking that the constraint is observed by replacing suffixal *l* with the already existing trill *r* rather than dissimilating it to some novel segment (say, [ɹ] or [ð]). Dissimilations whose effects are projected directly into underlying representations are very similar; for instance, the dissimilation of *r*'s in Spanish *árbol* 'tree' < Latin *arbor* likewise failed to yield a novel segment, and the same is true of the dissimilation of *d*'s that produced Latin *merīdiēs* 'midday' < *medii-diēs.[4] Equally striking is the dissimilatory loss of a segment in Hellenistic Greek *agɛ:okʰénai* ἀγηοχέναι 'to have led' from *agɛ:gokʰénai (modeled on older *enɛ:nokʰénai* ἐνηνοχέναι 'to have brought' by lexical analogy) and *pʰa:tría:* φᾱτρίᾱ '(religious) brotherhood' < *pʰra:tría:* φρᾱτρίᾱ; apparently the complete loss of a segment is easier than creating a new segment by dissimilation. It is true (as Polly Jacobsen reminds us) that a novel segment occurring in only one lexeme would be such an anomaly that native learners would probably assume it was an error, but the case of the Latin suffix is a little different: a novel dissimilation product of /l/ would occur in only one morpheme, but the morpheme is productive and common, and segments restricted to a single derivational morpheme are known (see Bloomfield 1962: 9–10 for a Menomini example on the level of underlying form). Possibly the phonological system is acting as a filter in a rather different way. A dissimilation product of /l/, for example, would continue to be parsed as an allophone of /l/ unless it began to overlap with the realization of some other segment; thus a novel outcome could not, under ordinary circumstances, become phonologically independent and would not appear in the historical record.

Further research on the nature of metathesis and dissimilation is clearly needed; for the moment we merely hold to the hypothesis stated at the beginning of this section, namely that these changes occur within the system of categorical phonological representations, not at the level of variable postlexical rules. In other words, they are not sound changes in the usual sense of the term – and that might ultimately be connected with the fact that they are so often irregular (cf. Hock 1991: 107–11).

Recently Ives Goddard has called attention to the fact that a wide range of regular sound changes which are *not* structure-preserving also do not appear to reflect low-level phonetic rules with gradient outputs. The most striking examples are unconditioned "saltatory" sound changes, in which the phonetics of a phoneme become very different in a single change. For instance, Proto-Polynesian *t has become *k* in most dialects of Hawaiian and in colloquial Samoan, and Proto-Algonkian *p became *k in the immediate ancestor of Arapaho and Gros Ventre (Goddard 2007: 118–19 with references). In both cases there were no conditioning factors and no merger (in the Polynesian languages cited because inherited *k had become the glottal stop, in Proto-Arapaho-Atsina because inherited *k had been lost unconditionally), and there is no evidence for any phonetically intermediate stage.

A somewhat different case is the conditioned sound change in the easterly dialects of Ancient Greek called the "third compensatory lengthening" (3CL, incidentally encountered in the Homeric Greek words for 'food' and 'end (of a rope)', cited above). In that sound change a sequence *VTw, where *T is a coronal consonant, was replaced by *V:T*; that is, the *w following the consonant was dropped and the vowel preceding the consonant was lengthened. For instance, Proto-Greek *kalwós 'beautiful' (of which the neuter *kalwon* καλϝον is actually attested in a Boiotian dialect inscription) appears as *ka:lós* κᾱλός in the Ionic dialect of the Homeric poems (whose meter guarantees the length of the vowel in the first syllable). This was a completely regular sound change; nearly twenty lexemes were affected, and there are no counterexamples. No plausible intermediate stage can be proposed. Metathesis was not involved, since *aulós* αὐλός (the name of a shawm-like wind instrument) underwent no change; neither was gemination of the coronal, since *allé:loisi* ἀλλήλοισι 'to one another' was also not affected. (All these words are well attested in Homer.) It looks as though the loss of *w was accompanied by a direct manipulation of the CV-skeleton, preserving the weight of the preceding syllable (so already Steriade 1982: 117–23). That was not a necessary development; in most dialects of Ancient Greek, including the very well-attested Attic, *w was lost without a trace (so that the example given above is *kalós* καλός with a short vowel in the first syllable – again guaranteed by numerous examples in metrical texts).

There has been no systematic study of how any of these types of change actually occur. Only such studies can reveal how these abrupt sound changes differ from the more familiar gradient sound changes and how the underlying structure of forms is involved.

Simplification of phonological rules

In the discussion up to this point we have encountered some examples of the conflation of two or more sound changes into a single phonological rule. That is an obvious simplification of the grammar. The phonology of a language can also be simplified in other ways. We first discuss the simplification of individual phonological rules.

A striking example of rule simplification is provided by the Attic dialect of Ancient Greek. Because most endings of the Ancient Greek mediopassive perfect and pluperfect begin with consonants, and because many stems to which those endings are suffixed end in consonants, forms of those tenses provide numerous examples of the assimilation of consonants in contact at morpheme boundaries. The endings variously begin with /t/, /s/, /st^h/, and /m/. (The "mediopassive" was used both as a passive and as an indirect reflexive; the pluperfect endings began with the same consonants as the corresponding perfect endings. On the inherited 3pl. see below.) The following ordered rules apply to the sequence of stem-final consonant plus ending-initial consonant(s):

(a)   dental stops → s before all the consonants in question;
(b)   ss → s;
(c)   s → ∅ between consonants;
(d)   stops (which at this point in the derivation can only be bilabial or velar) assimilate in voicing, aspiration, and nasality to an immediately following stop (including nasal stops).[5]

In Table 6.4 the mediopassive perfect 2sg. indicative, 3sg. indicative, infinitive, and participle of six verbs, each ending in a different bilabial or velar stop, illustrate the effects of (d). The traditional spellings, which largely represent the surface contrasts well, obscure the parallelism of these paradigms in one respect: ⟨γμ⟩ "gm" is phonetically [ŋm], in accordance with the rule stated under (d) above. We know that because ancient Greek grammatical tradition called the velar nasal – written ⟨γ⟩ "g" in all positions, even before velar stops – by the name ἄγμα; and since the principle governing the names of consonants in the Greek alphabet is that the first consonant of the name should be the way the letter was pronounced, the name must have been [áŋma], and /g/ must have been [ŋ] before /m/ (cf. Sturtevant 1940: 64–5, Allen 1987: 35–9).

Most of the rules given above, including most of the rules conflated under (d), are completely general phonological rules of Attic Greek. not only do they apply to all derived forms, they also operate as "morpheme structure constraints" (MSCs) on underlying forms. For instance, the /kt/ of *árktos* ἄρκτος 'bear' is a possible sequence of stops, but *gt and *k^{h}t are not; the /p^{h}t^h/ of *op^{h}t^{h}almós* ὀφθαλμός 'eye' is a possible sequence of stops, but *pt^h and *bt^h are not; and so on. That is the usual situation when a phonological rule arose by regular

Table 6.4 *Mediopassive perfect forms of six Ancient Greek verbs*

Med. -pass. pf. stem	/epi-trep-/ /epi-te-trap-/	/tri:b-/ /te-tri:b-/	/aleiph-/ /al-e:liph-/	/dio:k-/ /de-dio:k-/	/di-allag-/ /di-e:llag-/	/dekh-/ /de-dekh-/
Meaning	'have been entrusted'	'have been rubbed'	'have been annointed'	'have been pursued'	'be different'	'have received'
Indic. 2sg.	epitétrapsai ἐπιτέτραψαι	tétri:psai τέτρῖψαι	alé:lipsai ἀλήλιψαι	dedío:ksai δεδίωξαι	dié:llaksai διήλλαξαι	dédeksai δέδεξαι
Indic. 3sg.	epitétraptai ἐπιτέτραπται	tétri:ptai τέτρῖπται	alé:liptai ἀλήλιπται	dedío:ktai δεδίωκται	dié:llaktai διήλλακται	dédektai δέδεκται
Inf.	epitetráphthai ἐπιτετράφθαι	tetrî:phthai τετρῖφθαι	ale:líphthai ἀλήλίφθαι	dedio:khthai δεδίῶχθαι	die:llákhthai διήλλάχθαι	dedékhthai δέδεχθαι
Ptc.	epitetramménos ἐπιτετραμμένος	tetri:mménos τετρῖμμένος	ale:limménos ἀλήλιμμένος	de-dio:gménos δεδίωγμένος	die:llagménos διηλλαγμένος	dedegménos δεδεγμένος

sound change. The rule assimilating bilabial and velar stops to following nasals, however, is a different story, to which we must now give our attention (see Sommerstein 1973: 21–3).

It is true that the only bilabial which can precede *m* in Attic Greek is *m*; the sequences **pm*, **bm*, and **pʰm* do not occur. The subrule nasalizing bilabial stops before /m/ can be illustrated with numerous derived examples, of which some are adduced in (10).

(10)   a. *blémma* βλέμμα 'glance' ← /blep-/ 'look'
         b. *trî:mma* τρῖμμα 'experienced con man' (*'well-worn thing') and *tri:mmós* τρῑμμός 'beaten path' ← /tri:b-/ 'rub'
         c. *áleimma* ἄλειμμα 'ointment' ← /aleipʰ-/ 'anoint'

Intramorphemic examples of /mm/, illustrating that this is also an MSC, are not common, but at least *ámmos* ἄμμος 'sand' can be cited. This subrule, then, looks like the result of a regular sound change.

The sequence **bn* is also excluded, *mn* occurring instead – one finds not only derived examples like *semnós* σεμνός 'reverend, holy' ← /seb-nó-s/ (cf. *sébe:n* σέβειν 'to worship'), but also intramorphemic examples such as *prúmna* πρύμνα 'stern (of a ship)'. It also seems very likely that /gn/ was phonetically [ŋn] (at least intervocalically, see Sturtevant 1940: 64–5 with references; Allen 1987: 37 with n. 59 seems too hesitant to rely on the written evidence and phonetic likelihood), and there is good evidence that /gm/ was phonetically [ŋm] (see above). Thus the subrule nasalizing voiced bilabial and velar stops before nasals can also be the result of a regular sound change.

For other velar stops followed by *m* the situation is different. In other derived environments, including nouns productively derived from verb stems with the suffixes /-mat-/ and /-mó-/, all velar stops become [ŋ] before *m*, just as they do in the paradigm of the mediopassive perfect; thus nouns like those in (11) are precisely parallel to the derived nouns with [mm] listed above.

(11)   a. *dógma* δόγμα [dóŋma] 'opinion, (legislative) decree' ← /dok-/ 'seem good, be resolved (by a legislature)'
         b. *díɔ:gma* δίωγμα [díɔ:ŋma] and *diɔ:gmós* διωγμός [-ŋm-] 'pursuit' ← /diɔ:k-/ 'pursue'
         c. *diállagma* διάλλαγμα [diállaŋma] 'changeling' ← /di-allag-/ 'exchange'
         d. *táragma* τάραγμα [táraŋma] 'uneasiness, upset' and *taragmós* ταραγμός [-ŋm-] 'confusion, turmoil' ← /tarakʰ-/ 'disturb'

But in underived words only /gm/ surfaces as [ŋm]; the voiceless velar stops (aspirated and unaspirated) surface unchanged, as in (12).

(12)   *akmé:* ἀκμή '(highest) point'   *dokʰmé:* δοχμή 'span, handsbreadth'
         ákmɔ:n ἄκμων 'anvil'   *aikʰmé:* αἰχμή 'spear-point'
         ikmás ἰκμάς 'moisture'   *likʰmâ:n* λιχμᾶν 'to flick the tongue'
         likmâ:n λικμᾶν 'to winnow   (said of snakes)
            (grain)'

Since these forms are morphologically isolated, they must reflect the regular sound-change outcomes of these sequences.

Before *n* the situation is different again: both the bilabial and the velar voiceless stops (aspirated and unaspirated) surface unchanged, this time even in derived environments, as in (13).

(13)   a. *téknon* τέκνον 'child' ← /tek-/ 'give birth'
         b. *terpnós* τερπνός 'pleasant' ← /terp-/ 'enjoy'
         c. *sperkʰnós* σπερχνός 'hasty' ← /sperkʰ-/ 'hurry'
         d. *strupʰnós* στρυφνός 'astringent'

((13d) exhibits the same suffix as the two adjectives that precede it in the list, though the root is otherwise unattested; it is a Greek "cranberry word.")

Let us now assess this pattern of facts.

We can recognize the outcomes of two regular sound changes from the fact that they function as MSCs even in unanalyzable words: a rule changing all bilabial stops to *m* before *m*, which we can formalize as

$$[\text{labial}] \rightarrow [+\text{nasal}] \, / \, \_\_ \, [\text{labial}, +\text{nasal}],$$

and a change of all voiced noncoronal oral stops to nasals before nasals, thus:

$$[-\text{cor}, -\text{cont}, +\text{vce}] \rightarrow [+\text{nasal}] \, / \, \_\_ \, [+\text{nasal}].$$

Both rules apply to /bm/; it is not clear which applies first, and we do not know the order in which the sound changes that gave rise to those rules occurred. In addition, we have a rule that applies only in derived environments, namely

$$[\text{velar}] \rightarrow [+\text{nasal}] \, / \, \_\_ \, [\text{labial}, +\text{nasal}],$$

which changes other velar stops into the velar nasal before *m* (only). Operation only in derived environments is not characteristic of regular sound changes, but it is a known behavior of phonological rules. The conclusion seems inescapable: the nasalization of (all) velars before *m* in derived environments (only) did not result from regular sound change; instead it resulted from the extension of the rule nasalizing all bilabial stops before *m* (which *was* the reflex of a regular sound change). In terms of the rule itself this was a simplification: instead of applying to stops which were [labial], the rule now applied to all stops which were [−coronal]; in fact, if coronal stops had already become *s* before *m* (see above) by the point in the derivation at which this rule applied, the simplified rule could have applied to all stops before *m*.

But why should the rule changing bilabial stops to *m* before *m* have been simplified in this way? A further detail of the inflection of mediopassive perfects suggests a possible answer. The one member of the paradigm that had an ending beginning with a vowel was the 3pl. indicative, which originally ended in pf. *-atai*, plup. *-ato*. The relevant forms must originally have been made simply by combining the stem with the ending, so that the stem-final consonants would appear unaltered before these endings; but in attested forms a stem-final stop consonant which was not underlyingly aspirated was replaced by its aspirated counterpart before these two endings (!). In other words, the 3pl. endings had become underlying pf. /-hatai/, plup. /-hato/, and a rule combined the /h/ of the endings with stem-final labial and velar stops to yield [pʰ] and [kʰ] respectively on the surface. Attic examples are few, but since the same rule applied throughout the Attic-Ionic dialect group, we can also exemplify the rule from Herodotos (writing fifth-century East Ionic) and Homer (composing in a poetic dialect based on eighth-century East Ionic). Representative examples are listed in (14).

(14)   a. *epitetrápʰatai* ἐπιτετράφαται 'they are in the care (of), they have been entrusted (to)' *Iliad* 2.25, 62; *tetrápʰato* τετράφατο 'they kept facing' *Iliad* 10.189 (verb root /trep-/, compound /epi-trep-/, see above)

    b. *tetrípʰatai* τετρίφαται 'they exhibit abrasion, they have been bruised' Herodotos 2.93.3 (verb root /tri:b-/, see above)

    c. *gegrápʰatai* γεγράφαται 'they are written' *IG* 1.57.10, *an]agegrápʰatai* ἀν]αγεγράφαται 'they are enrolled' *IG* 1.66.2–3 (verb root /grapʰ-/ 'write', compound /ana-grapʰ-/ 'write up')

    d. *e:líkʰato* εἰλίχατο 'they were wrapped' Herodotos 7.90, *kate:líkʰato* κατειλίχατο (same meaning) 7.76 (verb root /(kat-)elik-/ 'wind, wrap (up)')

    e. *tetákʰatai* τετάχαται 'they are drawn up' (said of ships) Thoukydides 3.13.3; *antitetákʰatai* ἀντιτετάχαται 'they are deployed against' Xenophon, *Anabasis* 4.8.5 (verb root /tag-/ 'arrange, marshall' and cpd.)

    f. *tetéukʰatai* τετεύχαται 'they have been made' *Iliad* 13.22 etc. (verb root /teukʰ-/ 'make, fashion (as a craftsman)')

(There are quite a few other examples to roots ending in /-g-/, and a couple more to roots ending in /-pʰ-/ and /-kʰ-/.) We know that this was a prehistoric innovation of the Attic-Ionic dialect group: the endings were originally *-atai, -ato < *-n̥tai, *-n̥to (with no underlying /h/), and they still retain those inherited shapes in some other dialects. *Together* the two innovations – the reanalysis of the 3pl. endings so that they began with /h/ and the extension of the nasalization rule to velars – rendered the inflection of mediopassive perfects ending in noncoronal stops completely uniform, so that all corresponding forms made to roots in labials rhymed and all corresponding forms made to roots in velars also rhymed, regardless of whether the underlying root-final stop was voiced, voiceless, or aspirated. Unfortunately we don't know which innovation occurred first; but both appear to be the sort of learner errors that simplify the inflection of a relatively marginal morphological category characterized by unusual phonological complexity. No doubt the initial impetus for such an error was the fact that native learners did not hear the relevant forms often enough to learn them correctly, so that they produced (for example) *epitetrápʰatai* for *epitetrápatai and *dedeŋménos* for *dedekʰménos; but the effect was to simplify the inflectional system and, in the case of the nasalization rule, the phonology as well. The extension of the latter rule to productive word formation would then be natural enough.

```
ī   i        u   ū
ē                ō
ę̄   ę        ǫ   ǭ
         a
```

Figure 6.4 *Early southern Middle English vowels*

A rule simplification which must have had a rather different motivation can be cited from Middle English (ME). Sometime in the eleventh century the famous "trisyllabic shortening" rule entered the phonology of English; it shortened long vowels in stressed syllables provided that (a) the vowel was in at least the third syllable from the end of the word *or* (b) the vowel was followed by one of a large number of consonant clusters, including especially geminate consonants (Luick 1914–40: 324–30; the rule has already been introduced in the discussion of the GVS in Chapter 5). The examples in (15) (given as far as possible in late OE spelling, though it is known to have been somewhat archaizing) are typical.

(15) a. *hīdan, hidde* 'to hide, hid'
    b. *Crīst, Cristesmæsse* 'Christ, Christmas'
    c. *fēdan, fedde* 'to feed, fed'
    d. *frēond, freondscipe* 'friend, friendship'
    e. *lǣdan, lædde* 'to lead, led'
    f. *hēafod, heafodu* 'head, heads'
    g. *gāst, gastlice* 'spirit, spiritual'
    h. *hāliġ, haliġdæġ* 'holy, holy day'
    i. *blōma* 'ingot', *blostma* 'blossom'
    j. *sūþ, suðerne* 'south, southern'

The outputs of this rule were then overlaid by several mergers and other shifts of vowels in most dialects:

(a) short *æ* and *ea* merged with short *a* (ibid. pp. 346–52);
(b) long *ǣ* and *ēa* also merged, but became (or remained?) a lower mid vowel *ę̄* (i.e. /ɛ:/; ibid. pp. 341–5);
(c) long *ā* was rounded and raised to lower mid *ǭ* (i.e., /ɔ:/; ibid. pp. 358–63).

(Some other changes had no effect on the rule.) The result was a system with five short vowels but six long vowels (and no long *ā*) in which both the lower mid vowels underwent shortening to *a*. The short mid vowels were lower mid (a point that will become important below); the system of surface contrasts is charted in Figure 6.4 (lower mid vowels are marked with subscript hooks). Examples of the alternations between long lower mid vowels and *a* that survived for a significant period mostly involve verb paradigms in the case of the lower mid front vowel, but word-formation in the case of the lower mid round back vowel; typical examples are listed in (16):

(16)   a. *lẹ̄den, ladde* 'to lead, led'
           b. *rẹ̄den, radde* 'to read, read [past]'
           c. *sprẹ̄den, spradde* 'to spread, spread [past]'
           d. *mẹ̄ten, matte* 'to dream, dreamt' (impersonal)
           e. *lẹ̄ven, lafde* 'to leave, left'
           f. *dẹ̄len, dalte* 'to distribute, distributed'
           g. *clẹ̄ne, clansen* 'clean, to cleanse'
           h. *chẹ̄p, chapfare, chapman* 'bargain, trade, merchant'
           i. *gǭst, gastli* 'spirit, spiritual'
           j. *hǭli, halidai, halwen* 'holy, holiday, to sanctify'
           k. *wrǭth, wrappe* 'angry, anger'

Native learners must have conflated all this into a single shortening rule, but that rule had to be complicated to include backing of *ẹ̄*, unrounding of *ǭ*, and lowering of both. (In principle one or the other of those long vowels could have been underlying /ā/, but the potential evidence for that seems so weak that it is hard to believe that native learners would have come to such a conclusion.)

The rounding of *ā* to *ǭ* began south of the Thames before 1200 and spread northwards to the Humber during the thirteenth century (Luick 1914–40: 358–63). But already during that century the shortening rule began to be simplified: backing, unrounding, and lowering were eliminated, so that *ẹ̄* was shortened to *ẹ* and *ǭ* to *ǫ*. As expected, the simplification proceeded lexeme by lexeme, affecting inflection more completely than derivational morphology. All the past tenses in the above list exhibit alternative forms with *ẹ* (*ledde, redde,* etc.), which eventually crowded out the older forms with *a*; *clensen* also replaced *clansen*, and *holiday* replaced *halidai* (which survives only in the name *Halliday*), but otherwise the derived words with *a* survived as synchronically underived lexical relics: cf. Modern English *wrath, hallow, ghastly, Chapman,* and the derived verb *to chaffer*.

What is striking about this rule simplification is that it made the learning of inflectional morphology less straightforward. The crucial point is that there were no verbs with *ǭ* in the root that had past tenses to which shortening applied (note that ME *cladde* was the past not of *clǭthen* but of (Northern) *clẹ̄th(e)*, see the *OED* s.vv. *clead, clothe*); thus before the simplification of the rule a past tense with *a* in the root and no vowel between the root and the suffixal consonant (i.e. not ending in *-ede*) implied underlying *ẹ̄* in the root unambiguously. After the simplification of the rule, however, an otherwise identical past tense with *ẹ* in the root might imply either underlying *ẹ̄* or underlying *ē*; that is, since learners encountered both *lẹ̄den, lẹdde* and *blēden, blẹdde* 'bleed, bled', it might not be immediately obvious from a newly encountered past tense of this type what the rest of the paradigm should be. It appears that the simplification of the rule was an end in itself, so to speak, making the *phonology* of the language (only!) less complex.

It is possible that native learners were motivated to simplify the shortening rule by nothing more than the fact that the higher long vowels were shortened

Table 6.5 *Vowel length alternations in thirteenth-century Midlands Middle English*

Shortening	Lengthening
/ī/ ~ [i]	
/ē/ ~ [ẹ]	
/ę̄/ ~ [a]	/ę/ ~ [ę̄]
	/a/ ~ [ā]
/ǭ/ ~ [a]	/ǫ/ ~ [ǭ]
/ō/ ~ [ǫ]	
/ū/ ~ [u]	

more straightforwardly (/ī/ to *i*, /ū/ to *u*, /ē/ to *ẹ*, and /ō/ to *ǫ* – the last in very few examples, such as *gosling* and *goshawk*). Extension of this simple rule to /ę̄/ and /ǭ/ would automatically yield *ę* and *ǫ*, since there was no contrast between higher mid and lower mid short vowels. However, there was a further factor that might have encouraged learners to simplify the phonology in just this way. Also in the thirteenth century, but starting in the north and spreading southwards, stressed nonhigh short vowels in open syllables were lengthened; lengthening of *ę* and *ǫ* respectively yielded long lower mid *ę̄* and *ǭ*, giving rise to surface alternations between long lower mid vowels and short mid vowels rather than short *a* (Luick 1914–40: 397–404). The result in the Midlands dialects was the set of alternations given in Table 6.5 *before* the simplification of the shortening rule (with underlying vowels between slashes and lower mid vowels marked with hooks). The lengthening alternations were virtually all leveled in one direction or the other, but they must have existed for at least a few generations; during that time it could have been easy for native learners to confuse the two sets of quantitative alternations involving long lower mid vowels and so reduce them to a single surface pattern – which was, of course, easier to learn even though it made verb inflection a little harder to learn.

A quite different type of rule simplification is explored in Buckley 2009. A number of sound changes known from the historical record appear to have been phonetically natural in only some of the environments in which they occurred. An example is the Old High German shift of inherited *þ (i.e. */θ/) to *d* (Buckley 2009: 51–3). There is some evidence for an intermediate stage *[ð] (spelled *dh*), so it seems clear that we are witnessing two sound changes, [θ] > [ð] > [d]; but whereas the second change, the occlusion of the fricative, is natural in any phonotactic position, the first change, voicing, is not natural in word-initial position. Nevertheless word-initial *þ did eventually become *d* in Old High German. The most plausible analysis is that the allophonic rule voicing *þ in voiced environments was generalized to apply in all environments. In this case (though not necessarily in other cases) the next generation of learners would surely have learned the fricative as underlyingly voiced /ð/ (see the following section). Simplification of rules by the generalization of output allophones may be more common than we are currently aware of; Buckley adduces several cases, including the notorious Old French (OF) palatalization of Latin *c* /k/ before low /a/, only some of whose allophones had been fronted (Buckley 2009: 35–51). This is yet another subject that would repay further study.

It seems unlikely that these examples exhaust the range of possible motivations for rule simplification; this is an area of historical linguistics in which more work is needed.

Reordering of phonological rules and restructuring of underlying forms

Much of Paul Kiparsky's earlier work on language change (collected in Kiparsky 1982a) explored the reordering of phonological rules as a possible mechanism of phonological change. He argued that in general the justification for rule reordering must be that it simplifies the grammar, but exactly how it amounts to simplification proved elusive. At various times he suggested that rules tend to be reordered so that they are employed in as many derivations as possible (Kiparsky 1982a: 37–41), or so that paradigmatic allomorphy is minimized (ibid. pp. 65–6), or so that "transparency" is maximized (ibid. pp. 75–9) – that is, the phonology does not produce surface outputs which appear to contradict any of the rules. None of these hypotheses was fully satisfactory; the second and third, which are both plausible, can give different results, so that one needs to consider which takes precedence in particular cases (ibid. pp. 76–7). However, Kiparsky's approach was fundamentally sound in one crucial respect: he kept always in view the fact that any grammatical change must begin as a reanalysis on the part of native language learners. Let us examine a few possible cases of rule reordering from that perspective and see if we can make sense of their motivation from the learner's point of view.

An apparently ineluctable case of rule reordering is revealed by a comparison of two closely related northeastern dialects of Swiss German, those of Schaffhausen (the tiny northernmost canton) and of Kesswil (in the neighboring canton of Thurgau; Kiparsky 1982a: 19–20, 29, 76–7). Like all other German dialects, these two have a rule of i-umlaut which reflects an eighth-century (or earlier) sound change. In the earliest stages of its development the i-umlaut rule fronted all back vowels, and also raised short /a/ to *e*, when a high front vocalic occurred in the following syllable. However, the loss of postconsonantal *j* and the merger of posttonic short vowels in *ə* had made the German i-umlaut rule opaque by the eleventh century, since its phonological triggers could no longer be learned; since then i-umlaut has had multiple morphological triggers in German. One of these is a noun plural marker which ultimately reflects Old High German -*i*.

Table 6.6 *Umlaut and /o/-lowering in Schaffhausen*

	'bow'	'bows'	'floor'	'floors'
Underlying form	/bogə/	/bogə+PL/	/bodə/	/bodə+PL/
Umlaut		bøgə		bødə
Lowering			bɔdə	
Surface form	[bogə]	[bøgə]	[bɔdə]	[bødə]

Table 6.7 */o/-lowering and umlaut in Kesswil*

	'bow'	'bows'	'floor'	'floors'
Underlying form	/bogə/	/bogə+PL/	/bodə/	/bodə+PL/
Lowering			bɔdə	bɔdə+PL
Umlaut		bøgə		bœdə
Surface form	[bogə]	[bøgə]	[bɔdə]	[bœdə]

Much more recently the dialects of northeastern Switzerland underwent a sound change, and thereby acquired a rule, lowering /o/ to [ɔ] immediately preceding coronal obstruents and /r/ (see König 2001: 144–5); the rule does not lower [ø], the product of i-umlaut. In the dialect of Schaffhausen no further changes have occurred; thus the rules apply in their historical order, with the result that the plural of [bogə] 'bow', for example, is [bøgə] and the plural of [bɔdə] 'floor' is [bødə]. The relevant derivations are given in Table 6.6 (we give the plural marker in its abstract shape).

The dialect of Kesswil is similar, but it differs in one crucial point: in those paradigms in which it alternates with lowered [ɔ], the front vowel is lower mid [œ] rather than higher mid [ø]. The most straightforward way to account for this fact is the hypothesis that the rules have been reordered, as in Table 6.7. A skeptic might suggest that this is simply the result of a further sound change lowering *ø* in the same environments in which *o* had previously been lowered. But that cannot be the case, because non-alternating *ø* has not been affected (Enderlin 1913: 34). Thus the isolated word *frøʃʃ* 'frog', which is not derivationally related to any form containing a back vowel, exhibits higher *ø*, not lower *œ*, in the dialect of Kesswil; so does *gøtti* 'godfather', despite its apparent derivational relation to *gɔttə* 'godmother'. In these words the fronted vowel has been reanalyzed as underlying /ø/, and since the lowering rule does not apply to *ø*, they are not affected. A determined skeptic might counter that since the new lower mid front vowel appears only when it alternates with the lower mid back vowel, some sort of paradigmatic leveling must be to blame, even though its results appear to be purely phonological. But that cannot be true either, because of an interesting fact not mentioned by Kiparsky: not quite every [œ] is in alternation with [ɔ] in Kesswil. In particular, there is an impersonal verb *tættərlə*, which governs a dative experiencer, meaning 'be afraid'. Since it exhibits a lower mid front

Table 6.8 *Derivation of* tœttərlə *in Kesswil*

	'be afraid'
Underlying form	/tottər+l+INF/
Lowering	tɔttərlə
Umlaut	tœttərlə
Surface form	[tœttərlə]

Table 6.9 *Sound-change outcomes of inherited back round vowels in Kesswil*

	Inherited *u*	Inherited *o*
Before *T, r*	[o]	[ɔ]
Elsewhere	[u]	[o]

round vowel, one might expect to find in the lexicon a stem *tɔttər-* with a back vowel in the root. But the only lexeme of such a shape quoted for this dialect is *tɔttər* 'eggyolk' (Enderlin 1913: 33), which is most unlikely to be synchronically related to 'be afraid'. A verb *tottere(n)* 'to be afraid' is known from other Swiss dialects, but it is absent from almost the whole of the Thurgau, including all the villages near Kesswil for which the standard references report forms (see Wanner *et al.* 1973 s.v. *Totter* II, coll. 2077–81); in the vicinity of Kesswil only the suffixed, umlauted form appears to occur. There is only one way to account for this striking fact: since the suffix /-l-/ triggers umlaut, native learners must have inferred that the underlying form of the root still exhibits a back vowel, and the derivation must be parallel to that of 'floors', as in Table 6.8. This would seem to be an open-and-shut case of rule reordering.

However, there is a further possibility that we have not considered: native learners might have projected the lowered back vowel into underlying forms as /ɔ/; that would have the same effect as reordering the rules, and since we already know that native learners project the outputs of rules into underlying forms, such an explanation should be preferred. To a linguist that might seem crazy, since the complementary distribution of [o] and [ɔ] should be completely obvious. But a closer look at the vowel inventory of Kesswil reveals that it is not obvious at all, for an unforeseen reason: not only was inherited *o* lowered to *ɔ* before coronal obstruents and *r*, inherited *u* was lowered to *o* before coronal obstruents, *n*, and *r* (Enderlin 1913: 35–7). Leaving aside the position before *n* (where inherited *o* was lengthened), we have the distribution of the reflexes of inherited vowels in Table 6.9. Note that surface [o] appears in (roughly) the full range of phonological environments. From such a distribution native learners could only have concluded that surface [o] is a single underlying phoneme /o/; that follows from the ITH (see the preceding chapter). But that would automatically entail setting up /u/ and /ɔ/ as underlying phonemes too, since both contrast with /o/ in unanalyzable

words: cf. e.g. *torn* 'tower' vs. *tɔrn* 'thorn', *roft* 'waste pieces (of wood, etc.)'
vs. *rɔft* 'rust', and on the other hand *holts* 'wood' vs. *sults* 'brawn, boar's flesh',
truxxə 'dry' vs. *xnoxxə* 'bone', *fuxs* 'fox' vs. *oxs* 'ox' (perfect minimal pairs
between *o* and *u* are hard to find). The distributions of /u/ and especially of /ɔ/ are
oddly limited; but it seems clear that native learners do not always make use of
distributional facts in positing underlying forms. We conclude that native learners
in Kesswil did reanalyze [ɔ] as underlying /ɔ/ in precisely this way, with results
which superficially resemble the results that rule reordering would yield.

Why, then, did native learners assume that the underlying root of *tætterle* was
/tɔttər-/ rather than /tottər-/? It turns out that the umlaut product of inherited
u has remained [y] in Kesswil in most environments, including before coronal
obstruents (Enderlin 1913: 37–8); as a result, the surface umlaut alternation before
coronal obstruents is virtually always *o ∼ y*, never "*o ∼ ø*" (ibid. p. 39). Given
that learners had projected [ɔ] and [o] before coronals into underlying forms as /ɔ/
and /o/, when they decided that the [ø] of *tötterle* was derived (and not underlying
front /ø/), they could not imagine that it was the umlaut of /o/; the umlaut of /o/
could only have been [y] in such a word. The only alternative was /ɔ/, with the
result described above.

But then why did the dialect of Schaffhausen not undergo the same changes?
The answer is completely straightforward: in Schaffhausen inherited *u* was not
lowered, regularly remaining as [u] in all positions (Wanner 1941: 29–30); thus
it did not interfere with the distribution of [o] and [ɔ], and it remained clear to
native learners that the latter two are simply allophones of /o/ (ibid. pp. 26–9).
Since non-alternating examples of [o] and of [ɔ] do exist in Schaffhausen, this
might appear to violate the ITH, but it need not: possibly this complementary
distribution is so obvious that most native learners do restructure their grammars
toward the end of native language acquisition (NLA), reanalyzing the /ɔ/ that
they originally posited as /o/; possibly some native learners do hang onto /ɔ/, but
the constellation of sociolinguistic events that would be necessary to generalize
it has not yet appeared.

A further German example leads us to consider the process of learning German natively in more detail. A word-final obstruent devoicing rule entered the
language around 1100 CE. The result was that in Middle High German (MHG)
the endingless form of the adjective 'long', for example, was *lanc* [laŋk], while
the inflected forms were *lange* [laŋgə], *langen* [laŋgən], etc. In the modern language [g] has been lost throughout most of the German-speaking area when it
was immediately preceded by [ŋ] and and immediately followed by an obstruent,
unstressed vowel, or morpheme boundary. In roughly the northern half of the
country the two phonological rules still apply in their historical order (Wright
1907: 128), as in Table 6.10. In the more southerly dialects and in the standard
language, however, the order of devoicing and g-loss has been switched, with
the result that devoicing no longer has an opportunity to apply to any of the
relevant forms, as in Table 6.11. This example has traditionally been a problem for purely phonological explanations of rule reordering, since the rules are

Table 6.10 *Devoicing and g-loss in northern Germany*

	Uninflected	Inflected
Underlying forms	/laŋg/	/laŋg+ə/
Nasal assimilation	laŋg	laŋgə
Final devoicing	laŋk	
g-loss		laŋə
Surface forms	[laŋk]	[laŋə]

Table 6.11 *g-loss and devoicing in southern Germany*

	Uninflected	Inflected
Underlying forms	/laŋg/	/laŋg+ə/
Nasal assimilation	laŋg	laŋgə
g-loss	laŋ	laŋə
Final devoicing		
Surface forms	[laŋ]	[laŋə]

mutually bleeding (Kiparsky 1982a: 65–6, 102–5) and it is therefore difficult to see how reordering can simplify the phonology; it is often suggested that this is a good example of the elimination of alternations as a native-learner grammar optimization strategy (ibid.).

We might suggest that in this case, too, native learners have projected the absence of an oral stop into underlying forms, giving /laŋ/ 'long', for example. But it seems that that cannot be true, for the following reason. Prevocalic and morpheme-final surface [ŋ] in modern German not only exhibits the distributional restrictions of a cluster of nasal plus voiced stop, it is actually in complementary distribution with [ŋg], which appears on the surface in such words as *Tango, Ingrid, Angelika, Mongolien*, etc. before an unreduced vowel or a sonorant; further, an actual alternation between the two is discernible in such pairs as *Triangel* ([ŋ]) : *triangulär* ([ŋg]). The arguments for deriving surface [ŋ] from underlying /ng/ are actually quite strong (Lessen Kloeke 1982: 116–22), and that would seem to preclude the hypothesis advanced at the beginning of this paragraph.

However, a further fact undermines this counterargument. Most of the German words in which [ŋg] occurs on the surface, and virtually all the alternating pairs, are unlikely to be learned by a child of preschool age. For instance, a young native learner of German will ordinarily hear not *Triangel* and *triangulär*, the technical terms of geometry, but the usual words *Dreieck* and *dreieckig*. So for the first few years of native acquisition the evidence that surface [ŋ] might be underlying /ng/ boils down to the distributional facts which, as we have argued, native learners often overlook. Even if a child has a friend named *Angelika*, that isolated fact might not necessarily prevent her from sticking to the simple hypothesis that intervocalic and morpheme-final surface [ŋ] is underlyingly /ŋ/ for a long time. Eventually, of course, evidence for underlying /ng/ will accumulate until some adjustment of the grammar is required; but it is perfectly possible that by then, as Kiparsky observes in a different context, "the horses are already out of the barn" (Kiparsky 1982a: 230): isolated [ŋ] will remain underlyingly /ŋ/ and therefore 'long' will remain underlyingly /laŋ/ for this particular speaker.

Moreover, the existence of endingless [laŋk] 'long', familiar singular imperative [zɪŋk] 'sing!', etc., would not necessarily have been sufficient to make the scenario sketched above unlikely; if *Wange* 'cheek', etc., have been learned early in NLA as /vaŋə/, etc., the child might very well account for the endingless forms in [-k] with a rule *adding* [-k] to /-ŋ/ word-finally.[†] The subsequent loss of such a rule would not be surprising. It seems possible that some such sequence of events in the past is responsible for the generalization of word-final [ŋ].

Finally, there is yet another possibility: the devoicing rule too was lost in most vernacular dialects of southern Germany, and it might not be an accident that both that loss and the loss of [-k] in such forms as *lang* occurred in approximately the same geographical area. So far as we can discover, it is not known which change occurred first. We need to reckon with the possibility that in many southern dialects the devoicing rule was lost before the reordering under discussion could occur, so that there was no reordering. In that case [laŋk] would have reverted to [laŋg] upon the loss of the devoicing rule, and [laŋg] could then have become [laŋ] by the new rule of g-loss. Subsequently forms like [laŋ] could have spread into dialects in which the devoicing rule had not yet been lost – a process not at all the same as rule reordering within a single dialect. Given the magnitude of these uncertainties, we cannot be sure what really happened in this apparent case of rule reordering.

The hypothesis that apparent examples of rule reordering are actually just the projection of rule outputs into underlying forms is worth considering simply because it is surprisingly difficult to find a watertight counterexample in which the restructuring of underlying forms *could not* have happened. Perhaps the most promising case is the Finnish example discussed in Kiparsky 1982c (originally published in 1973). We here summarize some of the crucial arguments very briefly; readers are urged to consult Kiparsky's work for a fuller presentation.

In Proto-Baltic Finnic (PBF) the sequence *ti became *si by a sequence of sound changes; typical examples are adduced in Table 6.12. Subsequently Finnish acquired many new words containing the sequence *ti*; an obvious example is *äiti* 'mother', which was borrowed either from Gothic *aiþei* or from whatever language is the source of the Gothic word. However, the rule /t/ → *s* / __

[†] This is not an implausible alternative: one of the authors actually pronounces (variably) an excrescent [k] after the frequent English unstressed word-final coda [-ɪŋ], and such a pronunciation is not rare in New Jersey and on Long Island.

Table 6.12 *Assibilation in Proto-Baltic Finnic*

Proto-Finno-Ugric	PBF	Outcomes in daughters
*weti 'water' >	*wesi >	Finnish, Estonian *vesi*
*käti 'hand' >	*käsi >	Finn., Est. *käsi*
*kakti 'two' >	*kaksi >	Finn. *kaksi*, Est. *kaks*
*wi:ti 'five' >	*wi:si >	Finn. *viisi*, Est. *viis*

Table 6.13 *3sg. simple past tense forms in Finnish*

	'(s)he wanted'	'(s)he held'
Underlying form	/halut+i+∅/	/pitä+i+∅/
Assibilation	halus-i	———
Vowel deletion	———	pit-i
Surface form	[halusi]	[piti]

i continued to be part of the phonology of Finnish, applying only in derived environments. (The underlying stems of the Finnish words are /vete/, /käte/, /kakte/, /viite/, the final *-i* of the endingless forms of these and many other nominals is the result of a vowel raising rule, so the assibilation environment is derived.) The deletion of stem-final unround short vowels before suffixes beginning with *i* also gave rise to new sequences *ti*; since these are normally not subject to the assibilation rule, the vowel deletion rule must be ordered after assibilation in an ordered rules framework. We here reproduce Kiparsky's list of categories in which unassibilated *ti* occurs without exception, with his examples (Kiparsky 1982c: 171):

(a)   the past impersonal, e.g. *mentiin* 'one went' ← /men+tä+i+hen/;
(b)   the conditional, e.g. *tuntisin* 'I would know' ← /tunte+isi+n/;
(c)   derived verbs, e.g. *sotia* 'to wage war' ← /sota+i+ta?/;
(d)   derived adjectives, e.g. *vetinen* 'watery' ← /vete+i+nen/;
(e)   derived nouns, e.g. *sontiainen* 'dung beetle' ← /sonta+iai+nen/;
(f)   oblique plurals of nouns, e.g. *sotina* 'during wars' ← /sota+i+na/, *sotiin* 'into wars' ← /sota+i+hen/, *sodissa* 'in wars' ← /sota+i+ssa/.

For some verbs the same is true of the simple past in /-i/; thus there is a surface contrast between some verbs in which a sequence *ti* arises by vowel deletion and all those in which it arises by simple concatenation of morphemes, as in Table 6.13. But there are other verbs in which assibilation does apply in the simple past even though the sequence *ti* arose by vowel deletion, e.g. *piirsi* '(s)he drew' ← /piirtä+i+∅/, and others in which it applies variably, e.g. *kiiti* ~ *kiisi* '(s)he sped' ← /kiitä+i+∅/ (ibid. p. 167). The question is how to account for these facts.

Kiparsky adduces philological and distributional evidence that the last-mentioned class of assibilated forms are innovations: documents of the sixteenth and seventeenth centuries exhibit more unassibilated forms of these verbs than does modern Finnish (ibid. pp. 168–9), and in productive formations of this type assibilation has become the rule (ibid. pp. 169–70). What we can recover about the chronology of sound changes points in the same direction. The assibilation rule is very old, applying throughout the Baltic Finnic dialect continuum and thus reconstructable for PBF (see e.g. Fromm and Sadeniemi 1956: 39–40); the rule dropping unround short vowels before *i* is the result of a much later sound change, so we should expect it to be ordered after assibilation and counterfeed it. Thus Table 6.13 should reflect the inherited situation, and the spread of assibilation to *piirsi*, etc. should be more recent. But what was the structural change in the grammar that gave that result? Reordering the rules, so that assibilation applied after vowel deletion – the reverse of the historical sequence of sound changes – would certainly do the trick. Two other details make that an attractive solution. One is the fact that the assibilation of past tenses with deleted stem vowels has clearly gained ground over time; another is that many of the "holdouts" whose past tenses still end in *-ti(-)* on the surface would become homonymous with the past tenses of other verbs if assibilation did apply to them (e.g. *kynti* '(s)he plowed' would become homonymous with *kynsi* '(s)he scratched', Kiparsky 1982c: 169). We might suggest that the rules have in fact been reordered, with some past tenses marked not to undergo the assibilation rule even though they now fit its structural description; we would expect such lexical marking to be lost gradually over time, and it would make sense for it to be lost more slowly in exactly those cases in which its loss would lead to ambiguity. (This is similar to a proposal that Kiparsky entertains but rejects.)

But what about the six grammatical categories in which *-ti-* arising by vowel deletion never undergoes assibilation? They could be marked exceptions too, grammatical rather than lexical and perhaps more likely to persist for that reason. But how could native learners fail to learn the original ordering of the rules (first assibilation, then vowel deletion counterfeeding it) when it is exemplified in a wide range of morphological environments? Evidently they have dissociated the assibilation rule in the past tense from the other cases; that is, they somehow failed to learn that the rule applied uniformly in all grammatical environments, and the rule has been fragmented (see below). It appears that one part of the fragmented rule has been reordered, though most have not.

But at this point our argument is in danger of being undermined. Apparently we have to recognize at least two synchronic assibilation rules. In that case, how do we know that the later rule is not just another regular sound change that was arrested before going to completion? That is always a possible solution to apparent cases of rule reordering (as Jon Stevens reminds us). In this case such a solution doesn't seem particularly attractive, since there are many categories of forms that the new sound change (if that's what it is) never affected. But without better knowledge of Finnish dialects we cannot exclude the possibility that this is a

Table 6.14 */o:/-raising in Menomini*

Unraised /o:/	Raised /u:/
ko:n 'snow'	ku:nyak 'lumps of snow'
a:tɛʔno:hkɛw 'he tells a sacred story'	a:tɛʔnu:hkuwɛw 'he tells him a sacred story'
po:set 'when he embarks'	pu:setuaʔ 'when they embark'
kan opo:senene:nan 'he [obviative] does not embark'	kan nepu:seni:nawan 'we [exclusive] did not embark'

sound change which began in some nonstandard dialect and spread slowly through a dialect continuum, much like the tensing of /æ/ in North American English (see Chapter 3). We doubt that more can be said without further evidence. Evidence about how the assibilation rule first began to broaden its range of application would be especially important but might no longer be recoverable, since the change began so far in the past.

Other apparent cases of reordering known to us either are sketchily described in the literature or are more complex and uncertain than those discussed above. In the present state of our knowledge it isn't clear whether rule reordering per se is a possible type of phonological change. It is increasingly clear, however, that the projection of rule outputs into underlying forms is widespread even in circumstances in which a linguist might not expect it. We therefore turn to a discussion of that phenomenon in greater depth.

Unexpected underlying forms

In mid-twentieth-century Menomini, as recorded in Bloomfield 1962, the vowel [u:] did not occur underlyingly in normal native lexemes; it arose on the surface by raising of underlying /o:/ when a high vowel or a postconsonantal semivowel followed later in the word (ibid. p. 3). The pairs of examples in Table 6.14 are typical (ibid. pp. 96, 106–7). It can be seen that surface [o:] and [u:] were in complementary distribution.

But a number of "marginal" phenomena made this distribution less than perfect. For one thing, the borrowed lexemes *čo:h* 'Joe' and *ču:h* 'Jew' exhibited a contrast between these two vowels (Bloomfield 1962: 5), and since both were unanalyzable, /u:/ must have been underlying in the latter word. It looks like the contrast was the result of contact with English, and in the narrowest sense that is true; but why was it *possible* for speakers of Menomini to borrow this particular contrast, given that languages usually substitute their own phonemes for foreign ones in borrowed words? Moreover, there were also at least two native interjections with unexpected [u:], namely *čapu:ʔ* 'sploosh!' and *ku:h* 'stop that!'. Conversely, there were two onomatopoeic roots whose multiple /o:/'s were marked not to undergo raising: cf. *o:ho:hatimow* '(s)he weeps aloud', *o:ho:pi:wɛ:kat* 'there is a sound of whooping' (ibid. p. 97).

From these additional facts about Menomini raising we seem forced to conclude that [u:] had somehow achieved phonological independence, so that it could be underlying /u:/ in interjections and loanwords, *even though* it was fully predictable on the surface, since its only source was the raising rule. We need to explain how that is possible.

The crucial fact seems to be that some Menomini [u:] did not alternate with [o:] because they were followed by a high vowel or a postconsonantal semivowel in every form of the lexeme in which they occurred. The examples in (17) below (from Bloomfield 1962, 1975) are typical.

(17)   su:niyan 'coin' (*obviative* su:niyanan, *plural* su:niyanak)
         mu:čehkih 'blue jay' (*pl.* mu:čehki:hsak)
         tu:ti:s 'snipe' (*pl.* tu:ti:hsak ~ tu:ti:skok)
         seka:ku:hsyah 'onion' (*pl.* seka:ku:hsyak)
         nemu:hkehkwan 'my eyebrow' (kemu:hkehkwan 'your eyebrow', etc.)
         nɛhtu:hkwan 'my elbow' (*pl.* nɛhtu:hkwanan; ohtu:hkwan 'his/her elbow', etc.)
         ku:wiči:ʔsow 'she plays shinny'; ku:wiči:ʔsehɛw 'she invites her to play shinny'; ku:wiči:ʔsehewɛ:w 'she gives a shinny game'; ku:wiči:ʔswanak 'shinny bags'; ku:wiči:ʔswana:htek 'shinny stick'; etc., etc.

In the early stages of language acquisition a native learner might be expected to posit underlying /u:/ because there is no alternation in the morpheme that would suggest any other underlying vowel, according to the ITH proposed in Chapter 5. Fuller information should eventually lead the learner to conclude that these [u:] are underlyingly /o:/ even though they do not alternate, since the appearance of [o:] and [u:] on the surface is fully predictable. But it seems clear that a critical mass of some generation of native learners of Menomini – probably in the nineteenth century – did not do that. Instead they projected non-alternating surface outcomes into underlying forms and stuck with that analysis. What is striking about this case is that the new contrast can be described with the existing phonological distinctive features of the language – also in accordance with the ITH – since underlying /e:/ and /i:/ clearly did contrast (and, in addition, /e:/ was also raised to [i:] by the same raising rule, Bloomfield 1962: 5). The result of this learner error was a theoretically superfluous *and covert* underlying /u:/ which was available for use in interjections and loanwords.

It is not as clear how the nascent contrast between /o:/ and /u:/ contributed to the failure of /o:ho:h-/ 'call loudly' and /o:ho:p-/ 'whoop' to undergo raising at all. We can at least say that if the alternation between surface [o:] and [u:] had remained fully transparent, those developments should not have been possible; thus the acquisition of /u:/ was part of the process that undermined the exceptionless surface alternation inhibiting those developments. But we might expect some further factor to be necessary to account for the failure of /o:/ to undergo the raising rule in the verb roots just cited; the fact that they are onomatopoeic seems relevant, but we do not know whether that is the whole story.

We strongly suspect that learner errors of this kind – positing underlying segments which are phonologically derivable just because they do not alternate in the morphemes in question – are very common, though they become detectable only when further changes occur. As in Menomini, loanwords sometimes reveal that rule outputs have become covertly autonomous by using them to render foreign phonemes. The borrowing of Spanish voiced stops into Northern Chiapas Zoque, discussed briefly in Chapter 4, is another relevant case. Voiced stops and affricates occurred always and only immediately following a nasal. There were some lexemes in which a stop or affricate was always voiced because a nasal always preceded; typical examples include *wendi* 'candle', *sundunu* 'flannel moth caterpillar', *təʔmbits* 'Geomys species', *kandʒu* 'first cousin', *kaŋgoja* 'rabbit'. Positing underlying voiced stops in such words should have made it possible to borrow /b d g/ in other positions in Spanish loanwords. The eventual borrowing of such clusters as [mp], [nt] with voiceless stops (e.g. in *kampana həjə* 'bell flower' and *manta* 'cloak') could then have been facilitated by the underlying contrast between /p t k/ and /b d g/ in other positions, though it seems likely that extensive bilingualism is principally responsible for the unadjusted shapes of these loans. In other words, though this last phenomenon appears to be parallel to the odd non-raising of /o:/ in Menomini onomatopoeic roots, we have a plausible external explanation for the Zoque case.

A third example of this process, more thoroughly researched (because we have much more historical information), is the phonemic split of voiceless and voiced anterior fricatives in ME. In prehistoric OE the anterior fricatives *f, *þ (i.e. *[θ]), and *s had become voiced in fully voiced environments when the last preceding syllable nucleus was stressed (Luick 1914–40: 844–8, Campbell 1962: 179–80).[6] Throughout the OE period the surface alternations [f] ∼ [v], [θ] ∼ [ð], [s] ∼ [z] remained exceptionless and were seldom noted in spelling, since there were only three phonemes /f/, /þ/, /s/ under any analysis. However, in the generation before (n.b. not after) the Norman Conquest, OF words began to be borrowed into English; and OF had not only a sibilant which alternated in voicing much like the English one (e.g. [s] in *us* 'use' (noun), [z] in *user* 'to use') but also a non-alternating /s/, usually spelled *c*.[7] How the English pronounced this consonant in the earliest loanwords (such as *canceler* 'chancellor', borrowed in the reign of Edward the Confessor) cannot be discovered, as OE spelling conventions conceal it. But by the second half of the twelfth century French spelling conventions were becoming widely used, and we can be fairly certain that loanwords like *grace* (which first appears in the *Lambeth Homilies*) and *pece* 'piece' (first attested in the *Ancrene Riwle*, around 1200) were [grasə], [pe:sə], with intervocalic [s] immediately following a stressed vowel. Over the next couple of centuries a steadily increasing number of OF words with initial [v-] were borrowed into ME. These developments established an underlying contrast between /f/ and /v/, and

Table 6.15 *Alternating and non-alternating labiodental fricatives in Old English*

| | 'woman' | | 'boy' | |
	sg.	pl.	sg.	pl.
Nom.	wī**f**	wī**f**	cna*f*a	cna*f*an
Acc.	wī**f**	wī**f**	cna*f*an	cna*f*an
Gen.	wī*f*es	wī*f*a	cna*f*an	cna*f*ena
Dat.	wī*f*e	wī*f*um	cna*f*an	cna*f*um

between /s/ and /z/, in much the same way as the borrowing of 'Joe' and 'Jew' had begun to establish an underlying contrast in twentieth-century Menomini. They did not, however, disrupt the fricative voicing rule, on which see further below.

An explanation parallel to the one advanced above for Menomini and Zoque can account for the English data. There were numerous OE lexemes that exemplified the surface alternation [f ~ v], but also numerous others that exhibited only [v] because the fricative occurred in a voiced environment in all forms. The pair of nouns whose paradigms are given in Table 6.15 illustrates the situation. We give the forms in standard OE orthography, with [f] in boldface and [v] in italics. It is at least reasonable to suppose that some native learners posited underlying /v/ for non-alternating surface [v], and that that was what made the borrowing of OF initial /v/ possible. The borrowing of OF intervocalic /s/ *before* any other relevant changes had occurred is less easy to account for. The only non-alternating [s]'s in OE were word-initial, or adjacent to a voiceless consonant (including geminate /ss/), or word-finally in non-inflecting lexemes (such as the adverb *lǣs* 'less') or inflectional endings (e.g. gen. sg. *-es*) or suppletive forms (e.g. *is* 'is'). Variant spellings seem to show that geminate *ss* could be reduced to (apparently voiceless) *s* in allegro forms such as *þisum* 'to these' (beside unreduced *þissum*), but that seems an inadequate basis for learners to posit non-alternating /s/. It looks as though positing non-alternating /z/ in such words as *pise* 'pease', *hæsel* 'hazel', *ōsle* 'blackbird', etc. contributed toward making the borrowing of non-alternating /s/ possible for native learners, though exactly how that happened is not clear; once again we must probably posit extensive bilingualism for the immediate context of such loans. It does seem clear, though, that the lexical marking of the /s/ of ME *grace*, *piece*, etc. not to undergo the voicing rule is structurally parallel to the lexical marking of Menomini /o:ho:h-/, /o:ho:p-/ not to undergo the raising rule; thus a more solid explanation of the origin of one exceptional case, if it can be found, will probably shed light on the other.

The subsequent development that most commonly reveals covert underlying segments is probably not word-borrowing, however, but the destruction of conditioning environments in the process of "secondary split," discussed in Chapter 5. We noted there that when the conditioning environment for a phonological rule is destroyed, in whole or in part, we might reasonably expect the rule to cease working, so that the underlying segment reappears in place of the rule's output. But that is not what usually happens; typically the rule's output survives, and the destruction of the rule's conditioning environment makes the output contrastive. The cases we have just discussed strongly suggest that rule outputs become contrastive in secondary split *because they were already potentially contrastive*, since native learners had projected them into underlying forms in lexemes in which they did not participate in surface alternations, according to the ITH.

This is a testable hypothesis. It should be possible to examine all known cases of secondary split to see whether the rule outputs which they made contrastive were non-alternating in some lexemes at the time of the split. If that was true in every case, our hypothesis will be confirmed; if there are exceptions, further study of the exceptions will lead either to refinement of the hypothesis or to its replacement by a better hypothesis. We leave this for future research.

Rule fragmentation

Though it is uncertain whether phonological rules in an ordered sequence can be reordered, it is clear that they can evolve in several other ways. We deal with such changes in the next few sections.

When the phonological environment of a phonological rule is destroyed or obscured by further sound changes, the rule becomes morphologically conditioned; unless it originally applied only in a single morphological environment (because that was the only morphological environment in which the phonological trigger occurred), it will now have multiple morphological triggers. Under those circumstances a single rule can develop into a group of similar but distinct rules, roughly one for each relevant morphological environment, by the accumulation of further changes in each of the environments. We will call this process the "fragmentation" of a rule.

Whether and how fragmentation occurs must ultimately depend on how hard the rule is to learn as a single phonological rule. We discuss contrasting examples, beginning with a rule that has not been fragmented.

We have referred above to the German i-umlaut rule, which became fully morphologically conditioned some nine centuries ago. In modern standard German the rule occurs in many morphological environments; a partial list of the more important ones is the following (see also Wright 1907: 148–59, 163–4, 169, Drosdowski 1984: 239–40):

before a noun plural marker /-ə/ ∼ -∅ (i.e. -*e* after stressed syllables and zero after unstressed syllables) used with more than half of all masculine and about one-quarter of feminine nouns; typical examples are (masc.) *Gast* 'guest', pl. *Gäste*, *Vater* 'father', pl. *Väter*, (fem.) *Hand* 'hand', pl. *Hände*, *Tochter* 'daughter', pl. *Töchter*;

before a noun plural marker *-er* used with about 20 percent of neuter and a few
masculine nouns, e.g. (neut.) *Haus* 'house', pl. *Häuser*, (masc.) *Mann* 'man',
pl. *Männer*;

in the comparative and superlative of about two dozen adjectives, e.g. *lang* 'long',
länger 'longer', *das Längste* 'the longest';

in the present indicative 2sg. and 3sg. of most strong verbs, e.g. *fahren* 'travel',
pres. 2sg. *fährst*, 3sg. *fährt*;

in the past subjunctive of strong verbs, e.g. (3sg.) *führe* 'would travel';

before a suffix *-e* which forms feminine abstract nouns from adjectives, e.g. *Länge*
'length';

in neuter collectives formed with the prefix *ge-*, e.g. *Horn* 'horn', *Gehörn* '(set
of) antlers';

before the diminutive suffixes *-chen* and *-lein*;

before the suffix *-ling*, which forms nouns denoting persons typified by the
characteristic denoted by the root word.

Yet the operation of the rule is identical in all cases: only the vowel of the root
syllable is changed; back vowels are fronted, the low vowels are also raised, the
diphthong /aʊ/ is replaced by [ɔy], and the diphthongs /aɪ/ and /ɔy/ are not affected
(even though they have back nuclei). Evidently the uniformity and pervasiveness
of the rule make it easy to learn, and it has not undergone any fragmentation.
The only consequence of its multiple morphological triggers is that its lexical
scope has shifted differently over time in different word classes; for instance, the
number of nouns using the umlauting noun plural markers increased somewhat in
MHG, then much more in subsequent centuries, whereas the number of adjectives
with umlauted comparatives and superlatives increased in MHG but has fallen
sharply in recent centuries (see e.g. Wright 1907: 169–71, 197–8).

A completely different case is "Grassmann's Law" (GL) in Ancient Greek.
The sound change which gave rise to this phonological rule deaspirated aspirated
stops and deleted /h/ in syllable onsets if an aspirated stop followed anywhere in
the same phonological word. The lexicalized effects of the sound change can be
seen in numerous isolated words (the examples are all Attic):[8]

(18)   *péithetai* πείθεται '(s)he obeys, (s)he trusts' < *pheith-e- < PIE *bheydh- (cf.
        Latin *fīdit* '(s)he trusts'; Gothic *beidan*, OE *bīdan* 'to wait (for)')

        pɛ̂:khus πῆχυς 'forearm' < *phá:khus < PIE *bhāǵhus 'arm' (cf. OE *bōg* 'arm,
        shoulder, bough')

        têikhos τεῖχος 'wall' < *théikhos < PIE *dheyǵh- 'make out of clay' (cf. Oscan
        acc. pl. **feíhúss** 'walls')

        kephalé: κεφαλή 'head' < *khephalá: < PIE *ghebhal- (cf. OHG *gebal* 'skull')

        ekekhe:ría: ἐκεχειρίᾱ 'truce' < *hekhe-khe:ría: 'hold-hand' (*ékhe:n* ἔχειν 'to
        hold', *khé:r* χείρ 'hand'; see below on the initial *h- of the verb)

        akólouthos ἀκόλουθος 'following, accompanying, companion' < *ha-
        kólouthos 'one who walks the same path' (*ha-* ἁ- 'same', *kéleuthos* κέλευθος
        'path')

But in the synchronic grammar of Ancient Greek the operation of GL is far more restricted, and the single sound change has fragmented into several rather different rules, as follows.

The deaspiration rule of broadest application affects reduplicating syllables. These are frequently encountered because verbs beginning with single consonants or with clusters of a stop followed by a sonorant form their perfect stems in part by prefixing *Ce-*, where *C* is the initial consonant of the root. If the initial consonant of the root is aspirated, the consonant of the reduplicating syllable is deaspirated. The examples in (19) are typical (present and aorist infinitives of the same verbs are given in parentheses).

(19)   *tetʰnánai* τεθνάναι 'to be dead' ← /tʰe-tʰna-/ (*tʰné:iske:n* θνῄσκειν† 'to be dying', *tʰanê:n* θανεῖν 'to die')

tetʰukénai τεθυκέναι 'to have sacrificed' ← /tʰe-tʰu-k-/, *tetʰústʰai* τεθύσθαι 'to have been sacrificed' ← /tʰe-tʰu-/ (*tʰú:e:n* θύειν 'to be sacrificing', *tʰû:sai* θῦσαι 'to sacrifice')

pepʰε:nénai πεφηνέναι 'to have appeared' ← /pʰe-pʰa:n-/ (*pʰáinestʰai* φαίνεσθαι 'to seem; to clearly be', *pʰanê:nai* φανῆναι 'to appear')

pepʰeugénai πεφευγέναι 'to have escaped' ← /pʰe-pʰeug-/ (*pʰéuge:n* φεύγειν 'to be running away', *pʰugê:n* φυγεῖν 'to escape')

pepʰulakʰénai πεφυλαχέναι 'to have guarded' ← /pʰe-pʰulak-h-/, *pepʰulákʰtʰai* πεφυλάχθαι 'to be on one's guard' ← /pʰe-pʰulak-/ (*pʰulátte:n* φυλάττειν 'to guard', *pʰuláksai* φυλάξαι 'to take account of'; cf. noun /pʰúlak-/ φύλακ- '(a) guard')

kekʰε:nénai κεχηνέναι 'to gape' ← /kʰe-kʰa:n-/ (*kʰáske:n* χάσκειν 'to yawn', *kʰanê:n* χανεῖν 'to open the mouth')

kekʰrê:stʰai κεχρῆσθαι 'to use habitually' ← /kʰe-kʰrε:-/ (*kʰrê:stʰai* χρῆσθαι 'to use', *kʰré:sastʰai* χρήσασθαι 'to experience')

(It can be seen that other sequences of aspirated consonants in these forms are *not* subject to the dissimilation rule.) There is also a small class of present stems reduplicated with *Ci-*, of which one has a root beginning with an aspirated consonant and so undergoes the dissimilation rule:

(20)   *titʰénai* τιθέναι 'to put (repeatedly or distributively), to be putting' ← /tʰi-tʰe-/ (aorist *tʰê:nai* θεῖναι 'to put')

A second aspirate dissimilation rule (?; see below) has a much more restricted scope: it applies to roots of the shape /tʰV-/ (only) before the passive aorist suffix /-tʰε:-/ (only). There are two such roots:

(21)   *tetʰê:nai* τεθῆναι 'to be put' ← /tʰe-tʰε:-/ (see above)
        tutʰê:nai τυθῆναι 'to be sacrificed' ← /tʰu-tʰε:-/ (see above)

---

† On the diphthong in the present 'to be dying' see Threatte 1996: 505.

These two roots do not undergo aspirate dissimilation when followed by other suffixes or endings containing aspirated consonants; that can be seen from various forms of the aorist and present of 'put' and of the passive perfect of 'sacrifice':

(22)   *tʰéstʰe tà hópla* θέσθε τὰ ὅπλα 'ground arms!' (lit. 'put your own weapons (down)') ← /tʰe-stʰe/ (aorist stem /tʰe-/, 2pl. mediopassive /-stʰe/)

   etʰéstʰɛ:n ἐθέσθην 'the two of them put (their own)' ← /e-tʰe-stʰɛ:n/ (/e-/ past indicative prefix ("augment"), /-stʰɛ:n/ 3du. mediopassive)

   títʰestʰai τίθεσθαι 'to be putting (one's own)' ← /tʰi-tʰe-stʰai/ (/-stʰai/ mediopassive infinitive)

   tetʰústʰai τεθύσθαι 'to have been sacrificed' ← /tʰe-tʰu-ˊstʰai/ (see above)

Nor does the rule apply to other roots of the shape /CʰV-/ before the aorist passive suffix:

(23)   *kʰutʰɛ̂:nai* χυθῆναι 'to be poured' ← /kʰu-tʰɛ:-/ (/kʰew-/ ∼ /kʰu-/ 'pour')

Nor does it apply to other roots beginning with /tʰ-/ before the aorist passive suffix:

(24)   *tʰli:pʰtʰɛ̂:nai* θλῑφθῆναι 'to be squeezed' ← /tʰli:b-tʰɛ:-/ (*tʰlí:be:n* θλίβειν 'to squeeze', *tʰlî:psai* θλῖψαι 'to oppress')

   tʰraustʰɛ̂:nai θραυσθῆναι 'to be shattered' ← /tʰraus-tʰɛ:-/ (*tʰráue:n* θραύειν 'to break (something) up', *tʰrâusai* θραῦσαι 'to destroy')

Whether a process which applies to only two lexemes should be considered a synchronic rule is of course debatable; the examples might just as well be memorized individually. What matters in this context is that the phenomenon is one of the surviving fragments of an earlier phonological rule, regardless of its synchronic status. (On some other roots possibly beginning with /tʰ-/ see further below.)

A third fragment of the original rule, probably completely fossilized, is the dissimilation of the aspirates in the sequence /-tʰe:-tʰi/, the passive aorist suffix followed by the 2sg. imperative ending;[†] but in this case it is the second /tʰ/, not the first, that loses its aspiration, as in (25).

(25)   *entʰu:mé:tʰe:ti* ἐνθῡμήθητι 'think about it!' ← /en-tʰu:mɛ:-tʰɛ:-tʰi/

   hé:stʰe:ti ἥσθητι 'enjoy it!' ← /hɛ:d-tʰɛ:-tʰi/

   dialékʰtʰe:ti διαλέχθητι 'talk it over!' ← /dia-leg-tʰɛ:-tʰi/

   hɛ:tté:tʰe:ti ἡττήθητι 'yield!' ← /hɛ:tta:-tʰɛ:-tʰi/

The rationale seems to have been that the affix furthest from the root undergoes the dissimilation (a rough mirror image of the rule that dissimilates reduplicating syllables). Thus this phenomenon is probably a relic of a much earlier reanalysis of the phonological rule or of one of its fragments.

[†] An idiosyncracy of the passive aorist is that it selects active rather than mediopassive endings. Most of the plausible examples of passive aorist imperatives are made from passive "deponents," i.e. verbs which are passive in form but not in meaning.

A fourth class of related phenomena is more difficult to analyze. Six roots, including a basic noun, a basic adjective, and four verbs, exhibit a shape $t(R)VC^h$- when a vowel follows immediately, but a shape $t^h(R)VC$- when a consonant follows immediately; the forms in (26)–(31) are representative.

(26) a. nom. pl. *trík^hes* τρίχες 'hairs', gen. sg. *trik^hós* τριχός, etc.,
      b. nom. sg. *t^hríks* θρίξ 'hair', dat. pl. *t^hriksí* θριξί

(27) a. *tak^hús* ταχύς 'swift',
      b. comparative *t^há:tto:n* θάττων (*-tt-* < *-kj-*)

(28) a. *tap^hê:nai* ταφῆναι 'to get buried'
      b. *t^hápte:n* θάπτειν 'to be burying', *t^hápsai* θάψαι 'to bury', *tet^háp^ht^hai* τεθάφθαι 'to have been buried'

(29) a. *trép^he:n* τρέφειν 'to support, to raise (a child)', *tetrop^hénai* τετροφέναι 'to have raised', *trap^hê:nai* τραφῆναι 'to grow up'
      b. *t^hrépsai* θρέψαι 'to raise to maturity', *tet^hráp^ht^hai* τεθράφθαι 'to have been raised'

(30) a. *apo-trék^he:n* ἀποτρέχειν 'to run away; to run hard'
      b. *apo-t^hréksest^hai* ἀποθρέξεσθαι 'to be going to run hard'

(31) a. *epi-tú:p^hest^hai* ἐπιτύφεσθαι 'to be burned up', *epi-tup^hê:nai* ἐπιτυφῆναι 'to be consumed (by passion)'
      b. *epi-tet^hû:p^ht^hai* ἐπιτεθῦφθαι 'to be furious'

Historically all these roots were of the shape *$t^h(r)VC^h$-. The aspiration of the root-final stop was lost when another obstruent followed immediately; subsequently the aspiration of the initial *t^h- was lost by dissimilation, but of course only when the root-final aspiration survived before a vowel. The rule deaspirating stops before a following obstruent is still needed in the grammar of Classical Attic to account for many verb forms, such as:

(32) *grápsai* γράψαι 'to write' ← /graph-s-/ (*gráp^he:n* γράφειν 'to be writing')
      bápte:n βάπτειν 'to dip (repeatedly)' ← /bap^h-te-/ (*bap^hê:nai* βαφῆναι 'to get dunked')

(and, of course, the mediopassive perfect and pluperfect forms investigated in an earlier section of this chapter). It might seem that the most economical analysis would be to posit underlying forms of these roots with aspirated stops both initially and finally, to allow the last-mentioned rule to deaspirate their final stops before another obstruent, and to posit a further rule which subsequently dissimilates the first of two aspirated stops within a root.[9]

However, this is not the only possible analysis. It turns out that there were no inherited roots of the shape *$t(r)VC^h$- (because of a PIE constraint on the shape of roots), and thus no contrast between roots of the shape *$t^h(r)VC^h$- and those of the shape *$t(r)VC^h$-. It is therefore possible to posit underlying forms of the shape /$t(r)VC^h$-/ for these roots, in effect projecting the effects of GL into underlying forms, and to complicate the rule which assimilates stops to an immediately following obstruent as follows:

> when the root-final aspirated stop of a monosyllabic root is assimilated to a following obstruent, its aspiration is linked to a /t/ in the onset of the root-syllable, provided that that /t/ is not preceded by /s/.

(The condition is necessary to exempt the root /strep^h-/ 'turn' [cf. *strépsai* στρέψαι 'to turn (something)', etc.].) This seems just as plausible as the hypothesis of underlying two-aspirate roots. To the extent that native learners preferred this second alternative, they reanalyzed part of the original dissimilation rule into a rule of a very different kind.

It seems worth asking how such fragmentation of the aspirate dissimilation rule became possible. A complete answer does not seem attainable, but a partial answer can be found in the details of the language's inherited structure. The deaspiration rule originally applied in a large number of different morphotactic environments, and in each it was gradually altered by the accumulation of small linguistic changes – all of which were contingent events. That the rule has largely been lost in compound lexemes is understandable, since they are constantly vulnerable to reanalysis and re-formation on the part of language learners; the English replacement of *halidai* by *holiday* and then (in the word's original meaning) by *holy day* (at least in Catholic usage) is a comparable example. The other cases in which dissimilation originally applied were the following:

(a)   reduplicating syllables;

(b)   the initial consonants of two-aspirate roots followed by vowel-initial affixes;

(c)   aspirates in nominal stems followed by the instrumental plural ending -*p^{h}i* -φι or the adverb-forming suffixes -*t^{h}en* -θεν 'from', -*t^{h}i* -θι 'at';

(d)   aspirates in verb stems followed by the aorist passive suffix -*t$^h\varepsilon$:*- -θη-, the 2sg. imperative ending -*t^{h}i* -θι, mediopassive 1pl. -*met^{h}a* -μεθα, or any of several mediopassive endings beginning with -*st^h*- -σθ-: infinitive -*st^{h}ai* -σθαι, 2pl. -*st^{h}e* -σθε, imperative 3sg. -*st^{h}ɔ:* -σθω, imp. 3nonsg. -*st^{h}ɔ:n* -σθων, secondary 3du. -*st$^h\varepsilon$:n* -σθην, or default 2, 3du. -*st^{h}on* -σθον.

It can be seen that the rule has largely ceased to apply to the cases listed under (c) and (d). It seems surprising that the rule has been so widely lost in productive inflection; but in fact most of the suffixes and endings listed under (c) and (d) were relatively peripheral to the system. The instrumental case underwent syntactic merger with the dative sometime between 1200 and 800 BCE; in Classical Attic -*p^{h}i* -φι no longer occurs, and even in the Homeric poems it is used as an alternative dative ending and an adverb-forming suffix. The other items listed under (c) are derivational suffixes of adverbs, a relatively marginal word class. Nearly half the endings listed under (d) mark duals and third-person imperatives, which are very peripheral categories; most of the rest are endings of the mediopassive, the "marked" voice. Active 2sg. imperative -$t^h i$ -θι appears in only a minority of paradigms; in most the ending is zero. Only the passive aorist suffix is less marginal to the inflection of verbs – and it is only in that category that vestiges of the original aspirate dissimilation rule survive. These are all the sorts of categories in which native learners could easily make mistakes for lack of sufficient input, and since the mistakes involved non-application of a rule that obscured the shapes of morphemes, they evidently "made sense" and so survived and propagated.

The restriction of aspirate alternation in roots (whatever the correct analysis may be) to roots beginning with /t^h-/ is much more striking. Greek did inherit roots of the shape *p^h(r)VC^h- and *k^h(r)VC^h-, but in them the unaspirated output *p-*, *k-* has been projected back into underlying forms; for instance, the active aorist of /$peit^h$-/ (<*$p^h eit^h$-, see above) is *pêisai* πεῖσαι 'to persuade', not "*$p^h êisai$.*" A possible reason is that among two-aspirate roots that were subject to the alternation (because they were sometimes followed by consonant-initial suffixes or endings) those beginning with /t^h-/ happened to be more numerous. In any case, a learner hears examples of any particular lexeme less often than examples of a common and productive inflectional category; thus it is not surprising that the rule survived better in reduplicating syllables. Finally, one would expect the disintegration of such a phonological rule to leave opaque alternations in an isolated lexeme or two, and this one has; note the paradigm of 'have, hold, get':

(33)   *ék^{h}e:n* ἔχειν 'to hold, to have', *hékse:n* ἕξειν 'to be going to hold/have', *sk^{h}ê:n* σχεῖν 'to get'

The present and future clearly reflect earlier *hek^h-e- (in which *h- was lost by aspirate dissimilation) and *hek^h-se-. Their *h- reflects pre-Greek *s- before a sonorant (in this case, a vowel); in the aorist *sk^h-e-* the *s survives because it is followed by a stop. It is simply not credible that native learners of Classical Attic abduced rules from such a paradigm, given that the *h-* ∼ *∅-* alternation does not recur and the *s-* ∼ *h-* alternation recurs only in the reduplicated stems of /sta(:)-/ 'stand'; this is a lexical relic.

The reader can see that Greek aspirate dissimilation was much more vulnerable to fragmentation than German i-umlaut because it applied in fewer morphological environments, some of which were comparatively rare, and affected segments in more morphotactic environments – the German rule always alters the vowel of the root-syllable. Because its effects were scattered, different parts of aspirate dissimilation could be altered by different linguistic changes, and fragmentation was the result.

Rule restriction and loss

The application of rules can be restricted in a variety of ways. The fragmentation of the Greek aspirate dissimilation rule obviously involved increasing restrictions on parts of the original rule, for instance. But rules can also be restricted without losing their coherence; English provides an example.

As we noted two sections ago, late OE/early ME had inherited an automatic surface alternation between voiceless and voiced anterior fricatives, the voiceless fricatives being underlying. The alternation appeared frequently in final position in the stems of major lexemes, as well as in the derivation of verbs from nominals; the following ME examples are typical:

(34) a. *wulf, wulfes* [wɔlf, wɔlvəs] 'wolf, wolves'
  paþ, paþes [paθ, paðəs] 'path, paths'
  hūs, hūses [hu:s, hu:zəs] 'house, houses'

  b. *half, halfe* [half, halvə] 'half' (adj.)
  wrāþ, wrāþe [wra:θ, wra:ðə] 'angry'
  wīs, wīse [wi:s, wi:zə] 'wise'

  c. *drīfen, drāf* [dri:vən, dra:f] 'to drive, ((s)he) drove'
  queþen, quaþ [kwɛðən, kwaθ] 'to say, ((s)he) said'
  chēsen, chēs [ʧe:zən, ʧɛ:s] 'to choose, ((s)he) chose'

  d. *lēf, lēven* [lɛ:f, le:vən] 'permission, to permit'
  baþ, baþən [baθ, baðən] 'bath, to bathe'
  hūs, hūsen [hu:s, hu:zən] 'house, to house'

The last part of this pattern was reinforced by borrowing from OF, which also had nominals ending in voiceless *f* and *s* and derived verbs exhibiting the corresponding voiced fricatives instead (e.g. *us* 'use' : *user* 'to use'; *sauf* 'safe' : *sauver* 'to save'). A significant number of such pairs was borrowed already in the thirteenth century, or even a bit earlier. For instance, *grief* : *grieve* and *strife* : *strive* appear in the *Ancrene Riwle*, written around 1200, and *advice* : *advise* in Robert of Gloucester's chronicle of 1297; other thirteenth-century pairs include *safe* : *save*, *use* : *(to) use*, and *device* : *devise*; in the fourteenth century *relief* : *relieve* appears.

The first linguistic event that disrupted this consistent pattern was the borrowing from OF of words like *grace* [grasə] and *pece* [pe:sə] 'piece' in the second half of the twelfth century (discussed above), with voiceless [s] (written ⟨c⟩) between vowels. Those loanwords must have been lexically marked not to undergo the fricative voicing rule, but that did not disrupt the rule, which continued to apply in derived environments. The borrowing of French words with initial *v-* in the thirteenth century led to a clear contrast between underlying /f/ and /v/, at least in the East Midlands, which all subsequent native learners acquired, but that still had no effect on the rule. In fact, nouns ending in *-f* borrowed from OF before about 1350 were subject to the voicing rule: *beef*, which first appears in English around 1290, still has a plural *beeves*; the first attestation of *chief* is apparently *on the chive* 'on the head', *c*. 1330; and though the plural of *coif*, whose singular first appears in 1325, is not attested until the end of the fourteenth century (see below), we find *quaives* and *coives* in the seventeenth and eighteenth centuries (see the *OED* s.vv.). (The spelling of the other anterior fricatives does not reveal their voicing.)

In the middle of the fourteenth century word-final *-ə* began to be lost, at first variably, in London English; that is when reverse spellings like *mouse* for /mu:s/ (with no final /-ə/) begin to appear, showing that word-final *-e* could be phonetically meaningless. The immediate result was that voiced fricatives now appeared word-finally on the surface. When the process of loss was complete, within a generation or so after 1400,[10] the voicing rule became significantly opaque, since the word-final alternation [-f] ∼ [-v-ə] was now replaced by [-f] ∼ [-v]; and in fact it appears that such alternations as [half] ∼ [halv] 'half' in adjectives did not survive long.

The voicing rule became opaque in all positions because of three sound changes that occurred in the fifteenth century, the first already underway in 1400:

(a)   geminate fricatives, which had always been voiceless, were simplified (Jespersen 1909: 146);

(b)   fricatives were voiced when preceded by a fully unstressed syllable (ibid. pp. 199–206);

(c)   the vowel of the default plural ending (which was now [-əz] by change (b)) was lost except when a sibilant preceded immediately (ibid. pp. 188–9), and the ending [-z] was assimilated in voicing to a preceding consonant.

By the first change such plurals as *cuffes, mothes, masses* [kʊffəs, mɔθθəs, massəs] became [kʊfəs, mɔθəs, masəs], with voiceless fricatives between vowels; the relative handful of such nouns must at first have been marked as exceptions to the voicing rule. But the second and third sound changes created the fully opaque situation that still persists (to some extent) in modern English, with /wulf/ and /paθ/ subject to the voicing rule in the plural ([wʊlvz, paðz]) but /kuf/ and /moθ/ exempt ([kʊfs, mɔθs]). At that point the fricative voicing rule became vulnerable to being lost.

But the rule was not lost quickly, and in most dialects of English it still has not been lost completely. The rule still applies to noun plurals as follows. The only noun whose stem ends in /-s/ that is still subject to the rule is *house*. The rule affects only a few nouns in /-θ/, and there is considerable variation; one of the authors uses [ð], probably inconsistently, only in the plurals of *bath, path, mouth, sheath,* and *wreath*. However, about 40 percent of the monosyllabic nouns ending in /-f/ still undergo the voicing rule in most standard dialects of English. Not surprisingly, those that do are mostly inherited from OE (*half, calf, hoof, roof, thief, sheaf, leaf, knife, life, wife, loaf, wharf, turf, elf, self, wolf*); *beef* is so early a French loanword that its inclusion in this group is not surprising. However, at least two nouns borrowed later have also become subject to the rule. The plural of *shelf*, apparently borrowed from Low German late in the fourteenth century (when final /-ə/ was being lost), appears as *shelfes* and *shelves* in different manuscripts of Chaucer; both plurals continue to be found in the fifteenth century, but the the voiced plural eventually won out. The plural of *scarf*, which is first attested in the middle of the sixteenth century, was at first *scarfs*, and that form continues to occur down into the nineteenth century; *scarves* first appears in the middle of the eighteenth century and eventually became the norm. It thus seems clear that the rule remained marginally productive among noun plurals for many generations. On the other hand, many nouns in /-f/ that do not undergo the voicing rule in the plural entered the language after the rule became fully opaque; the list includes *skiff, clef, muff, ruff, fife, oaf, serf*, and a number of others. A few – *gaff, puff, cuff*, and apparently *reef* (originally *riff*) – contained geminate /ff/ in ME. A few others – *cough, trough, rough*, and *chough* – originally ended in /-aux/ or /-ɔux/ and acquired their modern /-f/ by a fifteenth- or sixteenth-century sound change (Jespersen 1909: 286–9; note that *laugh* was first used as a noun in the late seventeenth century, *tough* in the nineteenth, long after the rule had ceased to be fully productive). *Kerf* (OE *cyrf*) apparently is no longer subject to the voicing rule because its plural has always been rare; *cliff* (OE *clif*) was subject to the rule throughout the ME period except in the north, where /-ə/ was lost early and stem-final voiceless fricatives were generalized, and it is apparently the northern form that survives. A few alternating nouns have generalized /-v/ instead. *Grave* (OE *græf*) has apparently generalized an old dative in *-ə* that survived in such phrases as *in grave*; the reasons why /-v/ was generalized in *drove* and *grove* (OE *drāf, grāf*) are not clear. The most interesting development has affected *staff* (OE *stæf*). The plural was *staffs* in the north, but *staves* for many speakers of London English well down into the modern period, though *staffs* began to compete with it in the sixteenth century. Eventually a lexical split occurred: *staffs* won out as the plural of *staff*, but a new singular *stave* was backformed to *staves* in the specialized meaning 'wooden side-piece of a cask'.

In the derivation of verbs from nouns the rule no longer applies automatically; note that one *reefs* sails, that trees *leaf* out (since 1611 – they used to *leave* out, and one still *interleaves* pages), and so on. But though many of the examples with voicing go back to the fourteenth century or beyond, there are a few more modern additions. For instance, the noun *grease* was borrowed (from Old French *graisse*) with a non-alternating voiceless fricative (like *piece*), and the derived verb was still often spelled *to grece* at the beginning of the sixteenth century; an unambiguous example with a voiced fricative (spelled *z*!) first appears in 1575, and [s] and [z] have been in competition in that verb ever since. *To sheave* first appears in 1579, *to shelve* first in Shakespeare. Conversely, the noun corresponding to the verb *to believe* was originally also *believe*; the modern form *belief* begins to appear in the sixteenth century, backformed from the verb. (There are also more complex examples; see the *OED* s.vv. *close* v., *proof, thieve*.) It seems clear that in derivation the fricative voicing rule remained at least partly productive in early Modern English, though it no longer seems to be so; it is now firmly restricted to a (fairly large) class of lexical items. But the rule is still coherent – it is the same rule for derived verbs as for noun plurals – and it is certainly not yet dead.

A sharply contrasting case is the loss of the final devoicing rule in most of the southern dialects of German and in Yiddish. In most Swiss and Austrian dialects of German, in the dialects of southern Germany, and in Yiddish the rule has been lost completely; the only forms which still show its effects are those in which its output had been projected into underlying forms in the absence of alternations, such as Swiss *vek*, Yiddish *avek* 'away' (OHG *in weg* 'on one's way'). For instance, corresponding to standard German [tʰaːk, tʰaːgə] 'day, days' we find [tag, tag] in the Swiss dialect of Schaffhausen (Wanner 1941: 162) and Yiddish [tog, teg] (with an innovative umlauting plural, see above). It seems clear that such a paradigm as (nom.-acc. sg.) *taːk, (nom.-acc. pl.) *taːgə became *taːk, *taːg upon the loss of word-final *-ə, and that the devoicing rule was then lost because it was morphologically conditioned and therefore opaque. We need to ask how this process was different from the process of rule loss in the English case just discussed.

As in late ME, the loss of word-final *-ə was thoroughgoing in these dialects. For instance, though Yiddish has plenty of word-final ə's, few reflect MHG ə's (cf. Jacobs 2005: 102–4, 154–61). Yiddish nouns typically have no case endings, there are no noun plurals in -ə, and no verb forms end in -ə; quite a few attributive forms of adjectives do (ibid. pp. 172–3), but since they precede the noun, their -ə's are not phrase-final. It certainly looks like phrase-final *-ə was lost by a single sound change. The situation in Swiss German dialects is similar: though word-final -ə's do exist, most or all reflect earlier -ən (even in the 1sg. pres. indic. of verbs; cf. e.g. Keller 1961: 55–9, 61–4, 66, 69–70, 97–100, 102). Historical investigation reveals that inherited -ə was lost in most of the southern dialects of German by the sound change known as "Upper German apocope" (ibid. pp. 44, 204). Apocope is first recorded in twelfth-century Bavarian documents (König 2001: 159); by the end of the fifteenth century it had spread throughout Bavaria, Württemberg, and much of Switzerland and Austria (Besch 1967: 254–7). Since then it has spread across the Main and Rhine, down the Rhine, and to most of the southern border of the German-speaking area, as well as to Yiddish, leaving only isolated relic areas in southern Switzerland and southwestern Austria (König 2001: 159). In the eastern (i.e. Bavarian) half of the southern German-speaking area, the final devoicing rule has been lost in all and only those dialects in which word-final *-ə has been lost (Kranzmayer 1956: 79). In the western (i.e. Alemannic and Rhenish) half of the area, that is largely true as well (Jutz 1931: 177–8, 190, 225–8, Lessiak 1933: 35–6); for instance, all the High German dialects described in Keller 1961 have lost both final *-ə and the devoicing rule except for Lëtzeburjesch, the Rhenish dialect of Luxemburg, near the northwestern extremity of the High German speech area, which has generally lost *-ə but still shows devoicing.[11]

We suggest that the loss of word-final /-ə/ in these dialects was relatively rapid, and that language learners therefore found it too hard to learn the resulting alternation between word-final voiceless and voiced stops, which was completely opaque phonologically. Note that this is exactly parallel to the loss of the

Table 6.16 *Some Maori verbs and their derivatives*

Verb	Passive	Gerund
puri 'hold'	puritia	puritaŋa
hopu 'catch'	hopukia	hopukaŋa
kimi 'look for'	kimihia	kimihaŋa
inu 'drink'	inumia	inumaŋa
tatau 'count'	tatauŋia	tatauŋaŋa
mau 'carry'	mauria	mauraŋa

[-f] ~ [-v] alternation in English adjectives that likewise resulted from the loss of word-final /-ə/ and likewise appears to have been rapid. But the English fricative voicing rule applied in a wider range of environments. Why it should have been so hard for native language learners to acquire a word-final voicing alternation as a grammatical marker is not so clear; typologically it seems much less unusual than the Insular Celtic stem-initial consonant alternations, for example, which are likewise grammatically conditioned and have survived for centuries in all the languages in which they arose. Possibly the fact that many lexemes ended in non-alternating consonants encouraged the abandonment of the rule. As in so many cases, more work on this problem is needed.

A very different case of rule loss is provided by Maori, the Polynesian language of New Zealand. Like all Polynesian languages and most other Oceanic languages, Maori has no word-final consonants; all words end in vowels. But Proto-Austronesian, the earliest reconstructable ancestor of Oceanic, had numerous word-final consonants; in fact, most major lexemes were of the shape CVCVC. The loss of word-final consonants in Proto-Oceanic (or soon after that language began to diversify) gave rise to numerous alternations which still persist in many of the daughter languages, including Maori; note the Maori verbs and their derivatives in Table 6.16 (see Hohepa 1967: 106, 109–10, Hale 1973: 414–15). The stems of these verbs must once have been underlyingly /purit/, /hopuk/, etc. (or their ancestors), and the passive and gerund suffixes must have been /-ia/ and /-aŋa/ respectively; further, there must have been a rule deleting consonants word-finally. But that is no longer the correct analysis for modern Maori. Kenneth Hale's summary of the relevant facts regarding the formation of the Maori passive is worth quoting in full (Hale 1973: 417):

> (1) Stems which are basically nominal are often used verbally in spontaneous discourse; when they are so used, in the passive, they regularly take the ending /-tia/. (2) Derived causatives (formed with the prefix /whaka-/) take /-tia/ in the passive even if the basic verb stem takes another alternant when not in the causative. (3) There is a rule whereby certain adverbials are made to agree in voice with the verbs they modify; these adverbials take /-tia/ in the passive regardless of the shape of the passive ending which the verb itself

takes. (4) Borrowings from English, including unassimilated consonant-final ones, take the ending /-tia/ in the passive. (5) Compound verbs derived by incorporating a noun from an adverbial phrase regularly form their passives in /-tia/. (6) In general, /-tia/ can be used when the conventional passive termination for a given verb is not remembered.

(An example of (1) is *wharetia* 'be housed' from *whare* 'house' [Hohepa 1967: 50].) The facts regarding the formation of gerunds are parallel (so far as the syntax of the language allows). It is clear from this pattern of facts that the entire system has been reanalyzed in Maori: lexemes end in vowels not only on the surface, but also underlyingly; the default alternants of the passive and gerund suffixes are /-tia/ and /-taŋa/ respectively, but closed classes of verbs instead use alternants beginning with other consonants (always the same consonant for both suffixes for any given verb). The rule deleting word-final consonants has been lost incidentally to this reanalysis, because there are no longer any word-final consonants (at any stage of the derivation) for it to delete (Kiparsky 1982a: 203).

The great differences between the three mechanisms of phonological rule loss discussed here suggest that rules might also be lost in other ways. Much more work must be done before we can suggest even a catalogue of typical mechanisms of rule loss.

Morphological influence on the development of phonological rules

Modern High German has lost many instances of inherited word-final /-ə/, but the losses in recent centuries have been heavily conditioned by morphology. For instance, the dative singular ending /-ə/ has been lost almost completely within the past two centuries, the homonymous plural suffix has been retained with little or no variation, and one currently hears considerable variation in the pronunciation of the present indicative 1sg. ending – even though all three were already phonetically identical /-ə/ in MHG, more than half a millennium ago. This is not a typical case of regular sound change; but then what is it?

The development of -ən in the southern and midland dialects of early ME was very similar. The merger of OE unstressed vowels in ə in the eleventh century (Luick 1914–40: 320, 489–92) and the late OE replacement of the inflectional ending -um by -ən (ibid. pp. 923–4) made the inflectional ending -ən exceptionally polyfunctional; it marked the following grammatical categories:

(35)   a. the oblique cases of the singular of n-stem nouns;
        b. the plural of n-stem nouns, except the genitive plural (which ended in -ənə);
        c. the dative singular masculine and neuter of strong adjectives;
        d. most of the caseforms (singular and plural) of weak adjectives;

     e. the dative plural of all nouns and adjectives;
     f. the plural of the subjunctive, both present and past, of all verbs;
     g. the plural of the past indicative of all verbs;
     h. the plural of the present indicative of a small, closed class of verbs, the
          so-called "preterite-presents";
     i. the past participle of strong verbs;
     j. the infinitive of all verbs.

Throughout the area south of the river Humber the *-n* of this inflectional syllable was lost variably; different early ME texts exhibit different degrees and patterns of loss, but in all the *-n* is missing more often in some grammatical categories than in others (Moore 1927: 232–4). By the early thirteenth century, when ME texts become extensive enough for more than tentative analysis, the loss of *-n* was well under way, so that they reveal little about the process of loss. However, Samuel Moore observed that the final *-n* of inflectional syllables is frequently omitted in twelfth-century copies of OE texts, evidently because the scribes no longer always pronounced it. His examination of the omission of *-n* in nominal endings in fifteen twelfth-century copies found substantially more omission in singular forms of n-stem nouns than in noun plurals in every text, and in some texts (though by no means all) substantially more omission of *-n* in weak adjective forms than in nouns (Moore 1927: 235–41). Since the loss of *-n* must have been greater in speech than in copies of older texts, it is clear that the process of loss must already have been well under way in the twelfth century and is likely to have begun before that. Omission of final *-n* in eleventh-century texts is uncommon, but there are enough examples to show that the process of loss had already begun, and the distribution of omissions is similar to that in twelfth-century copies (ibid. pp. 241–7). Evidently the loss of *-n* in unstressed syllables in English occurred over much more than a century, though the process probably was not as prolonged as the loss of *-ə* in Modern High German.

    These two cases are of interest because they are clear exceptions to the generalization that sound changes are conditioned only by phonological factors. In principle it would be possible to treat them as combinations of a sound change and morphological changes ("analogy"; so Moore 1927: 248–56 in considerable detail). But the fact that the morphological conditioning took place while the sound change was still in the variable stage seems significant. It is reasonable to hypothesize that morphological conditioning was possible in these cases *because* the variable stage of the sound change lasted for more than two or three generations (unlike the course of typical vowel rotations, for instance, and very unlike the course of typical mergers). Apparently if a sound change that affects a range of different inflectional markers stabilizes, even temporarily, at the variable stage for a long enough period, native learners can reanalyze the variation differently for different inflectional markers. It is not clear that the usual mechanisms of morphological change operate in these circumstances. For instance, if the loss of dative singular -ə in modern German is supposed to be modeled on some other, related inflectional form, what form could that possibly be? The dative plural always ends in -ən; nouns that have had no ending in the dative singular for some centuries are feminine and/or end in unstressed syllables, whereas dative singular -ə was restricted to masculines and neuters ending in a stressed syllable. It seems much more likely that native learners, presented with variation between -ə and ∅ for this category, increasingly decided that the ending was dispensable (whereas the noun plural ending, for example, was not).

The obvious question is what relation this phenomenon has to the structure of the grammar. Kiparsky proposed that "the morphology of a language is subject to overall paradigmatic conditions of a functional nature," of which one consequence is that functionally important markers tend to be preserved in language change whereas redundant markers tend to be lost (Kiparsky 1982a: 88–99, including consideration of the two cases discussed here). But if changes begin as learner errors, it is not clear that we should expect them to bear any relation to the structure of adult native-speaker grammars.

On the other hand, the fact that native learners *can* reanalyze stable variable phonological rules along morphological lines might lead us to ask whether those rules are really superficial phonetic implementation rules, regardless of the fact that they obviously have gradient outputs. The answer is not obvious, if only because modern work in phonology and morphology shows that the relationship between the two is not hierarchical. Mismatches between phonological and morphological structure are commonplace; a standard example is the English adjective *unhappier*, which is phonologically [un][happier], with two stress-based feet, but morphologically [[[un][happy]]er] (the meaning is 'more [not happy]', not 'not [more happy]'). The only way to account for this pervasive phenomenon is the hypothesis that phonology and morphosyntax are parallel computational systems complexly linked. We may therefore need to ask, in effect, how close to the phonetic surface a phonological process has to be in order to render it inaccessible to morphological analysis and manipulation on the part of native learners.

Some of these phenomena have recently been dealt with in the context of homophony avoidance by Jean-François Mondon (Mondon 2009). Mondon concludes that homophony avoidance is one of the strategies that native learners employ to minimize ambiguity in the language(s) they are learning. Since surface homophony of morphosyntactically distinct forms is a significant source of ambiguity, this NLA tactic can appear to cause morphological interference in the implementation of a sound change, even though the motivation for the use of the tactic was purely phonological (i.e. the preservation of a useful phonological contrast). An immediate desideratum for future work is to sort out which apparent examples of morphological interference in sound change can be explained as purely phonological in this way and which ones must reflect real morphological interference.

In Chapter 8 we will address changes that are unarguably morphological in nature from a modern perspective. In order to do so, however, we must first discuss morphological structure in Chapter 7.

Notes

1 Though higher mid long vowels are spelled ει and ου in our standardized Ancient Greek orthography, early inscriptions of many dialects, including Attic, spell them with single vowel letters, which shows that they were not diphthongs; see Allen 1987: 69–79 for discussion. Unfortunately there were also real diphthongs that are also spelled ει and ου; one has to know all attested forms of a word to determine whether it contains a real or a "spurious" diphthong. These long vowels and diphthongs merged early in the fourth century BCE; that is the reason for the unetymological standard spellings.

2 The feminine suffix of 'all' (and many other adjectives) was originally *-ja; what its underlying form in Classical Attic was is unclear. In our discussion of the 2CL we give it as /-sa/ for simplicity's sake, since it became -sa at some point in the derivation.

3 Classical Latin *lingua* appears to have been remodeled by lexical analogy with the unrelated verb *lingere* 'to lick'. A similar remodeling seems to have occurred independently in Lithuanian and in Armenian.

4 That dissimilation in Iberian Latin 'tree' was intramorphemic seems surprising: we might expect the two *r*'s of Latin *arbor* to have been a single melodic feature bundle linked to two C-slots – note that Latin had no constraint against adjacent *r*'s – in which case the dissimilation appears to be a violation of the Obligatory Contour Principle. However, see the discussion of Kenstowicz 1994: 532–7 with references.

5 However, geminates (which do not arise in the inflection of these verb stems) apparently have only a single aspiration feature, noted in writing on the second member, as in the names *Sappʰó:* Σαπφώ and *Bákkʰos* Βάκχος (as one would expect, given that geminates are not clusters but single articulations occupying two C-slots). That in turn suggests that the aspiration of the first members of the clusters *pʰtʰ* φθ and *kʰtʰ* χθ is real, though what its phonetic realization was might be beyond recovery.

6 The conditioning of OE fricative voicing by stress seems peculiar, but the fact that the abstract noun suffixes *-þ(u)* and *-s* did not undergo it, at a time when they must still have been *-iþu and *-isi, seems to demand the restriction; so does the voicelessness of the cluster in *bletsian* 'to bless' < *blōdisōjan 'to sprinkle with (sacrificial) blood'. It is also clear that fricatives in the onsets of stressed syllables preceded by prefixes, e.g. in *beforan* 'in front (of)', were not voiced. The positive exceptions mentioned by Campbell (1962: 179–80) must reflect later episodes of intervocalic fricative voicing – of which there are naturally few examples, since most potential inputs had already been voiced. This problem would repay further study.

7 Great care is needed in assessing the impact of OF loanwords on ME phonology, for several reasons. In the first place, some nouns now spelled with word-final *-ce* were borrowed without word-final /-ə/; for instance, *pais* 'peace' is attested from 1154 and *vois* 'voice' from the 1290's. On the other hand, *service* was probably first borrowed with [-zə]: it appears as *serfise* in the entry of the *Peterborough Chronicle* for the year 1070 and as *servise* in several twelfth-century compositions, and throughout the middle ages spellings with *s* and with *c* both remain common (see the *OED* s.v.). Both spellings also occur in OF, and it appears that some French dialects had /s/ and others /z/ in this word. In the case of word-initial *v-* the pitfalls are different. South of the Thames and in the lower Severn valley word-initial anterior fricatives were voiced sometime in the eleventh century (Luick 1914–40: 933–8); thus OF loanwords with initial *v-* would not necessarily have altered the phonology of those dialects (it would depend on how loanwords with initial *f-* were treated). In the north the coexistence of spellings such as *voys* and *woys* for 'voice' strongly suggests that OF *v-* was borrowed into those dialects as /w/, again with no impact

on the phonology of the language. The crucial evidence must thus come from the East Midlands – and from before *c*. 1350, because around that time word-final /-ə/ began to be lost, and that too would have created a contrast between voiced and voiceless anterior fricatives. As it happens, quite a few OF loanwords with initial *v-* are attested from the East Midlands between about 1250 and about 1340; they include at least *veil* (*Genesis and Exodus*, ca. 1250), *venison* (*Havelok the Dane*, late thirteenth century), *vacant, vanity, venomous, versle* ('to sing psalms'), *very, vestiment, vile, violence, virgin, virtue, vision, visit, void*, and *vow* (all in the works of Robert Manning of Brunne, active 1303–1338).

8   To evaluate the cognates cited from other languages the reader needs to know that in word-initial position PIE aspirated stops became voiced stops in Germanic, but fricatives in the Italic languages; in both cases the outcomes are etymologically unambiguous. The Greek and Oscan nouns meaning 'wall' must originally have referred to earthen ramparts or mud-brick walls; cf. also Sanskrit *dehī́* 'earthwork', *déhat* '(s)he will daub'.

9   This "two-aspirate root" solution is not quite as simple as the text suggests. Note that stops actually *assimilate* in voicing and aspiration to a following obstruent, as mediopassive perfect infinitives in /-sthai/ demonstrate, but that the aspiration of such an assimilated stop does *not* trigger dissimilatory loss of the root-initial aspiration. This can be handled by exception features (so e.g. Sommerstein 1973: 45–6), but an account which relies on the fact that the aspiration is not strictly internal to the root (because it is also linked to a C-slot outside the root) seems preferable.

10   Word-final *-e* must be consistently pronounced to make the verse of Chaucer, who died in 1400, scan; in the verse of his younger imitators there is no such consistency. The only plausible explanation for this pattern of facts is that Chaucer was linguistically conservative in this respect – that is, he made no use in his verse of the variable loss of /-ə/ that was current in the speech of his generation – and that his imitators were not. For further details see Jespersen 1909: 186–90.

11   There is a further fact that necessarily complicates any assessment of the loss of devoicing in High German: most of the more northerly High German dialects, including the other relevant dialects that Keller describes (Alsatian and the dialect of Darmstadt), have largely merged the voiced and voiceless obstruents as a result of the "binnenhochdeutsche Konsonantenschwächung" (Lessiak 1933: 13); they could have lost the devoicing rule as a result of that merger, and it is generally difficult to tell whether they lost it before the merger occurred.

7   Morphology

Traditional historical linguists have amassed a large body of facts about specific morphological changes in particular languages, yet there is very little literature on the subject that takes modern advances in theory into consideration. This chapter will briefly describe some aspects of a recent approach to morphology, Distributed Morphology (DM), in the generative tradition. In the following chapter we will use those concepts to analyze well-attested types of morphological change.

Morphological theory and morphological change

When it became clear in the 1870s that sound change is normally regular in phonological terms, historical linguists undertook to separate regular sound changes from other types of change in the forms of words. The latter were classed together as "analogy," defined as the influence of forms on other forms. It became generally accepted that analogical change typically operates in terms of proportions between sets of forms. For instance, the replacement of English *besought* by *beseeched* (attested as an alternative at least since John Milton) can be explained by the following analogical proportion, given that the past tense of *preach* is *preached*:

(1)   *preach* : *preached* : : *beseech* : X; X = *beseeched*.

But this approach was always empirically inadequate, because a substantial minority of morphological changes cannot be explained convincingly by proportions. For instance, the replacement of *digged* by *dug* (first as a past participle in the sixteenth century, then also as a finite past tense in the eighteenth), or of *sticked* by *stuck* (first in the sixteenth century), might conceivably be explained by proportional analogy with verbs like *sting* : *stung*, in spite of the fact that all the older examples have roots ending in nasals, and *struck* (seventeenth century) might originally have been the past participle of northern English *strick*, only later accepted into the paradigm of standard *strike* (cf. Seebold 1966: 18 with n. 49). But no proportion can be constructed to explain past tenses like *hung* (first in the sixteenth century) and *snuck* (nineteenth century, North American), because their roots *hang* and *sneak* do not contain the vowel /ɪ/. Conversely, it is not difficult to construct proportions that give utterly implausible results. For instance, the plural of *moose* (borrowed into English from Eastern Abnaki, an Algonkian language) is usually *moose*, apparently on the model of native *deer* : *deer*. A proportion *goose* : *geese* : : *moose* : X is just as acceptable formally, yet the result "*meese*" is a joke. Attempts to constrain this theory have been disappointing. Jerzy Kuryłowicz's celebrated "laws" of analogy (Kuryłowicz 1949) are far from exceptionless; Witold Mańczak's work on analogical tendencies (Mańczak 1958) provides plenty of good information on what is likely to happen but amounts to no more than a set of statistical observations.

Since 1960 further reasons to doubt the traditional approach to morphological change have accumulated. Many "analogical" changes can be shown to be phonological (see the preceding chapter). Others are fundamentally syntactic; for instance, the process by which the functions of the inherited dative, locative, and ablative cases were assigned to a single case (called the dative) in Proto-Germanic was a reduction in the number of morphosyntactic categories, not just a change in morphology. There are also purely morphological changes; for instance, in Old English (OE) a single ending came to be used for the nominative plural and accusative plural in each class of nominals (except the first- and second-person pronouns), a single set of forms came to be used for all three genders in the plural of pronouns and determiners, and the 3pl. form came to be used for all three persons in the plural of finite verb paradigms. But the morphosyntactic categories did not change, and for the most part these "syncretisms" cannot be explained as the result of sound changes; therefore they must have been purely morphological changes. A theory of linguistic change which does not distinguish between these different types of change cannot be correct. But the most serious shortcoming of the traditional approach is that it does not take native language acquisition (NLA) into account. It has long been clear that children acquire their native language(s) by constructing systems of rules. Since most changes in linguistic structure must begin as native-learner errors, a model of morphological change must be based on the systems of rules that native learners construct. Recently Charles Yang has investigated how well models based on surface analogy and on rules account for the actual performance of children in learning English irregular verbs (Yang 2002: 59–100). His rule-based model accounts for the pattern of the children's errors much better than a surface analogy model.

Confronting actual studies of acquisition with data from the historical record leads almost immediately to interesting questions; here is an example. Reported morphological acquisition errors are mostly of two types: failure to express a morphosyntactic category that is obligatorily expressed in the target language, and overuse of default or other productive patterns of inflection. Use of forms which are incorrect in other ways appears to be rare. For instance, Xu and Pinker report that among 20,000 English past tense forms used by nine children drawn from several databases only 0.2 percent – one in every 500 – was an *incorrect irregular* form like *brung* (Xu and Pinker 1995: 531). This is not an isolated finding; studies of the acquisition of German and Italian yield similar results (Yang 2002: 69 with n. 7 and references). Yet the written record of English is littered with innovative irregular verb forms. Regular verbs that have become irregular within the attested history of English include at least *catch, dig, dream, kneel, ring, stick, string, strive, wear,* and in the USA *dive* (see the *OED* s.vv.; there are also several more involved examples). And those are only the innovative irregularities that have become part of the standard dialect; a full list of attested forms would be much longer. Some such forms have almost certainly arisen repeatedly. For instance, a past participle *brungen* occurs half a dozen times in OE poetry, and a corresponding *brung* occurs in traditional Appalachian ballads (as sung by Jean Ritchie), but there does not seem to be a continuous historical link between the two; such a past participle must somehow be a natural and repeatable error.

It will be easier to account for unexpected morphological innovations if we take several facts into account. First of all, it is not accurate to describe all the "weird past tense forms" of Xu and Pinker 1995 as irregular. A large proportion of non-default English past tense forms are formed by lexically restricted rules (Yang 2002: 59–100), and a large proportion of Xu and Pinker's unexpected forms use just two of those rules, namely replacement of the the root syllable coda /-ɪŋ/ with /-æŋ/ and replacement of the root vowel /ɪ/ with /ʌ/ (Xu and Pinker 1995: 540–3). Genuine irregularization may be very rare, but the incorrect generalization of minor rules might not be.

Moreover, it is possible that studies of native acquisition errors are not counting events of the relevant kind. In order to become a historical change a native-learner error must persist beyond the window for NLA. What matters, then, is not how often children in general produce incorrect irregular past tenses, but *how many children* persist in using *even one* such form into middle childhood. Xu and Pinker did ask whether there are children who systematically irregularize, but found that "[t]he CHILDES transcripts simply do not contain enough samples from any child to rule out systematic irregularizations of particular verbs at particular ages by particular children" (Xu and Pinker 1995: 544). It might also be observed that a sample of nine children, or even several dozen children, is utterly inadequate: if even one in a thousand children produces such an innovative irregularity consistently, what we see in the historical record would not be surprising, and if one in a hundred does so we might well wonder why we do not find more forms of this type. In short, we might need much more data, and the sample might need to be constructed very differently.

The above is a very "quick and dirty" discussion of a straightforward problem in reconciling data from the historical record and data from NLA, yet it shows clearly that further study along the same lines is very likely to yield progress in solving old puzzles. Since progress can only be made within a coherent theory of morphology, we next need to ask what a theory of morphology needs to account for. (At this point readers who are familiar with only morphology-poor languages such as Modern English would do well to read the first two chapters of Spencer 1991, which present basic morphological concepts in a pretheoretical way.)

Morphological patterns

We here offer a brief discussion of several basic ideas that became influential in generative thinking about morphology, some of which have been adopted by DM while others have been rejected.

Chomsky 1970 pointed out that there is a pervasive constellation of differences between English deverbal nouns like *destruction* and gerunds like *destroying*, both in their syntactic behavior and in the way that they are formed; what is most relevant to morphology is that gerunds are formed by a single fully productive rule, while the formation of deverbal nouns is lexically idiosyncratic. It seemed to follow that while the formation of gerunds could be handled by the syntax, a different set of rules is needed for derivational morphology, and those rules ought to be located in the lexicon, where all the idiosyncrasies of the grammar are housed. The necessary enrichment of the lexicon (which obviously was not just a list) was explored in Jackendoff 1975 and Aronoff 1976; Paul Kiparsky evolved a theory, lexical phonology, in which morphological and phonological rules alternated in a cycle within the lexicon (Kiparsky 1982b).

The place of inflectional morphology in native-speaker grammars seemed less clear. Halle 1973 placed it too within the lexicon. But because inflection is, in effect, morphology which is relevant to the rules of syntax, locating it in the lexicon entails allowing complex interactions between syntactic rules and the lexicon. Obvious alternatives are to make inflection (or at least regular inflection) part of the syntax itself (see Spencer 1991: 205–8 with references) or to locate it among the rules of the phonology (see especially Anderson 1982). A range of variations on both approaches is discussed in Spencer 1991. Recognizing a separate component of the grammar to house inflection seems to have been resisted by appeal to Occam's Razor (cf. Aronoff 1994: 165). Disagreements about the nature of inflection entailed disagreements about the theoretical status of inflectional paradigms. But regardless of one's position on that question, it is possible to state a number of constraints on paradigms that hold up reasonably well cross-linguistically. That line of research was pursued especially by Andrew Carstairs-McCarthy; Carstairs 1987 is a full presentation of his arguments and conclusions. If paradigms are not a feature of grammars, some other explanation for the generalizations that can be made about them must be found.

A different set of questions bears on the relationship between form and meaning. Mark Aronoff pointed out that there are formal units that must be recognized as morphemes but have no definable meanings (Aronoff 1976: 11–15). An example is English /-si:v/ (or /-sijv/) *-ceive*, which must be a unit because it has an idiosyncratic allomorph /-sɛp-/ *-cep-* that appears before obstruents; some examples of compounds of this morpheme are given in (2):

(2)   a. conceive : conception, concept
            b. deceive : deception, deceptive
            c. perceive : perception, perceptive, percept
            d. receive : reception, receptive, receptacle

(Note also *precept* and *contraception*.) But *-ceive* has no definable meaning; only its compounds have meanings, and there is no semantic common denominator between them. In inflectional paradigms we even encounter morphemes which are completely empty semantically. A standard example is the Navajo morpheme *yi-* which is prefixed to verbs if and only if there is no other vowel in the prefix complex to the right of the disjunct boundary (Kari 1976: 36–45, 104–14 with references); this "peg prefix" has a phonological function rather than a meaning. In so familiar a language as Latin we find a more complex example. Aronoff 1994: 34–9 argues persuasively that the "third stem" of a Latin verb – the fourth "principal part" – is a semantically empty stem to which a very diverse set of forms is constructed, and he points out that cases of this kind are good evidence for an autonomous module of morphology, not reducible to phonology and syntax.

Conversely, just as there are "pieces" of words with no meaning or function, so there are meanings and functions which are expressed not by any piece, but by a process. Familiar examples are English *men*, *women*, *feet*, *teeth*, *geese*, *mice*, *lice* and the large class of German plurals exemplified by *Väter*, *Mütter*, *Brüder*, *Töchter*, in which plurality is indicated by changing the vowel of the root (in German by means of a pervasive phonological rule; see the preceding chapter). Almost every conceivable analysis of this last phenomenon has been proposed in the generative tradition at one time or another.

Finally, some account must be taken of the internal structure of words. There is a long line of work in the generative tradition on the constituent structure of derivationally complex words (see Spencer 1991: 183–90, 197–205 with references). A solid result of this line of research is that derivational morphology is hierarchical and can be represented by trees that share many of the properties of syntactic trees. Most strikingly, it is clear that one component of each derived word is the word's "head," which determines the lexical class of the word and interacts with the rules of syntax, including inflection; the head is normally the last category-changing affix that is added in derivation (Williams 1981, Spencer 1991: 184–7). For instance, the head of the verb *withstand* is the basic verb *stand*; the prefix *with-* does not change the lexical class of the lexeme, so that the structure of the word is [with+stand]$_V$ (i.e., it is compounded, not derived) and the past tense is *withstood*. However, because the verb *grandstand* is derived from the noun *grandstand* by zero affixation, the structure of this verb is [[grand+stand]$_N$∅]$_V$; the head is the zero affix, which triggers default past tense morphology, and as a result the past is *grandstanded* (see Spencer 1991: 184–6). There are obvious similarities between these structures and syntactic phrase structure trees, and the link between the heads of words and the heads of X-bar phrases naturally awakens the suspicion that derivational morphology is in fact word-internal syntax.

The proposal that word formation might literally be syntax receives strong support from Mark Baker's spectacular work on lexical incorporation (Baker 1988a). Baker argues persuasively that productively derived causatives, applicatives, antipassives, and possessor ascension constructions result from the incorporation into a verb of lexical heads which the verb dominates; he even suggests such an analysis for passives. Most importantly, Baker proposes the "Mirror Principle," which states that the order of morphological affixation is identical to the order of syntactic operations because the affixes are the result of the syntactic operations (Baker 1985, 1988a: 12–15, 22–3). Though counterexamples to the Mirror Principle can be found, it is supported by a large majority of examples from a wide range of languages. Baker's work makes sense of so much morphological structure as word-internal syntax that the hypothesis that all piecebased morphology is syntax becomes worth serious exploration. It appears that many of the inferences drawn from Chomsky 1970 were premature (see Siddiqi 2009: 10–13 with references).

A theory of morphology that accommodates all these facts and conclusions must analyze most morphology as syntax, yet recognize an autonomous module of morphology for those phenomena that cannot be syntactic; it must also give an account of morphological processes as well as pieces and must deal with a number of issues not raised above, such as the place of defaults in morphological systems and the existence of rigid "templates" in some inflectional systems (e.g. Semitic imperfective verbs, see Noyer 1997: 3–57). Above all, it must be a theory of the architecture of natural-language grammars, since syntax, phonology, autonomous morphology, and the lexicon are all involved. In our estimation the most promising approach that does all these things is Distributed Morphology.

Some useful aspects of Distributed Morphology

No book-length introduction to DM has yet appeared. Short introductions to the theory are Harley and Noyer 1999, Embick and Noyer 2007, Rolf Noyer's web page "Distributed Morphology" (www.ling.upenn.edu/ ~rnoyer/dm), and Siddiqi 2009: 7–26. Book-length discussions of particular issues in DM are Noyer 1997 and Siddiqi 2009. We do not here present a full description of the theory, for which the reader should consult the references given; instead we outline specific claims and analyses of DM which we find useful in explicating morphological change.

DM adopts the hypothesis that structure within words is hierarchical in the same way that sentential structure is, and that all hierarchical structures are generated by the syntax. Moreover, all syntactic structure, including morphosyntactic categories, is held to be autonomous and abstract. No syntactic structure is projected from lexemes, and no phonologically relevant material (such as the shapes of inflectional markers) is present in syntactic trees as generated; all such material is inserted after the tree is in place. This makes intuitive sense for a reason that every experienced linguist is aware of. Like the argument structures and case frames of (sentential) syntax, the structures of words are not idiosyncratic to the same degree that unanalyzable roots are idiosyncratic; in each language there is a fairly small number of fixed patterns into which compounds and derived lexemes fit, and affixes expressing comparable morphosyntactic categories are usually found in the same positions in the inflected word. If syntactic structure, external or internal, were projected from lexemes, we might expect a much greater variety of structures, given the highly idiosyncratic meanings of lexical material. Of course the word-internal structures and the word-external structures are often different in detail, but generating them with the same "machinery" is still the most economical approach.

This necessitates a substantial shift in the way we think about morphology. Most obviously, DM gives a complex answer to the thorny question, "What is a word?" Words have no theoretical status in DM; word boundaries are consequences of superficial morphological and phonological constraints which can differ substantially from language to language, and mismatches between hierarchical structure and word boundaries are not surprising. Anyone whose linguistic experience extends beyond a single family of languages or a single area of the world should find this realistic. Moreover, changes in exactly where the boundaries of words fall – such as the univerbation of postpositions with nouns, or the cutting loose of an inflectional marker as a clitic – are not exceptional phenomena requiring special explanations. We will return to these points in the following chapter.

DM modularizes the lexicon, much as the rules of the grammar fall into separate modules with different properties. Meaningful units, called "idioms," are listed in an Encyclopedia; they can be roots, affixes, free-standing phonological words, or groups of words in construction with one another (i.e. idioms in the pretheoretical sense). By contrast, information about which phonological pieces can be inserted at which syntactic terminal nodes is given in a separate list, the Vocabulary. Some terminal nodes are marked with morphosyntactic categories, or bundles of such categories; for instance, the trees corresponding to the English words *dogs* and *feet* include a rightmost node marked [pl]. Other nodes, called root nodes, are filled with what are usually called members of the major word classes (verbs, nouns, adjectives). In the latter case the insertion of any of a large number of phonological strings will yield a grammatical utterance, but in the former case there is typically only one that will do. Morphemes for which there is no choice of what to insert are called "f-morphemes" ("functional morphemes"); those for which there is a choice are "l-morphemes" ("lexical morphemes"). They roughly correspond respectively to the grammatical markers and lexemes of other analyses. The Vocabulary is a list of all the phonological strings that can be inserted at syntactic terminal nodes, each string paired with a specification of

$$[[[\sqrt{\text{Arrive}}]\ N]\ pl]$$
$$|\qquad\quad |\ \ \ |$$
$$[\text{ərayv}\quad +\text{əl}+z]$$

Figure 7.1 *Syntactic structure of the word* arrivals

the information that must be present at the syntactic terminal node at which it is inserted. For instance, the /-z/ of *dogs* is paired with the morphosyntactic feature [pl] which must be present at the node at which it is inserted, and that pairing is a Vocabulary item. Thus the Vocabulary encodes the sound-to-morphosyntax matchings of the language, and the Encyclopedia encodes the sound-to-meaning matchings of individual meaningful elements. Mismatches between sound units and morphosyntactic or semantic units are not exceptional, or even uncommon: consider the cross-linguistic prevalence of polysemy and of multiword idioms, and the notorious quirkiness in the meanings of derived words (emphasized by Jackendoff 1975). Presumably they are not even more common than they are because the system as a whole must be learnable.

The controversial distinction between inflection and derivation is not recognized as such by DM. It is a practically useful distinction in a large number of cases, but intermediate cases (such as participles and gerunds, especially in languages with rich nominal inflection) are so common that DM is surely right to abandon any attempt to draw a line between the two.

At the point of Vocabulary insertion a word thus has a double structure: a tree dominating terminal nodes with morphosyntactic information at each, and a string of phonological forms which are inserted at the nodes. Representing the tree by bracketing, the noun-deriving suffix by N, and the root by $\sqrt{}$ we can represent the structure of English *arrivals* as in Figure 7.1. Whereas the syntactic structure is hierarchical – in other words, it's a tree – the phonological structure is a one-dimensional ordered string at this point in the derivation. Phonological rules, some of them sensitive to the status of particular pieces of the string, can impose a hierarchical structure on the phonological representation, but any such structure is *not* simply read off the syntax. This analysis gives a maximally general and optimal account of the mismatches between syntactic constituent structure and phonological constituent structure noted by Williams 1981 and many others.

Two questions immediately arise. In cases where there is more than one Vocabulary item that is paired with the same morphosyntactic feature, how does the grammar determine which one is inserted? And how does the theory handle instances in which there is no one to one matching between morphosyntactic features and phonological strings? To both questions DM gives interesting answers that are relevant to morphological change. The most extensive and detailed discussion of these questions is still Noyer 1997, on which the following exposition is largely based. As usual, we will concentrate only on those findings of Noyer's that are likely to be most useful in accounting for morphological changes.

What happens in the morphological module of the grammar will be easiest to understand if we follow a hypothetical derivation from the output of syntax to the underlying phonological representation. In the default case Vocabulary insertion occurs at once, with one Vocabulary item inserted at each syntactic terminal node, but in more complex cases several quite different things can happen before Vocabulary insertion occurs. First, morphosyntactic features which are not present in the output of syntax can be added to nodes by a variety of operations that read the syntactic tree; these are called "dissociated morphemes" (Embick 1997: 7–8, 26–61). Depending in part on one's model of syntax, these include concord or agreement markers, case features, and [passive], among others. Secondly, adjacent nodes can fuse into a single node which then bears all the morphosyntactic features of the fused nodes; familiar examples are the fused (gender-)number-and-case endings of nominals in conservative Indo-European languages. Thirdly, the addition of "empty" nodes can be required by morphological well-formedness conditions; these are often called "thematic" affixes, generalizing a traditional term of Indo-European philology. For instance, all but a tiny handful of Latin verbs have present stems that end in a functionless vowel which is often absent from the perfect stem: *-ā-* for the first conjugation, *-ē-* for the second, *-ī-* for the fourth, short *-i-* for the (fewer than twenty) third-conjugation verbs with citation forms in *-iō* or (deponent) *-ior*, and some other short vowel, possibly underspecified, for the remaining third-conjugation verbs (Aronoff 1994: 48–53 suggests /-e-/, while Embick and Halle 2003 opt for /-i-/). It is reasonable to infer from that distributional fact that regular Latin present stems require the addition of an f-morpheme as a sister to the Root (or the Root plus any other present-stem-forming affix, such as the nasal infix or the suffix *-ess-*), and that the "theme vowels" are inserted at that node. It is also possible for the morphology to specify that a particular type of morphological word must have a fixed number of affixes in specified positions relative to the Root – in effect, a template – as in the Classical Arabic imperfective (Noyer 1997: 3–57). Finally, feature impoverishment can occur before Vocabulary insertion. How those two processes interact is best explained in the light of an example; we choose the Ancient Greek mediopassive verb endings to illustrate.

Ancient Greek verb endings are fused suffixes that mark the person and number of the subject. There are two complete sets, traditionally called "primary" and "secondary." The latter occur in the past tenses of the indicative (imperfect, aorist, and pluperfect) and in the optative mood; the primary tenses occur in nonpast indicative tenses and the subjunctive mood. There is also a set for the imperative mood which lacks first-person members, since the syntax does not generate first-person imperatives. Since the range of nonpast tenses is widest, we accept the hypothesis (implied by the traditional terminology) that the primary endings are the default endings.[1] Neither primary nor secondary endings directly express tense or mood; past tenses and the subjunctive and optative moods are clearly marked by other means, and the nonpast tense made from each stem is the default category. Thus the most economical analysis is that the secondary

Table 7.1 *Attic Greek mediopassive verb endings*

		Primary		Secondary		Imperative	
sg.	1	-mai	-μαι	-mɛːn	-μην	—	
	2	-(s)ai	-(σ)αι	-(s)o	-(σ)ο	-(s)o	-(σ)ο
	3	-tai	-ται	-to	-το	-stʰɔː	-σθω
du.	1	-metʰa	-μεθα	-metʰa	-μεθα	—	
	2	-stʰon	-σθον	-stʰon	-σθον	-stʰon	-σθον
	3	-stʰon	-σθον	-stʰɛːn	-σθην	-stʰɔːn	-σθων
pl.	1	-metʰa	-μεθα	-metʰa	-μεθα	—	
	2	-stʰe	-σθε	-stʰe	-σθε	-stʰe	-σθε
	3	-ntai	-νται	-nto	-ντο	-stʰɔːn	-σθων

endings are inserted in the context of other markers. Whether the imperative endings directly express mood is not so clear. Since several are shared with other sets of endings, we adopt the hypothesis that they too are inserted in the context of an imperative marker, which occupies the position of the other mood suffixes but is zero.

The sets of mediopassive endings in the Attic dialect of *c.* 400 BCE are given in Table 7.1. (The presence or absence of /s/ in the 2sg. endings is a phonological complication which has nothing to do with the morphological processes at issue here.) It can be seen that there are a number of syncretisms – that is, instances in which different bundles of morphosyntactic features are expressed by the same ending – in this table. The question is how to account for them. DM does so in the context of a universally unmarked hierarchy of features, in which person is ranked higher than number, which in turn is ranked higher than gender and other features (Noyer 1997: lxxv; the hierarchy is not absolutely universal, but deviations from it on the part of particular languages are held to be marked). Also relevant to the analysis is the hypothesis that duals are special, marked types of plurals, with a feature complex [du pl], so that when no Vocabulary item marking the dual is available the grammar defaults to the unmarked plural (Noyer 1997: lxxv). This latter hypothesis is strongly supported by the Indo-European facts; in every ancient or medieval Indo-European language which has dual verb endings for only some person(s) and/or marks duals more widely on nominals than verbs or vice versa – namely, in Ancient Greek, Germanic, Old Irish, and Tocharian – one always defaults to the corresponding plural marker in the absence of a suitable dual. The same phenomenon appears in Classical Arabic (Noyer 1997: lxviii).

One syncretism in the table of endings above involves the nonsingular first person: dual is not distinguished from plural, and that is a general fact about Greek verb inflection. This fact can be accounted for by means of an impoverishment filter, informally stated as

*[1 du] / T,

which prohibits feature bundles including first person and dual in finite verbs (i.e. in the presence of Tense; a more formal statement would specify that the filter applies when the finite verb has been Merged with Tense). The filter obviously applies after the fusion of terminal nodes, and it applies only to verb forms, since there are 1du. pronouns in Ancient Greek. The filter merely states that one of the relevant features must be changed, but since duals are marked [du pl], the redundant feature [du] is dropped, causing a default to plural. A similar solution might be proposed for the nonsingular third-person imperative endings, but in that case there is a further complication. Third-person finite verb forms are normally considered to be unmarked for person, since they exhibit default agreement (i.e. they agree with any subject NP that doesn't include the speaker or the addressee). However, it seems clear that the second person is the default for imperatives, and that other persons must be marked. Therefore we can propose an impoverishment filter

*[3 du] / [imperative],

which will lead to the 3pl. ending being used for the 3du. as well. However, we will see below that a third-person feature may also be needed to handle the pattern of syncretism in primary and secondary endings.

The remaining syncretisms can be handled by a system of defaults. Vocabulary insertion obeys the "subset principle" (Halle 1997 – essentially the "elsewhere condition," first employed by Pāṇini) as follows. A Vocabulary item must match all or a subset of the morphosyntactic features present at the terminal node at which it is inserted; if more than one Vocabulary item meets that description, the one that matches the greatest number of features must be chosen. (If a Vocabulary item is specified for any feature not present at the terminal node, it cannot be inserted at that node.) If the subset relation does not obtain between the features of two Vocabulary items, the one referring to the feature higher on the hierarchy is inserted first (Noyer 1997: 44–5). Bearing these principles in mind, the Vocabulary items of Table 7.1 might be ordered for insertion as listed below, with first person taking precedence over second, second over third (but see further below), and defaults last (thus plural after dual; see Noyer 1997: 42, 54).

-metʰa	1 pl
-mɛ:n	1 / secondary
-mai	1
-stʰe	2 pl
-(s)o	2 / secondary, imperative (see further below)
-(s)ai	2
-stʰɛ:n	3 du / secondary
-stʰɔ:n	3 pl / imperative
-nto	3 pl / secondary
-ntai	3 pl

-stʰɔ:	3 / imperative
-to	3 / secondary
-tai	3
-stʰon	du

This will work, but the details are problematic in two ways. First, the ending *-(s)o* is to be inserted under two disjunct conditions (in categories for which secondary endings are appropriate and in imperatives); a more parsimonious analysis would make it the default ending. Since imperative endings seem unlikely to be default endings, that would entail making the secondary endings default endings. There is no doubt that at some earlier stage of the language they were exactly that, but the architecture of the Ancient Greek verb system suggests strongly that the primary endings have become default endings instead.[2] We might therefore ascribe the disjunction in the Vocabulary item *-(s)o* to its survival from an earlier organization of the system in which it made more sense. Much more worrisome is the fact that a feature "3" must be recognized not only in imperatives (see above) but in the other sets of person-and-number endings. This is necessary in order to specify (by the subset principle) that secondary 3du. *-stʰɛ:n* is an exception to the generalization that dual forms are marked by the default ending *-sthon;* that *-sthon* is a default ending is in turn suggested by the fact that it marks all second-person duals and the 3du. in categories that take primary endings. If we abandon the latter hypothesis, we will no longer need to mark *-stʰɛ:n* as an exception, and it will follow that we no longer need to recognize the third-person feature for non-imperative finite verbs. Our ordered list will then be:

-metʰa	1 pl
-mɛ:n	1 / secondary
-mai	1
-stʰon	2 du
-stʰe	2 pl
-(s)o	2 / secondary, imperative (see above)
-(s)ai	2
-stʰɔ:n	3 pl / imperative
-stʰɔ:	3 / imperative
-stʰɛ:n	du / secondary
-stʰon	du
-nto	pl / secondary
-ntai	pl
-to	*elsewhere / secondary*
-tai	*elsewhere*

The last two endings (the 3sg. endings) are defaults in this analysis, *-to* being inserted when the relevant terminal node contains no features in the "secondary" context and *-tai* being inserted elsewhere. This accords better with the usual status of third-person verb forms cross-linguistically, but at the expense of recognizing two homonymous Vocabulary items which (suspiciously) just happen to be second-person dual and default dual.

We have presented these alternative analyses to make a point. As Indo-Europeanists have long suspected, there is no optimal analysis of the Ancient Greek person-and-number endings, nor of the similar systems to be found in other archaic Indo-European languages; not all the details "make sense," and a modern analysis does not make much better sense of them. It does, however, suggest a reason why they might be vulnerable to change: different native learners are likely to have arrived at different grammars on the basis of the surface input data. Whether the specific alternative analyses that DM makes available lead to enlightening explanations of attested changes remains to be seen, but it is at least clear that any less precise analysis will be unable to make more than general suggestions about the reasons for particular changes.

The discussion of DM up to this point has focused on morphological "pieces"; we need to describe briefly how the theory handles "process morphology." Since morphosyntactic features are generated at synctactic terminal nodes, it is not possible for [pl], for example, to be paired directly with the vowel change of English *feet*; instead there must be a zero affix (as in *sheep*, *deer*, etc.) accompanied by the vowel change. Processes like the latter are effected by "readjustment rules." Noyer 1997: liii–lxii explores this hypothesis, suggests how it can be tested, and deals with some apparent counterexamples. (Note that this is fully compatible with experimental evidence bearing on how speakers of English learn and access irregular past tenses; see e.g. Yang 2002: 59–100, Stockall and Marantz 2006, both with references.)

How to handle suppletion in DM is an unresolved question. The suggestion that only f-morphemes can exhibit suppletion seems difficult to reconcile with the facts; for instance, it seems impossible that the suppletive verbs of Old Irish, which number at least fourteen, are all f-morphemes.[3] We will explore suppletion in the next chapter.

Finally, we should note that DM does not recognize paradigms as part of the grammar. To some extent they are an automatic consequence of the organization of morphology and to some extent they appear to result from constraints on learnability, as a brief review of the most important findings of Carstairs 1987 will show. The fact that paradigms can be constructed at all is a straightforward consequence of the fact that each root-morpheme can be in close construction with only a limited number of f-morphemes, so that the possible combinations can all be listed. The fact that each root selects only one of the possible exponents of a given morphosyntactic feature or feature bundle (Carstairs 1987: 31) is a straightforward consequence of the subset principle. Carstairs' "paradigm economy principle," according to which the number of paradigmatically distinct lexical classes is always at or close to the minimum made possible by the number of alternative inflectional endings (ibid. pp. 47–52), is of a quite different nature. The fact that Carstairs found it necessary to revise the principle several times, allowing for infractions of specific kinds (ibid. pp. 56–83), strongly suggests that it is not a consequence of any formal mechanism of grammar. However, it is clear that an inflectional system which complies with the paradigm economy principle is easier to learn, and it is therefore reasonable to hypothesize that the principle is somehow a consequence of native language acquisition. The most puzzling of Carstairs' findings is the fact that a large majority of paradigms appear to obey the "peripherality constraint" (ibid. p. 193), according to which allomorphy is normally sensitive only to morphosyntactic features marked closer to the root – again, with some exceptions. As Carstairs notes (ibid. pp. 201–3), this does not follow from Baker's "Mirror Principle," though there seems to be some connection between the two. More study of these last points, especially by specialists in language acquisition, is needed; but it seems clear that none of them requires us to recognize paradigms as a part of native-speaker grammars.

In the following chapter we will examine a number of well-attested types of morphological change and attempt to analyze them in terms of the concepts of DM. Readers should be warned that for some types of change (such as the origin of lexical classes) simple examples are not to be found; we will do our best to offer as much information as may be needed to understand the changes under discussion, and that will sometimes be a large amount of information. This is unavoidable. Those who wish to study morphological change must get used to dealing with large and complex inflectional systems.

Notes

1 The pattern of category expressions which we exemplify by the Greek mediopassive endings recurs in the active endings, but they exhibit much more conditioned allomorphy; thus the mediopassive endings provide a simpler illustration. For simplicity we gloss over the fact that these endings appear both in middle paradigms and in (most) passive paradigms; that might also have to be accounted for by impoverishment, but until the nature of the middle voice is better understood we prefer to reserve judgment. We treat each ending as an indivisible unit in our analysis. It would also be possible to try to divide them into smaller pieces to which individual morphosyntactic features might be assigned. However, the resulting system would be full of complex irregularities; even the order of the markers for voice and person/number would vary from ending to ending. For the sake of exposition we prefer to use the simpler unitary analysis, though we recognize that splitting the endings up might ultimately be correct and should be explored.

2 The strongest evidence that the Ancient Greek primary endings are the default endings comes from the active voice of the optative mood of thematic and sigmatic stems. The inherited 1sg. forms ended in -οια /-oia/ and *-σαια */-saia/ (the former is actually attested in Arkadian εξελαυνοια /ekselaunoia/ 'I would drive out'); but in nearly all the dialects for which relevant forms are attested, 1sg. -α /-a/ has been replaced by -μι /-mi/, so that the attested forms end in -οιμι /-oimi/ and -σαιμι /-saimi/. The optative is a category which selects secondary endings (see the text above), but -μι /-mi/ is an inherited primary ending; its spread to a secondary category shows that primary endings had become the default set of endings by the time the change occurred.

3 Old Irish verbs that are unarguably suppletive include the following (cited in the present indicative 3sg., as there is no infinitive): the copula *is* and the substantive verb *atá*, both 'is' (but used in different syntactic contexts); *ad·cí* 'sees', *agid* 'drives', *at·baill* 'dies', *berid* 'carries', *do·beir* 'gives', *do·beir* 'brings' (the two verbs *do·beir* have different perfective

paradigms, both suppletive), *do·tét* 'comes', *do·tuit* 'falls', *fo·ceird* 'puts', *fo·gaib* 'finds', *ibid* 'drinks', and *téit* 'goes'; verbs which are suppletive under at least some analyses include *ad·cota* 'obtains', *bronnaid* 'injures, damages', *con·oí* 'protects', *do·bidci* 'shoots, casts, hurls', *gataid* 'steals', *ithid* 'eats', *tinaid* 'melts', and *tongid* 'swears'. See Veselinović 2003 for extensive discussion. Some other Indo-European languages also exhibit significant amounts of suppletion; for instance, Ancient Greek and the Tocharian languages each have at least nine or ten suppletive verbs.

8 Morphological change

Since the study of morphological change in a Distributed Morphology (DM) framework has hardly begun, we do not attempt to construct an overarching framework for this chapter; instead we treat topics of interest one by one, demonstrating how the machinery of DM helps explain morphological changes of different types.

Resegmentation and reinterpretation of terminal nodes

Reinterpretation of the feature content of word-internal syntactic terminal nodes by native learners is a universal type of change. English provides some straightforward examples. Modern English *-dom*, *-hood*, *-ship* are destressed forms of Old English (OE) *dōm* 'judgment, rule, power', *hād* 'person, rank, station (in life)', *scipe* 'state, condition' (the first surviving also as the noun *doom*). The shift from major lexeme to suffix did not happen directly. The following stages of development can be distinguished (see Meid 1967: 218–21).

(a)   Fully transparent compounds were formed; at this stage OE *wīsdōm*, for instance, still meant 'wise judgment' or 'discretion', *cynedōm* 'royal authority', and so on.[1]

(b)   Learners reinterpreted the meanings of the compounds; thus they acquired idiosyncratic meanings (Encyclopedia entries, in DM terminology), in these cases 'learning, knowledge, wisdom' and 'area subject to royal authority, kingdom' respectively.

(c)   On the basis of the shifted meanings of the compounds, later generations of learners increasingly reinterpreted the second element as a noun-forming suffix; eventually some began to use it productively, in this case yielding, e.g., *boredom, martyrdom*, and *officialdom*, among other innovative forms (see the *OED* s.v. *-dom*).

Stage (c) is almost inevitable if the lexemes which gave rise to the suffixes cease to be used as independent words or undergo substantial shifts in meaning, but that does not seem to be a necessary precondition for reanalysis. For instance, the adjective-forming suffix English *-ly*, German *-lich* reflects OE *līč*, OHG *līh*, both 'body', and the oldest examples of such adjectives were compounds meaning 'shaped like X' or 'looking like X', where X represents the first member of the compound (Meid 1967: 226–7); but whereas the independent English word has largely been lost (see the *OED* s.v. *lich*), the corresponding German word survives with only modestly restricted meaning as *Leiche* 'corpse' (see Kluge 1995 s.v.). This kind of interplay between major lexemes and affixes seems to be typical.

Functional morphemes are also subject to reinterpretation, as a sketch of the history of Ancient Greek /-ske-/ ~ /-sko-/ -σκε- ~ -σκο- will demonstrate. The Greek suffix was inherited from Proto-Indo-European (PIE); in the parent language it seems to have formed iterative and habitual stems, of which at least the ones listed in (1) below are securely reconstructable (Zerdin 2000: 39–41, Ringe 2002: 418).[2]

(1)   a. *g^wm̥-ské/ó- 'be walking' ('take one step after another'; *g^wem- 'step')
       b. *ǵn̥h₃-ské/ó- 'know (a person)' ('recognize on sight'; *ǵneh₃- 'recognize')
       c. *h₁-ské/ó- 'be (customarily), used to be' (*h₁es- 'be')
       d. *h₂i-ské/ó 'keep looking for' (*h₂eys- 'look for')
       e. *mi-ské/ó- 'be mixing' (repetitive motion; *meyḱ- 'put together')
       f. *pr̥-ské/ó- 'keep asking' (*preḱ- 'ask')
       g. *ph₂-ské/ó- 'pasture (animals)' ('protect habitually'; *peh₂- 'protect')

In Ancient Greek the function of this suffix had been generalized, so that it was just one of many affixes used to form imperfective aspect stems (traditionally called "present stems"). For instance, among the roughly two dozen such presents attested in the Homeric poems (our earliest substantial Greek texts) there is nothing *necessarily* iterative or habitual about *t^hrɔ́:iske:n* θρώισκειν 'be leaping, each leap, leap repeatedly', *pásk^{h}e:n* πάσχειν 'undergo, be suffering', *mimné:ske:n* μιμνήσκειν 'be/keep reminding', etc., and it is more than a little difficult to read such an interpretation into *t^hné:iske:n* θνήισκειν 'be dying'.

Two of these imperfective stems, however, coexisted with imperfectives that exhibited a zero affix (so-called "root-presents," because it appears superficially that further inflectional markers are added to the verb root rather than to a fully characterized aspect stem), and the verbs in question were very common; the relevant stems are in (2):

(2)   a. /éske/ ἔσκε '(s)he used to be, (s)he was'   : /ê:en/ ἦεν '(s)he was'
          (stem /e-ske-/ ~ /e-sko-/)   (stem /es-/ ~ /eh-/)

       b. /ép^{h}aske/ ἔφασκε, /p^{h}áske/ φάσκε '(s)he   : /ép^{h}ɛ:/ ἔφη '(s)he said'
          used to say, (s)he said'   (stem /p^{h}ɛ:-/ ~ /p^{h}a-/)
          (stem /p^{h}a-ske-/ ~ /p^{h}a-sko-/)

As the translations given suggest, these stems sometimes do and sometimes do not have a habitual meaning in Homer; while that is strictly true of any imperfective stem in Greek, these seem to have habitual force much more often than usual (Zerdin 2000: 311–16, 319–22), and that is probably the last vestige in Greek of the suffix's original function before the reanalysis (see below). The

$[[\sqrt{p^{h}a:-}]\ -pf]$ $[[\sqrt{p^{h}a:-}]\ -pf]$

   | | | |

  $p^{h}a$- $\emptyset$ $p^{h}a$-   -ske-

Figure 8.1 *Ionic dialect 'say' before reanalysis*

$[[\sqrt{p^{h}a:-}]\ -pf]$ $[[[\sqrt{p^{h}a:-}]\ -pf]\ +iter]$

   | | | | |

  $p^{h}a$- $\emptyset$ $p^{h}a$- $\emptyset$ -ske-

Figure 8.2 *Ionic dialect 'say' after reanalysis*

stem /eske-/ ~ /esko-/ was clearly inherited from PIE, being cognate with Palaic imperative *iska* 'be!', Old Latin *escit* 'is', and the Tocharian B copula 3sg. *star-*, 3pl. *skentar-* (see Keller 1985, Hackstein 1995: 277–82 with references, Zerdin 2000: 40, 310–11). The stem /pʰa-ske-/ ~ /pʰa-sko-/ has no clear cognates outside of Greek, but like clearly inherited stems of this type it has a respectably wide distribution within Greek; in particular, it provides the participle *pʰáskɔ:n* φάσκων 'saying' for the stem /pʰɛ:-/ ~ /pʰa-/ 'say' in Classical Attic. This shows that it was not restricted to poetic language nor to the Ionic dialect; the significance of that fact will become clear immediately below.

It appears that in the Ionic dialect, in some generation prior to the composition of the Homeric poems, one or (more likely) both of these stems in *-ske/o-* was reanalyzed as follows (see Zerdin 2000: 282). Before the reanalysis 'say', for instance, had the terminal nodes and the phonological strings in Figure 8.1 assigned by Vocabulary insertion (abstracting away from the suffixal alternation between *e* and *o*). After the reanalysis the same stem had the structure diagrammed in Figure 8.2. In other words, native learners supposed that the root in the stem on the right actually had an imperfective zero suffix, and that the suffix *-ske/o-* was a further suffix with specifically iterative/habitual function; that amounted to a reinterpretation of *-ske/o-* in these two stems not only in terms of meaning, but also in terms of its position in the word-internal syntactic tree, since it was now added to fully characterized aspect stems. In the archaic Ionic dialect of the Homeric poems the suffix *-ske/o-* became productive in this new function, marking iterative/habitual stems derived from aspect stems. We find it added to more than ninety imperfective ("present") stems and more than thirty perfective ("aorist") stems (Zerdin 2000: 278–81); typical forms are *aristéueske* ἀριστεύεσκε 'he used to be preeminent' (imperfective *aristeu-e-* ἀριστευ-ε-) and *éiksaske* εἴξασκε 'it would yield it (repeatedly)' (perfective *eik-sa-* εἴξα-). The status of *-ske/o-* as a fossilized marker of imperfective aspect (see above) was not affected by this creation of a new iterative/habitual *-ske/o-*. Productive iterative/habitual *-ske/o-* also occurs in the Ionic of Herodotos (cf. Zerdin 2000: 303–7), but there is no evidence that it ever spread beyond the Ionic dialect or survived beyond the Classical period.

Interestingly, this reinterpretation of /-ske- ∼ -sko-/ is probably more or less the reverse of one which occurred much earlier in the prehistory of Greek, in which the PIE iterative suffix was reinterpreted as an imperfective marker. Unfortunately that change cannot be reconstructed in comparable detail, since the structure of the PIE verb system cannot be reconstructed with enough certainty. That the new Ionic Greek suffix wound up with just about the same meaning as its distant ancestor probably reflects the (partial) survival of the old suffix's original meaning in the only two inherited stems that could be reanalyzed to yield the new suffix.

A more involved example of reinterpretation gave rise to the English default adverb-forming suffix *-ly*. Etymologically this suffix is more or less descended from OE *-lić* (and its Old Norse cognate *-lig-*, which occurred in Norse loans); but as we noted at the beginning of this section, that suffix originally formed adjectives, and there are still numerous English adjectives in *-ly* formed from nouns and some formed from other adjectives (*manly, kingly, timely, goodly, dastardly*, etc.; see the *OED* s.v. *-ly*[1]). In OE the productive adverb-forming suffix was originally *-e* (cf. e.g. *beorhte* 'brightly', *lange* 'for a long time', *wīse* 'wisely', *grame* 'angrily', etc.), and of course it was added to adjectives in *-lić* to yield adverbs in *-lice* (e.g. *cynelić* 'royal' : *cynelice* 'royally'; *lēoflić* 'lovable, lovely' : *lēoflice* 'lovingly'). But we also find a few adverbs in *-lice* for which we can quote no adjective in *-lić*, only a basic adjective without the suffix *-lić*. An example is *bealdlice* 'boldly', apparently formed directly from *beald* 'bold' and in competition with *bealde*; even more striking is the pair *hwæt* 'quick' : *hwætlice* 'quickly', to which we can quote neither an adjective **hwætlić* nor an adverb **hwate*. That could reflect accidental gaps in our attestation of OE vocabulary; but since adjectives in *-lić* were no longer being formed productively *from other adjectives* in OE (*OED*, s.v. *-ly*[1]), the correct conclusion is probably that *-lice* had been reanalyzed as an adverb-forming suffix and had begun to be used productively (so Campbell 1962: 275). Such a development must have begun as an error on the part of native learners who had (for example) heard the adjective *lēof* 'beloved' and the adverb *lēoflice* but had not yet encountered the adjective *lēoflić*. (There does not seem to be an adverb "*lēofe*.") The adverb-forming suffix *-ly* gained ground in Middle English (ME), as productive formations typically do over time (*before* the loss of *-e*, which does not seem to have been an important factor).

These examples of feature reinterpretation also involve the resegmentation of forms, which merits further discussion. The most obvious type of resegmentation splits a single terminal into two, assigning partly new content to at least one of the two terminals and part of the phonological string to each. The fourteenth-century development of such ME word pairs as *move* and *movable*, borrowed from French, that we noted in Chapter 4 involved such a split: a small class of lexemes (roots, in DM terms) was split into sequences of lexeme + suffix (root + f-morpheme), yielding an adjective-forming head *-able* with a meaning 'which can be Xed', because (a) all the split roots had a similar semantic structure, (b) they all ended in the same phonological string, and (c) the remainder of each could be identified, both semantically and phonologically, with another root.

Superficially similar to the process just described is backformation, which can be defined as the use of a word-formation process in reverse to derive a simpler word from a more complex one. The usual raw material for backformation is a word of which the head is a recognizable affix but the apparent root does not occur independently; a typical result is that the latter comes to be used without affixes as a head in its own right. This process, too, typically affects loanwords. For instance, the noun *donation* was borrowed into English from French (which had in turn borrowed it from Latin) in the fifteenth century; but while the noun-forming suffix *-ion* (or *-tion* or *-ation*), which was the word's head, was already a prominent affix (Vocabulary item, in DM) at that date, the root appeared elsewhere only in the derived words *donative* and *donator*, which were also borrowed around the same time. In the nineteenth century native speakers backformed a verb *donate* to one of these lexemes, probably to *donation*, since that was by far the commonest; the verb appears first in print in 1845 in the USA. Many members of the large class of English verbs in *-ate* arose by the same process in earlier generations (see Jespersen 1954: 447).

The same process of reverse derivation can lead to a shift in the boundaries of affixes. For instance, the English verb *to orient* was borrowed from French early in the eighteenth century, and in the middle of the nineteenth century a noun *orientation* was derived from it. Almost at once a verb *orientate* was backformed to the noun, and in British English *orientate* has become standard (though in North America it is stigmatized). As this example shows, backformation tends to be maximally transparent. An even more striking example is the verb *self-destruct* (not "*self-destroy*"!), backformed to the noun *self-destruction* in the 1960s. Note that these examples do not involve reinterpretation.

Simpler shifts in the boundaries of affixes – the phonological strings manipulated by Vocabulary insertion in DM – are also common. Latin verb conjugation provides a typical example. Most "first conjugation" verbs (the class with present stems in -$\bar{a}$-) seem to be fairly recent creations, but the few that are old reflect very diverse origins (cf. Sihler 1995: 528–30). For instance, some were formed to roots ending in short *-a-* by adding a suffix *-ye- ~ *-yo-; thus *sonā-* 'resound' reflects earlier *swena-e/o- from still earlier *swena-ye/o-, and its root *swena- reflects PIE *swenh$_2$- and is cognate with Sanskrit *svani-*. (The root-final short vowel of 'resound' also appears in the past participle *sonitus* < *swena-to-s and the perfect stem *sonu-* < *swena-w- instead of expected "*sonātus*" and "*sonāv-*.") But the largest class were derived from nouns ending in *-ā- by the addition of the suffix *-ye- ~ *-yo- (ibid. pp. 511 15). Though there are no clear examples with PIE etymologies, some are old enough to have cognates in other Italic languages; for instance, *cūrā-* 'take care of, administer' reflects prehistoric Latin *koisā-ye/o-, whose basis *koisā survives in the noun *cūra* 'care, administration' and whose formation is paralleled by Paelignian *coisa-* (of which the present infinitive, if attested, would be **coisaom*; actually attested is the perfect

3pl. *coisatens* 'they administered, *cūrāvērunt*'). But the loss of intervocalic **y*
and the subsequent contraction of vowels (**-a-ye/o- > *-a-e/o- > *-ā-*), or deletion of a short vowel after a long vowel (**-ā-ye/o- > *-ā-e/o- > *-ā-*), made the
original verb-forming suffix **-ye- ~ *-yo-* unrecoverable by native learners. Its
function was transferred to the contracted vowel *-ā-* (part of which was originally
the last segment of the stems to which the original suffix had been added), and
-ā- was then added to nouns of all stem classes to form verbs. For instance, we
find *nōminā-* 'name' derived from the noun *nōmen*, *dōnā-* 'give, present' derived
from *dōnum* 'gift' (stem *dōno-*), and so on. This development also occurred in
related languages of ancient Italy; cf. e.g. Oscan **duunated**, Venetic *donasto*
'(s)he gave, *dōnāvit*'.

As might be expected, ambiguity can also lead to shifts in the boundaries of
phonological pieces; the Ancient Greek verb system offers a simple example.
There was a class of perfective ("aorist") stems formed with a suffix /-ε:-/ -η-,
still largely intransitive in the Homeric poems, which acquired passive function;
typical examples are /kʰar-ε:-/ χαρη- 'rejoice', /pʰan-ε:-/ φανη- 'appear', /mig-ε:-/
μιγη- 'get mixed, have sex', /hrag-ε:-/ ῥαγη- 'get broken'. But already in Homer
this inherited type is greatly outnumbered by an alternative type in /-tʰε:-/ -θη-
with an identical pattern of inflection, e.g. /ager-tʰε:-/ ἀγερθη- 'be gathered',
/klin-tʰε:-/ κλινθη- 'get bent, swerve', /do-tʰε:-/ δοθη- 'be given', /pelas-tʰε:-/
πελασθη- 'approach', /meikʰ-tʰε:-/ μειχθη- 'get mixed' (apparently in competition with /mig-ε:-/; see Risch 1974: 250–4). The only plausible source for this
longer suffix is resegmentation, the final /-tʰ-/ -θ- of some root having been reinterpreted as the initial consonant of the suffix; we need to find the source of this
error. There is a handful of pairs of homonymous roots with and without final
/-tʰ-/; an intransitive perfective stem made to the root with this final consonant
might be mistaken for such a stem made to the alternative root without the final
consonant, and resegmentation would follow automatically. The most plausible
such pair is transitive /plε:-/ πλη- 'fill', which in the passive means 'get filled'
and 'be full' (depending on the aspect of the stem), and intransitive /plε:tʰ-/ πληθ-
'be full' (of which a perfective stem could only mean 'get filled'). The difference
in form and meaning is precisely what is required to account for the reinterpretation: an intransitive perfective **plε:tʰ-ε:- **πληθ-η- 'become full, get filled'
could easily be reinterpreted as **plε:-tʰε:- **πλη-θη-, a marked intransitive perfective formed to the transitive root. Unfortunately **plε:tʰε:- did not survive to be
attested (even in Homer); it was subsequently remodeled to /plε:stʰε:-/ πλησθη-
by a more complex process which does not concern us here. (This explanation is essentially that of Chantraine 1925: 105–6, Risch 1974: 253–4, though
we think we have identified a more plausible root as the starting point of the
innovation.)

A similar, but more dramatic, type of resegmentation involves shifts in the
boundaries of phonological words. The most familiar examples are provided
by the "univerbation" of verbs and adverbial particles ("preverbs") in conservative Indo-European (IE) languages. Such a process seems to have been arrested

halfway in the case of the modern German "separable prefixes." When the verb form is finite, the verb and the particle, which constitute an idiom (i.e., a multi-root Encyclopedia entry) with a specific and often idiosyncratic meaning (e.g. *aufführen* 'to perform': *auf* 'on, on top, up', *führen* 'to lead'), are distinct phonological words and are often separated, since the finite verb is the second major constituent while the particle remains at the end of the VP:

(3)   *Sie   führ-en   das Spiel auf.*
        they lead-3PL the play up
        'They're performing the play.'

However, when the verb form is a participle or infinitive, so that it does not move to second position, univerbation occurs:

(4)   *Sie   hab-en   das Spiel auf-ge-führ-t.*
        they have-3PL the play up-PTCP-lead-PTCP
        'They performed the play.'

(5)   *Sie   werden   das Spiel auf-führ-en.*
        they become-3PL the play up-lead-INF
        'They will perform the play.'

It is clear that *aufführen* and *aufgeführt* are single phonological words because each exhibits only a single primary stress (on *auf-*). Interestingly, this is the second round of univerbation, so to speak, that has occurred in the history of German verbs. There is also a class of "inseparable prefixes" which are always unstressed and always part of the same phonological word as the verb root, e.g.:

(6)   *Ich zerlege den Braten.   Ich wird den Braten zerlegen.*
        'I'm carving the roast.'   'I'm going to carve the roast.'

(7)   *Ich gebrauche das Wörterbuch.   Ich habe das Wörterbuch gebraucht.*
        'I'm using the dictionary.'   'I used the dictionary.'

These prefixes, too, were once independent particles which could be separated from the verb root. No direct ancestor of German is attested early enough to demonstrate that. However, in texts written in Gothic, a Germanic language fairly well attested from the fourth century which has left no descendants (so that it is a "great-aunt" of all modern Germanic languages), we do occasionally find clitics interposed between verb roots and prefixes which are inseparable in every other attested Germanic language, e.g.:

(8)   *frah-Ø   i-na   ga-u-ƕa-sēƕ-i-Ø*
        ask.PST-3SG him-ACC.SG PFV-?-anything-see.PST-SBJV-3SG
        'he asked him whether he could see anything' (*Gospel of Mark* 8.23)

The verb is a form of *gasaíƕan* 'to catch sight of, to see', a compound of *saíƕan* 'to see' with the perfective preverb *ga-* (cognate with German *ge-*); between the prefix and the verb have been inserted not only the interrogative clitic *-u* but also the indefinite pronoun *ƕa*. Other examples can be cited, including some others with two clitics interposed; cf.

(9)   *diz-uh-þan-sat-Ø*   *ij-ō-s*   *reirō*   *jah usfilmei*
       apart-and-then-sit.PST-3SG them-F-ACC.PL shaking and amazement
       'for trembling and amazement seized them' (ibid. 16.8)

with a conjunction and an adverb between the components of *dissitan* 'to settle on'. Similar patterns of facts can be found in the development of the Ancient Greek verb system.

The kind of simple univerbation just discussed probably reflects a simple type of learner error: native learners suppose that complex idioms are single phonological words because their components are adjacent in a large proportion of the examples heard and because an idiom "ought to be" a "word" (given that so many Encyclopedia entries actually are). The "V2" constraint of German, which keeps the tensed verb and the particle non-adjacent in a large proportion of examples heard, is evidently the reason why univerbation of verb roots and separable prefixes has not become categorical in that language.

A more unusual type of univerbation transformed DPs composed of an adjective and a noun in an adverbial case into adverbs derived from the adjectives, the noun losing its lexical meaning completely in the process; that was how the Romance adverbs marked with the suffix *-mente* in Italian and Spanish, *-ment* in French, etc., arose. Several peculiarities of the formation converge on that account of its origin. The suffix is normally added to the feminine form of the adjective, though feminine is the marked gender in Romance languages and is not normally the basis of derived forms; that is difficult to explain unless the suffix were originally a feminine noun with which the adjective had to agree.[3] The adverbial suffix appears "outside" of the (admittedly very few) other suffixes that adjectives can bear – that is, it is further from the root; note the following Italian pattern, which is both productive in that language and typical of Romance languages as a whole:

(10)   a. *chiara* 'clear' (fem.)   *chiarissima* 'as clear as possible' (fem.)
        b. *chiaramente* 'clearly'   *chiarissimamente* 'as clearly as possible'

That is the position one would expect the adverbial suffix to occupy if it had originally been a separate word. Finally, and most strikingly, in some Romance languages the conjoined syntagm [ADV & ADV] is realized as [ADJ(fem) & ADJ(fem)-SUFFIX] (Meyer-Lübke 1895: 687). For instance, from the conjoined Spanish adjectives *temerario y loco* 'wild and crazy' is formed the conjoined adverb pair *temeraria y locamente* (not "*temerariamente y locamente*"). By far the most economical explanation of all these facts is that the suffix was originally a feminine noun. In fact it was Classical Latin *mēns, ment(i)-* 'mind, judgment, opinion, feelings, intentions', one of a fairly large number of nouns of general meaning used in descriptive phrases (Bauer 2010 with references). The phrases were in the ablative case, which has various adverbial meanings, including 'with...' (in an abstract sense); the form of the phrases was ... *ā mente* or ... *ī mente* (depending on the lexical class of the adjective), and they meant 'with...mind' or 'with...intentions'. The number of individual examples which can be plausibly explained by a very modest semantic shift is surprisingly large, e.g. *serēnā mente* 'with cloudless mind' → 'serenely', *humilī mente* 'with a submissive attitude' → 'humbly', *clārissimā mente* 'with intentions most clear' → 'as clearly as possible'. Though the noun survives in some Romance languages (e.g. Italian *mente* 'mind', Spanish plurale tantum *mientes* 'thoughts'[4]), the ablative case survives in none, and that development might have contributed to the learner errors that must underlie this univerbation.

An inverse process, in which an inflectional affix is "cut loose," typically as a phrasal clitic, also occurs; the relatively recent history of English provides a notorious example. To understand what happened we need to begin with the OE situation. OE had a robust system of case-marking on nominals and a number of inflectional classes of nouns. Most (but not all) masculine and neuter nouns exhibited an ending *-es* in the genitive singular; so did all masculine and neuter "strong" adjectives (i.e., adjectives with no preceding determiner or possessive). Thus in phrases like *ōðres mannes* 'another man's' and *mīnes hūses* 'of my house' the ending appears on both noun and adjective because the nouns are masculine and neuter respectively and the syntax demands a strong adjective; but the adjective has a different ending in *þæs mōdigan mannes* 'the brave man's' and *þæs hēan hūses* 'of the lofty house' because the syntactic context demands weak adjectives, and both noun and adjective have different endings in *æðelre cwēne* 'of a noble queen' because the noun is feminine. Genitive plurals ended in *-ena*, *-ra*, or *-a*. By the end of the OE period nouns were increasingly being inflected according to the majority masculine paradigm, with nominative–accusative plurals in *-as* and genitive singulars in *-es* (Clark 1958: xlix–li, lvii–lviii); in the entry of the *Peterborough Chronicle* for 1123, for instance, we find the phrase *þes cwēnes canceler* 'the queen's chancellor' (ibid. p. 44; "standard" OE *þēre cwēne cancelere*). By about 1200 uninflected adjectives and determiners before fully inflected nouns had become usual (Mossé 1952: 64, Jespersen 1954: 282, Bennett and Smithers 1968: xxvi–xxx), so that one finds *i þiss middellærdess lif* 'in this world's life', *onn eche lifess bokess writt* 'in the roster of the book of eternal life' in the *Orrmulum* (OE *in þisses middangeardes līf, on ēces līfes bōce ġewrite*) and *a mihti kinges luve* 'a mighty king's love', *efter kene cnihtes deað* 'after a bold knight's death' in the *Ancrene Riwle* (OE *mihtiġes cyninges lufu, æfter cēnes cnihtes dēaðe*). That is important, because in a DP with a recognizable case marker only on the noun at its right edge it is ambiguous whether the ending forms a constituent with the noun root or with the DP as a whole – that is, whether it is an inflectional "ending" or a phrasal clitic. The most innovative dialect attested around 1200, that of the *Orrmulum*, has already undergone a further reanalysis: the genitive singular marker *es* (spelled *ess* by Orrm) is added to fully inflected plural forms, so that we find *manness* 'man's', *menness* 'men's' (though if the plural already ended in *-es* no further *-es* was added – exactly as in modern English; Bennett and Smithers 1968: xxvi–xxx). In this dialect the form *menness* already had the structure given in Figure 8.3. (The plural affix triggered vowel change in the root in this noun, as it still does.) Since

$$[[[\sqrt{\text{MAN}}]\ +\text{pl}]\ +\text{gen}]$$
$$|\qquad\ \ |\qquad\ \ |$$
$$\text{man}\ +\ \emptyset\ +\ \text{ɔs}$$

Figure 8.3 *Morphological structure of* menness *in the dialect of the* Orrmulum

the old masc. and neut. gen. sg. ending now occurred only on nouns, typically at the right edge of the DP, and was now an "agglutinative" marker added at the end of a sequence of markers, it should have been reinterpretable as a clitic by native learners. Whether that had already happened in Orrm's dialect is unclear; in such examples as *ure Laferrd Christess hird* 'our Lord Christ's company', *i Daviþþ kingess chesstre* 'in King David's city', the first two nouns might conceivably be analyzed as a compound. By the middle of the fifteenth century it was definitely occurring; Jespersen 1954: 283 cites from Caxton an example *of [the quene his modr]es owne brestis*, in which the marker *-es* is clearly adjoined to the bracketed DP 'the queen his mother' as a whole. Caxton's approximate contemporary Mallory, like earlier authors, still postposes a prepositional phrase, as in *the dukes wyf of Tyntagail* 'the duke of Tintagel's wife' (Jespersen 1954: 286); the significance of that fact is not clear. But in any case examples with the clitic *'s* following a DP-internal PP were normal a century or so later; examples like *the Duke of Gloucester's purse* can be cited from Shakespeare and the other Elizabethan dramatists (Jespersen 1954: 287).

Implausible alternative analyses of this development have been proposed because of a conviction that the obvious solution is somehow "unnatural." In particular, some linguists have tried to take seriously spellings like *for Jesus Christ his sake* (quoted from the *Book of Common Prayer* by Jespersen 1954: 301; note that Jespersen corrects to *Christès* pp. 301–2) as an indication that possessive *'s* is historically a reduced form of *his*. It is true that in thirteenth-century ME one finds collocations of a noun followed by coreferential *his*, but only when the noun is the dative object of a verb or preposition; an example occurs in the well-known dream of King Arthur in Laȝamon's *Brut*:

> And ich i-grap mi sweord leofe mid mire leoft honde
> and smæt of Modred is hafd þat it wond a þene veld.

A fairly literal translation is:

> 'And I grasped my beloved sword with my left hand
> and smote off Modred his head so that it rolled on the field.'

(The later manuscript reads *and smot of Modred his hefd*, which makes it clear that *is* in the earlier manuscript should be taken as the possessive pronoun, not the genitive ending; see Brandl and Zippel 1949: 3–4.) But if we agree that native learners acquire a coherent syntax of their language, we cannot also believe that such a collocation could be generalized out of context. For instance, in John of Trevisa's late-fourteenth-century translation of the *Polychronicon* we read:

> Also, gentilmen children buþ y-tauȝt for to speke Freynsch fram tyme þat
> a buþ y-rokked in here cradel and conneþ speke and playe wiþ a child hys
> brouch; . . .

Literally:

> 'Also, well-born children are taught to speak French from the time that they
> are rocked in their cradle and can talk and play with a child's toy; . . . '

The object of *wiþ* in this sentence is clearly *brouch* 'toy', and there is no governing
verb or preposition to assign dative case to *child*; it follows that *child hys* can only
be a spelling for *childes* 'child's'. Moreover, such spellings first become common
in the fifteenth century (Brunner 1948: 51), when the only English dialect that
still might have had a dative case was the archaic Kentish. Some scribes took
the spelling *his* seriously and generalized from it, creating such monstrosities
as the much-quoted heading *The wyf of Bathe hir tale*; but medieval scribes
were not necessarily competent linguists, and what they wrote was not always
linguistically real. (A similar example of scribal confusion are the forms of
'eleven' in Mallory's works, in which the initial unstressed syllable was mistaken
for the indefinite article ["*a leven*"] and subsequent scribes "corrected" the result
to the ungrammatical "*an eleven*" [Ann Taylor, p.c.]. For comprehensive and
thorough discussion see Allen 2008: 223–72.)

The development of an inflectional affix into a clitic seems unnatural only if we
misconceive inflectional morphology as a kind of graveyard in which fossilized
bits of phonology and syntax come to rest, cemented in place by the sheer opacity
of the system. DM maintains that since the difference between affixes and clitics
is a purely phonological one, it should be just as easy for an affix to become a
clitic as vice versa. The historical record supports that hypothesis in the case of
English *'s*.

Fusion, readjustment rules, and empty morphs

In two types of cases a morphosyntactic property can fail to have any
string of phonological segments associated with it alone: f-morphemes can be
fused, so that two or more occupy a single head at which a single Vocabulary
item is inserted; and a morphosyntactic property can be marked superficially by
an alteration of some segment of the lexeme with no overt affix. Occasionally we
encounter the converse situation, in which some string of phonological segments
seems to have no identifiable function. In this section we briefly review the little
that is known about the origins and development of these phenomena.

Fused markers of gender, number, and case are familiar because they are typical of IE languages, but they are not particularly common among the languages
of the world. An unfortunate result of this distribution is that there are hardly

any examples whose development out of an earlier, more transparent system we can observe in the historical record. For instance, the noun class prefixes of Niger-Congo (including Bantu) languages, which are unanalyzable markers both of number and of concord class, are reconstructable to such an early stage of the family's prehistoric development that there is no clear indication of how they arose. Similarly, it is wholly mysterious why the PIE gen. sg. should have been marked by *-és (with ablaut variants *-os and *-s), but the gen. pl. by *-óHom (Ringe 2006: 41), two unanalyzable endings sharing no diagnostic phonological material. The changes that we are able to observe allow the following limited conclusions about such systems. First, once a system of fused markers has arisen it tends to persist; for instance, though the date of PIE remains a matter of dispute, most specialists would agree that the Russian system of fused nominal markers, directly descended from the PIE system, has persisted for at least five millennia with changes only in detail, not in the overall nature of the system. Secondly, the fact that regular sound changes can make the boundaries between markers unlearnable is one source of new fusions (not surprisingly). For instance, it is easy to show that in PIE the feminine gender of adjectives was marked by a clearly segmentable suffix that preceded the case-and-number endings (Ringe 2006: 50–2); but in the daughter languages phonological changes obscured the boundaries of that suffix, with the result that in Latin, for example, many feminine adjectives simply have "different endings" from their masculine and neuter counterparts – so that the endings now mark gender as well as number and case. Finally, because fused systems tend to persist, new unanalyzable items can apparently be attracted into them. A striking example is a PIE marker containing the distinctive breathy-voiced stop *-bʰ-, which must originally have meant something like 'two sides' since it appears in words meaning 'both' (Greek /ámpʰɔ:/ ἄμφω, Sanskrit ubʰā́, Proto-Germanic (PGmc.) *ba-, etc.; see Jasanoff 1976 for discussion). But it also appears in the instrumental plural ending *-bʰí (and perhaps in some other oblique nonsingular endings, though that is disputed); the connection between the two seems certain, since we can also reconstruct a fossilized adverb *h₂n̥t-bʰí 'on both sides' (*h₂ent- 'face, side', see Jasanoff 1976: 124–7; reflexes include Greek /ampʰí/ ἀμφί and PGmc. *umbi > OE *ymbe* 'around'). Yet the reconstructable instrumental singular ending is *-éh₁ (~*-h₁), obviously of completely different origin. It looks like a postposition has been attracted into the case-and-number system and assigned a fused function. (A more complex and more definite hypothesis along the same lines can be found in Jasanoff 2009.)

Verb inflection tends to be both more complex and more transparent than nominal inflection. To the extent that fused markers occur, they are easier to explain in one respect. It seems natural for a single marker to express both the person and the number of the subject or object because very many languages have unanalyzable pronouns that likewise express both person and number. That person-and-number agreement markers were originally independent pronouns is probably a reasonable hypothesis in most instances. In a few cases we can actually demonstrate that subject pronouns have become agreement markers; for instance, within the last few centuries independent subject pronouns have become clitics marking agreement in most North Italian dialects (i.e. those north of the La Spezia–Rimini line) and in the Rhaeto-Romance languages Ladin and Friulian (see e.g. Haiman 1991, Poletto 1995, both with references). Though comparable documentation is lacking in most other cases, the obvious resemblance between pronouns and agreement markers in many language families (such as Athabaskan and IE) suggests that this is a fairly common type of reinterpretation of terminal nodes (see above).

In other respects fusion in verb endings seems to originate and behave in much the same ways as in nominal endings, so far as we can tell. Thus complex sets of fused verb endings have persisted for millennia in IE languages just as fused nominal endings have. Replacement of endings usually does not alter the system. For instance, in Latin the old passive 2pl. ending did not survive; instead it was replaced by a phrase consisting of the present passive participle and the 2pl. of 'be', so that the inherited 2pl. passive of *dūcere* 'to lead', for example, was replaced by

(11)   *dūc-i-min-ī es-tis
         lead-V-pass.ptcp-nom.pl be-2pl
         'being-led you-are'

(where "V" indicates the theme vowel; see the discussion in Chapter 7). But the present indicative of 'be' can be omitted in Latin, as in many conservative IE languages; when the present passive participle was lost in its original function, learners reinterpreted ellipses like *dūciminī* as 2pl. forms, and the result was a 2pl. passive ending *-minī* – unanalyzable, like many of the inherited endings (Buck 1933: 252).

The presence of "readjustment rules," which alter phonological features of the lexeme in the presence of particular affixes (which can be ∅), is a clear case of the morphologization of phonology. The eventual fate of i-umlaut in English is a case in point. Old English had an i-umlaut rule like that of modern German (see Chapter 6), with uniform effects on the vowels of root-syllables but multiple morphological triggers. The most important categories in which the OE rule applied were the following:

- in the (mostly endingless) dative singular and nominative-accusative plural of about two dozen nouns (Campbell 1962: 251–5, 257), e.g. *bōc* 'book', dat. sg. *bēċ*, nom.-acc. pl. *bēċ*;
- in the comparative and superlative of about half a dozen adjectives (ibid. pp. 273–4), e.g. *lang* 'long', *lengra, lengest*;
- in all forms of regular class I weak verbs, which were probably still being derived productively from nouns and adjectives in the OE period (ibid. pp. 321–9), e.g. *fyllan* 'to fill', derived from *full*;
- in the dialects spoken south of the Thames, in the present indicative 2sg. and 3sg. of strong verbs (ibid. pp. 299–301), e.g. *stentst* '(you) stand', *stent* '((s)he) stands', inf. *standan*;

Table 8.1 *Typical Old English examples of i-umlaut*

	Base forms	Umlauted forms
Nouns	*mūs* 'mouse', *tōþ* 'tooth'	*mȳs* 'mice; to a mouse', *tēþ* 'teeth; with a tooth'
Weak verbs	*fūs* 'eager', *blōd* 'blood'	*fȳsan* 'to urge', *blēdan* 'to bleed'
Strong 3sg.	*brūcan* 'to use', *fōn* 'to take'	*brȳcþ* 'uses', *fēhþ* 'takes'

- in a number of derivational categories, such as feminine abstract nouns in *-þ* formed from adjectives, e.g. *lengþ*, derived from *lang*.

(The rule also applied, sometimes variably, in quite a few other forms, many of them more or less isolated.) The examples in Table 8.1 show that i-umlaut was still a single phonological rule in OE, with uniform effects much like those of the modern German rule.[5] In ME, however, the scope of the rule was steadily narrowed in the following ways. Even in the dialects south of the Thames the rule ceased to apply in strong verb paradigms; for instance, whereas the present indicative 3sg. of Kentish OE *healdan* 'to hold' was *helt* 'holds' (with i-umlaut of the root vowel, syncope of the ending, and assimilation /-d-þ/ → [t]), in Kentish ME documents of the thirteenth and fourteenth centuries we find not *helt* (with umlaut) but un-umlauted *halt* (with *a* < *ea* by regular sound change). Class I weak verbs ceased to be productive; the surviving inherited examples derived from surviving nouns and adjectives gradually became fewer, and the semantics of some diverged from those of their bases. The lists of nouns and adjectives to which the rule applied also grew steadily shorter, and the derivational categories in which it applied ceased to be productive. The resulting pattern in modern English is the following. Seven nouns still have umlauted plurals (*women, men, feet, teeth, geese, mice, lice*), not counting a couple of archaisms (*kine, brethren,* the last in specialized religious usage); the only comparative and superlative still affected are *elder, eldest,* which are now restricted to use with kinship terms and in fixed phrases (*elder statesman,* etc.); the only inherited class I weak verbs whose relation to their bases is still clear are probably *feed, bleed, breed, tell* (if the relationship to *tale* is still felt) and the causatives *fill* and *fell*; and derivational examples have been reduced to *strength, length, breadth,* and perhaps a few more.[6] It seems impossible that native learners of modern English could still be learning a single phonological rule, or even several rules, from seventeen examples exhibiting nine different vowel changes. They must instead be learning readjustment rules for specific f-morphemes in construction with specific roots; that is what the OE i-umlaut rule has become in modern English.

Phonological strings that do not correspond to any morphosyntactic feature or any single derivational head are likewise the result of historical accidents. Latin verb inflection provides a clear example, the "third stem" (Aronoff 1994: 37–9), formed either from the root or from the present stem with a variety of suffixes containing *-t-* or *-s-*, e.g. *duc-t-* (*dūc-* 'lead'), *lāp-s-* (*lāb-* 'slip'), *am-ā-t-* (present stem *am-ā-*, root *am-* 'love'). From the third stem are formed the perfect participle, which is passive unless the verb is deponent or intransitive (*ductus* 'led', *lāpsus* 'having slipped', *amātus* 'loved'), the future active participle 'about to X' (*ductūrus, lāpsūrus, amātūrus*), a verbal noun called the "supine" which is used in two different and highly restricted syntactic environments (*mīlitēs ductum vēnī, sed difficile factū est* 'I came to lead the troops, but it's hard to do'), and a range of derivational formations (*ductim* 'continuously', *ductāre* 'to bring [a bride] home', *ductus* 'line, shape', *lāpsāre* 'to stumble', *lāpsus* 'sliding motion, error', *lāpsiō* 'tendency', *amātor* 'lover', etc.). Since there is no semantic or functional common denominator among these formations, the third-stem suffix is empty of content; yet it is a recognizable entity, consistently appearing as *-s-* with some roots, *-t-* with others, *-it-* with still others, and so on. The contingent events which gave rise to this situation can be summarized as follows. PIE had a large number of derivational suffixes beginning with *-t-, including verbal adjectives in *-tó-, derived action nouns in *-tu- and in *-ti-, and agent nouns in *-ter- (Ringe 2006: 61, 63). The first two were integrated into Latin verb inflection as the past participle and the supine respectively; the last three survive as masculine action nouns in *-tu-* (nominative singular *-tus*), feminine action nouns in *-tiōn-* (nom. sg. *-tiō*), and masculine agent nouns in *-tōr-* (nom. sg. *-tor*); and a number of new formations were derived from these inherited ones within the separate prehistory of Latin. The same sound changes affected the initial *-t-*'s of all these suffixes, so that any phonological peculiarity in one was reflected in all the others; for instance, just as pre-Latin *kād-to-s 'fallen' became *cāssus*,[†] so also *kād-tu-s '(a) fall, event' and *kād-tiō '(a) fall' became *cāssus* and *-cāssiō* (the latter in compounds like *occāssiō* 'favorable event, opportunity'). Native learners evidently reanalyzed the third-stem suffix as a unit, so that when the root *lāb-* 'slip' acquired a historically irregular third stem in *-s-* all the relevant formations were affected alike (as the examples cited above demonstrate).

Syncretism

The literature on syncretism is extensive (cf. Carstairs 1987: 87–102 with references), and various somewhat different definitions of the term are in use. We define syncretism as the systematic expression of distinct morphosyntactic features, or distinct sets of features at fused terminal nodes, by the same phonological string. Thus we restrict the term to mean homonymy of the exponents of functional morphemes (f-morphemes), as Carstairs does, and we accept his demonstration that systematic and accidental homonymy can be distinguished in a large proportion of instances (ibid. pp. 93–102), but we do not follow him in

---

[†] Latin geminate *ss* after long vowels and diphthongs was not simplified until the first century CE; we here use the older forms because they are more transparent.

Table 8.2 *1pl. and 3pl. forms of an Old High German verb*

	Pres. indic.	Pres. subj.	Past indic.	Past subj.
1pl.	farēm	farēm	fuorum	fuorīm
3pl.	farant	farēn	fuorun	fuorīn

Table 8.3 *1pl. and 3pl. forms of a Middle High German verb*

	Pres. indic.	Pres. subj.	Past indic.	Past subj.
1pl.	faren	faren	fuoren	füeren
3pl.	faren	faren	fuoren	füeren

distinguishing "syncretism" in fused morphemes from "takeovers" in other cases (see further below).

How syncretisms arise and how they develop are separate questions which we will address in turn. The origins of some syncretisms are unknown because they are already present in the earliest stage of a language that can be reconstructed; well-known examples in the IE family are the syncretism of dative plural and ablative plural in all nominal paradigms and the syncretism of nominative and accusative (in each number) in all neuter nominal paradigms. Later syncretisms can be shown to have arisen in several different ways, as follows.

The most straightforward way in which homonymies of f-morphemes arise is through phonemic merger. Homonymies that arise by merger are of course accidental at first, but if they are pervasive enough, native learners can reinterpret them as systematic homonymies – that is, syncretisms. The attested history of German provides an example. In Old High German (OHG), 1pl. verb forms ended in -*m*;[†] 3pl. verb forms ended in -*nt* in the present indicative, but in -*n* in the past and the subjunctive. The starting point for the developments under discussion here can be exemplified by the strong verb *faran* 'travel', whose relevant forms are given in Table 8.2. Within the OHG period word-final -*m* in unstressed syllables became -*n* (Braune and Reiffenstein 2004: 120), giving rise to an accidental homonymy of 1pl. and 3pl. in the past and the subjunctive. Then in the Middle High German (MHG) period the indicative 3pl. ending -*nt* was replaced by the default 3pl. ending -*n* of the past indicative and the present and past subjunctive; this happened earliest in the northern High German dialects ("Middle German"; Paul *et al.* 1969: 186). The result was that -*n* expressed the feature bundles [1, pl] and [3, pl] in nearly all verb forms in the language. Since unstressed vowels had all merged, the partial paradigm of Table 8.2 had become the partial paradigm in Table 8.3.

The exception was 'be', which had quite different forms in the 1pl. and 3pl. of the present indicative. In OHG these were 1pl. *birum* (> *birun*) and 3pl. *sint*.

[†] In the present indicative this ending was in competition with an alternative -*mēs*, but -*m* ultimately won out; see Braune and Reiffenstein 2004: 261–3.

Table 8.4 *Classes of non-neuter nominals with nom.–acc. pl. syncretism in Attic Greek*

	Nouns	Adjectives, numerals
i-stems	/pólis/ πόλις 'city'	/trê:s/ τρεῖς 'three'
u-stems	/présbus/ πρέσβυς 'ambassador'	/hɛ:dús/ ἡδύς 'pleasant'
s-stems	/trié:rɛ:s/ τριήρης 'trireme'	/alɛ:tʰέ:s/ ἀληθής 'true'
Comparative	—	/mé:sdɔ:n/ μείζων 'bigger'

Table 8.5 *Actual and expected nom. and acc. pl. endings of the Attic Greek classes of nominals with nom.–acc. pl. syncretism*

	Actual ending	Expected ending
Type *pólis*		
nom. pl.	*-e:s*	*-e:s* < **-ees* < **-eyes*
acc. pl.	*-e:s*	*-i:s* < *-ins*
Type *présbus*		
nom. pl.	*-e:s*	*-e:s* < *-ees* < **-ewes*
acc. pl.	*-e:s*	*-u:s* < *-uns*
Type *trié:rɛ:s*		
nom. pl.	*-e:s*	-e:s < -ees < *-ehes
acc. pl.	*-e:s*	*-ɛ:s < -eas < *-ehas
Type *mé:sdɔ:n*		
nom. pl.	*-o:s*	-o:s < *-oes < *-ohes
acc. pl.	*-o:s*	*-ɔ:s < *-oas < *-ohas

In MHG those forms at first survived as *birn* and *sint* respectively. However, in the thirteenth century the 1pl. form began to be replaced by other forms, one of which was 3pl. indicative *sint*, and this process too began in the northern dialects that had eliminated 3pl. *-nt* in all other verbs (Wright 1907: 274, Paul *et al.* 1969: 125 6); the eventual result was that modern German *sind* is both the 1pl. and the 3pl. form. In other words, native learners of MHG interpreted the homonymy of 1pl. and 3pl. forms as a systematic syncretism, since it was nearly exceptionless, and extended it to the present indicative of 'be' (eventually under the form of the 3pl., marked only for number).

Syncretisms that must be attributed to native-learner errors also seem to be frequent in the historical record. The Attic dialect of Ancient Greek offers an unusually clear set of examples (Ringe 1995: 52–6). Whereas the nom. pl. and acc. pl. of neuter nominals are always the same in Ancient Greek, the nom. pl. and acc. pl. of masculine and feminine nominals are nearly always different in form (often very different). However, in Classical Attic they are the same in four lexical classes of stems, namely those exemplified by the nominals in Table 8.4.[7] A comparison of the actually occurring endings with those which would be expected to have developed by sound change alone, given in Table 8.5,

Table 8.6 *Partial paradigm of a Latin third-conjugation verb*

		Present indicative	Future indicative	Present subjunctive
sg.	1	agō	agam	agam
	2	agis	agēs	agās
	3	agit	aget	agat
pl.	1	agimus	agēmus	agāmus
	2	agitis	agētis	agātis
	3	agunt	agent	agant

shows what has happened. In each of these lexical classes the expected nom. pl. and acc. pl. ended in *-s* preceded by a long vowel and differed only in the quality of those vowels, and in every instance the nom. pl. form took over acc. pl. function as well. The change must have begun as a learner error in one or more of these classes and spread to the rest; a reasonable guess is that the second class, in which the original vowels were very different, was the last to be affected. That this is a systematic syncretism is argued by its exceptionlessness: there are no attested Attic nominals with nom. pl. and acc. pl. ending in *-V:s* and distinguished only by the quality of the long *V:*. In fact the only remaining class of nominals with nom. pl. and acc. pl. distinguished only by the vowel in the ending was the very large class with nom. pl. in (short) *-es* and acc. pl. in (short) *-as*. One would expect them eventually to be affected by the same syncretism, and that is what happened: in the Attic koiné of the Hellenistic period we begin to find occasional examples of acc. pl. *-es* (the old nom. pl. ending) for expected *-as*, and in the second century BCE they become fairly common (Ringe 1995: 57 with references). The conservatism of the literary tradition ensures that acc. pl. *-as* continues to be written until the end of the ancient world and beyond, but we know that this syncretism eventually became categorical because in Modern Greek both the nom. pl. and the acc. pl. of this lexical class end in *-es* (see Householder *et al.* 1964: 46–52).

Often a combination of phonological changes and learner errors eventually leads to exceptionless syncretism; that is what happened in the late prehistory and early attested stages of the West Germanic languages, in which nom. pl. and acc. pl. forms became identical except in the first- and second-person pronouns (cf. the paradigms and discussion in van Helten 1890, Campbell 1962, Brunner 1965, Gallée 1993, Braune and Reiffenstein 2004; see Ringe 1995: 57–62 with references).

A quite different type of syncretism is observable in Latin verb inflection. For the most part the morphosyntactic categories of Latin verbs are very clearly marked, but in the future of the third and fourth conjugations we find an exception. The situation can best be appreciated by comparing the present indicative, future indicative, and present subjunctive active of a relevant verb, such as *agere* 'to drive, to do', given in Table 8.6. (The pattern is the same in the passive; only

Table 8.7 *Thematic present indicative and subjunctive of an Ancient Greek verb*

		Present indicative		Present subjunctive	
sg.	1	/ágɔ:/	ἄγω	/ágɔ:/	ἄγω
	2	/ágeis/	ἄγεις	/ágɛ:is/	ἄγηις
	3	/ágei/	ἄγει	/ágɛ:i/	ἄγηι
pl.	1	/ágomen/	ἄγομεν	/ágɔ:men/	ἄγωμεν
	2	/ágete/	ἄγετε	/ágɛ:te/	ἄγητε
	3	/ágɔ:si/	ἄγουσι	/ágɔ:si/	ἄγωσι

the shapes of the endings are different.) While the stem vowel of the present indicative is variable and difficult to specify (see Chapter 7), that of the future indicative is normally long /-e:-/ and that of the present subjunctive is long /-a:-/, both vowels being shortened by general phonological rules before word-final -*m* and -*t* and before *nt*. However, the 1sg. of the future indicative is obviously the present subjunctive form, with /-a:-/ rather than /-e:-/. We need to explain why this one subjunctive form acquired future function as well.

A plausible motivation can be found in the reconstructable prehistory of the paradigm (Cowgill 1965: 44). The Latin future indicative is the PIE present subjunctive, which functioned both as a future and as a modal form in PIE. (The Latin subjunctives, in turn, are PIE optatives, a different modal form.) In the classes of PIE verbs that were ancestral to these Latin declensions, the subjunctive was formed by *lengthening* the stem vowel (Ringe 2006: 29–30). Compare the present indicative and subjunctive active of the Ancient Greek verb /áge:n/ ἄγειν 'to lead', which is cognate with Latin *agere*, in Table 8.7. Though the endings are partly different from the Latin ones and some details are obscure, the subjunctive obviously has long /ɛ:/ η (< PIE *ē) wherever the indicative has /e/ ε and the subjunctive has long /ɔ:/ ω (< PIE *ō) wherever the indicative has /o/ o. (The /o:/ of indicative 3pl. -*o:si* arose by the "second compensatory lengthening," already encountered at the beginning of Chapter 6; inherited /-onsi/ -ονσι is actually attested in Arkadian inscriptions.) The Greek long /ɛ:/ η is etymologically identical with the long /-e:-/ of the Latin future, which has been generalized at the expense of *-ō-. But in Greek the 1sg. present indicative and subjunctive are homonymous, because the 1sg. of the indicative, exceptionally, has a long vowel in the ending. The same was true in the prehistory of Latin, and that must be the motivation for the use of the 1sg. subjunctive as a 1sg. future: homonymy of future and subjunctive was less dysfunctional than homonymy of future and present indicative. Exactly how the change took place is not recoverable; possibly native speakers used ambiguous future 1sg. forms in *-ō and then clarified by repeating themselves using a subjunctive instead, so that native learners took the inherited future forms to be errors and the subjunctives to be the correct future forms.

Table 8.8 *The development of some gen. sg. and abl. sg. endings in Italic*

	PIE[†]	Latin	Oscan
o-stems			
gen. sg.	*-osyo?	-osio, -ī	**-eís**
abl. sg.	*-ead > *-ād → *-ōd	-ōd > -ō	**-ud**
eh$_2$-stems			
gen. sg.	*-eh$_2$s > *-ās	-ās → -āī > -ae	**-as**
abl. sg.	*-eh$_2$s > *-ās	-ād > -ā	**-ad**
i-stems			
gen. sg.	*-eys	-is	**-eís**
abl. sg.	*-eys	-īd > -ī	**-id**
u-stems			
gen. sg.	*-ews	-ous > -ūs	-ous
abl. sg.	*-ews	-ūd > -ū	-id

[†] The "PIE" stage given here is actually reconstructable only for the non-Anatolian, non-Tocharian branches of the family (see Ringe 2006: 4–6).

However they arise, syncretisms tend to persist, probably for several reasons. On the one hand, syncretism of fused markers clearly reduces the burden on a learner's memory (Carstairs 1987: 91–2, 109–14). On the other hand, learners typically do not find in the language they are learning the formal means to "undo" its syncretisms. In addition, the mere fact that children are so good at learning quirky morphology tends to militate against change. But there are a few known instances in which syncretisms have been reversed; one of the clearest involves the ablative singular in ancient Italic languages, including Latin. In PIE the ablative case had almost no distinctive markers. In the plural it was always syncretized with the dative, in the dual with the dative and instrumental; in the singular it was syncretized with the genitive in "athematic" nominals, one of the two large lexical classes (see Ringe 2006: 41–4, 50–2). Only in the "thematic" class of nominals ("o-stems," the etymological source of the Latin "second declension") did the ablative singular have a distinctive ending, which ended in *-d. Sanskrit preserves this inherited system virtually unchanged. In the Italic languages, however, the distinctive ablative singular marker was extended to further lexical classes of stems. Table 8.8 illustrates this by a comparison of some PIE, Latin, and Oscan endings.[8] Evidently the inherited o-stem abl. sg. ending was analyzable as underlying */-:d/, i.e. lengthening of the stem vowel plus /d/. Native learners apparently extracted it and used it to form distinctive abl. sg. endings for the other lexical classes of stems that ended in vowels – an obviously felicitous error.

Discussion of a couple of further examples of the undoing of syncretism, from Italian and Georgian, can be found in Carstairs 1987: 128–32.

Impoverishment, defaults, syncretism, and leveling

In the preceding section we have avoided using the concept of impoverishment filters, and of morphological defaults generally, because it seems clear that not every instance of syncretism involves the generalization of default markers. A consideration of some straightforward case syncretisms will illustrate.

In all the cases of nominative–accusative syncretism that arose in the history of Attic Greek the nominative marker was generalized. We could plausibly suggest that the nominative is the unmarked case and that since the accusative case is the other "direct" case it is distinguished from the nominative only by the presence of an additional feature, noncommittally [+acc] for the purposes of this discussion. The syncretisms could then be represented by an impoverishment filter

$$*[\text{acc pl}] / X\_\_,$$

where X is a root of the relevant lexical class; since an inherent feature such as [pl] ranks universally higher than a dissociated feature such as a case, the result would be the use of nom. pl. forms in acc. pl. functions. We could hypothesize that language learners posited that filter to account for the effects of their phonetic misperceptions and/or for adult errors which were not perceived as such. The same analysis will work for very many nom.–acc. syncretisms, including a large majority of the West Germanic examples (Ringe 1995: 57–62).

But there are also instances in which that analysis cannot be made to work because the accusative marker was generalized. Examples (ibid. pp. 56, 61–2) include:

(12)   Heraklean Greek nom.-acc. *tri:s* τρῑς 'three' (see above on the ending)

(13)   OHG masculine a-stem noun nom.-acc. pl. *-a* (the old nom. pl. ending apparently survives in Old Saxon nom.-acc. pl. *-os*)

(14)   OHG feminine ō-stem nom.-acc. sg. *-a* (the old nom. sg. ending *-u > ∅ survives in fem. strong adjectives)

(15)   OHG feminine ō-stem nom.-acc. pl. *-a* (the old nom. pl. ending *-o* survives as the nom.-acc. pl. ending of fem. strong adjectives)

Of course the *results* of these syncretisms can be analyzed as impoverishment, but that analysis became possible only after the syncretism was complete. In other words, there were two historical changes: first the accusative marker was generalized because of learner errors, then the new syncretism was (presumably) reanalyzed as impoverishment.

But though "inverse" cases like these prevent us from hypothesizing that syncretism always occurs by the (incorrect) acquisition of impoverishment filters, many syncretisms do involve the generalization of default markers, often by

Table 8.9 *Present indicative passive paradigms of 'call'*

		Gothic	Latin	Ancient Greek	
sg.	1	haitada	vocor	/kalô:mai/	καλοῦμαι
	2	haitaza	vocāris	/kalê:i/	καλῇι
	3	haitada	vocātur	/kalê:tai/	καλεῖται
du.	1	haitanda	—	—	
	2	haitanda	—	/kalê:sthon/	καλεῖσθον
	3	—	—	/kalê:sthon/	καλεῖσθον
pl.	1	haitanda	vocāmur	/kaló:metha/	καλούμεθα
	2	haitanda	vocāminī	/kalê:sthe/	καλεῖσθε
	3	haitanda	vocantur	/kalô:ntai/	καλοῦνται

means of straightforward impoverishment. The rest of this section will present and discuss a range of cases.

A spectacular example of syncretism by the generalization of defaults occurred repeatedly in the history and reconstructable prehistory of Germanic languages. The syncretism occurred first in the passive endings. Like Latin, PGmc. inherited a full set of mediopassive person-and-number endings from PIE but restricted them to passive function (in Germanic, though not in Latin, deponent verbs were also eliminated). Most of the attested daughters of PGmc. replaced the inherited passive forms with phrases, except for a few lexical relics, but in Gothic, the Germanic language which is adequately attested earliest, there is still a full passive paradigm in the present tense. When we compare the passive endings of Gothic with those of Latin or Greek, however, we get a surprise. Table 8.9 gives the present indicative passive of 'call' in Gothic (*haitan*), Latin (*vocāre*), and Ancient Greek (/kalê:n/ καλεῖν). (Person-and-number combinations which are never expressed by a distinctive ending in any paradigm in the language are represented here by blanks; all are duals, for which plurals are used instead by straightforward impoverishment [see Chapter 7].) The Gothic paradigm exhibits massive syncretism: its eight cells are filled by only three endings (as compared with seven in the present indicative active, in which the 3sg. and 2pl. have accidentally homonymous endings). The syncretism of 1sg. and 3sg. will be discussed below; here we are concerned with the syncretism of all the nonsingular forms. Their ending is the inherited 3pl. ending; its *-nd-* corresponds exactly to the *-nt-* of the Latin and Greek 3pl. endings. Since third-person forms are unmarked for person, and since duals are specially marked plurals, the 3pl. is the default nonsingular form, and this syncretism is a clear instance of defaulting to a maximally unmarked form when markers for more complex morphosyntactic features are lost. How that loss occurred is not so clear; possibly the relative rarity of passive forms did not provide native learners with enough examples, but we do not have enough evidence to advance any hypothesis with much confidence.

Table 8.10 *Present and past indicative paradigms in some West Germanic languages*

		Old English	Old Saxon	Old High German
Pres. indic.				
sg.	1	weorþe	wirđu	wirdu
	2	wierst	wirđis	wirdis
	3	wierþ	wirđid	wirdit
pl.	1	weorþaþ	werđađ	werdumēs (→ -ēm)
	2	weorþaþ	werđađ	werdet
	3	weorþaþ	werđađ	werdant
Past indic.				
sg.	1	wearþ	warđ	ward
	2	wurde	wurdi	wurti
	3	wearþ	warđ	ward
pl.	1	wurdon	wurdun	wurtum
	2	wurdon	wurdun	wurtut
	3	wurdon	wurdun	wurtun

A second instance of this syncretism, affecting all active finite paradigms, occurred in the northern West Germanic dialects long after PGmc. had diversified into several languages. By that point dual forms as well as passive forms had been lost. The effects of this second round of nonsingular syncretism can be seen by comparing typical present indicative and past indicative paradigms of OE and Old Saxon – the two northern West Germanic languages which are attested in the early Middle Ages – with their close relative OHG, as in Table 8.10. Our sample verb is the common strong verb 'become'. (The subjunctive nonsingular forms were exactly like those of the past indicative, but with different vowels preceding the endings.) Again the inherited 3pl. form has come to be used with all nonsingular subjects (since the 1du. and 2du. subject pronouns are used with pl. verb forms in Germanic languages other than Gothic, as expected). In this case, however, we can suggest a possible scenario for the process of syncretism. The northern 3pl. present indicative ending was *-ãþi < *-anþi, originally differing from OHG -*ant* < *-andi only in the identity of its obstruent consonant. We might therefore expect the 2pl. ending (in all categories) to have been *-þ, differing from OHG -*t* < *-d in the same way. But that need not have been so: such "Verner's Law alternants" occurred extensively in PGmc. verb endings, and a daughter language that generalized one particular alternant in one ending did not always generalize the same alternant in other endings. (For further explanation see Ringe 2006: 102–5, 182–4, with exemplification on pp. 237–9.) If the northern dialects generalized *-d in the 2pl., the relevant endings must have been as in Table 8.11. In the last three columns the plural forms differ only in their final consonants, and – crucially – the consonants of the 1pl. and 2pl. forms each differ from that of the 3pl. forms by only one distinctive feature (*d was always a stop in

Table 8.11 *Inherited pl. verb endings in northern West Germanic*

	Pres. indic.	Pres. subj.	Past indic.	Past subj.
1pl.	*-um	*-ēm	*-um	*-īm
2pl.	*-id	*-ēd	*-ud	*-īd
3pl.	*-ąþi	*-ēn	*-un	*-īn

PWGmc.). Misperception of these consonants by native learners could have led to the generalization of a single form, and it is not surprising that the form not marked for person was generalized. The syncretism could then have spread to the present indicative, again with the "non-person" form generalized. The final result would have been learnable as an impoverishment filter.

A third, more limited instance of this syncretism was mentioned early in the preceding section. We noted that in late OHG the 1pl. and 3pl. endings of past and subjunctive verb paradigms fell together as *-n* by sound change, and that in MHG the leveling of 3pl. *-n* into the present indicative (replacing inherited *-nt*) rendered the 1pl. and 3pl. of all verb paradigms accidentally identical, except for the present indicative of 'be'. The subsequent spread of 3pl. *sind* '(they) are' to 1pl. function is yet another example of plural syncretism under the form of an inherited 3pl. (though the 2pl. familiar form remains the distinctive *seid*).

Intuitively these syncretisms make sense: if the morphosyntactic category "person" is no longer marked, the form not marked for person – i.e. the "third-person" form – should be used. But the feature hierarchy required is not the one suggested as a universal default by DM (see Chapter 7). In the default hierarchy person is higher than number; therefore a filter *[1 pl], for instance, should suppress [pl] in the prohibited feature bundle and lead to the use of the 1sg. form with 1pl. subjects, which is not what happened. It seems clear that in early Germanic languages the hierarchy of features was different, with number outranking person.

The reader should note that this does not necessarily have anything to do with the development of Germanic dual forms. In all the Germanic languages except Gothic, dual verb forms were lost in the prehistoric period, but 1du. and 2du. pronouns survived into the historical period (except in OHG) and were used with 1pl. and 2pl. verb forms respectively. Because duals were doubly marked as [du pl], a filter prohibiting the expression of [du] in finite verbs would cause default to the plural regardless of the feature hierarchy.

Note also that in all these Germanic syncretisms the nonsingular forms collectively are behaving more or less like what Carstairs-McCarthy calls a "slab," i.e. a subparadigm corresponding to a superordinate morphosyntactic category (see Carstairs 1987: 77–83, where the concept is introduced and applied in a completely different way). That suggests that "slab behavior" in general might prove to be a consequence of the hierarchy of morphosyntactic features, a hypothesis that deserves further investigation.

Table 8.12 *Partial PIE paradigm of the determiner 'that'*

	Masc.	Neut.	Fem.
nom. pl.	*tóy	*téh$_2$	*téh$_2$es
acc. pl.	*tóns	*téh$_2$	*téh$_2$ns (apparently *[tā́s])
gen. pl.	*tóysoHom		*téh$_2$soHom
dat. pl.	*tóymos		*téh$_2$mos

A further syncretism in the Gothic present passive might be the result of very different factors. The ending -*ada* of the 1sg. and 3sg. is the inherited 3sg. form – i.e., the default form for the entire paradigm; formally we can say that an impoverishment filter

> *[1] / passive

has been acquired, so that the "personless" 3sg. form surfaces. (We know that this change happened within the separate prehistory of Gothic because a Runic Norse 1sg. *h[a]itē* 'I am called' with a quite different ending is attested [Krause 1971: 122].) It just so happens that the 1sg. and 3sg. of the (active) *past* indicative are always identical in Gothic (because of earlier sound changes); possibly native learners extended that pattern to the marginal present passive in the absence of sufficient evidence to the contrary – though in this case too we do not have enough evidence to be confident in our suggestions.

A cluster of syncretisms which is both easy to understand and straightforward to model (as impoverishment) is the erosion of gender marking in the plurals of adjectives and determiners in Germanic languages. PGmc. and its daughters had a rule that nouns of different genders which were conjoined triggered neuter plural concord (Streitberg 1920: 166 with references, Ringe 2006: 171); we can thus infer that the neuter gender was the default – at least for the purposes of concord – and the development of PIE paradigms in Germanic has to be evaluated in that light. In PIE all forms of feminine adjectives, quantifiers, and determiners were distinct from the corresponding forms of the other genders; masculines and neuters were usually distinct in the direct cases but identical in the oblique cases. In PGmc. that was still largely true, but one significant syncretism had developed: in the paradigms of determiners, quantifiers, and strong adjectives, in each of the oblique cases of the plural there was only a single form for all three genders, and it was the inherited masculine/neuter form. A comparison of the plural forms of the default determiner 'that' in the two protolanguages will illustrate (omitting oblique cases which were lost in PGmc. or whose markers are difficult to reconstruct); we present the PIE partial paradigm in Table 8.12 and the corresponding PGmc. paradigm in Table 8.13. (Vowels with two macrons are "trimoric" vowels; what their phonetic realization was is unclear. For discussion see Ringe 2006: 73–4 with references.) The sound changes which the PGmc. forms underwent are straightforward enough that the reader can see

Table 8.13 *Partial PGmc. paradigm of the determiner 'that'*

	Masc.	Neut.	Fem.
nom. pl.	*þai	*þō	*þōz
acc. pl.	*þanz	*þō	*þōz
gen. pl.		*þaizõ̃	
dat. pl.		*þaimaz	

which PIE form is the ancestor of which PGmc. form. Conspicuously missing are fem. gen. pl. "*þōzõ̃" and dat. pl. "*þōmaz," the expected reflexes of the PIE feminine forms; they have been replaced by the corresponding masculine/neuter forms with *-ai- (reflecting PIE *-óy-). The learner errrors which gave rise to this change are likely to have involved misanalyses of conjoined concord situations; the change can be represented as the acquisition of an impoverishment filter

    *[fem obl] / [pl],

which would trigger defaulting to the neuter form in the oblique cases of the plural – provided that case outranks gender on the feature hierarchy.

The expected next step in this development would be gender syncretism in the direct cases of the plural as well, i.e. the simplification of the filter to *[fem pl] and the addition of a filter *[masc pl]. In PGmc. only the numeral 'four' had undergone that change. As expected, it is the PIE neuter form that survives: PGmc. nom.–acc. *fedwōr 'four' (all genders) reflects PIE neuter *kʷetwór (Stiles 1985: 85–8, Ringe 2006: 204, 287). The earliest attested stages of most Germanic languages retain the PGmc. situation. However, in OE the third-person pronoun and the determiners also exhibit gender syncretism in the direct cases of the plural (see e.g. Campbell 1962: 289–92). Though the expected phonological developments of the inherited forms are not entirely clear, it appears that in the determiners the inherited masculine forms survive, while in the third-person pronoun there is variation between the inherited masculine and neuter forms; that probably indicates a shift in the default gender from neuter to masculine within the separate prehistory of OE.

In later stages of some Germanic languages gender syncretism in the plural became complete; modern German is an example. A similar development occurred independently in the history of Russian and of other Slavic languages. It appears that syncretism by the generalization of defaults is a widespread type of morphological change.

In different circumstances the generalization of a default marker can result in a type of change called "leveling." Leveling can be defined as the elimination of an alternant which occurs in a specific morphosyntactic environment. An example which was mentioned in passing above will illustrate the process. In OHG the 3pl. ending was -nt in the present indicative but -n in the past indicative and the present and past subjunctive. Clearly -*n* was the default ending, since the categories in which it appeared had nothing in common except that they were 3pl. forms. Moreover, there was a small class of common verbs called "preterite-presents" whose present tenses were inflected like ordinary past tenses; in their paradigms all 3pl. forms ended in -*n*. Not surprisingly, -*n* replaced -*nt* within the MHG period, thus "leveling out" the functionless difference between the 3pl. endings. A precisely parallel change occurred in the Midlands dialects of ME, with default 3pl. -*en* replacing present indicative -*eþ* (see Brunner 1948: 74–5, Mossé 1952: 76). Leveling of markers characteristic of one lexically determined inflectional class into another is commonplace, and it naturally leads to the erosion of lexical classes; examples will be given in a later section.

Paradigms and suppletion

The examples adduced in the last paragraph above involve the elimination of "suppletive" alternants, i.e. phonological strings which express the same morphosyntactic categories but do not have the same underlying phonological form. Among f-morphemes suppletion is so commonplace that it is seldom remarked on (see Carstairs 1987: 15, 147–8). But root-morphemes also occasionally exhibit suppletion; a familiar example is English *went*, the suppletive past tense of *go*. It turns out that suppletion among roots is harder to define than suppletion among f-morphemes. A typical traditional definition might be that forms made to different roots (or etymologically unrelated forms) belonging to the same paradigm are suppletive. Such a definition obviously depends on the concept of the paradigm. A paradigm, in turn, might be defined as a complete set of inflectional forms of a single lexeme – and that definition, in turn, depends on the concept of inflection. Unfortunately it proves impossible to draw a clear distinction between inflectional morphology and derivational morphology; there are plenty of instances that fall clearly into one category or the other, but also not a few that seem to be "borderline" in one way or another (see Carstairs 1987: 4–5 with references). This is one of the reasons that DM does not recognize the distinction – nor the linguistic reality of paradigms that depends on it. But in that case, how are we to define suppletion of roots?

A consideration of the suppletive verbs in use in Classical Attic Greek suggests one possible answer. Many are of the expected type, with tense-and-aspect stems formed from different roots that fit neatly into a single paradigm; in Table 8.14 are some typical partial paradigms. (The perfect stems and the aorist passive stem [from which the future passive stem is formed by further suffixation] are typically made to one or more of the roots exemplified by the stems listed here.) But there are also several sets of defective verbs in partial competition, none of which has a full paradigm of forms; in a sense they are suppletive, but together they do not make a single tidy paradigm. The most striking case involves verbs meaning 'say', presented in Table 8.15.

Table 8.14 *Some suppletive verbs in Attic Greek*

	Aorist (nonpassive)	Present	Future (nonpassive)
'carry, bring'	/enenkê:n/ ἐνεγκεῖν	/pʰére:n/ φέρειν	/óise:n/ οἴσειν
'see'	/idê:n/ ἰδεῖν	/horâ:n/ ὁρᾶν	/ópsestʰai/ ὄψεσθαι
'eat'	/pʰagê:n/ φαγεῖν	/estʰíe:n/ ἐσθίειν	/édestʰai/ ἔδεσθαι
'take'	/helê:n/ ἑλεῖν	/haire:n/ αἱρεῖν	/hairé:se:n/ αἱρήσειν
'run'	/dramê:n/ δραμεῖν	/trékʰe:n/ τρέχειν	/dramê:stʰai/ δραμεῖσθαι

Table 8.15 *'Say' in Attic Greek*

Present	Fut. nonpass.	Aor. nonpass.	Perf. active
/pʰánai/ φάναι	/pʰé:se:n/ φήσειν	(/pʰê:sai/ φῆσαι)	—
/lége:n/ λέγειν	/lékse:n/ λέξειν	(/léksai/ λέξαι)	—
—	/erê:n/ ἐρεῖν	—	/eirɛ:kénai/ εἰρηκέναι
—	—	/eipê:n/ εἰπεῖν	—

The stems in parentheses are very rarely used in Classical Attic. (They do not occur at all in Attic inscriptions, which in some ways reflect Classical Attic speech more closely than literary documents [see Threatte 1996: 529–30, 619].) The aorist passives are /lekʰtʰê:nai/ λεχθῆναι and /hrɛ:tʰê:nai/ ῥηθῆναι; the perfect mediopassives are /lelékʰtʰai/ λελέχθαι, /eirɛ:sthai/ εἰρῆσθαι, and an isolated 3sg. imperative /pepʰástʰɔ:/ πεφάσθω 'let it be said'. A present /agoréue:n/ ἀγορεύειν, appearing mostly in compounds in place of /lége:n/, also occurs. By far the commonest stems are present /pʰánai/ and aorist /eipê:n/. Several verbs meaning 'hit, beat' present a similar picture of partial competition and partial suppletion; so do a pair meaning 'ask' and another pair meaning 'sell'. All these examples show that suppletion of the familiar kind is part of a larger phenomenon: the inflected forms of defective lexemes *can* dovetail neatly to form a single paradigm, but they *need not* do so. We might therefore define suppletive lexemes as synonymous defective lexemes which are never in functional competition; such a definition would allow for a cline of intermediate situations between full competition and "clean" suppletion. This is yet another indication that paradigms are epiphenomena.

However, it seems possible that the "messy" situation just described is genuinely different from a case like English *go* : *went* : *gone*, in which there is clearly only a single verb in the native speaker's grammar. If that is true, we might analyze the latter as follows in DM. We recognize only a single root √Go, but unlike most roots, this one is paired in the Vocabulary with phonologically unrelated strings whose insertion is conditioned by the f-morphemes in construction with it: /wɛnt/ is inserted in the context of [past], but /goʊ/ in most other contexts. (The past participle /gɔn/ is clearly a form of /goʊ/, though the phonology is irregular.) As we will see immediately below, sets of defective lexemes like the Greek examples adduced above can develop into neat suppletive paradigms, and

Table 8.16 *'Go' in Latin and three of its descendants*

		Latin	Spanish	French	Italian
Pres. indic.					
sg.	1	eō	voy	vais	vado
	2	īs	vas	vas	vai
	3	it	va	va	va
pl.	1	īmus	vamos	allons	andiamo
	2	ītis	vais	allez	andate
	3	eunt	van	vont	vanno
Pres. subj.					
sg.	3	eat	vaya	aille	vada
Pres. inf.		īre	ir	aller	andare
Impf. indic.					
sg.	3	ībat	iba	allait	andava
Fut. indic.					
sg.	3	ībit	irá	ira	andrà
Perf. indic.					
sg.	3	iit	fué	alla	andò
Perf. ptc.		itum	ido	allé	andato

it seems likely that that occurs when native learners reanalyze them as single roots with the exceptional property just described.

Few examples of suppletion have arisen within the recorded history of languages. A clear example is the verb 'go' in Romance languages. Comparison of a partial paradigm in Latin and several of its descendants, given in Table 8.16, will show what has happened. The Latin verb was irregular but not suppletive, with a present stem /i:-/ ~ /e-/, a perfect stem /i-/, and a third stem /it-/. In late Latin it was partly replaced by *vādere* 'to walk' and partly by other verbs (*ambulāre* 'to walk' in parts of Gaul, *ambitāre* 'to make a circuit' in parts of Italy, etc.). In the long run, different patterns in the frequency of use must have led native learners to acquire some forms of each competing verb and not others in each area of the former Roman Empire. The inherited verb evidently survived best in the Iberian peninsula, but the most interesting survival is the French future *ira*. The Latin future tense was everywhere replaced by a phrase consisting of the infinitive and the present indicative of *habēre* 'to have'; that is still the situation in Sardinian and in the Sicilian dialects of Italian, but elsewhere the phrase underwent univerbation. The French future thus contains a fossilized infinitive and shows that univerbation of the phrase preceded replacement of the inherited infinitive *īre* 'to go'. That confirms what we would have suspected in any case: that the constitution of the Romance suppletive paradigms was a gradual and lengthy parallel process.

So far as we can reconstruct, a similar process gave rise to the multiple suppletive verbs of many conservative IE languages; but it appears that a particular

development in the prehistory of that family made suppletion a more likely outcome. For the last common ancestor of the non-Anatolian subfamilies we can
reconstruct many verbs with two or three stems expressing different aspects; for
instance, it seems clear that PIE *telh$_2$- 'lift' had not only a basic perfective
("aorist") with zero-affixation (3sg. *télh$_2$-t '(s)he lifted') but also a nasal-infixed
imperfective ("present;" 3sg. *tl̥-né-h$_2$-ti '(s)he's lifting') and a reduplicated stative ("perfect;" 3sg. *te-tólh$_2$-e '(s)he's holding [it] up'). But there are also quite
a few verb roots for which only a single aspect stem can be reconstructed; for
instance, *bʰer- 'carry' seems to have made only an imperfective *bʰér-e/o-, and
that is why 'carry' is suppletive in Latin, Ancient Greek, and both Tocharian languages. (See Ringe 2006: 24–41 for a sketch of the reconstructable system.) That
seems puzzling until we examine the verb system of the Anatolian languages. A
basic Anatolian verb has only one stem. It is possible to construct additional stems
with specialized meanings (imperfective, causative, etc.), but each is clearly a
derived lexeme; they do not all together constitute a single inflectional paradigm.
It seems likely that Anatolian preserves the PIE system, more or less, and that
the other daughters have incorporated an inherited system of lexical derivation
into the inflection of their verbs.[9] In the course of such a development it would
be natural for etymologically different verbs to be incorporated into a single
inflectional paradigm for functional reasons, and we suggest that that is what
happened.

Regardless of how they arise, suppletive paradigms tend to persist over long
periods of time, even when parts of them are replaced. The inflection of 'go' in
English illustrates this process. A present *ganganã 'to go' can be reconstructed
for PGmc. (Seebold 1970: 213–6); a competing present *gānã (stem *gai- ~ *gā-)
might or might not be reconstructable for PGmc. but had certainly entered the
language by the Proto-West Germanic period (Seebold 1970: 216–17, Guðrún
Þórhallsdóttir 1993: 35–7, Ringe 2006: 264–5). A past stem is reconstructable
for neither verb; instead there was a past whose PGmc. shape is difficult to reconstruct but which certainly began with the sequence *ijj- (Seebold 1970: 174–6
with references). The same situation persists in OE prose: the present is usually
gān, less often gangan, and the past is ēode, probably a remodeled reflex of the
PGmc. suppletive past. In ME gōn gradually out-competed gang (except in the
north), but yēde survived as the suppletive past (see the OED s.v. yode, yede v.[1]).
In the fifteenth century, however, the latter was replaced by went, the past tense of
wend, whose present subsequently ceased to be used; thus the PGmc. suppletion
persists even though none of the modern forms is certainly a direct reflex of any
of the PGmc. forms.

Concord classes and lexical classes

Suppletion of roots is an extreme case of irregularity in inflection; it
is therefore not surprising that, though many languages exhibit a few cases of

root-suppletion, not many exhibit more than a few. The division of lexemes into arbitrary classes for one or more inflectional purposes, which also complicates the grammar, seems to be more common, though different types of classes of lexemes are not equally so.

Concord classes of nouns appear to be a relatively common type of root-class. The familiar "genders" of IE and Afro-Asiatic languages are concord classes; so are the noun classes of Niger-Congo languages. Comparable systems are found in Algonkian and Northeast Caucasian languages and a wide range of other families; Aronoff 1994: 89–121 adduces examples from the Torricelli family (Arapesh) and the Lower Sepik family (Yimas) of New Guinea, and Corbett 1991 provides a good worldwide survey. The defining characteristic of concord classes is that adjectives and determiners which are part of the same DP as a noun, as well as third-person pronouns which corefer, are marked with its concord class marker; in some cases verbs are also marked for concord if the noun is the subject (or another argument; see the Chichewa examples in Chapter 1), and other patterns of concord-marking are occasionally found. Thus concord systems are one of the principal loci of "dissociated" morphemes (see Chapter 7) not generated by the syntax.

Very little is actually known about the origin of concord classes; they are typically in place in the earliest reconstructable stage of any language family that has them. It is reasonable to infer that concord markers were originally deictics and/or classifiers of some sort which underwent univerbation with phrasal heads (see Corbett 1991: 310–12 with references), but the evolution of a system of concord from such beginnings has not been observed. More can be said about how existing concord systems develop. The overall structures of concord systems seem to be stable over long periods of time, but changes in detail are not rare. Occasionally a new concord class is created, virtually always reflecting a transparent semantic classification (see Corbett 1991: 313). For instance, Russian has split each of its inherited three genders into "subgenders" on the semantic basis of animacy (ibid. pp. 165–8): the accusative plural is identical with the genitive plural if the noun is animate, but with the nominative plural if it is inanimate; the same pattern recurs in the singular of masculine nouns ending in a nonpalatalized consonant (though not in the singular of other genders, nor in the singular of other classes of masculine nouns). Note the partial paradigms in Table 8.17. See further Corbett 1991: 42–3, 165–8. This development apparently had a syntactic origin. Some direct objects are actually marked with the genitive case rather than the accusative in Russian, e.g. in negative sentences. This rule was extended to some singular nouns denoting male human beings in contexts in which the accusative was required, namely to those whose acc. sg. was identical with the nom. sg., as a means of marking the direct object more clearly; native learners reinterpreted these genitives as accusatives, and later generations of learners spread the pattern to masculine plurals, then to all plurals (Corbett 1991: 98–9 with references). Other Slavic languages have undergone similar developments; Old Church Slavonic exhibits only the beginning of the process, in which only masculine o-stems denoting free adult male human beings have an

Table 8.17 *Partial paradigms of some Russian nouns*

		Masculine		Feminine		Neuter	
		Inanimate	Animate	Inanimate	Animate	Inanimate	Animate
		'tooth'	'husband'	'hand'	'wife'	'face'	'child'
sg.	nom.	зуб /zub/	муж /muʒ/	рука /ruˈka/	жена /ʒeˈna/	лицо /lʲiˈtso/	дитя /dʲiˈtʲa/
	acc.	зуб /zub/	мужа /ˈmuʒa/	руку /ˈruku/	жену /ʒeˈnu/	лицо /lʲiˈtso/	дитя /dʲiˈtʲa/
	gen.	зуба /ˈzuba/	мужа /ˈmuʒa/	руки /ruˈkʲi/	жены /ʒeˈnɨ/	лица /lʲiˈtsa/	дитяти /dʲiˈtʲatʲi/
pl.	nom.	зубы /ˈzubɨ/	мужья /muʒˈja/	руки /ˈrukʲi/	жёны /ˈʒonɨ/	лица /ˈlʲitsa/	дети /ˈdʲetʲi/
	acc.	зубы /ˈzubɨ/	мужей /muˈʒej/	руки /ˈrukʲi/	жён /ʒon/	лица /ˈlʲitsa/	детей /dʲeˈtʲej/
	gen.	зубов /zuˈbov/	мужей /muˈʒej/	рук /ruk/	жён /ʒon/	лиц /lʲits/	детей /dʲeˈtʲej/

Table 8.18 *Partial paradigms of some noun phrases in Tocharian B*

	'great king' (masc.)	'great queen' (fem.)	'large fire' (neut.)
sg. nom.	orotstse walo	orotstsa lāntsa	orotstse puwar
obl.	orocce lānt	orotstsai lāntso	orocce puwar
pl. nom.	orocci lāñc	orotstsana lantsona	orotstsana pwāra
obl.	oroccem lāntäm	orotstsana lantsona	orotstsana pwāra

Table 8.19 *Partial paradigms of some noun phrases in Romanian*

	'the good man' (m.)	'the good house' (f.)	'the good thread' (n.)
sg.	bărbatul bun	casa bună	firul bun
pl.	bărbaţii buni	casele bune	firele bune

acc. sg. identical with the gen. sg. (Ronald Kim, p.c.). This process resembles the early Latin disambiguation of 1sg. future forms by the use of subjunctives (see above).

Reduction of the number of concord classes seems to be more common. The three genders of PIE have survived to the present in some daughters (e.g. Icelandic and German, Greek, and Slavic languages generally), but in others they have been reduced to two (non-neuter and neuter in mainland Scandinavian; masculine and feminine in, e.g., Baltic, Celtic, and most Romance languages), and in some daughters grammatical gender has been lost altogether (e.g. Armenian). This can only be the result of learner errors, occasioned by the phonological erosion of markers and/or preexisting gender syncretisms. In some cases, such as the wholesale transfer of late OE nouns into the masculine class (see below), the reduction of genders was apparently straightforward. A few cases can be shown to be more complex; one phenomenon in particular deserves mention.

In the Tocharian languages nouns are still classified into three genders, but neuter adjectives, determiners, and quantifiers exhibit a curious split syncretism: their endings are always identical with those of masculines in the singular and with those of feminines in the plural. In Table 8.18 we present three typical Tocharian B noun phrases in the nominative and oblique cases of the singular and plural. Since the two languages exhibit the same system in considerable detail, this development probably occurred in (or before) Proto-Tocharian. Astonishingly, the same pattern recurs in Romanian – a language whose speakers cannot have been in contact with those of Tocharian, since the latter were already in Central Asia by the time the Romans conquered the Balkans. In Table 8.19 we present three Romanian noun phrases in the direct case, singular and plural. The syncretism of neuter and masculine in the singular makes sense, since the two genders were originally distinguished only in the nominative and accusative cases, but the syncretism of neuter and feminine in the plural is difficult to account for; in particular, phonological mergers seem to have played no role in either Romanian or Tocharian. Evidently we must accept this as a "natural" way for gender systems to develop, though so far its rationale remains unclear. But there is a further fact of interest: Italian too exhibits relics of this development in a handful of common nouns, all descended from Latin neuters (e.g. *l'uovo* 'the egg', pl. *le uova*, Latin neut. *ōvum*; *il ginocchio* 'knee', pl. *le ginocchia*, diminutive of Latin neut. *genū*). There were more such relics in Old Italian. It thus appears that in Italian, at least, the reduction of three genders to two occurred after an initial stage in which a Romanian-type syncretism took place.

A quite different type of lexeme classes is exemplified by the "declensions" and "conjugations" of Latin grammar. These are not concord classes but arbitrary classes of lexemes which exhibit partly different inflectional markers for identical functions. Following Aronoff, we will simply call them "inflectional classes" (see Aronoff 1994: 64). Languages with a small number of well-defined inflectional classes occupy a kind of middle ground between those like Turkish or Greenlandic, in which most or all lexemes of each major lexical category are inflected alike, and those like Ancient Greek or Navajo, in which there are so many different patterns that recognizing inflectional classes is not always more useful than treating each lexeme separately. How lexical classes arise and develop can be illustrated by a very brief historical sketch of the Latin system.

The development of the Latin noun system was comparatively straightforward. In PIE there were already two lexical classes, "thematic" nouns, which ended in the ablauting vowel *-e- ~ *-o-, and "athematic" nouns, which ended in obstruents or sonorants (including the high vocalics *i and *u); their number-and-case endings were partly different, and athematic nouns exhibited half a dozen different patterns of accent and ablaut (i.e. vowel alternation within the root; see Ringe 2006: 41–50). The first change of importance was the split of the athematic class into four or five lexical classes,[10] which happened for the following reasons. Regular sound changes gradually obscured the boundaries between stems and endings and the original parallelism of the different subclasses of stems. For instance, among the non-neuter nominative plural forms, i-stem *-ey-es lost its intervocalic *y and contracted to -*ēs*, but u-stem *-ew-es > *-owes (which eventually became Classical Latin -*ūs*). The development of dative singular endings was similar: i-stem *-ey-ey > *-*ēy* > *-ei (> Classical -*ī*) – identical with the consonant-stem ending *-ey > -*ei* (cf. Old Latin *rēcei* 'to the king') – but u-stem *-ew-ey > *-owei (> Classical -*uī*). Especially disruptive was the contraction of *-eh$_2$- and *-eh$_2$e- to *ā, the sound change which gave rise to a distinctive class of feminine ā-stems. At an early date (roughly, in Proto-Italic) a partial paradigm of the non-neuter athematic classes must have looked something like Table 8.20. The inflection of the classes is still obviously parallel, and it is still clear that the various classes of vowel stems underlyingly exhibit the consonant-stem endings preceded by something further, but not all the details can still be handled by phonological rules that would be straightforward for native learners to acquire. There is thus an incipient divergence of one lexical class into four. The divergence of the ā-stems from the other classes was increased by morphological

Table 8.20 *Nascent stem classes of nouns in early Italic*

		C-stems	i-stems	u-stems	ā-stems
sg.	nom.	*-s, ∅	*-is	*-us	*-ā
	acc.	*-em	*-im	*-um	*-ām
	gen.	*-es	*-eis	*-ous	*-ās
	dat.	*-ei	*-ei	*-owei	*-āi
pl.	nom.	*-es	*-ēs	*-owes	*-ās
	acc.	*-ens	*-ins	*-uns	*-ās

changes from two sources, beginning already in the Proto-Italic period. On the one hand, the inflection of ā-stem nouns was influenced by the partly different inflection of ā-stem determiners; in particular, the genitive plural in *-āsōm, with its distinctive "pronominal" *-s-, spread to ā-stem nouns (whence Oscan **-asúm**, *-azum*, Classical Latin *-ārum*; cf. Skt. *tásām*, Homeric Greek /táːɔːn/ τᾱ́ων 'of those (fem.)' < PIE *téh₂soHom). On the other hand, the fact that the largest class of adjectives had o-stem masculine and neuter forms, but ā-stem feminines, encouraged the repeated mutual influence of those two classes on each other. In the Proto-Italic period the syntactic merger of the instrumental case with the ablative led to the use of *-ois (< PIE instrumental plural *-ōys; cf. Oscan **-úís**, *-ois*) as the dative-ablative plural ending of o-stems; the corresponding ā-stem ending, which must have been *-āfos or the like,[11] with the same ending *-fos as the other athematic stems (> Latin *-bus*), was remodeled as *-ais (cf. Oscan **-aís**; by later sound changes both endings became Classical Latin *-īs*). Somewhat later, within the individual history of Latin, an ā-stem nominative plural *-ai (Classical *-ae*) was created on the model of o-stem *-oi (> Classical *-ī*);[12] later still the genitive singular *-ās* (which survives in *pater familiās* 'father of (the) household') was replaced by *-āī*, the o-stem ending evidently being tacked onto the stem vowel. By that point the ā-stems had lost all connection with the other athematic classes, and their inflection was roughly parallel to that of the o-stems.

It might be supposed that the i-stems, u-stems, and consonant stems would also have continued to diverge over time. The u-stems did become a separate "declension" (the "fourth"), but the i-stems and consonant-stems re-converged. (We know that they had become distinguishable classes in Proto-Italic because they are still largely separate in Oscan and Umbrian; see e.g. Buck 1928: 124–31.) That development might have been encouraged by the syncope of i-stem nom. sg. *-is to *-s* in disyllables when preceded by a heavy syllable ending in *-t-* or *-d-* (cf. Sommer 1948: 369–70), but for the most part the convergence was clearly the result of native-learner errors, specifically the confusion of similar-sounding endings with identical functions. The following changes occurred:

(a)   consonant-stem acc. sg. *-em* was leveled to most i-stems (though inherited i-stem *-im* survives as an alternative for a few nouns in the Classical period);

(b)   consonant-stem gen. sg. *-es (> -is) was leveled to all i-stems, ousting inherited i-stem *-eis (the reverse happened in Oscan, see e.g. Buck 1928: 124–5);

(c)   consonant-stem abl. sg. *-i (> -e) was leveled to most non-neuter i-stems, though the inherited i-stem ending *-īd (> -ī) survives in neuters (and adjectives), and as an alternative for a few non-neuter nouns (e.g. *ignī* 'with fire');

(d)   i-stem non-neuter nom. pl. -ēs was leveled to all non-neuter consonant stems, ousting inherited *-es;

(e)   conversely, consonant-stem non-neuter acc. pl. -ēs was leveled to the i-stems, where it is still in competition with inherited -īs in the Classical period;

(f)   i-stem dat.-abl. pl. -ibus was leveled to all consonant stems, ousting inherited *-bus.

The result was not a complete merger of the two classes; in Classical Latin neuter i-stems and consonant stems are still clearly distinguishable, and even non-neuter i-stems can still be distinguished from consonant stems by their gen. pl. -ium (vs. consonant-stem -um), optional acc. pl. -īs, and sometimes nom. sg. -is or -ēs. But the two classes have become so similar that it makes sense to treat them as subclasses of the "third declension."

What generalizations can be made about this complex series of developments (including further details that we have glossed over here)? The broadest generalization is that the origin and development of lexical classes are the result of contingent events that have nothing to do with the classes themselves. Regular sound change plays a significant role, both in giving rise to lexical classes and in providing the raw material for learner errors that affect them. Also important are morphological changes that reflect the larger structure of the language (such as the functional relation between o-stems and ā-stems in adjective inflection). All these changes occur one at a time, so that the overall picture changes only slightly from one generation to the next; it is the cumulative effect of individual changes that increases or reduces the number and independence of lexical classes in the long run. Paradigms do not seem to play any clear role in these processes; on the contrary, many of the most important changes are those that cut across paradigms.

The development of lexical classes of Latin verbs was far more complex, and considerations of space forbid a detailed discussion here. A few observations, however, will give some idea of how the Latin "conjugations" arose. Though each conjugation includes verbs of several originally different types, the principal sources of first-, second-, and fourth-conjugation verbs were PIE derived presents. The first conjugation includes verbs in *-yé- ~ *-yó- derived from ā-stem nominals (see the discussion earlier in this chapter), a few old factitives in -ā- < PIE *-eh₂- (e.g. *novā-* 'to renew' = Hittite *newahh-*; cf. Latin *novos* 'new' = Hittite *nēwas*), and very many more recent denominatives; the second

conjugation includes statives in -ē- < PIE *-éh₁- (e.g. *rubē-* 'be red' = Old Irish
ruidi- 'blush', and cf. also OHG *rotē-* 'be red') and causatives and intensives in
*-éye- ∼ *-éyo- (e.g. Old Latin *lūcē-* 'cause to shine' = Sanskrit *rocáya-*); the
fourth conjugation includes denominatives in *-(i)yé- ∼ *-(i)yó- (most of which
were created within the separate prehistory of Latin, but cf. *sepelī-* 'bury' = Sanskrit *saparyá-* 'honor'). All these types of derived verbs had one thing in common
in PIE: they formed only imperfective ("present") stems. But in the prehistory
of Italic, as in all the other non-Anatolian daughters, most verbs were eventually
provided with a full range of three aspect stems (see Rix 1992: 225); moreover,
the original aspect system gradually developed into a mixed aspect-and-tense
system, so that the traditional appellations of the stems, "present, aorist, perfect,"
become increasingly apt (and we will use them in the rest of this discussion). It
appears that the innovative aorist stems of these derived verbs were formed by
adding the inherited suffix *-s-; that formation might actually survive in Classical Latin in supposedly "contracted" forms like *amāstī* 'you loved' (Rix 1992:
226–7). But the perfects of these verbs were apparently periphrastic, constructed
with a perfect active participle in *-wus-i- and appropriate forms of the verb
'be' (ibid. pp. 227–9). The participial suffix was added to the stem that preceded
the perfect passive participle in *-to-; thus active *koisāwus- 'having taken care
of' was parallel to passive *koisāto-, active *monewus- 'having reminded' to
passive ⁺moneto-, and so on. A complex and messy process of univerbation,
of which not all the details have been worked out (ibid. pp. 229–37), led to a
resegmentation in which the initial *-w- of the old participial suffix was reinterpreted as the suffix of the perfect stem. Finally, the functional distinction between
aorist and the perfect collapsed, yielding a single "perfect" stem with both functions for each verb.[13] The result was three large classes of verbs with regular
inflection:

(16)   1st conjugation 2nd conjugation 4th conjugation
            Present stem -ā- < *-ā(ye)-   -ē- < *-ē-, *-eye- -ī- < *-iye-
            Perfect stem -ā-v-   -u- < *-e-w-[14]   -ī-v-

Those classes are the crucial framework of the Latin system of conjugations.
(Some underived verbs appear in the first, second, and fourth conjugations
because various phonological developments resulted in their having present stems
ending in long vowels; many originally derived verbs became synchronically
underived lexemes when the words they had originally been derived from were
lost, or when the link between base and derived verb became unrecoverable
because of phonological or semantic changes.)

Of course it did not necessarily follow that most underived verbs would be
reduced to a single conjugation, more or less, namely the third. But a completely
different development contributed heavily to that outcome. PIE verb stems, like
PIE noun stems, fell into two large classes, "thematic" stems which ended in an
ablauting vowel *-e- ∼ *-o- and "athematic" stems which ended in an obstruent
or sonorant. In all the daughters except Anatolian and Tocharian, the thematic

class has expanded at the expense of the athematic class, though the process has
gone less far in Indo-Iranian and Greek than in the other daughters. In Latin
the athematic present stems have been reduced to a handful of relics, and all
other non-derived present stems are thematic; most of them constitute the third
conjugation, and the inherited thematic vowel is the third-conjugation stem vowel.
The third conjugation is still less homogeneous than the others. In addition to
presents in which the stem vowel is simply added to the root, it includes some
with initial reduplication or a nasal infix, and a productive subclass with a suffix
-sc- (cognate with the Greek suffix discussed earlier in this chapter, but with
inchoative meaning). The present-forming suffix *-ye- ∼ *-yo- actually gave rise
to a different stem vowel /-i-/ which has only partly merged with the old thematic
vowel by sound change; that is why there is a subclass of "third-conjugation verbs
in -iō." The formation of the perfect stem is also diverse, partly because some
third-conjugation perfects reflect inherited aorists while others reflect inherited
perfects. But there is enough uniformity of inflection in the third conjugation to
make it reasonable to regard it as a single lexical class with subclasses (not unlike
the third declension).

The crucial factor in the development of Latin lexical classes of verbs can
be summarized as follows. Classes of derived lexemes are typically productive,
and they typically have uniform inflection. Their productivity ensures that over
time they accumulate member lexemes (so long as they remain productive). In
the long run they can become very large, and their sheer size can prompt the
reorganization of an inflectional subsystem around them. In the course of such
a development it is possible for one productive class to become a *default* lexical
class to which new lexemes of the relevant lexical category are automatically
assigned. That is the last phenomenon we will discuss in this section.

We note first that it is not necessary for a system of lexical classes to include a
genuine default class. A system which clearly does not include one is the modern
German system of noun inflection. (Our discussion is based on Drosdowski (ed.)
1984: 238–52; see also the detailed analysis of Wegener 1999.) German nouns
are divided into lexical classes on the basis of plural formation, with subclasses
based on the inflection of the singular. Native nouns ending in stressed syllables
(mostly consonant-final) fall into four classes:

Class 1:   plural in -ə without i-umlaut;
Class 2:   plural in -ə with i-umlaut (see Chapter 6);
Class 3:   plural in -ər with i-umlaut;
Class 4:   plural in -ən without i-umlaut.

Nouns ending in unstressed syllables fall into the same four classes, but the
ending is adjusted by various phonological rules; for instance, -ə is dropped after
an unstressed syllable containing ə and after the diminutive suffix -lein, and -ən
is reduced to -n after an unstressed syllable containing ə. The assignment of
nouns to the classes exhibits weak correlation with concord classes: plural class 1
includes a large number of masculines and a majority of neuters; class 2 includes

a large number of masculines and a significant minority of feminines, but only a tiny handful of neuters; class 3 includes about 20 percent of the neuters and a few masculines; class 4 includes about three-quarters of the feminine nouns, a significant minority of masculines, and a few neuters. There is a fifth plural class, in -*s* (without i-umlaut), and its membership is interesting; it includes:

- nouns ending in an unstressed but unreduced vowel or diphthong (e.g. *Opa* 'grandpa', *Risiko* 'risk'), whether native or foreign;
- personal names;
- acronyms, abbreviations, and a few technical terms (e.g. *Hoch* 'high', i.e. 'high-pressure weather cell');
- some compound nouns whose last element is not a noun (e.g. *Stelldichein* 'rendezvous', literally 'put-yourself-in');
- some loanwords from French, English, Netherlandic, and Low German (e.g. *Deck, Park, Pier, Haff* 'lagoon').

The last point, especially, might lead one to suppose that this is the default class, to which new nouns such as loanwords are automatically assigned. But two types of evidence argue strongly that that is not the case. In the first place, most foreign nouns in German have not been assigned to the class with plurals in -*s*. Most masculine and neuter loanwords belong to plural class 1 or 2 (pl. *Antiquare, Altäre, Generale* or *Generäle*, etc.); most feminines belong to class 4 (pl. *Universitäten*, etc.), as do masculines ending in certain suffixes (pl. *Professoren, Kandidaten*, etc.). It is especially non-native-sounding loanwords from English and French that have plurals in -*s* (pl. *Hobbys, Gourmets, Hotels*, etc.), though some monosyllables do likewise (see above); a polysyllabic English loanword that sounds "German enough" is typically assigned to one of the other plural classes (e.g. pl. *Dschungel* or *Dschungeln* 'jungles', depending on the gender to which the noun is assigned – that varies, but the plural is always of a native type!). Secondly, an analysis of native-learner errors does not show any strong tendency to generalize -*s* (see especially the careful review of studies in Dąbrowska 2001: 552–7). We are forced to conclude that the class of plurals in -*s* is a residual class, but not the default class. There is no genuine default class.

In English the situation is clearly different: the plural class in -*s* is both the default class and the majority class, and has been so since at least the twelfth century. That seems to have been the result of a straightforward development. Though early Latin loanwords in OE often retain their Latin genders and are assigned to an appropriate OE lexical class, some shifts do occur, and a shift into the masculine a-stem class with nom.-acc. pl. in -*as* is the most frequent (see Campbell 1962: 207 9), which suggests that that lexical class might already have been the default class for nouns. Among later Latin loanwords this shift becomes more pronounced (ibid. pp. 218–19), and the default status of that lexical class is fairly clear (see the discussion of the possessive clitic earlier in this chapter; for the OE facts cf. Welna 1980). The reasons for this development are not clear, but it may be significant that the masculine a-stem class is the largest class of nouns in OE (though not a majority class), including about one-third of the native nouns in the language; that statistical fact might have led successive generations of native learners to posit it as the default class, and its continued productivity over time would naturally have led it to become the majority class as well.

A similar development among lexical classes of verbs is both very common and easy to motivate. We noted above that regular verbs of the Latin first conjugation are the most productive group; Aronoff 1994: 43 calculates that the first conjugation includes just over half the attested verbs of Classical Latin, and that 96 percent of them are completely regular. That is partly because they are nearly all derived verbs – most are still obviously derived synchronically, and most of the rest originated as derived verbs – and partly for more specific reasons. Whereas synchronically derived verbs of the second conjugation are clearly statives, first-conjugation derived verbs are of all semantic types (including statives, e.g. *albicāre* 'to be coated white'). The same is true of derived verbs of the fourth conjugation, but they are far fewer (not more than one-sixth as numerous, see Aronoff 1994: 43). That must ultimately be the result of an accident of history: at some point the first conjugation overtook the fourth in productivity, for reasons that cannot now be recovered. The result is that the first conjugation is the default lexical class of Latin verbs, to which loanwords are routinely assigned (e.g. *atticissāre* 'to speak Attic Greek' ← Greek /attikísde:n/ ἀττικίζειν, late Latin *baptizāre* ← Greek /baptísde:n/ βαπτίζειν), and it has remained so in the Romance languages.

An exactly parallel development took place in the prehistory and history of English. PGmc. had half a dozen lexical classes of verbs, including strong verbs (basic verbs, corresponding closely to the Latin third declension), "class I" weak verbs with a present-stem suffix *-i- ~ *-ja- (mostly derived verbs, corresponding to the Latin fourth conjugation and part of the second), "class II" weak verbs (all derived, corresponding to the Latin first declension), and several smaller "weak" classes, each with specific semantics (see Ringe 2006: 235–60; the small closed classes are not relevant here). To judge from the reconstructable examples, all these classes – even the strong verbs – were productive in the PGmc. period and for some time subsequently (considering the distribution of strong verbs across daughter languages in Seebold 1970). But the relative productivity of the classes shifted over time, and the development of weak class II underwent an important shift. Originally verbs of that class had been formed only from feminine ō-stem nouns (just as Latin first-conjugation verbs had been formed only from feminine ā-stem nouns; see above). But already in the PGmc. period they had begun to be formed from nouns of other classes, from adjectives, and from basic verbs (see Ringe 2006: 255–6, 292). In all those areas they competed with weak verbs of class I. But the latter tended to have definable semantic relationships to their bases (factitives formed to adjectives, causatives formed to basic verbs; ibid. pp. 252–4), while the semantic relationship of a class II weak verb to its base was most often pragmatically defined. Class II therefore gradually overtook class I in productivity. By the time OE is actually attested it was clearly no longer possible

Table 8.21 *Case mergers in some daughters of PIE*

Ancestral system	Proto-Greek	Proto-Italic	Proto-Germanic
genitive	genitive	genitive	genitive
ablative	genitive	ablative	dative
instrumental	instrumental	ablative	instrumental
dative	dative	dative	dative
locative	dative	locative	dative

to create or borrow a new strong verb. Some Latin loans were still being assigned to weak class I (e.g. *āspendan* 'to spend' ← *expendere* 'to weigh out', *dihtan* 'to arrange, to dictate' ← *dictāre*), but most were assigned to weak class II (e.g. *offrian* 'to offer' ← *offerre*, *predician* 'to preach' ← *praedicāre*, etc.), and it is clear that weak class II was the default class of verbs. By this point the reader will have guessed that it is the source of the modern English class of "regular" verbs, which (like the class of nouns with plurals in -*s*) is both the default class and the majority class.

The loss of morphosyntactic categories

Finally, something should be said about the loss of morphosyntactic categories. We have seen above that the loss of duals and the reduction of the number of concord classes, for instance, can be modeled as impoverishment. Moreover, learner errors that might give rise to the relevant impoverishment filters are easy to imagine, since duals are a special (and much less frequently used) type of plural and concord classes are essentially arbitrary. The loss of most other types of categories, however, does not seem to be so simple.

It is well known that case systems have undergone extensive attrition in most (though not all) IE languages. It is often suggested that phonological changes which made the case endings progressively less distinct are responsible for that development. But it can be shown that several mergers of cases in various daughters of the family occurred so early that phonological mergers cannot be responsible. The relevant facts are as follows. The reconstructable case system of the last common ancestor of most IE languages – the ancestor of all the subgroups except Anatolian (and possibly Tocharian) – included eight cases, namely those actually attested in Sanskrit. In all the immediate daughters the direct cases – that is, the nominative, accusative, and vocative – remained distinct, as one would expect. In Proto-Greek (i.e., the ancestor of all the attested Greek dialects), Proto-Italic, and Proto-Germanic, the remaining five cases have undergone mergers as indicated in Table 8.21. None of these intermediate protolanguages had undergone *any* sound changes which ought to have obscured the distinctions between the case endings, yet each has merged at least one pair of cases. Moreover, further mergers occurred at an early period in the further development of these subgroups, before phonological erosion of the case endings had become extensive. The instrumental is attested as a separate case in Greek only in the Mycenaean dialect written in the Linear B syllabary before about 1200 BCE; in all later Greek dialects it has merged with the dative. In Gothic, the daughter of PGmc. that is well attested earliest (from the middle of the fourth century CE), the instrumental has likewise merged with the dative, though it survives (somewhat marginally) in the West Germanic languages attested in the eighth and ninth centuries. In Latin, though not in Oscan and Umbrian, the locative has likewise become a marginal case, its use restricted to a few frequently used nouns and certain types of place names; otherwise it has been replaced by various prepositions which govern the ablative.

What sort of learner errors could have given rise to these mergers? Misinterpretation of syncretism is an obvious candidate, and a plausible one for the mergers of the ablative case. The most bizarre feature of the inherited system – fully preserved in Sanskrit – was that the ablative had almost no distinctive markers: in the plural (and dual) it was always syncretized with the dative, while in the singular it was syncretized with the genitive except in the thematic lexical class (i.e., the o-stems), in which it did have a distinctive ending. It is reasonable to hypothesize that that situation led to the merger of the ablative with the genitive in Greek and with the dative in Germanic – two mergers which do not make much sense in semantic terms – through the repeated misparsing of ablative caseforms as forms of the other cases on the part of native learners. In Italic, on the other hand, those syncretisms clearly had no effect on the development of the system; on the contrary, in the singular the distinctive ablative ending was extended to all lexical classes (as described in an earlier section of this chapter), while in the plural the syncretism with the dative persisted even through the merger of ablative and instrumental – of which one consequence was the use of the inherited o-stem inst. pl. ending as an abl. pl. *and dat. pl.* ending! That merger, and the remaining mergers in Table 8.21, cannot be blamed on the misinterpretation of syncretisms. What must have happened instead is revealed by the way the locative case was subsequently restricted in Latin. All these languages developed prepositions; apparently inherited adverbs used with cases for greater precision (as still, for the most part, in Sanskrit) were reanalyzed as prepositions governing the cases. Thus some inherited cases came to be effectively in competition with various prepositions. Since we know that native learners overgeneralize productive patterns in various ways, and since the construction of prepositional phrases (like all phrase structure) is obviously productive, it is not surprising that prepositions might have encroached on inherited cases to such an extent that the cases were no longer learned. An indication that that is partly responsible for the loss of cases is the fact that the genitive and dative cases, which mark relationships – adnominal and indirect object respectively – that cannot be paraphrased with prepositional phrases in these languages, survived everywhere. The details of the process of merger are likely to have been idiosyncratic and complex in each instance, and we might not be able to reconstruct most of them, but the general picture is more or less clear.

Competition between practically alternative expressions can also be shown to be responsible for the loss of various categories of verb inflection. The aspect called the "perfect" in the non-Anatolian subgroups of IE is a case in point. It was originally a stative, with no implication about prior events; we know that because it is still a stative in attested Homeric Greek (see Chantraine 1927) and because numerous stative relics survive in Indo-Iranian, Germanic, Latin, and (especially) Classical Greek. But in all the daughters it developed into an "anterior" tense resembling the English present perfect, and in most it developed further into a simple past. That brought it into competition with the "aorist," the inherited perfective past tense. The various daughters resolved the competition in various ways, e.g.:

- in Balto-Slavic and Armenian the perfect was lost and the aorist survived;
- in Germanic the aorist was lost and the perfect survived;
- in Latin and Celtic the two were conflated into a preterite tense, which for some lexemes was etymologically an aorist while for others it was etymologically a perfect;
- in Sanskrit the two past tenses were redifferentiated, the perfect becoming the the default past tense while the aorist referred to the recent past.

It can be seen that most of these developments involved loss of a category under competition. It is unclear how much of that development is attributable to shifts in adult usage and how much to learner errors, but it seems clear that both must have been involved.

As in every area of morphological change, more work needs to be done on the loss of morphosyntactic categories; but we have tried to lay out some general lines that such inquiries might pursue.

Our discussion of morphological change has been long and involved – more so than any other part of this book – but it should be clear that we have barely scratched the surface. On the one hand, morphology is the most idiosyncratic part of a language's grammar, and in large and complex inflectional systems a large number of complex changes are possible. On the other hand, discussion of morphological change in a modern theoretical framework has barely begun. This is an area of historical linguistics to which we hope and expect that future generations will contribute very largely.

Notes

1 The first part of OE *cynedōm* is an archaic noun stem from which *cyning* is itself derived; see the *OED* s.v. *kine-*[1] for discussion. In late OE the compound was regularized to *cyningdōm*.
2 On the semantics of this suffix see Zerdin 2000: 288–94. The PIE stems given all have "zero-grade" roots, in which the underlying *e of the root has been deleted. In 'be (customarily)'

and 'keep looking for', underlying */ss/ has been reduced to surface *s by a regular PIE phonological rule (Mayrhofer 1986: 120–1, Ringe 2006: 18); in 'be mixing' and 'keep asking', underlying */ḱsḱ/ has been reduced to surface *sḱ by another regular PIE phonological rule (Ringe 2006: 20).

3 French adverbs like *constamment* 'contantly', in which the suffix is apparently added to the masculine form of the adjective (in this case *constant*) instead of the feminine (*constante*), are in large part archaisms: in Old French, as in Latin, the feminine of present participles was identical with the masculine. See Meyer-Lübke 1895: 687–8 for discussion.

4 The Spanish noun *mente* 'mind' must have been borrowed from written Latin at a later date, since its stressed vowel has not undergone the regular "breaking" of short *e* (in contrast to the stressed vowel of inherited *mientes*). How the suffix evaded breaking is not entirely clear. Probably it acquired secondary stress when it was "demoted" from being a separate phonological word and that inhibited breaking, since only fully stressed vowels were subject to the sound change (cf. *pensar* 'to think' with stress on the second syllable, but pres. 3sg. *piensa* 'thinks' with stress on the first syllable).

5 The West Saxon OE i-umlaut rule affected all the back vowels and diphthongs as follows: *æ, a, o → e; u → y; ā → ǣ; ō → ē; ū → ȳ; ea, eo → ie; ēa, ēo → īe*. In other dialects the details were slightly different. In the text we exemplify the rule with West Saxon forms exhibiting two common underlying vowels, neither of which happens to occur in the few comparatives and superlatives to which the rule applies.

6 Among the inherited i-umlauted forms in Modern English, *set* and *lay* are still obviously related to *sit* and *lie*, but the relationship is more indirect; *deal* and *heal* are no longer usually associated with *dole* and *whole*; *deem* is obsolete; *filth* no longer seems to be associated with *foul*; *health* is associated with *heal* rather than *whole*.

7 'Three' is the only example of the first class of these stems that is not a noun. The comparatives exemplified by 'bigger' are a closed class of about twenty members; they usually have stems in *-n-*, but in these forms and a few others the *-n-* is lacking and the vowels of stem and ending contract (see Smyth 1956: 78, 87–9).

   Of the expected endings listed, *-i:s, -ees* (both classes), *-eas* are attested in other dialects, including Homer; *-u:s* is attested as a variant reading in Homer (see Ringe 1995: 54–6); *-ins* and *-uns* are attested in Cretan Doric; for *-eyes, *-ewes cf. Skt. *tráyas* 'three', *bahávas* 'many'; for *-oes cf. Mycenaean Greek *me-zo-e* 'bigger' (Linear B syllabary, thirteenth century BCE).

8 Latin gen. sg. ending *-osio* is attested on the Old Latin *Lapis Satricanus* (de Simone 1980: 81–3). On the origin of the usual ending *-ī* see Devine 1970, Nussbaum 1975: 127–30. Oscan **-eís** is the i-stem ending, which has spread to the o-stems in the whole Sabellic subgroup of Italic. The o-stem abl. sg. ending is reconstructed with an e-vowel to account for Lithuanian gen. sg. *-o* < Proto-Baltic *-ā < post-PIE *-ād; on the origin of the ending see Ringe 2006: 43 with references. Latin gen. sg. *-ās* survives only in a few fossilized phrases, especially *pater familiās* 'father of the household'. Uncontracted gen. sg. *-āī*, with the *-ī* of the o-stems added to the stem vowel, is well attested in early Latin and is still used occasionally for metrical purposes by Vergil. Latin abl. sg. *-ōd, -ād, -īd, -ūd* are attested in Old Latin inscriptions. Latin i-stem gen. sg. *-is* is actually the old consonant-stem ending, which has been generalized to all "third-declension" nominals. Oscan *-id* could be the regular sound change outcome of *-ūd, but it could also be the old i-stem ending *-īd.

   A similar extension of the thematic abl. sg. ending occurred in Hispano-Celtic, the Celtic language spoken in northeastern Spain at the time of Roman contact (Villar 1997: 920–5), and in Avestan, the ancient Iranian language in which the Parsi scriptures are written (see e.g. Hoffmann and Forssman 2004: 116); the Italic, Celtic, and Iranian developments differed in detail.

9 Melchert 1997 suggests that traces of an inherited inflectional contrast between perfective and imperfective stems do survive in Anatolian, but in all his potential examples the imperfective suffix is *-ye- ~ *-yo-; even if he is correct, the rest of the scenario sketched here could be correct as well.

10 The Latin "fifth declension" reflects an originally disparate collection of irregularities and may have become a unified class fairly late; see e.g. Sommer 1948: 394–401, Ringe 1995: 50 with references. We omit it for simplicity's sake.

11 The inherited ending *-āfos probably survives in Classical Latin fem. *duābus* 'to/with two', *ambābus* 'to/with both' (cf. Sommer 1948: 465); but similar forms of nouns, e.g. *filiābus* 'to/with (the) daughters', are probably later innovations, prompted by the practical need to distinguish feminines from masculines (ibid. pp. 331–2).

12 Nom. pl. *-ai should also have become "-ī" in polysyllables (cf. the development of *-ais); Classical -ae was reintroduced from the monosyllabic determiner *hae* 'these (fem.)' and interrogative/relative *quae* 'which (pl. fem.)'.

13 The fact that subjunctives in embedded clauses sometimes follow "primary" sequence of tenses and sometimes "secondary" sequence when the matrix verb is a perfect indicative is one of the last vestiges of the distinction between perfect and aorist in Latin. Another functional relic of the aorist is the use of the perfect subjunctive with *nē* in prohibitions (e.g. *nē crēdiderīs* 'don't believe [it]!').

14 Since in the suffix complex *-e-w- the *-w-, like the past participial suffix *-to-, is obviously added to the first part of the causative present suffix *-eye-, we might expect also to find perfects in "-ēv-" and past participles in "-ētus" made to stative presents. They may once have existed – cf. the fossilized noun *acētum* 'vinegar', for instance, obviously derived from *acē-* 'be sharp' – but because the two present suffixes had become indistinguishable, a single formation was generalized in the other stems as well.

9   Syntactic change

The study of syntax has not usually received much attention from historical linguists. Many historical grammars either give very little consideration to syntax or do not include a section on it at all.[†] Historically oriented works that do treat syntax, including important early volumes such as Delbrück 1888 and 1893–1900 and Wackernagel 1920, are largely descriptive and confine themselves to the interaction of morphology and syntax. Another approach has been to employ typology to attempt to explain syntactic change, notable examples including Lehmann 1974, Friedrich 1975, and Miller 1975, the first two of which are fairly extreme in their attempts to motivate syntactic change in the interest of typological consistency (see the telling criticisms of Watkins 1976).

The reason for the lack of serious attention to syntax in historical linguistics, no doubt, is that it is hard to know what to compare between two synchronic states of a language from different time periods (so, recently, Longobardi 2003: 127). One compares phonemes in phonology, morphemes in morphology, but what in syntax? In the history of many Indo-European languages, a shift from Object-Verb (OV) to Verb-Object (VO) or Genitive-Noun to Noun-Genitive order is manifest in the documentary record, but, as noted by Longobardi 2003: 109, such changes have multiple causes and cannot be reduced to a single shift in linguistic structure.[‡] The difficulty lies in the fact that syntactic structures and operations are not 'visible' in the way that phonemes and morphemes are. As a child acquires a language, as noted by Hale 1998: 9 and Embick 2008: 60, among others, she does not have direct access to the syntactic structures of the speakers of the previous generation as she does for phonemes and morphemes, only the syntactic output that they produce. It is for this reason, then, and because of gaps and other limitations in the historical documentary record, as well as variations due to sociolinguistic factors (which may not be obvious to contemporary researchers), that, as Kroch 2001: 700 puts it, "conclusive results have been hard to come by."

It is the view of generative linguists interested in syntactic change today that, in fact, the rules of syntax do not change from generation to generation.

[†] Fortson's highly commendable 2009 handbook of Proto-Indo-European includes a chapter on syntax, but treats only a small number of surface features.

[‡] Harris and Campell 1995: 347–53 propose that one can compare surface patterns, but while such a comparison can reveal that syntactic change has occurred, it does not explain why it has occurred. Others who advocate this approach include Watkins 1976 and Hock 1991: 611–17; see also Campbell and Harris 2002 and Harris 2008.

Changes in phonology, morphology, and the lexicon trigger syntactic change (see e.g. Lightfoot 1999, Longobardi 2001, and Keenan 2003) when they cause the features of functional heads to change (Hale 1998: 14). Under this view, which we hold to be correct, it is not, then, that the rules of syntax change, but that they operate under different conditions in different synchronic states of a language.[†]

Syntactic change can, of course, also be caused by external forces, i.e. contact. There is an important distinction between syntactic change via contact versus intergenerational syntactic change via acquisition. In situations of language contact, it is normally adults who acquire a new language imperfectly or import structures from their native language and subsequently pass their imperfectly learnt grammar to the next generation (see Chapter 4). Some examples from the so-called Celtic Englishes are given in (1) through (3).

(1)   Hiberno-English (Filppula 1999: 99–107)

   a. Irish
      Tá   sé   tréis imeacht.
      be.3.SG.PRS 3.SG.M.NOM after go.VBLN
      'He has just gone.'

   b. Hiberno-English
      He is after going.

(2)   Hebridean English (Odlin 1997: 41–4)

   a. Scottish Gaelic
      "Seall   sios," ars esan,   "co leis   siod."
      look.2.SG.IMP down said 3.SG.M.EMPH who with3.SG.M there

      Chaidh a fear   ad sios 's sheall   e.
      go.PRT DEF man.NOM.SG down and look.3.SG.PRET 3.SG.M

      "Tha,"   ars esan,   "leibh   péin."
      be.3.SG.PRS said 3.SG.M.EMPH with.2.PL REFL
      '"Look down," he said, "and see whose they are." The man went and looked. "It's yours," he said.'

   b. Cf. Hebridean English
      "Go down and have a look whose cask is that that throw the hinges."
      This man went down. "It belongs to yourself."

(3)   Cambro-English (Thomas 1997: 79)

   a. Welsh
      Dyna   od   oedd   ef!
      There is strange be.3.SG.IMPRF 3.SG.M
      'How strange it was!'

   b. Cambro-English
      There's strange it was!

[†] This approach has resulted in considerable activity in syntactic change in recent years, e.g., Hale 2007, Roberts 2007, Miller 2010, and many of the papers collected in Ferraresi and Goldbach 2008 and Crisma and Longobardi 2009.

Each of these constructions, the *after*-perfect of Hiberno-English, the unbound reflexive of Hebridean English, and exclamative *there* of Cambro-English, appear to be direct tranfers of syntactic structures from Irish, Scottish Gaelic, and Welsh, respectively, by interference.

Our primary concern in this chapter, however, is intergenerational change via acquisition. A look at the documentary record of any language with sufficient historical depth will reveal that visible changes in syntax from one synchronic state to a later one are not wholly implemented overnight, but over a(n often extended) period of time, a change occurring, at first, at a fairly low rate, eventually increasing significantly, and then only being fully completed over what may be a lengthy period of time. It has often been noted, for example, that the use of periphrastic *do* in interrogative and negative clauses in English began in the fourteenth century, but, even centuries later, in 1700, had still not completely replaced its antecedent structures. Yet, should it be the case that a syntactic parameter changes its setting from one generation to the next via imperfect learning in the acquisition process, we have to ask why we find that change takes place only gradually in the documentary record. This seeming paradox has been solved by Kroch 1989, who points out that a parameter for which only a small amount of data is present in the primary linguistic data heard during the period of acquisition can lead two learners to acquire different grammars. This has given rise to Kroch's Grammars in Competition Hypothesis, in which parameter settings, not entire grammars, compete; it is manifested in the variation found in the documentary record as the reflex of an innovative parametric setting competes with and eventually supplants the reflex of the older parametric setting.[1] This may seem counterintuitive, but, as Embick 2008: 65 succinctly and clearly puts it, "[i]f there is one input N to a syntactic derivation, and we find two distinct forms derived from this N, then there must be distinct grammars at play." Kroch 1994 discusses a number of examples of morphosyntactic change within this model.

As an illustration of the Grammars in Competition Hypothesis, we will review Taylor's 1994 treatment of the evolution of OV to VO order in ancient Greek. Under Kayne's 1994 Antisymmetry Hypothesis, underlying VO order is fundamental and OV languages are the result of leftward movement of the object DP around the verb to a specifier or adjoined position. The change of OV to VO order within the history of a language, then, amounts to the loss of the feature that triggers the object DP movement.

Taylor 1994: 7–10 notes that surface word order in all periods of ancient Greek is highly flexible, i.e. a lot of movement is possible, presumably for pragmatic and stylistic reasons. Drawing upon samples from Books I, III, and VIII of the *Iliad* of Homer (generally dated to *c*. 750 BCE), the beginning of Book III of the *Histories* of Herodotos (mid- to later fifth century BCE), and the Koiné Greek of the first 18 books of the Acts of the Apostles of Luke (second half of the first century CE), she compiles the statistics on the placement of the verb in these texts given in Table 9.1 (a simplified version of Taylor's Table 1, which breaks down the distribution of clause types by the arguments that they contain).

Table 9.1 *Position of the verb in three
Ancient Greek texts*

	Homer	Herodotos	Luke
V-final	44%	27%	8%
V-medial	44%	57%	62%
V-initial	12%	17%	31%

But Taylor is able to identify two diagnostics to determine the underlying order at these three stages in the history of Greek. The first, which applies only to Herodotos and Luke, is the position of the non-emphatic third-person pronoun *auton*, which never appears after a verb preceded in its VP by more than one constituent. (This use of *auton* probably did not exist in Homeric Greek, in which it was employed as a reflexive; see Taylor 1994: 15, 35 n. 9.) This informs us that *auton* does not postpose, i.e. move rightward, and so its position in the clause relative to the verb is diagnostic of underlying OV or VO order; see example (4) (= Taylor's example [32]; note that "IPF" stands for "imperfect," the imperfective past tense, and "AOR" for "aorist," the perfective past tense).

(4) a. Herodotos III.52.6
Periandros men toutoisi   <u>auton</u>   katelambane
P.NOM.SG PTCL DEM.DAT.PL 3.ACC.SG.M coax.IPF.3SG
'P. coaxed him with these things.'

b. Herodotos III.75.1
sugkalesantes   Persas   hoi   magoi
collect-together.PTCP.NOM.PL Persian.ACC.PL DEF.NOM.PL magus.NOM.PL
anebibasan   <u>auton</u>   epi purgon
mount.AOR.3PL 3.ACC.SG.M on tower.ACC.SG
'. . . having collected together the Persians, the magi mounted him
on a tower.'

c. Acts 1.9
kai   nep^{h}elē   hupelaben   <u>auton</u>   apo tōn
CONN   cloud.NOM.SG take-up.AOR.3SG 3.SG.ACC from DEF.GEN.PL
op^{h}t^{h}almōn   autōn
sight.GEN.PL 3.GEN.PL
'. . . and a cloud took him up from their sight.'

As indicated in the clauses in (4a) and (4b), the position of *auton* demonstrates the presence of both underlying OV and VO order in Herodotos. This turns out to be true of Luke, too, but at a different relative proportion. Taylor's 1994: 15 statistics are given in Table 9.2. It is clear that while Herodotos exhibits OV order at a rate of 55 percent based upon this diagnostic, Luke exhibits a rate of OV order that has diminished to only 5 percent.

The second diagnostic is the position in which clitics appear; this diagnostic can be applied to the Homeric data. Taylor 1994: 15–19 demonstrates that clitics

Table 9.2 *Position of* auton *in*
Herodotos and Luke

	Herodotos	Luke
Preverbal *auton*	55%	5%
Postverbal *auton*	45%	95%

appear in two positions in ancient Greek, either adjoined to the left edge of TP or
to the left edge of VP; see examples (5) and (6) (= Taylor's examples [33] and
[34], adapted; "MD" is the "middle" voice):

(5)   Clitic attached to TP
        a. Homer IV.157
            [CP autar [TP =hoi   [TP Proitos   kaka   mēsato
                but   3.DAT.SG.M   P.NOM.SG evil.ACC.SG plan.AOR.MD.3SG

            tʰumōi   ]]]
            heart.DAT.SG
            '. . . but P. planned evil against him in his heart.'

        b. Herodotus I.111.2
            [CP hoti [TP =min   [TP houtō protʰumōs Harpagos
                why   3.ACC.SG   so   eagerly   H.NOM.SG

            metepempsato]]]
            sent-for.AOR.MD.3SG
            '. . . why H. sent for him so eagerly.'

(6)   Clitic attached to VP
        a. Herodotos I.146.1
            Minuai   de   Orkʰomeniou [VP =spʰi [VP anamemikʰatai]]
            M.NOM.PL PTCL O.GEN.SG   3.DAT.PL mix-together.PF.PASS.3PL
            'The M. of O. are mixed together with them.'

        b. Gospel of St. John XVIII.34
            ē alloi   [VP eipon   =soi   peri emou   ]†
            or other.NOM.PL   say.AOR.3PL 2.DAT.SG about 1.GEN.SG
            '. . . or did others say it to you about me?'

Taylor argues that when the underlying order of the VP is OV, the verb governs
to the left and the clitic floats to the left edge of TP, but that when it is VO, the VP
acts as a barrier and the clitic must remain within it. An analysis of the position
at which clitics adjoin at the various stages of ancient Greek yields the result in
Table 9.3 (excerpted from Taylor's Table 3): It is noteworthy that the proportional
distribution of clitic adjunction for Herodotos and Koiné Greek is so similar to
that of the distribution of the pronoun *auton* – in fact, as shown by Taylor 1994:

---

† This clause exhibits Prosodic Inversion, a process by which the clitic moves one word to the right;
  see Taylor 1996 for a discussion of this phenomenon with reference to Ancient Greek.

Table 9.3 *Clitic adjunction in Homer, Herodotos, and the New Testament*

	Homer	Herodotos	New Testament
Adjunction to TP	99%	60%	6%
Adjunction to VP	1%	40%	94%

Table 9.4 *Underlying verb and object order in Homer, Herodotos, and Luke*

	Homer	Herodotos	Luke
Underlying OV	99%	60%	5%
Underlying VO	1%	40%	95%

18, the difference is not statistically significant. When we combine the results of the two diagnostics, then, we arrive at the proportion of underlying OV versus VO order in Homer, Herodotos, and Luke given in Table 9.4 (excerpted from Taylor's Table 4).

It seems clear that Homeric Greek is essentially a verb-final language, while Koiné Greek, attested at least 800 years later, is close to being a consistent verb-medial language. Interestingly, Herodotos, who wrote in a period between the two but closer to that of Homer, exhibits a mix of orders. What are we to make of this? Can the mix of orders somehow be squared with either the OV grammar of Homer or the VO grammar of Koiné Greek?

Taylor 1994: 20 and 28–30 notes that the non-verb-final surface orders in Homer can be derived straightforwardly via a rule of postposition and that, once the remnant underlying OV tokens are removed from the Koiné corpus, the remaining verb-final surface orders can be derived via a rule of preposing, respectively. Here it is important to note Taylor's demonstration that subject postposing occurs at about the same rate in both the OV and VO grammars. (That is not surprising; that syntactic mechanisms such as postposing are triggered by pragmatic or stylistic factors whose rates of application remain constant over time has been demonstrated by Kroch 1989 and Santorini 1993.) Were one to propose that the mixed order of Herodotos can be accounted for by preposing as in Homer, one would find that the rate of postposing increased from 43 percent in Homer to 60 percent in Herodotos. This is not an appealing solution because, as noted by Taylor 1994: 31–2, not only do we expect the rate of postposing not to increase, but the assumption of an underlying OV grammar for all of Herodotos does not accord with the distribution of *auton* or object clitic placement (see Tables 9.2 and 9.3 above). It is clear, then, that the language of Herodotos cannot be made to fit either the grammar of Homer or of Koiné Greek.

Table 9.5 *Estimated distribution of verb-final and verb-medial clauses in Herodotos compared with observed distribution assuming 62 percent verb-final tokens (Subjects are symbolized by S, and complements by X or Y)*

Pattern	Estimated verb-final clauses	Estimated verb-medial clauses	Total estimated clauses	Total observed clauses
SXv	35	3	38	34
XYv	1	0	1	2
SvX	25	30	55	59
XvS	11	2	13	16
XvY	2	0	2	1
vSX	8	14	22	20
vXY	1	2	3	2
N	83	51	134	134

The Grammars in Competition Hypothesis does provide a solution, however. Taylor 1994: 32–4 provides a quantitative model that calculates the distribution of part of the data as though it is verb-final and the remainder as though it is verb-medial. Her result, reproduced here as Table 9.5 (= Taylor's Table 20), reveals that an estimation of 62 percent of the clauses as verb-final in Herodotos, i.e. 83 out of 134, provides the best fit to the attested data.

That the rate of 62 percent OV structure is nearly identical with the 60 percent rate indicated by the diagnostics of the distribution of *auton* and clitic placement is remarkable and provides significant reason to believe that OV and VO grammars were in competition in the language of Herodotos; it demonstrates a change in progress that was barely incipient in Homer and was close to having run its course in Koiné Greek *c.* 800 years later.

In the Ancient Greek example of syntactic change just discussed, a clear instance of a change in syntax between different synchronic states is seen. But a syntactic change need not always result in a change in syntax between different synchronic states. We turn now to an example from Old Irish in which syntactic change instead results in morphological change.

Old Irish, attested from *c.* 600 to *c.* 900 CE, is a VSO language known for its dual system of verbal inflection. In simplex verbs, absolute inflection is used when the verb occurs in absolute initial position in the clause, conjunct inflection when it is preceded by one of a number of 'conjunct' particles, a category that includes negators, complementizers, and connectives, here illustrated with the verb *guidid* 'pray'.[2]

(7)   a. Absolute inflection (gloss 27$^\mathrm{d}$7 from the Würzburg glosses on the
            Pauline epistles):
            <u>guidid</u>   dia   eruib   =si   dogress
            pray.3.SG.PRS.ABS god.NOM.SG for.2.PL   EMPH.2.PL continually
            'God prays for you continually.'

b. Conjunct inflection (gloss 42^a4 from the Milan glosses on the commentary to the Psalms):

ni= <u>guid</u>   digail   du= thabairt
NEG pray.3.SG.PRS.CNJ punishment.ACC.SG to   inflict.VBLN.DAT.SG

foraib
on.3.PL

'He does not pray that punishment is inflicted upon them.'

With both simplex and compound verbs, there is a productive process whereby object agreement affixes are positioned prior to the stressed syllable, preceded by the initial preverb in compound verbs and a dummy prefix *no=* in simplex verbs, e.g.:

(8)   a. Simplex verb (Milan gloss 55^a5)
               no-t·erdarcugub
               PREV-2.SG.OBJ·celebrate.1.SG.FUT
               'I will make you famous.'

           b. Compound verb (Würzburg gloss 9^a4)
               do-<u>nn</u>·éicci
               PREV-1.PL.OBJ·behold.3.SG.PRS
               'It beholds us.'

(These morphemes are traditionally referred to as infixed pronouns and are assumed to be referential. Eska 2009–10 and Griffith 2011 argue that they are instead non-referential exponents of object agreement.) Beside this pattern, object agreement affixes may also be suffixed to simplex verbs that bear absolute inflection, e.g.:

(9)   a. béirth-i (Würzburg gloss 23^a19)
               bear.3.SG.FUT.ABS-3.SG.N.OBJ
               'He will bear it.'

           b. mórs-us (l. 132 of the Prologue to the *Martyrology of Oengus*)
               magnify.3.SG.PRT.ABS-3.SG.F.OBJ
               'It magnified her.'

It has traditionally been assumed that the infixing and suffixing patterns existed side by side and that the suffixing pattern was gradually yielding to the infixing pattern because of the redundancy of having two patterns for a single purpose (so e.g. Quin 1975: 43–4 and Sims-Williams 1984: 149);[†] but that cannot be the explanation, because Cowgill 1987 demonstrated that a full infixing pattern and a full suffixing pattern did not exist side by side in Old Irish.[‡] That is, there was

---

[†] In Middle Irish, roughly dated to the period *c.* 900 to *c.* 1250 CE, suffixed object affixes become quite rare.
[‡] The following exposition is an abbreviated version of facts laid out in Cowgill 1987 and Eska 2003.

no **n-a·beir* beside *beirth-i* '(s)he bears it' in Old Irish. The suffixing pattern was required in the following configurations:

(a)   1sg. future verbs with 3sg. masculine or neuter object affix;
(b)   3sg. verbs with 3sg. masculine or neuter object affix;
(c)   1pl. verbs with 3sg. masculine or neuter object affix;
(d)   3pl. verbs with 3sg. masculine or neuter object affix.

In texts composed before *c.* 700 CE, the following additional configurations required the suffixing pattern, but this was only optionally the case afterwards:

(a)   3sg. verbs with 3sg. feminine or 3pl. object affixes.
(b)   The consuetudinal present, subjunctive, and future of the substantive verb with 1sg./pl. or 2sg./pl. object affix.

Likewise, there are many combinations of person and number marking, as well as certain verbal categories, in which only the infixing pattern occurs (see Cowgill 1987: 2–3 for examples).[3]

The opposition between the infixing and suffixing pattern is of interest in a chapter on syntactic change because the object agreement affixes continue unstressed clitic referential pronouns. Therefore, under the widespread assumption that such clitics are adjoined to TP (Kayne 1991),[†] the verb must occupy C when object agreement affixes occur in the suffixing pattern, but T when such affixes occur in the infixing pattern. Since the infixing pattern is productive and expanding at the cost of the suffixing pattern with simplex verbs bearing absolute inflection, we are seeing the loss of V-to-C movement. It is likely, then, that the suffixing pattern was original. But what triggered the loss of V-to-C movement and the gradual loss of the suffixing pattern? Cowgill 1987 offers no explanation for the distribution of the infixing vs. suffixing pattern or the ongoing change towards the infixing pattern, but Breatnach 1977: 99–101 has proposed that the extensive amount of phonological change that occurred in pre-Old Irish resulted in the merger of a number of verb–object agreement affix forms creating significant ambiguity. Breatnach does not attempt to work out the mergers that occurred, but Eska 2003: 30–1 does so, employing *beirid* 'bears' as an example, with the results reported in Table 9.6.[4] As can be seen, aside from the 3sg. masc. and neut. affixes attached to the 1pl. and 3pl. verb, the expected forms are attested in the 3sg. verb. Phonological changes have created some mergers, e.g. *biri* 'you (sg.) bear' with **biri* 'you (sg.) bear him/it', and some near mergers, e.g. *biru* 'I bear' with **birū* 'I bear him/it', but, by and large, there has not been so much reduction that the expected paradigms lead to excessive ambiguity. There must be more going on. It appears likely that the availability of the semantically void preverb *no=* provided the means for the infixing pattern to become available as an alternative to the suffixing pattern for object agreement affixes.[5] As previously noted by Watkins 1963: 7, pressure to adopt such an alternative would have come not only from compound verbs, in which the infixing pattern was the only

---

[†] Or, under the articulated CP model of Rizzi 1997, in the lower reaches of the articulated CP.

Table 9.6 *Expected development of Old Irish verbs with suffixed object agreement markers*

	1sg. *biru* < *berū=t*			1pl. *bermai* < *beromas=et*		
+ 1sg.obj.	*berū=t=mV	>	**birūm	*beromas=et=mV	>	**bermaī(u)m
+ 2sg.obj.	*berū=t=tV	>	**birūt	*beromas=et=tV	>	**bermaī(u)t
+ 3sg.m.obj.	*berū=t=en	>	**birū	*beromas=et=en	>	*bermait*†
+ 3sg.n.obj.	*berū=t=e	>	**birū	*beromas=et=e	>	*bermait*†
+ 3sg.f.obj.	*berū=t=san	>	**birūs	*beromas=et=san	>	**bermaī(u)s
+ 1pl.obj.	*berū=t=(s)ni	>	**birū(i)nn	*beromas=et=(s)ni	>	**bermaīnn
+ 2pl.obj.	*berū=t=(s)ui	>	**birū(i)b	*beromas=et=(s)ui	>	**bermaīb
+ 3pl.obj.	*berū=t=sus	>	**birūs	*beromas=et=sus	>	**bermaīus

	2sg. *biri* < *berisi=t*			2pl. *beirthe* < *beretes=et*		
+ 1sg.obj.	*berisi=t=mV	>	**birī(u)m	*beretes=et=mV	>	**beirthē(u)m
+ 2sg.obj.	*berisi=t=tV	>	**birī(u)t	*beretes=et=tV	>	**beirthē(u)t
+ 3.sg.m.obj.	*berisi=t=en	>	**biri	*beretes=et=en	>	**beirthe
+ 3.sg.n.obj.	*berisi=t=e	>	**biri	*beretes=et=e	>	**beirthe
+ 3.sg.f.obj.	*berisi=t=san	>	**birī(u)s	*beretes=et=san	>	**beirthē(u)s
+ 1pl.obj.	*berisi=t=(s)ni	>	**birīnn	*beretes=et=(s)ni	>	**beirthēnn
+ 2pl.obj.	*berisi=t=(s)ui	>	**birīb	*beretes=et=(s)ui	>	**beirthēb
+ 3pl.obj.	*berisi=t=sus	>	**birīus	*beretes=et=sus	>	**beirthēus

	3sg. *beirid* < *bereti=t*			3pl. *berait* < *beraddi=t*		
+ 1sg.obj.	*bereti=t=mV	>	*beirthium*	*beraddi=t=mV	>	**bertom
+ 2sg.obj.	*bereti=t=tV	>	*beirthiut*	*beraddi=t=tV	>	**bertot
+ 3.sg.m.obj.	*bereti=t=en	>	*beirthi*	*beraddi=t=en	>	*bertait*†
+ 3.sg.n.obj.	*bereti=t=e	>	*beirthi*	*beraddi=t=e	>	*bertait*†
+ 3.sg.f.obj.	*bereti=t=san	→	*beirthius*	*beraddi=t=san	>	**bertos
+ 1pl.obj.	*bereti=t=(s)ni	→	*beirthiunn*	*beraddi=t=(s)ni	>	**bertainn
+ 2pl.obj.	*bereti=t=(s)ui	>	*beirthib*	*beraddi=t=(s)ui	>	**bertaib
+ 3pl.obj.	*bereti=t=sus	>	*beirthius*	*beraddi=t=sus	>	**bertos

† Final *-t* originated as a secondary addition after the 3pl. desinence, and then spread
  to first-person forms.

one available, but also from syntagmata in which the suffixing pattern was not
available with simplex verbs, including the following:

(a)   negated verbs, e.g.
        ní-n·berat 'they do not bear us';
(b)   verbs following certain connectives and complementizers, e.g.
        ara-don·berat 'in order that they bear us';
(c)   tenses and moods in which absolute inflectional forms do not exist,
        e.g.
        (i) imperfect *no-n·beirtis* 'they used to bear us',
        (ii) conditional *no-n·béirtais* 'they would bear us';

(d)   relative verbs, e.g.

      no-n·bertae 'who bear us';

(e)   passive verbs, e.g.

      no-n·berar 'we are borne'.

(In the passive paradigm, first- and second-person object affixes are attached to the 3sg. form of the verb.)

As such pressure caused the suffixing pattern to become less common in pre-Old Irish – a period when the object agreement morphemes would still have been clitics – there would have been increasingly less evidence for V-to-C movement for children acquiring the language. Moreover, Newton 2008 notes that once the Cowgill particle, which evidently cliticized to TP, had been apocopated in verbs that did not bear an object agreement morpheme, evidence for V-to-C movement would likewise have been diminished for native language learners.

The syntactic change whereby V-to-C movement was lost in pre-Old Irish, then, appears to have been motivated by phonological changes and paradigmatic pressure, but it did not result in further superficial syntactic change. In particular, the language retained its VSO clausal order. However, the loss of V-to-C movement *was* responsible for the morphological change whereby the suffixing object agreement pattern was eventually lost in the language. With the loss of V-to-C movement, the forms which used the suffixing pattern would no longer have been regularly generated by the syntax and would therefore have been learnt as morphological irregularities. Why they were retained longest in the 3sg. of the paradigm is a matter for further research.

We will examine one further example of syntactic change in this chapter, the growth of *do*-periphrasis in the history of English. It provides another example of the Grammars in Competition Hypothesis; moreover, since it occurs in a number of clause types, it exemplifies the fact that though change may start at different rates in different contexts, it progresses at the same rate in all. This is known as the Constant Rate Effect (discovered by Kroch 1989) and it provides evidence for the fact that syntactic change occurs at the abstract level of parameter change.

In Middle English (ME), unlike Modern English (ModE), negative and interrogative clauses do not make use of *do*-periphrasis. In clauses without auxiliary verbs, the matrix verb is followed by the negator *not* in the surface order in negative clauses, and subject–verb inversion occurs in interrogative clauses, as in (10).[†]

(10)   a. Negative clause (310:31:45)

       . . . spoile him of his riches by sondrie fraudes, whiche he [$_T$ perceiueth not.]

    b. Interrogative clause (310:166:10)

       How great and greuous tribulations [$_C$ suffered] [$_{SpecTP}$ the Holy Appostyls . . . ?]

[†] These examples are adapted after Kroch's examples (19a) and (18a), respectively. Kroch's examples are primarily drawn from Ellegård 1953, whose numbering system is reproduced throughout.

Table 9.7 *Increase of periphrastic* do *in clauses of different types*

	Neg. decls.	Neg. quests.	Aff. transs. adv. & yes/no quests.	Aff. intrans. adv. & yes/no quests.	Aff. *wh*-obj. quests.
1400–25	0.0%	11.7%	0.0%	0.0%	0.0%
1425–50	1.2%	8.0%	10.7%	0.0%	0.0%
1450–75	4.8%	11.1%	13.5%	0.0%	2.0%
1475–1500	7.8%	59.0%	24.2%	21.1%	11.3%
1500–25	13.7%	60.7%	69.2%	19.7%	9.5%
1525–50	27.9%	75.0%	61.5%	31.9%	11.0%
1550–75	38.0%	85.4%	73.7%	42.3%	36.0%

Neg. = negative, decs. = declaratives, quests. = questions, aff. = affirmative, trans. = transitive, adv. = adverbial, intrans. = intransitive, *wh*-obj. = *wh*-object

But beginning in the fourteenth century, and at an increasing rate subsequently, clauses of these types begin to be attested in which periphrastic *do* bears tense and the matrix verb remains in VP, e.g. (adapted after Kroch's example (20)):[6]

(11)   a. Negative clause (318:194:567)
        . . . bycause the nobylyte there commynly [$_T$ dothe] not [$_{VP}$ exercise them in the studys therof.]

        b. Interrogative clause (304:97:15)
        Where [$_C$ doth] the grene knyght [$_{VP}$ holde him?]

The rise of periphrastic *do* was occurring at the same time that V-to-T movement was being restricted to modal auxiliaries (Kroch 1989: 217),[7] which previously had behaved like matrix verbs. This increasing restriction, then, led to competition between grammars in which V-to-T movement of matrix verbs was still possible and those in which it was not, which resulted in the generation of periphrastic *do* to bear tense. Kroch's data appear to show that this competition was completed by the third quarter of the sixteenth century, when the restriction of modals to T was fixed, and V-to-T movement was lost (though Warner 1997 and Lightfoot 1999 believe that the loss of V-to-T movement was somewhat later). An examination of the percentage of clauses in which periphrastic *do* occurs by clause type, given in Table 9.7, reveals the increasing rate at which it is manifested over time and provides a basis to examine the Constant Rate Effect. (The data are from Kroch's Table 3, which contains more information, itself based upon data from Ellegård 1953's Tables 7 and 20.)

The first thing to notice is that as *do*-periphrasis began to compete with V-to-T movement, it occurred with different frequencies in different clause types. The Constant Rate Effect formulated by Kroch proposes that over the time periods listed above, the rate of increase was the same across all clause types. This is

Table 9.8 *Slope of the logistic for the categories in Table 9.7*

Neg. decls.	Neg. quests.	Aff. trans. adv. & yes/no quests.	Aff. intrans. adv. & yes/no quests.	Aff. *wh*-obj. quests.
3.74	3.45	3.62	3.77	4.01

so because the increasing percentage of *do* periphrasis is the result of a single underlying grammatical change.

In order to demonstrate this, Kroch employs a mathematical function known as the logistic (see Kroch 1989: 203–6) that describes the s-shaped curve of linguistic change. The s-shaped curves that describe the increasing use of *do*-periphrasis in the clause types in Table 9.7 appear to be different when plotted out, but as Kroch 1989: 224 notes, this is because the vertical part of the s-shaped curves occurs at different times. When the slopes of the different curves are calculated by fitting the data for each clause type to the logistic, the result in Table 9.8 is obtained (cited after Kroch's Table 4, which also provides information on intercept points). It is clear that the values for the slopes are close together, and, indeed, nearly the same in the first, third, and fourth columns, for which the most data is available (see Kroch's Table 3 for the figures). The single best slope for all clause types is 3.70, and a χ^2 test shows that the probability of random fluctuations being responsible for deviations as large as those found in Table 9.8 is over 95 percent.[†] The slope of the s-shaped curve for all five clause types, then, is plausibly the same underlyingly, i.e. the rate of change is constant across them.

This result is bolstered when one examines an independent reflex of the loss of V-to-T movement, the position of unstressed adverbs, which Kroch illustrates with Ellegård's data on the position of *never*, as in example (12):

(12)   a. ME (l. 1744 of Chaucer's *Merchant's Tale*)
            Quene Ester looked [$_{VP}$ never with swich an eye.]

        b. ModE
            Queen Esther [$_{VP}$ never looked with such an eye.]

In ME the matrix verb exhibits V-to-T movement, whereas in ModE the verb remains in VP. The change started in late ME in which, beside the matrix verb + *never* order which was categorical earlier in the language, *never* + matrix verb and *do* + *never* + matrix verb orders are attested, both of which provide evidence for the loss of V-to-T movement. The number of tokens of each of these is given in Table 9.9 (Kroch's Table 7, compiled with data from Ellegård 1953: 184). After applying the logistic function to these data, Kroch finds that the slope for the loss of V-to-T movement in clauses containing *never* is –3.76, which is very

---

[†] It is important to note that this does not mean that the probability that the Constant Rate Effect as proposed by Kroch is true is over 95 percent, but that the probability of finding deviations as large as those attested is over 95 percent if it is true.

Table 9.9 *Position of* never

	do + *never* + verb	*never* + verb	verb + *never*
1425–75	3	52	99
1475–1500	4	80	102
1500–25	1	80	28
1525–35	3	151	16
1535–50	14	125	13
1550–75	9	71	8
1575–1600	6	152	5

Table 9.10 do-*periphrasis in unemphatic affirmative declarative clauses (Kroch's analysis)*

	Per cent with *do*-periphrasis
1390–1400	0.014%
1400–25	0.23%
1425–50	0.27%
1450–75	1.78%
1475–1500	1.37%
1500–25	2.27%
1525–50	7.05%
1550–75	8.13%

close to the 3.70 for the increase in *do*-periphrasis identified above.[8] (The value is negative because it expresses the loss of V-to-T movement, unlike Table 9.8, which records the increase of *do*-periphrasis.) It seems very likely, then, that all of the clause types which have been discussed show that V-to-T movement was being lost at the same rate.

There is still the matter of the rise of *do*-periphrasis in unemphatic affirmative declarative clauses as exemplified in note 6. As in the other clause types, the rate of *do*-periphrasis increases steadily until 1575, as in Table 9.10 (cited after Kroch's Table 8, which provides additional information). Kroch 1989: 230–1 finds that the application of the logistic function to these data results in a slope of 2.28, which is considerably different from that found for other clause types in which V-to-T movement was being lost. Though *do*-periphrasis increases for precisely the same period of time in unemphatic affirmation declarative clauses as in the other clause types, Kroch takes the different rates to reflect not a competition between V-to-T movement and *do*-periphrasis, but one between V-to-T movement and both *do*-periphrasis and tense lowering. This may not be necessary, however. Warner 2006: 54–5 argues that a reassessment of the

Table 9.11 do-*periphrasis in unemphatic affirmative
declarative clauses (Warner's analysis)*

	Slope
Affirmative transitive *wh*-adverbial and yes/no questions	3.76
Affirmative intransitive *wh*-adverbial and yes/no questions	3.71
Affirmative *wh*-object questions	4.33
Negative questions	3.81
Negative declaratives	4.14
Overall (without affirmative declaratives)	3.79
Affirmative declaratives	3.76

philological analysis of the data is in order and yields a different result. He suggests that the data from before 1425 should be omitted from consideration because these texts are primarily western, while the data from the sixteenth century come from texts that are primarily central and eastern, i.e. the data compiled by Ellegård contains a mix of dialects. When an appropriate adjustment is made, Warner arrives at the slopes for clause types evincing an increase in *do*-periphrasis in Table 9.11 (cited after Warner's Table 3.2). It is clear that affirmative declarative clauses pattern with all other clause types, a result which lends yet more weight to the credibility of the Constant Rate Effect. But it is important to note that it would not have been possible to discover this without the detailed philological analysis that is traditional in historical linguistics.

In this chapter we have reviewed some examples of how contemporary theoretical approaches can be applied to the study of syntactic change and can achieve meaningful results that philological analysis alone could not. We have seen that the Grammars in Competition Hypothesis can explain why parameter change that occurs between two generations often, nonetheless, is realized only over long periods of time and that syntactic change sometimes does not result in a change in surface syntax; and, furthermore, that the Constant Rate Effect can explain how a single parameter change proceeds at the same rate through different clause types. Much more work on these approaches to syntactic change remains to be done, but immediate prospects are encouraging for the analysis of an area of linguistic structure frequently overlooked in diachronic research.

Notes

1 There are, of course, many examples of diachronically stable variation known in the languages of the world. Pintzuk 2003: 509–10 mentions object shift in contemporary Scandinavian languages (e.g. Bobaljik and Thráinsson 1998), heavy constituent shift in Old English (e.g. Pintzuk and Kroch 1989), and postposition in Yiddish (Santorini 1993) and ancient Greek (Taylor 1994). The type of variation that leads to syntactic change, on the other hand, is inherently unstable.

2 Compound verbs exhibit a similar dual system in which a verb in absolute initial position in the clause takes deuterotonic (second syllable) stress and a verb preceded by a conjunct particle takes prototonic stress (first syllable), e.g. 3sg. prs. deut. *do·beir*, prot. *tabair* 'gives'.

3 The listed statements are deliberately simplified, in that the following have been omitted. In three categories the suffixing pattern remained in use even in person and number configurations in which the infixing pattern otherwise obtained:

(a) The stereotyped use of the substantive verb and object affix to indicate possession, e.g., 1sg. prs. *táthum* 'I have' (lit. 'there is to me'), 2sg. *táthut* 'you have', 3sg. m. *táithi* 'he has', 3sg. f. *táthus* 'she has', 1pl. *táithiunn* 'we have', 2pl. *táthuib* 'you have', 3pl. *táthus* 'they have'.

(b) Stereotyped phrases such as complexes of 3sg. subjunctive verbs with 1st-person object affix in prayers (as per Hamp 1984:1 40), e.g., *snáidsiunn* 'may he protect us.'

(c) Texts composed in a highly stylized and often obscure register known as *rosc*.

4 In Table 9.6 we employ the so-called Cowgill particle, first proposed by him in 1975. We follow Schrijver 1994: 181–4 in identifying this particle as the reflex of a clitic form of the connective **eti* (> =*et via apocope and =*t post-vocalically), and we follow Schumacher 2004: 100–4 in the reconstruction of its phonological development. Expected, but unattested, forms are marked with **. Not all forms listed as attested with a suffixed object agreement affix occur with *beirid*, but all can be inferred with confidence from other attested forms.

5 *no=* continues the adverb *nu* 'now' which is attested as such in Continental Celtic. Its semantic bleaching and grammaticalization as a preverb parallels that of the most common of Old Irish preverbs, *do=*, which continues a sentence connective *to which was also used in Continental Celtic to provide a host for second position clitics.

6 Kroch also notes that, up to the sixteenth century, periphrastic *do* likewise appears at an increasing rate in unemphatic affirmative declarative clauses, e.g. (adapted after his example (21)):

(a) They worshipped the sonne whanne he [$_T$ dede] [$_{VP}$ arise.] (78:327:8)

(b) When he [$_T$ dyd] [$_{VP}$ se[e] that Crist schold be dede ...] (167:188:2)

(c) Me think I [$_T$ doe] [$_{VP}$ heare a good manerly Beggar at the doore ...] (346:5:17)

7 Kroch 1989: 222 notes that *be* and *have*, whether in their auxiliary or matrix verb use, also always raised to T, even after V-to-T movement began to be lost, which is confirmed by the fact that they never occur with periphrastic *do*.

8 In analyzing the data of Table 9.9 it is necessary for Kroch to factor out tokens in which *never* is adjoined to TP rather than VP, e.g. (ll. 20–1 of "The Bee and the Stork"):

For many are that never [$_{TP}$ kane halde the ordyre of lufe ...]

He estimates that 16 percent of *never* + matrix verb tokens are so constructed (Kroch 1989: 227–8).

10 Reconstruction

In Chapter 5 we noted that a sound change which has "gone to completion" might become a phonological rule, or that its outcome might be projected into underlying forms. The former, which we discussed at length in Chapter 6, is of interest to linguists studying phonological systems. Instances in which sound changes alter underlying forms are important for a completely different reason. In those cases the effects of regular sound change can become fossilized, so to speak, because isolated underlying forms, to which no phonological rules apply, are relatively immune to every kind of historical change *except* regular sound change (and complete loss of the word, on which see below). The effects of regular sound change accumulate in underlying forms like geological strata, unperturbed by other, less regular kinds of historical change. We can then exploit the regularity of sound change by the "comparative method" (see below), comparing the sound-change outcomes in divergent lineages to reverse the changes and recover prehistoric ancestral forms. That is the subject of this chapter.

Before we can discuss linguistic comparison in any detail, we need to define some terms. We begin with linguistic "descent":

> Language or dialect Y of a given time is descended from language or dialect X of an earlier time if and only if X developed into Y through an unbroken sequence of instances of native language acquisition.

Of course any language or dialect also contains some non-native linguistic material, possibly even material from an imperfectly learned dialect whose descent was not unbroken (see Chapter 4). But a precise and rigorous definition of descent helps us sort out the linguistic phenomena that we must deal with. Most importantly, we can rely on the regularity of sound change *only* within lines of descent, since some sound changes acquire lexical conditioning when borrowed from dialect to dialect (see Chapter 3).

We can now define linguistic "relatedness" and "families" of languages:

> Two languages are said to be related if and only if they are descended from a common ancestor.

> All the languages descended from a common ancestor are said to constitute a family of languages.

Related languages are sometimes referred to as "sisters"; the languages descended from an earlier language are usually called its "daughters."

Of course there are families within families; for instance, the Germanic family and the Romance family are both part of the larger Indo-European family, since Proto-Germanic and Proto-Romance were themselves descended from Proto-Indo-European. We therefore recognize "subfamilies" or "subgroups" within families; some linguists use terms such as "stock" or "phylum" to refer to families which have been diverging for at least four millennia (as opposed to "shallow" families like Germanic and Romance, both about two millennia old).

A reconstructed ancestor language is usually called a "protolanguage" and named "Proto-X," where X is the name of the family to which the protolanguage is ancestral.

Finally, there are standard terms for the classes of words, affixes, and sounds that are used in comparative reconstruction. Words or affixes in related languages that have been inherited from their common ancestor by unbroken linguistic descent (see above) are called "cognates." Other sets of words or affixes are *not* cognates, no matter how similar they may be from language to language; in particular, any item that has been borrowed into a language – even from a related language – at any time after their common protolanguage began to diversify is by definition not cognate with anything else in any other language. (On the other hand, words borrowed *into the protolanguage* are cognates in the daughters of *that* protolanguage, since they are inherited from the last common ancestor of those daughters.)

Monomorphemic cognates develop (mostly) by regular sound change. Given a regular development of an ancestral sound x to y in one lineage, and a regular development of the same sound x to z in another, diverging lineage, we expect to find a regular "sound correspondence" $y = z$ in cognate words and affixes in those two lineages. Regular sound correspondences are the input for comparative reconstruction.

Uses of linguistic reconstruction

Linguistic reconstruction is a test of our hypotheses regarding language change, especially the regularity of sound change. The test has been applied many times in the past, typically with highly satisfactory results. Suitably rigorous comparative reconstruction normally yields coherent proto-grammars, or rather fragments of grammars, and more or less extensive proto-lexica. The reconstructed ancestor of the Romance languages can be compared with actually attested Classical Latin; the experiment reveals that Proto-Romance was a dialect of first-century CE Latin, not identical with the upper-class urban Latin of our texts, but only modestly different from it in unremarkable ways. The Proto-Germanic word for 'chieftain' has been reconstructed as *kuningaz (whence Modern English *king*, etc.); though the word is not attested in exactly that shape in any Germanic language, the reconstruction is confirmed in startling detail by

Finnish *kuningas* 'king' and Lithuanian *kùningas* 'lord, priest', evidently very early loanwords from Germanic. Examples of this kind can be multiplied.

But though the conceptual basis and the practical methods of linguistic comparison have long since been proved correct, we can still learn from the attempt to apply them to new sets of linguistic data. Most obviously, if we cannot reconstruct a coherent grammar fragment and a convincing lexicon fragment from a given set of languages using the same rigorous methods that have given provable results in the past, the relationship(s) between those languages must remain doubtful at best. But even when it is clear that the languages being compared are related, strict application of the comparative method can tell us a good deal about how the parent language diversified. If reconstruction from attested languages A, B, and C yields a protolanguage, reconstruction from A and B also yields a (different) protolanguage, and we can demonstrate that Proto-AB developed from Proto-ABC by regular sound changes, we will have established a subgroup (A, B) within the language family ((A, B), C) (Hoenigswald 1960: 146). If it is clear that language D is a member of an established family, but some sounds of the protolanguage seem to have evolved in D in two different and incompatible ways – some words exhibiting one development, other words the alternative development, in no clear pattern – we can conclude that the prehistory of D included at least one period of intensive dialect contact, since regular sound changes are characteristic of particular lines of descent (see above).

In addition to yielding information about particular languages and families, linguistic reconstruction significantly increases the evidence for language change in general that we have our disposal. Of course evidence gleaned by reconstruction is much less detailed than evidence from the historical record, just as evidence from the historical record is less detailed than evidence from fieldwork on languages still spoken. But reconstruction extends the range of historical evidence in much the same way that the written record extends the range of linguistic change beyond what has been learned from the past half-century or so of sociolinguistic fieldwork. It should be obvious that evidence recovered by linguistic reconstruction must be used with great care, since it is necessarily more impoverished and more qualified by uncertainty than any other kind of linguistic evidence we have; but it is useful nonetheless.

Finally, the results of linguistic reconstruction are often of great interest to colleagues in other fields, especially archaeology, history, and population genetics. That is an important reason for reconstructing protolanguages – and for doing so as rigorously and reliably as possible, since there is a considerable risk of misleading colleagues who wish to use our results but do not have the expertise to check our work.

Goals and limits of linguistic reconstruction

The ideal aim of comparative reconstruction is to recover the entire grammar and lexicon of a prehistoric language that has left multiple descendants.

In practice that is impossible. All languages gradually lose and replace old words and affixes as they are transmitted from generation to generation. The turnover is quickest among less commonly used lexical items, but even "basic" words are replaced at a slow but significant rate. Phonological and morphological rules are also lost or replaced; even underlying phonemes undergo mergers which destroy the contrasts between them. By chance some linguistic material may be lost in all the daughters, or in all but one, in which case reconstruction of those details for the protolanguage will be impossible; and the more time elapses, the greater the attrition will be.

Moreover, the branching structure of linguistic evolutionary trees has an impact on the reconstructability of protolanguages. If a protolanguage has only two immediate daughters, a lexical item or morphological category must be preserved in *both*, or in some further daughter(s) of both, in order to be reconstructable for the protolanguage; only greater-than-binary "speciations" obviate this problem. Unfortunately, binary branching structures are by far the commonest among the linguistic evolutionary trees of the world (Nichols 1990).

Finally, the accuracy of comparative reconstruction is strictly limited by a basic fact about language change. Only sound changes which have "gone to completion" (see Chapter 5) are regular enough to be the basis of a mathematically reliable method of reconstruction. For that reason the basic algorithms of phonological reconstruction, collectively called the "comparative method," loom very large in the methodology of linguistic reconstruction, and they will occupy a central place in this chapter. It is important to remember that the utterly reliable but strictly limited results of the comparative method are not the whole story, certainly not an end in themselves; they are simply the first and most indispensable tool for the reconstruction of proto-grammars and lexica. But every other kind of development – changes in meaning, changes in phonological rules, loss of morphological markers, and so on – fails to exhibit the kind of recurrent regularity that we can exploit mathematically. In practice we are reduced to reconstructing as many roots and affixes as we can by the comparative method, then making informed inferences about what their meanings, functions, and paradigmatic relations in the protolanguage were – and the more the daughter languages disagree on those points, the less secure our inferences will be.

We must therefore begin with a consideration of the phonological patterns that regular sound change produces, both within lineages and across related lineages.

Sound change and sound patterns

Let us return to the example of sound change in French that we adduced in Chapter 5. The outcomes of Latin /eː/ in modern French that we found were the following:

unstressed /ə/ or ∅;
stressed /ɛ/ before surviving /n/,
/ɛ̃/ before *n that did not survive,
and /u̯a/ elsewhere.

The distribution of these outcomes is for the most part clear even in modern French, because the syllables that were stressed in Latin are still stressed in French and the nasalization of /ɛ̃/ betrays the former presence of a nasal after the vowel; only the distribution of the two unstressed outcomes /ə/ and ∅ is difficult to see. The phonetics of the outcomes, however, are far from obvious; though /ɛ/ and /ɛ̃/ are obviously similar, neither resembles /u̯a/, and /ə/ is more or less dissimilar to all stressed vowels.

This situation – a clear phonological distribution of outcomes, but opaque phonetics – is fairly typical of long-term outcomes of regular sound change. The reasons for this pattern are straightforward. On the one hand, the phonologically definable classes of sounds to which sound changes apply often (though not always) persist for many generations; for instance, all the changes eventuating in French /u̯a/ applied to stressed vowels. On the other hand, even if every sound change in a series is phonetically natural – as in the case under discussion – a long sequence of changes can change the phonetics of a given sound dramatically.

From these considerations follows a generally applicable rule of thumb in phonological reconstruction: distribution of outcomes is normally a better guide to what has happened than phonetics is; if the languages of a family have been diverging for millennia, distribution of outcomes is almost invariably a *much* better guide than phonetics. The reader should keep this in mind throughout the discussion that follows.

Let us reexamine the types of phonemic splits and mergers discussed in Chapter 5 in terms of their impact on the input data for phonological reconstruction.

Purely phonetic changes that do not alter the pattern of contrasts, such as the change of [w] to [v] in the Romance languages and (independently) in High German, do not alter the pattern of regular correspondences between the sounds of related languages at all. The kind of pattern that results can be seen in the cognates from Fox and Shawnee, two closely related Algonkian languages, adduced in Table 10.1. Since Fox has no /θ/, Shawnee has no /s/, and neither phoneme participates in any other regular sound correspondence between these two languages, it is clear that only one inherited phoneme is represented. The only question is whether the sound in the protolanguage was phonetically *[s] or *[θ], and that would be a matter of guesswork in any case (see above; comparison with related languages strongly suggests *[s]).

Unconditioned merger produces a pattern in which one phoneme in a language regularly corresponds to two in related languages, and – crucially – those two are not in complementary distribution. The comparison of the Cree sibilant with its Fox and Shawnee correspondents in Table 10.2 will illustrate. In the first thirteen items in Table 10.2 (through 'my older sister') Cree /s/ corresponds to Fox /s/ and

Table 10.1 *Some Fox and Shawnee cognates*

	Shawnee	Fox
outside	θa:kiči	sa:kiči
he spits	θekwi	sekwiwa
river	θi:pi	si:po:wi
I grab his leg	niθakika:na	nesakika:na:wa
your foot	kiθiči	kesiči
its tail	hoθowa:lwi	osowa:nowi
he gets up	paθekwi	pasekwi:wa
he defecates	mi:θi	mi:si:wa
shoe	mkiθe	mahkese:hi
tobacco	lθe:ma	nese:ma:wa
my younger sibling	nθi:me:θa	nesi:ma
three	nθwi	neswi
my father	noʔθa	no:sa
he breathes	leʔθe	ne:se:wa
my son	nikwiʔθa	nekwisa
my older sister	nimiʔθa	nemise:ha
ten	metaʔθwi	meta:swi

Shawnee /θ/; in the last ten (from 'needle') it corresponds to Fox and Shawnee /š/ (i.e., /ʃ/; see the Introduction). Most importantly, the two correspondences are not in complementary distribution: though minimal pairs are difficult to find in Algonkian languages, note that both correspondences occur word-initially before /e/ = /e/ = /i/ in the similar verbs 'he spits' and 'he urinates', and there is no clear pattern of distribution among the other lexical items. We have to conclude that there were two sibilant proto-phonemes which have been merged unconditionally in Cree; there is a high probability that the first was */s/ and the second */š/.

A similar pattern appears in the comparison of some modern English and German stressed vowels. Consider the cognate sets in Tables 10.3 and 10.4.[1] In this case we have an actual minimal pair, 'life' vs. 'loaf', which forces recognition of two different vowels in the protolanguage and a merger in German. But even without that pair, the fact that both vowel correspondences occur before and after so many of the same consonants in no discernible pattern would lead to the same conclusion. In this case, however, it is very doubtful that any linguist could recover the phonetics of the two proto-vowels from modern data alone; this is a case in which the phonemic oppositions of the protolanguage are recoverable, but not the phonetics. Fortunately we do not need to rely on modern data, since Old English (OE) and Old High German (OHG) are well attested. The modern correspondence /aɪ/ : /aɪ/ is OE ī : OHG ī, leading to a reconstruction of Proto-West Germanic *ī; modern /oʊ/ : /aɪ/ is OE ā : OHG ei, and evidence of various kinds (including evidence from other Germanic languages) leads to a reconstruction of Proto-West Germanic *ai. We cannot expect to be so lucky in every case.

Table 10.2 *Sibilant merger in Cree*

	Shawnee	Fox	Cree
he spits	θekwi	sekwiwa	sihkiw
river	θi:pi	si:po:wi	si:piy
pin	θakho:we		sakahikan 'nail'
your foot	kiθiči	kesiči	kisit
its tail	hoθowa:lwi	osowa:nowi	osoy
he gets up	paθekwi	pasekwi:wa	pasikow
it is heavy	koθekwanwi		kosikwan
he defecates	mi:θi	mi:si:wa	mi:si:w
it is bitter	wiʔθakanwi		wi:sakan
shoe	mkiθe	mahkese:hi	maskisin
my younger sibling	nθi:me:θa	nesi:ma	nisi:mis
my son	nikwiʔθa	nekwisa	nikosis
my older sister	nimiʔθa	nemise:ha	nimis
needle	ša:ponika	ša:ponikani	sa:ponikan
he urinates	šekiwa	šekiwa	sikow
skunk	šeka:kwa	šeka:kwa	sika:k
duck	šiʔši:pa	ši:ši:pa	si:si:p
wildcat	pešiwa	pešiwa	pisiw
I shoot him	nimešwa	nemešwa:wa	nimiswa:w
two	ni:šwi	ni:šwi	ni:so
day	ki:škwe	ki:šekwi	ki:sik 'sky'
my eye	nški:šekwi	neški:šekwi	niski:sik
it is big	mša:wi	meša:wi	misa:w

Conditioned mergers lead to a more complex pattern. As we saw in Chapter 5, the merger of intervocalic *s with *r* in Latin led to a skewed distribution of *s* and *r* in that language: for some generations the two consonants contrasted everywhere except in intervocalic position, where only *r* was found (and for many more generations intervocalic *s*, apparently reintroduced in loanwords, remained very rare). One would expect related languages that had not undergone the change to exhibit *s* in all environments, so that in the merged environment there are two correspondences, *r* = *r* and *r* = *s*, whereas elsewhere there are only *s* = *s* and *r* = *r*. That is what we find; see the Latin and Sanskrit cognates in Table 10.5.[†] (The retroflex *ṣ* of Sanskrit 'burn (it)', 'daughter-in-law', and 'Dawn' is the result of a productive rule retracting /s/ after vowels other than /a/ and /a:/. That outcome is not represented word-finally in 'twice' because word-final syllables (only!) are traditionally cited in underlying form.)

[†] See the Introduction for the values of the Latin symbols. In our transliteration of Sanskrit, long vowels are likewise marked with a macron; the acute accent indicates high pitch. Dotted coronal consonants are retroflex; *ś* is approximately [ç].

Table 10.3 *Some English and German cognates, first set*

	English	German
by	/baɪ/	bei /baɪ/ 'at, near'
Friday	/ˈfraɪdeɪ/	Freitag /ˈfraɪtaːg/
pipe	/paɪp/	Pfeife /pfaɪfə/ 'whistle, pipe'
ripe	/raɪp/	reif /raɪf/
life	/laɪf/	Leib /laɪb/ 'body'
wife	/waɪf/	Weib /vaɪb/ 'woman'
drive	/draɪv/	treiben /traɪbən/
shrive	/ʃraɪv/	schreiben /ʃraɪbən/ 'write'
(bird)lime	/laɪm/	Leim /laɪm/ 'glue'
slime	/slaɪm/	Schleim /ʃlaɪm/ 'slime, mucus'
bite	/baɪt/	beißen /baɪsən/
smite	/smaɪt/	schmeißen /ʃmaɪsən/ 'fling, hurl'
white	/waɪt/	weiß /vaɪs/
write	/raɪt/	reißen /raɪsən/ 'tear'
glide	/glaɪd/	gleiten /glaɪtən/
idle	/aɪdəl/	eitel /aɪtəl/ 'conceited'
ride	/raɪd/	reiten /raɪtən/
side	/saɪd/	Seite /zaɪtə/ 'side, page'
wide	/waɪd/	weit /vaɪt/ 'far'
iron	/aɪərn/	Eisen /aɪzən/
ice	/aɪs/	Eis /aɪz/
wise	/waɪz/	weise /vaɪzə/
like (adj.)	/laɪk/	gleich /glaɪx/ 'same, equal, even'
light (adj.)	/laɪt/	leicht /laɪxt/ 'easy'
(pig)sty	/staɪ/	Steige /ʃtaɪgə/ 'stall, fold, sty'
line ('flax')	/laɪn/	Lein /laɪn/
mine (adj.)	/maɪn/	mein /maɪn/
shine	/ʃaɪn/	scheinen /ʃaɪnən/ 'appear'
swine	/swaɪn/	Schwein /ʃvaɪn/
thine	/ðaɪn/	dein /daɪn/
wine	/waɪn/	Wein /vaɪn/
file ('rasp')	/faɪl/	Feile /faɪlə/
mile	/maɪl/	Meile /maɪlə/
pile ('stake')	/paɪl/	Pfeil /pfaɪl/ 'arrow'
while (nn.)	/waɪl/	Weile /vaɪlə/

In cases like this comparison with a related language helps to clarify two things. In the first place, the etymological sources of merger products that participate in no alternations, like the *r*'s of Latin *nurus* 'daughter-in-law', *Aurōra* 'Dawn', *ferunt* 'they carry', etc., can be identified only by comparison with a non-merging related language. Secondly, if a marginal contrast in the merging environment has been reestablished by loanwords or words of obscure origin, the non-merging

Table 10.4 *Some English and German cognates, second set*

soap	/soʊp/	*Seife* /zaɪfə/
loaf	/loʊf/	*Laib* /laɪb/
foam	/foʊm/	*Feim* /faɪm/
home	/hoʊm/	*Heim* /haɪm/ 'home, hostel, asylum'
goat	/goʊt/	*Geiß* /gaɪs/
woad	/woʊd/	*Waid* /vaɪd/ (/vaɪt/?)
clothes	/kloʊðz/	*Kleider* /klaɪdər/
loathe	/loʊð/	*leiden* /laɪdən/ 'suffer, endure, allow'
oath	/oʊθ/	*Eid* /aɪd/
ghost	/goʊst/	*Geist* /gaɪst/ 'spirit'
most	/moʊst/	*meiste* /maɪstə/
oak	/oʊk/	*Eiche* /aɪxə/
spoke (nn.)	/spoʊk/	*Speiche* /ʃpaɪxə/
dough	/doʊ/	*Teig* /taɪg/
own (adj.)	/oʊn/	*eigen* /aɪgən/
bone	/boʊn/	*Bein* /baɪn/ 'leg, (fish)bone'
stone	/stoʊn/	*Stein* /ʃtaɪn/
dole (nn.)	/doʊl/	*Teil* /taɪl/ 'part'
holy	/hoʊli/	*heilig* /haɪlɪg/
whole	/hoʊl/	*heil* /haɪl/ 'unhurt, healthy'

language will confirm the late entry of those items into the merging language by failing to offer cognates for them. Sure enough, there are no Sanskrit cognates of Latin *rosa* 'rose', *miser* 'wretched', etc.

Unless they give rise to unusually robust and pervasive alternations, conditioned losses can be discovered only by comparison with a related language that has not undergone the change. The English change of word-initial /kn-/ to /n-/ is a case in point. Consider the English–German cognate sets in Table 10.6. Though there are no minimal pairs, there is also no clear phonological distribution of German /n-/ and /kn-/; it is clear that German preserves a contrast which English has lost by conditioned merger of /k-/ with zero in the initial cluster /kn-/. The only alternating member of the /kn-/ set in English is *knowledge* /nɑlədʒ/ : *acknowledge* /əknɑlədʒ/ (derived from *know* /noʊ/, which has no exact cognate in German), and it is questionable whether native speakers would be able to recognize in this pair a potential word-initial underlying /kn-/ without the ludicrously archaic orthography.

In cases of secondary split the situation is still more involved: two phonemes which contrast in the language which has undergone the split are shown to have been allophones of a single phoneme *by environments preserved in their cognates*. Cases of this kind are usually complex, but once again English and German provide a simple illustration, as in Table 10.7. There is no doubt that /θ/ and /ð/ contrast in English, but both correspond to German /d/. Leaving aside several complications – this is a simplified example – we can say that when

Table 10.5 *Inherited *s and *r in Latin and Sanskrit*

	Latin	Sanskrit
'seven'	septem	saptá
'(s)he follows'	sequitur	sácatē
'it crawls'	serpit	sárpati
'(s)he buries'	sepelit	saparyáti '(s)he honors'
'sun'	sōl	súar
'they are'	sunt	sánti
'(s)he is'	est	ásti
'(s)he will be'	erit	ásati
'nostrils'	nārēs	nāsā
'(s)he burns (it)'	ūrit	óṣati
'daughter-in-law'	nurus	snuṣā́
'Dawn' [goddess]	Aurōra	Uṣā́s
'of bronze'	aeris	áyasas 'of iron'
'horse'	equos	áśvas
'three'	trēs	tráyas
'twice'	bis	dvís
'wheel'	rota	ráthas 'chariot'
'king'	rēx	rā́ṭ
'red'	ruber	rudhirám 'blood'
'they roar'	rudunt	rudánti 'they cry'
'(s)he turns (it)'	vertit	vártati
'(s)he dies'	moritur	mriyátē
'they carry'	ferunt	bháranti
'four'	quattuor	catvā́ri [neuter]
'udder'	ūber	ū́dhar
'between, among'	inter	antár 'inside'
'sister' [acc. case]	sorōrem	svásāram

German /d/ is intervocalic the English correspondent is /ð/, but when German /d/ is in other positions the English correspondent is /θ/. This is the sort of pattern that is needed to recognize and "undo" a secondary split.

Let us now exploit these correspondence patterns in a demonstration of comparative reconstruction.

Phonological reconstruction by the "comparative method"

The immediate goal of comparative phonological reconstruction is to identify the splits and mergers that have occurred in divergent lines of descent and reverse them, so to speak, so as to reconstruct the phonological shapes of the

Table 10.6 *Inherited *kn- in English and German*

	English	German
'knave'	/neɪv/	Knabe /knɑ:bə/ 'boy'
'knead'	/ni:d/	kneten /kne:tən/
'knee'	/ni:/	Knie /kni:/
'knight'	/nɑɪt/	Knecht /knext/ 'servant'
'knot'	/nɑt/	Knoten /kno:tən/
'nail'	/neɪl/	Nagel /nɑ:gəl/
'name'	/neɪm/	Name /nɑ:mə/
'navel'	/neɪvəl/	Nabel /nɑ:bəl/
'need' (nn.)	/ni:d/	Not /no:t/ 'distress, trouble, danger'
'nether-'	/nɛðər-/	nieder /ni:dər/ 'down'
'new'	/nu:/	neu /nɔʏ/
'night'	/nɑɪt/	Nacht /nɑxt/

Table 10.7 *Reconstructing the secondary split of Old English þ in Modern English*

	English	German
'bath'	/bæ:θ/	/bɑ:d/
'bathe'	/beɪð/	/bɑ:dən/
'cloth'	/klɔθ/	/klɑɪd/ 'dress, garment'
'clothe'	/kloʊð/	/klɑɪdən/
'lo(a)th'	/lɔθ/	/lɑɪd/ 'injury, pain'
'loathe'	/loʊð/	/lɑɪdən/ 'suffer, endure, allow'

items in the protolanguage which are ancestral to the cognate sets. We here give an extended example with discussion in depth.

Table 10.8 is a list of cognates in two divergent dialects of Mańśi (Vogul), an Ob-Ugric language spoken in southwestern Siberia; the data were extracted from Steinitz 1955 and Munkácsi and Kálmán 1986. Note that /ɲ ʎ tʲ sʲ ʧʲ/ represent palatalized consonants; /j/ is the palatal semivowel; /w/ is not entirely frictionless; /ɨ ɜ/ are nonfront unrounded vowels.[2] Though the data have been restricted to make this problem manageable, it is not a "toy" problem; we will encounter the full range of patterns and difficulties typical of working with exact cognates.

The first task is to make a list of the recurrent sound correspondences and the cognate sets in which they occur and notes on the phonotactic positions in which they occur, if there are any restrictions. We list them in the format "Tavda = Sosva"; we also note word-initial examples of consonants, since often (though by no means always) it is easy to establish contrasts between consonants in word-initial position. We find the following consonant correspondences:

Table 10.8 *Cognates in two Mańśi dialects*

	Tavda	Sosva	Meaning
1.	æːriˑ	aːri	fenced backwater (for fishing)
2.	ætiˑ	ati	(s)he gathers
3.	tʃˠanɜˑ	sʲoni	(s)he kneads
4.	tʃˠæːlyˑw	sʲaːliɣ	thin, watery
5.	tʃˠæŋtʃˠiˑ	sʲaŋsʲi	sparrow
6.	eːryˑw	eːriɣ	song
7.	jaltɜˑ	jolti	(s)he is suspicious; (s)he works magic
8.	jænyˑw	janiɣ	big
9.	jæriˑ	jari	(s)he gnaws
10.	jiliˑ	jali	(s)he goes around
11.	jilpəˑŋ	jalpəŋ	holy
12.	jiltiˑ	jalti	it (a wound) heals
13.	jis	jis	(s)he came
14.	jonsɜˑ	junsi	(s)he dozes
15.	kaːlɜˑ	xoːli	(s)he dies
16.	kal	xal	cleft, chink
17.	karoˑwlɜ	xariɣli	it (fire) goes out
18.	katɜˑ	xati	(s)he tears
19.	kæˑt	kaːt	hand
20.	keːriˑ	keːri	(s)he plaits; (s)he yokes
21.	kɜːr	xaːr	male (of reindeer)
22.	kiːtiˑ	keːti	(s)he sends
23.	kitʲiˑ	kitiɣli	(s)he asks
24.	kol	xol	morning, dawn
25.	koʎtɜˑ	xuʎti	(s)he stays behind
26.	koɲiˑ	xoɲi	(s)he closes his/her eyes
27.	koːl	xuːl	fish
28.	koːr	xuːr	riverbank; edge (of a container)
29.	kyl	kol	house
30.	kyn	kʊn	out
31.	liːpiˑ	leːpi	(s)he covers
32.	ʎiːŋ	ʎeːŋk	wooden wedge, peg
33.	miɲiˑ	mini	(s)he goes
34.	naːn	noːn	vulva
35.	nat	not	lifetime
36.	natəˑŋ	notəŋ	grown up
37.	niː	neː	woman
38.	ɲaːtɜˑ	ɲoːti	(s)he helps
39.	ɲal	ɲol	nose
40.	ɲæːr	ɲaːr	naked
41.	ɲeːl	ɲaːl	arrow
42.	ɲeːr	ɲaːr	swamp
43.	ɲeːroˑw	ɲaːriɣ	cartilage
44.	ɲolɜˑ	ɲuli	silver fir
45.	onʃɜˑ	unsi	(s)he crosses over

(cont.)

Table 10.8 (*cont.*)

	Tavda	Sosva	Meaning
46.	oːrɜ·	uːri	(s)he waits, (s)he guards
47.	or	ur	forest; hill
48.	paːʎi·	poːʎi	(s)he freezes to death
49.	paːrɜ·	poːri	(s)he hollows (something) out
50.	pæːl	paːl	bench, shelf for sleeping
51.	pæːrt	paːrt	board
52.	pælə·m	paləm	horsefly
53.	pænti·	panti	(s)he covers (a container)
54.	peːrsi·	peːrsi	(s)he wraps up
55.	piːti·	peːti	(s)he cooks; (s)he puts (it) in a kettle
56.	piʎi·	pili	(s)he is afraid
57.	polə·m	poləm	the Pelymka (river)
58.	pon	pun	hair, feather
59.	ponʃɜ·	ponsi	it ripens
60.	poŋo·wtɜ	poŋiɣti	(s)he presses
61.	poːl	puːl	piece, bite
62.	porɜ·	puri	(s)he bites
63.	porʃ	pors	rubbish
64.	sarɜ·	sori	narrow place; isthmus
65.	sæːm	saːm	region
66.	sæːt	saːt	seven
67.	sɜːlɜ·	saːli	it (lightning) flashes
68.	sɜːʎ	saːʎ	goldeneye (duck)
69.	sɜːm	saːm	scale (of treebark)
70.	syŋ	saŋkʷ	wedge
71.	ʃaʎ	soʎ	hoarfrost
72.	ʃæːny·w	saːniɣ	nit
73.	ʃɜːn	saːn	birchbark bowl
74.	ʃiːmə·l	seːməl	black
75.	ʃiːny·w	seːniɣ	rotten birchwood
76.	ʃiʃ	sis	back [noun]
77.	ʃon	sun	sled
78.	taːr	toːr	cloth
79.	tatɜ·	toti	(s)he brings, (s)he fetches
80.	tæːl	taːl	winter
81.	tæːr	taːr	root
82.	tæl	tal	lap, embrace
83.	teːrpi·	teːrpi	bait; medicine
84.	ti	ti	this
85.	tiːli·	teːli	(s)he is born
86.	tɜːro·w	taːriɣ	crane
87.	tol	tul	cloud
88.	toːlɜ·	tuːli	(s)he brings in
89.	waːt	woːt	wind
90.	wɜːtɜ·	waːti	(s)he picks (berries)

p = p	items 11, 31, 48–63 (word-initial), 83
m = m	33 (word-initial), 52, 57, 65, 69, 74
w = w	89, 90 (only word-initial)
w = ɣ	4, 6, 8, 17, 43, 60, 72, 75, 86 (only in the coda of noninitial syllables)
t = t	2, 7, 12, 18, 19, 22, 25, 35, 36, 38, 51, 53, 55, 60, 66, 78–88 (word-initial), 79 (also intervocalic), 89, 90
tʲ = t	23
n = n	3, 8, 14, 30, 34–7 (word-initial), 34 (also word-final), 45, 53, 58, 59, 72, 73, 75, 77
ɲ = n	33
ɲ = ɲ	26, 38–44 (word-initial), 60
l = l	4, 7, 10–12, 15–17, 24, 27, 29, 31 (word-initial), 39, 41, 44, 50, 52, 57, 61, 67, 74, 80, 82, 85, 87, 88
ʎ = l	56
ʎ = ʎ	25, 32 (word-initial), 48, 68, 71
r = r	1, 6, 9, 17, 20, 21, 28, 40, 42, 43, 46, 47, 49, 51, 54, 62–4, 78, 81, 83, 86 (never word-initial)
s = s	13, 14, 54, 64–70 (word-initial)
ʃ = s	45, 59, 63, 71–7 (word-initial), 76 (also word-final)
ʧ = sʲ	3–5 (word-initial), 5 (also word-medial)
j = j	7–14 (only word-initial)
k = k	19, 20, 22, 23, 29, 30 (only word-initial)
k = x	15–18, 21, 24–8 (only word-initial)
∅ = k	32 (only word-final after ŋ = ŋ)
∅ = kʷ	70 (only word-final after ŋ = ŋ)
ŋ = ŋ	5, 11, 32, 36, 70 (only in the syllable coda)

There are a few words which begin with vowels (1, 2, 6, 45–7) and a very few monosyllables which end in vowels (37, 84), as well as numerous polysyllables which end in vowels (see below); but there are no sequences of vowels without an intervening consonant. We find the following vowel correspondences in initial syllables:

y = o	29, 30 (only after k = k)
y = a	70 (between s = s and ŋ = ŋkʷ)
æ = a	2, 5, 8, 9, 52, 53, 82 (never after k = x or k = k)
a = a	16–18 (only after k = x)
a = o	3, 7, 35, 36, 39, 64, 71, 79 (never after k = x, k = k, or p = p)
o — o	24, 26, 57, 59, 60, 63 (only after k – x and p = p)
o = u	14, 25 (after k = x), 44, 45, 47, 58, 62, 77, 87
i = i	13 (after j = j), 23 (after k = k), 33, 56, 76, 84
i = a	10–12 (only between j = j and l = l)
i: = e:	22 (after k = k), 31, 32, 37, 55, 74, 75, 85 (never before r = r)
e: = e:	6, 20 (after k = k), 54, 83 (only before r = r)

e: = a:	41–3 (only after ɲ = ɲ; 42 and 43 before r = r)
ɜ: = a:	21 (after k = x), 67–9, 73, 86, 90
æ: = a:	1, 4, 19 (after k = k), 40, 50, 51, 65, 66, 72, 80, 81
a: = o:	15 (after k = x), 34, 38, 48, 49, 78, 89
o: = u:	27, 28 (both after k = x), 46, 61, 88

In noninitial syllables, however, the range of vowels is far more restricted. The most pervasive pattern is found in Tavda: the vowel of the second syllable, regardless of its identity or phonotactic position, is half-long (and stressed). Since that is a completely automatic consequence of syllable count, we should disregard it in setting up our correspondences; in effect, the Tavda data are incompletely phonemicized, and by ignoring half-length we are phonemicizing them more completely. We find the following correspondences:

i· = i	1, 2, 5, 9, 10, 12, 20, 22, 26, 31, 33, 48, 53–6, 83, 85 (only word-final)
ɜ(·) = i	3, 7, 14, 15, 17, 18, 25, 38, 44–6, 49, 59, 60, 62, 64, 67, 79, 88, 90 (only word-final)
y· = i	4, 6, 8, 72, 75 (only before w = ɣ)
o· = i	43, 60, 86 (only before w = ɣ)
ə· = ə	11, 36, 52, 57, 74 (only before sonorants; m = m, ŋ = ŋ, l = l are attested)

There is one word in which the unstressed syllables do not match, namely 23 (Tavda *kit̕i·*, Sosva *kitiɣli*). There are also quite a few monosyllabic words (13, 16, 19, 21, 24, 27–30, 32, 34, 35, 37, 39–42, 47, 50, 51, 58, 61, 63, 65, 66, 68–71, 73, 76–8, 80–2, 84, 87, 89).

We need to find the contrasts and complementary distributions among these correspondences so that we can reconstruct the splits and mergers that occurred in each line of descent. The dialects are closely enough related that phonetics will be of some use in figuring out which correspondences might be split products of original single phonemes. However, since sound changes can accumulate so as to alter the phonetics of segments drastically (see above), our most important guides to possible splits and mergers will be correspondences that are partially similar, i.e. that exhibit the same outcome in one language or the other, and we have ordered the above lists with that in mind.

Let us begin with the vowels of noninitial syllables, since that seems to be a particularly simple subunit of the phonology. In fact, there are so few potentially contrastive vowels in noninitial syllables that we can reasonably infer that they are unstressed, or were unstressed in the protolanguage (see endnote 2), and we will refer to them as such in what follows. You can see at a glance that there are at most two contrastive units. The first two correspondences occur only word-finally, the third and fourth only before a unique correspondence of fricatives, and the last only before sonorants. Thus those three units are in complementary distribution and cannot contrast with each other; the five correspondences represent at most two proto-phonemes. The next question is whether the first and second correspondences contrast, and whether the third and fourth correspondences do.

The second correspondence turns out to have an even more restricted distribution than we noted above. Its occurrence is apparently determined by the vowel of the preceding syllable:

> ɜ(·) = i after first-syllable a = a (18), a = o (3, 7, 64, 79), o = o (59), o = u (14, 25, 44, 45, 62), a: = o: (15, 38, 49, 88), o: = u: (46), ɜ: = a: (67, 90), and after medial-syllable o· = i (17, 60)

All the first-syllable vowels in question are nonfront vowels in both dialects; the Tavda reflex in the medial-syllable correspondence is also nonfront. It appears that Tavda exhibits some kind of vowel harmony. We should then expect the correspondence i· = i to occur following syllables with front vowels, at least in Tavda, and for the most part that is what we find:

> i· = i after first-syllable æ = a (2, 5, 9, 53), i = a (10, 12), i = i (33, 56), æ: = a: (1), e: = e: (20, 54, 83), i: = e: (22, 31, 55, 85)

Clearly it is the frontness of the preceding vowel in Tavda that matters, since in some of these correspondences Sosva has *a* or *a:*. We posit the following hypothesis:

> Tavda exhibits frontness agreement of unstressed vowels with the vowel of the preceding syllable. If there were any shifts of vowel frontness in the development of Tavda, they occurred *before* the modern agreement rule entered the language.

However, there are two exceptional words that exhibit i· = i even after nonfront first-syllable vowels:

> 26 koɲi· = xoɲi
> 48 pa:ʎi· = po:ʎi

But both words exhibit palatalized consonants immediately before the final vowel. If we reexamine the words with final ɜ(·) = i, we will find that none of them exhibit palatalized consonants before that vowel correspondence. It appears that final vowels in Tavda also assimilate in frontness to a preceding palatalized consonant, and that that rule entered the language later than, applies after, and so overrides the frontness agreement rule. Since the difference between unstressed ɜ(·) and *i·* in Tavda can be explained by positing regular sound changes, we do not want to project it back into the protolanguage; we reconstruct one vowel, presumably *i. In fact, at this point we might reasonably wonder whether the Tavda data are still incompletely phonemicized, since the occurrence of *i·* and ɜ(·) can be predicted from Tavda facts alone.

The third and fourth correspondences of the five listed above are much rarer. By now we expect the choice between them to be determined by the vowel correspondence of the first syllable, and that is what we find:

y· = i after first-syllable æ = a (8), æ: = a: (4, 71), e: = e: (6), i: = e: (75)
o· = i after first-syllable o = o (60), e: = a: (43), ɜ: = a: (86)

For the most part these are the familiar correspondences that determined the
choice between ɜ· and i· in Tavda, but there is one surprise. The back correspondence, not the front correspondence, follows first-syllable e: = a: even though
the Tavda reflex in that correspondence is a *front* vowel. (Though we have no
examples of a word-final unstressed vowel after first-syllable e: = a:, we would
correspondingly expect it to be ɜ(·) rather than i·. So the data are not incompletely
phonemicized after all; the unstressed vowels do contrast in Tavda, though only
after first-syllable e:.) By now the neat pattern of frontness in unstressed high
vowels is so widespread – item 43 is the only counterexample – that we should
be willing to adopt further hypotheses in order to save it. We posit the following
development for Tavda:

1   shifts of vowel frontness, if any (to be determined by further work
        below);
2   assimilation of unstressed vowels to vowels of preceding syllables in
        frontness, with lowering of the back allophone from *[i] to *[ɜ];
3a   some long nonfront vowel > e: in the correspondence e: = a: (items
        41–3);
3b   assimilation in rounding of *i to y and of its back allophone *[ɜ] to o
        before w;
4   assimilation of unstressed vowels to preceding palatalized conso-
        nants;
5   shift of stress to the second syllable, with non-contrastive lengthening
        of the second-syllable vowel.

The sound changes occurred, and the rules apply, in the order given, except that
we cannot determine the chronology and ordering of (3a) and (3b) or of (3a)
and (4); (4) must follow (3b), since the second vowel in item 60, poɲo·wtɜ, is
not i nor y. It would be possible to restate (3b) in such a way that we would not
need to order it after (2), but the alternative given here appears to be the simplest
attainable. Note that (3a) is a plausible change because that vowel correspondence
has a highly restricted distribution: it occurs only after ɲ = ɲ. We will need to
return to that point in analyzing the stressed vowel correspondences.

   It turns out that we are able to reconstruct only one unstressed vowel. We
might reasonably call it *i or *ɔ (remembering that the phonetics of proto-
segments is informed guesswork). But since unstressed vowels often become [ə],
*i is possibly the more realistic choice. The changes that it underwent in Tavda
have been outlined above, except that we need to add

0   unstressed vowels became ə before sonorants;

it seems simplest to order it first (and state the other changes so as to exempt
ə), but in fact we can only say for certain that it preceded (5). In Sosva it is the

only change of unstressed vowels that occurred. We might reasonably guess that unstressed *i already had an allophone *[ə] in the protolanguage, but the data do not force that conclusion, since change/rule (0) is natural and could have occurred repeatedly.

Now we turn to the consonants, which seem less bewildering than the stressed vowels. The bilabial correspondences p = p and m = m resemble nothing else, share reflexes with nothing else, and do not appear to be in complementary distribution with anything else (or with each other); there are a few minimal pairs which confirm their contrasts with some other consonants (e.g. 50 vs. 80, 61 vs. 27, 58 vs. 77, 65 vs. 66, 69 vs. 68, and note that 33 vs. 56 is a near-minimal pair for these two correspondences), but even without that evidence we could not justify claiming that either one is a split product of some proto-phoneme. We reconstruct *p and *m respectively.

The voiced bilabial approximant is another matter. w = w occurs only in word-initial position, while w = ɣ occurs only in the codas of unstressed syllables. It makes sense to hypothesize that both reflect a single proto-phoneme. An obvious guess at its phonetics is *w, especially since preceding unstressed vowels are rounded (to y and o) in Tavda, which suggests that this was originally a round segment. On the other hand, the postvocalic reflex [ɣ] in Sosva suggests that this consonant might originally have been *[ɣʷ]. *w is rare enough (in these data) that we could try to claim a complementary distribution with various other consonants, but the fact that both *p and *w occur word-initially before back vowels (even though they are not the same back vowels) argues for the cautious solution of keeping them separate.

The next two correspondences in our list present us with a complementary distribution that is hard to miss:

t = t occurs word-initially before æ = a, a = o, o = u, i = i, æ: = a:, a: = o:, o: = u:, ɜ: = a:, i: = e:, and e: = e:;

 following æ = a, a = a, a = o, a: = o:, ɜ: = a:, i: = e:, l = l (7, 12), ʎ = ʎ (25), n − n (53), or *w (60) and preceding the unstressed vowel;
 following a = o, a: = o:, æ: = a:, and r = r (51) word-finally;

tʲ = t occurs following i = i and preceding the unstressed vowel (23).

It seems clear enough that we have a single proto-phoneme *t of very wide distribution that has been palatalized between two i's in Tavda by a very natural regular sound change. We might expect the same change to have affected other alveolars, and that is what we find:

n = n occurs word-initially before a = o, a: = o:, and i: = e:;

 following æ = a, a = o, æ: = a:, or i: = e: and preceding the unstressed vowel;
 in stressed syllable codas between o = u and s = s (14) or ʃ = s (45), between o and ʃ = s (59), and between æ = a and *t (53);
 following o = u, y = o, a: = o:, and ɜ: = a: word-finally;

ɲ = n occurs following i = i and preceding the unstressed vowel (33);

similarly,

l = l occurs word initially before iː = eː;

> following i = a, æ = a, o = o, u = o, æː = aː, aː = oː, oː = uː, ɜː = aː, iː = eː,
> or *w (17) and preceding the unstressed vowel;
> in stressed syllable codas between a = o and *t (7); between i = a and *p (11)
> or *t (12);
> following æ = a, a = a, a = o, o = o, o = u, y = o, æː = aː, oː = uː, eː = aː,
> and the unstressed vowel (74) word-finally;

ʎ = l occurs following i = i and preceding the unstressed vowel (56).

Clearly these two proto-phonemes, occurring in most of the possible phonotactic positions, are *n and *l respectively.

But an obvious question now asserts itself: are ɲ = ɲ and ʎ = ʎ also split products of those two proto-phonemes? We can come to that conclusion *only* if they can be shown to have developed from *n and *l by regular sound change. That proves to be infeasible. Though there are no perfect minimal pairs, there are no clear complementary distributions either; for *n vs. *ɲ note the following:

34. naːn = noːn	vs.	38. ɲaːtɜ· = ɲoːti	
35. nat = not		39. ɲal = ɲol	

and for *l vs. *ʎ note the following:

7. jaltɜ· = jolti	vs.	25. koʎtɜ· = xuʎti	
31. liːpi· = leːpi		32. ʎiːŋ = ʎeːŋk	
88. toːlɜ· = tuːli		48. paːʎi· = poːʎi	

In the first set of pairs adduced, if the two nasals were split products of a single *n, the outcomes would have to depend on the consonants following the vowels – and *t would have to have different effects depending on whether it was followed by an unstressed vowel (or depending on whether the stressed vowel was long or short). In the pair 31 vs. 32 the outcome would again have to depend on the consonants following the stressed vowel; in 7 vs. 25 and 88 vs. 48 it would have to depend on the preceding vowel, though all the vowels in question are nonfront vowels – and the effects would have to be opposite depending on the length of the vowel. None of this makes any sense at all. We are constrained to recognize two further proto-phonemes *ɲ and *ʎ.

It also seems obvious to ask whether r = r is a split product, especially since it never occurs word-initially. But the only other correspondence which resembles it phonetically is l = l, and there are no fewer than three minimal pairs: 27 koːl = xuːl vs. 28 koːr = xuːr; 41 ɲeːl = ɲaːl vs. 42 ɲeːr vs. ɲaːr; 80 tæːl = taːl vs. 81 tæːr = taːr. There is also a virtual minimal pair with ʎ = ʎ: 48 paːʎi· = poːʎi vs. 49 paːrɜ· vs. poːri. We have no choice but to recognize an ancestral *r, which apparently did not occur word-initially.

The sibilants s = s and ʃ = s are also obvious candidates for split products of a single proto-phoneme. Once again there are no minimal pairs, but no good complementary distribution either; note the following:

13. jis = jis	vs.	76. ʃiʃ = sis
14. jonsɜ· = junsi		45. onʃɜ· = unsi, 59 ponʃɜ· = ponsi
66. sæ:t = sa:t		72. ʃæ:ny·w = sa:niɣ
69. sɜ:m = sa:m		73. ʃɜ:n = sa:n

It can be seen that in this case too the sound changes that would be needed to derive these two correspondences from a single proto-phoneme would be as implausible as those rejected above. We must reconstruct both *s and *ʃ, positing a merger of the two as *s* in Sosva. The rare correspondence ʧʲ = sʲ, occuring only in items 3 through 5, must also be reconstructed as a separate proto-phoneme; the only other correspondences that it at all resembles are ʃ = s and j = j, and all occur word-initially before some of the same vowels. The likeliest phonetic guess for this correspondence is *ʧʲ, since affricates often develop into fricatives, but seldom the other way around.

Though j = j occurs only word-initially, there is nothing with which it can be plausibly combined; we reconstruct *j. It is true that j = j is in perfect complementary distribution with r = r, and the two might conceivably be split products of a single *r. On the other hand, this is just as likely to be a case like modern English /h/ and /ŋ/, which are also in perfect complementary distribution but certainly do not constitute a single phoneme. Reconstructing both *j and *r is preferable because it is the more cautious course. The same can be said of ŋ = ŋ: though it occurs only in the syllable coda and is thus in complementary distribution with j = j, its phonetic distinctiveness argues that we should reconstruct *ŋ, with a limited distribution, as well.

That leaves the four correspondences involving voiceless velar stops. Two of them, Ø = k (32) and Ø = kʷ (70), appear in one word each word-finally after ŋ = ŋ; since the status of single examples is always problematic – we can make them "regular" by default, but such hypotheses can hardly inspire confidence – we postpone consideration of them until we have discussed the other cases. Interestingly, the correspondences k = k and k = x, both occurring only in word-initial position, are actually in complementary distribution:

k = k occurs before i = i (23), y = o (29, 30), æ: = a: (19), e: = e: (20), and
   i: = e: (22);
k = x occurs before a = a (16–18), o = o (24, 26), o = u (25), a: = o: (15), ɜ: =
   a: (21), and o: = u: (27, 28).

Obviously k = x occurs before nonfront vowels. We expect k = k to occur before front vowels, and it does – provided that the ancestor phonemes of y = o and æ: = a: were front vowels! In Tavda they still are, but not in Sosva; the split must have occurred in Sosva before those two vowels became nonfront. This is a case of secondary split: /k/ and /x/ contrast in Sosva, because both occur before /a:/, but the environments preserved in Tavda allow us to "undo" that split and reconstruct a single proto-phoneme *k. Obviously the correspondence ∅ = k could also be *k, with loss of the stop word-finally after *ŋ* in Tavda. But there is also another possibility: *k* could have been added in Sosva word-finally after a stressed syllable ending in *ŋ*.[†] To this dilemma the correspondence ∅ = kʷ adds another. It occurs in the same word as the unique vowel correspondence y = a. In effect, one language has "docked" the rounding in this word on the vowel, the other on the word-final velar; we can be pretty sure that the protoform exhibited rounding somewhere, but a more definite statement than that may not be possible. We will revisit that question when we deal with the stressed vowels. Finally, it should be pointed out that *ŋ and *k are, strictly speaking, in complementary distribution, though they are different enough that it would be surprising if they reflected the same proto-phoneme. If we reconstruct word-final *k after *ŋ in items 32 and 70, the hypothesis that they are split products of a single proto-phoneme becomes wildly implausible, since a change of *kk to *ŋk* (or a development of a single *k to *ŋk* at the end of a stressed syllable) is very unnatural.

Finally we turn to the stressed vowel correspondences. So far we have discovered two things about them:

(a)   the correspondence e: = a: must reflect a back vowel, because it is followed by *o·w* rather than *y·w* in Tavda;

(b)   the correspondences y = o and æ: = a: must reflect front vowels, since they are preceded by *k* rather than *x* in Sosva.

From the last it can be reasonably (though not quite necessarily) inferred that æ = a reflects a front vowel too. For the moment we should leave aside the unique correspondence of item 70. The long vowel correspondences we need to account for are the following:

e: = e:, front (see item 20), which occurs only before *r
i: = e:, front (see item 22), which never occurs before *r
e: = a:, back (see item 43), which occurs only after *ɲ
ɜ: = a:, back (see item 21), which never occurs after *ɲ
æ: = a:, front (see item 19)
a: = o:, back (see item 15)
o: = u:, back (see items 27, 28)

Clearly the first two correspondences are in complementary distribution, and so are the third and fourth; each of those pairs reflects a single proto-phoneme. The last three show no clear distributions. There are some minimal pairs, as follows:

[†] See the footnote on p. 128 in Chapter 6.

85. tiːliˑ = teːli	vs.	88. toːlɜˑ = tuːli
42. ɲeːr = ɲaːr	vs.	40. ɲæːr = ɲaːr
21. kɜːr = xaːr	vs.	28. koːr = xuːr
69. sɜːm = saːm	vs.	65. sæːm = saːm
1. æːriˑ = aːri	vs.	46. oːrɜˑ = uːri
50. pæːl = paːl	vs.	61. poːl = puːl
81. tæːr = taːr	vs.	78. taːr = toːr

We can make a deduction about the phonetics of the proto-phoneme reflected by iː = eː and (before *r) eː = eː from information already in hand. Since *t, *n, and *l were palatalized in Tavda between high front unround vowels (see above), the *lack* of palatalization in 22 *kiːti* and 85 *tiːli* can only mean that their stressed vowels were not high front vowels when palatalization occurred. The obvious alternative is *eː, preserved before *r in Tavda and everywhere in Sosva. Plausible reconstructions of the five stressed long vowels are the following:

iː/eː = eː	*eː
eː/ɜː = aː	*ɜː or *aː
æː = aː	*æː
aː = oː	*aː or *oː
oː = uː	*oː or *uː

Since the five long vowels contrast with each other, alternative reconstructions must be chosen so as not to confuse them: if the fifth correspondence is *oː, then the fourth must be *aː and the second *ɜː; if the second is *aː, the fourth must be *oː and the fifth *uː. The short vowel correspondences are the following:

i = i, front (see item 23), occurring after *j, but only when *s follows (item 13)
i = a, occurring only between *j and *l
æ = a, not found after *k; occurring after *j, but only when *n or *r follows
  (items 8 and 9)
a = a, back (see items 16–18), occurring only after *k
a = o, not found after *k or *p
o = o back (see items 24 and 26), occurring only after *k and *p
o = u, back (see item 25), occurring after *k and *p (and other consonants)
y = o, front (see items 29 and 30), occurring only after *k

Minimal pairs and sets are surprisingly few, but the following can be cited:

16.	kal = xal	vs.	24. kol = xol vs. 29. kyl = kol
18.	katɜ = xati	vs.	23. kitʲi = kiti(ɣli)
52.	pæləˑm = paləm	vs.	57. poləˑm = poləm
82.	tæl = tal	vs.	87. tol = tul

(There are also minimal pairs between the long and the short vowels, but since it seems clear that those two subsets of vowels are stable, with no mismatches, we would reconstruct them differently in any case.) The challenge is to find the complementary distributions that can be exploited to reconstruct the most economical system of short vowels for the protolanguage. We might consider

Table 10.9 *Phonemes of Proto-Mańśi*

Consonants				Short vowels		Long vowels		
p	t	ʧʲ	k	i, y	u			
	s	ʃ			o	e:	ɜ:	o:
m	n	ɲ	ŋ	æ	a	æ:		a:
	l	ʎ						
w	r	j						

hypothesizing that i = a, which occurs only between *j and *l, is a split product of *i, which we would reconstruct for i = i, were it not for the fact that *l was palatalized in Tavda between high front unround vowels (see above). The first vowel of the Tavda form in the cognate set 10 jili· = jali therefore cannot have been *i throughout the prehistory of Tavda; it must have been some other vowel. The obvious candidate is *æ, which we should reconstruct from the correspondence æ = a because we reconstructed *æ: from æ: = a: (other things being equal); note that the Sosva reflex of both correspondences is the same. Since the next four correspondences in our list are back vowels in both dialects, we won't want to suggest that any of them is a split product of *æ. But a = o is in complementary distribution both with a = a and with o = o (though those two are not in complementary distribution with each other, nor with o = u); which of those alternatives should we combine it with? In either case one of the proto-phonemes which we posit will be left with a limited distribution, but if we "strand" a = a by combining the other two, the situation will be maximally marked, since a = a occurs only after *k. It seems better to combine a = a and a = o as *a, leaving *o (whose reflexes are o = o) with a moderately limited distribution. In any case o = u must be *u. (Note that this suggests reconstructing long o: = u: as *u: but a: = o: as *a: – from which it follows that e:/ɜ: = a: must be *ɜ:.) The remaining recurrent correspondence y = o has such a limited distribution that it is in complementary distribution with several other vowels; but since it must be a front vowel, and since its reflexes are very different from those of *i and *æ, we can only reconstruct it as *y.

We now have the optimal segment inventory for Proto-Mańśi, given in Table 10.9. The consonant system clearly makes typological sense; the vowel system is somewhat marked. The lack of a short *e and the presence of a short *y seem especially odd. But this is the best we can do with the information at our disposal.

We now have a least a fighting chance of making sense out of item 70, *syŋ* = *saŋkʷ*. If we propose that the rounding in this word appeared on the word-final velar in the protolanguage, we must reconstruct a very rare labiovelar stop, or else a unique word-final cluster *kw. However, if we propose that the rounding was on the vowel, this can be another case of *y, thus *syŋk, and that vowel becomes a bit less rare and its distribution a bit less limited. We can then suggest that the reflex of this vowel in Sosva is unround *a* precisely because the rounding was transferred to the following velar. But this is still mostly speculation – usually the best we can do with a unique datum.

The phonemic shapes of the Proto-Mańśi forms as we have reconstructed them are the following:

1. æːri	31. leːpi	61. puːl
2. æti	32. ʎeːŋk	62. puri
3. ʧani	33. mini	63. porʃ
4. ʧæːliw	34. naːn	64. sari
5. ʧænʧi	35. nat	65. sæːm
6. eːriw	36. natiŋ	66. sæːt
7. jalti	37. neː	67. sɜːli
8. jæniw	38. ɲaːti	68. sɜːʎ
9. jæri	39. ɲal	69. sɜːm
10. jæli	40. ɲæːr	70. syŋk
11. jælpiŋ	41. ɲɜːl	71. ʃaʎ
12. jælti	42. ɲɜːr	72. ʃæːniw
13. jis	43. ɲɜːriw	73. ʃɜːn
14. junsi	44. ɲuli	74. ʃeːmil
15. kaːli	45. unʃi	75. ʃeːniw
16. kal	46. uˑri	76. ʃiʃ
17. kariwli	47. ur	77. ʃun
18. kati	48. paːʎi	78. taːr
19. kæːt	49. paːri	79. tati
20. keːri	50. pæːl	80. tæːl
21. kɜːr	51. pæːrt	81. tæːr
22. keːti	52. pælim	82. tæl
23. kiti	53. pænti	83. teːrpi
24. kol	54. peːrsi	84. ti
25. kuʎti	55. peːti	85. teːli
26. koɲi	56. pili	86. tɜːriw
27. kuːl	57. polim	87. tul
28. kuːr	58. pun	88. tuːli
29. kyl	59. ponʃi	89. waːt
30. kyn	60. poɲiwti	90. wɜːti

For item 23 we reconstruct only the portion shared by both dialects.

Comments on comparative phonological reconstruction

It can be seen that the comparative method recovers the constrasts between the phonemes of the protolanguage – and *only* the contrasts. The inferences we make are guided and limited by the fact that sound change is regular, and that the only kind of phonemic change is therefore merger (conditioned or not). Those inferences are a matter of simple mathematics. By contrast, the actual phonetics of the proto-segments must be inferred from their reflexes in the daughters by a completely different type of inference, based solely on our collective experience about how sounds are *likely* to develop phonetically. It follows that, on a formal level, every reconstruction that posits the same contrasts, or an equivalent set of contrasts, is equally acceptable. We indicated that in the discussion above by noting plausible alternatives at various points.

We treat large classes of sounds (consonants, stressed vowels, etc.) across both languages, or rather all the languages, more or less simultaneously; if we had five languages to compare, our correspondences would be of the form p = p = p = p = p. This is the most efficient way to analyze phenomena in which a pattern in one language is illuminated by the environment preserved in a related language, such as secondary split and conditioned loss. In effect, we are phonemicizing on correspondences rather than on allophones. But because correspondences are not, in fact, allophones, and because the phonetics of the members of a correspondence can diverge widely, outcomes shared by two or more correspondences in a single language are the best guide to complementary distributions between the correspondences. In the problem above that became clear especially in the analysis of the stressed vowels. We therefore work with large amounts of linguistic data at every stage of the process – and if we are to succeed, it is absolutely imperative to keep track of the data accurately. Inadvertent errors in "bookkeeping" are a significant source of errors in the final analysis.

It should also be clear that comparative reconstruction cannot be pursued successfully without prior preparation of various kinds. Seeing the phonological patterns in the data is crucial, and a thorough grounding in basic phonetics and phonology is what makes the patterns visible. Internalizing the principle of phonological contrast is particularly important. In addition, experience with a wide variety of languages is helpful because it presents the researcher with diverse examples of phonological inventories, patterns, rules, and changes. Though comparative reconstruction is exclusively the property of diachronic linguistics, prior mastery of relevant synchronic facts remains essential.

There is a further pitfall that is more difficult to avoid. In the Mańśi problem the phonological patterns are interlocked; different decisions about consonants, for instance, will lead to increasingly divergent decisions about stressed and unstressed vowels. The result can still be a coherent reconstruction, and it will still be mechanically convertible into the reconstruction outlined above (unless mistakes have been made), but it will be significantly less economical and less plausible: not only will the system be more complex, but there will be more segments with surprisingly restricted distributions. We structured the demonstration above in such a way as to arrive at an optimal or near-optimal solution as quickly as possible. But what if we had entered the problem by a different route and arrived at a less optimal solution? There is no easy remedy for such an accident; if the solution one has arrived at seems too improbable, the only recourse is to try to figure out why and then start over, preferably beginning with a different class of sounds, making different decisions, and paying close attention to their consequences for the result.

Finally, we should state the obvious: if all the daughters have undergone a particular change, we will not be able to reconstruct it and will necessarily project its output into the protolanguage. Romance philology provides some well-known examples. Latin *h*, for instance, has been lost in all Romance languages and so cannot be recovered by the comparative method. Though different Latin vowels and diphthongs usually develop differently in the daughters, short *a* and long *ā* always have the same outcome, as do short *e* and the diphthong *ae*. The result is that Proto-Romance is reconstructable with an odd system of *nine* vowels and one diphthong (*au). Of course it is possible that the odd vowel system we have reconstructed for Proto-Mańśi is likewise the result of unrecoverable changes in both dialects.

Internal reconstruction

Traditional historical linguistics recognizes a method of "internal" reconstruction, in which alternations within a single language are exploited to reconstruct aspects of its prehistory. From a modern point of view this amounts to exploiting the phonological rules that generative phonology posits – and the exceptions to those rules. We have already exemplified this at some length in Chapters 5 and 6, and it seems superfluous to add further discussion here.

It should be pointed out, however, that internal reconstruction is almost always less reliable than comparative reconstruction, both because changes in phonological rules after they have achieved categorical status can obscure the effects and the scope of regular sound changes and because loss of words, affixes, and categories in a single line of descent can be recognized only by comparison with other lines of descent. In practice internal reconstruction is used only when provably related languages are unavailable. For a demonstration of what can be recovered under favorable circumstances see e.g. Trask 1997: 124–95 with references to earlier work (especially that of Luís Michelena).

Reconstruction of morphosyntax and the lexicon

There is no method for reconstructing morphology or syntax comparable to the "comparative method" for phonology. The reasons for that disappointing fact are simple and straightforward. Morphemes (the units of morphology) and the rules of syntax are not meaningless items distributed arbitrarily through the utterances of a language; in consequence morphological and syntactic changes cannot and do not exhibit *mathematically exploitable recurrent* regularity in the way that phonological changes do. An easy way to illustrate this is to take our statement of the regularity of sound change, namely:

either all examples of sound x in a dialect at the time of the change become x',
or, if x becomes x' only under certain conditions, those conditions can be stated *entirely* in phonological terms

and replace all the phonological terms with morphosyntactic ones, thus:

either all examples of morpheme x in a dialect at the time of the change become morpheme x',
or, if x becomes x' only under certain conditions, those conditions can be stated *entirely* in morphosyntactic terms.

The statement is probably still true, as can be seen from almost any list of examples. For instance, the English plural marker [+umlaut] was replaced by /-əs/ in the context of the morpheme *bōk* 'book' (i.e., *bēċ* became *bōkes*) in the decades around 1200; in the Midlands dialects the indicative plural subject marker /-əθ/ was replaced by the default plural subject marker /-ən/ in the twelfth century; and so on. Yet the "regularity" of these replacements is not useful, because the items undergoing change do not recur arbitrarily in a large number of semantically and functionally unrelated contexts, as phonemes do. Since syntax is a system of rules rather than a set of pieces, syntactic change cannot even be discussed in the same terms as regular sound change.

Nevertheless some progress has been made in understanding morphological and syntactic change, as we have discussed at length in Chapters 8 and 9. In practice, the reconstruction of morphology begins with the phonological reconstruction of functional morphemes and then attempts to understand the observed patterns in terms of what is known about morphological change. Since we are just beginning to understand how syntactic rules develop, syntactic reconstruction depends more heavily on agreement between the phenomena of the daughter languages.

Change in lexical semantics is well enough understood on a practical level; for instance, we know that words meaning 'human being' often shift their meaning to 'man' (i.e., 'adult male human being'), and words meaning 'man' often shift to 'husband'. But so far as we can see, such changes are driven by extralinguistic factors – or, if there is a linguistic component to such changes, we do not understand it. Reconstruction of the meanings of proto-lexemes is still very much a matter of guesswork informed by experience.

Notes

1 The cognates are listed in underlying form (thus German final devoicing is not represented). This is a reasonably complete list of English and German cognates exhibiting these correspondences; we have included words that are literary or obsolescent, but have (mostly) omitted doubtful cases and pairs exhibiting further complications. Though *shrive, line, wine, mile*, and *pile* and their cognates are all ultimately loans from Latin, all can be reconstructed

for Proto-West Germanic (*skrīban, *līn, *wīn, *mīliju, *pīl); thus it is reasonable to suppose that they were borrowed into the last common parent of English and German while it was still a single (though probably dialectally diverse) language.

2 In Table 10.8 glosses separated by commas indicate the range of meaning of the form. Where two meanings separated by a semicolon are given, the first is the meaning of the Tavda form, the second the meaning of the Sosva form. The verb forms glossed as 3sg. present are 3sg. nonpast in Sosva (Murphy 1968: 64), but in the (extinct) Tavda dialect they no longer expressed an ongoing action or state in the present (since that function had been assumed by present progressive forms) and were therefore relegated to future time and general statements, much like the English simple present of non-stative verbs (see Honti 1975: 49). Second-syllable vowels were more or less lengthened in Tavda (see Steinitz 1955, Honti 1975 passim) and apparently were usually stressed (Kálmán 1964. 31), but there does not seem to have been a contrast between long and short vowels in that position; we write "half-long" vowels with a following raised dot.

The Tavda dialect evolved in isolation from the others for many generations and was strongly divergent (Kálmán 1964: 5, Honti 1988: 148). Mutual intelligibility between these two dialects appears to have been limited at best – i.e. they are perhaps better regarded as "different languages."

11 Beyond comparative reconstruction

Subgrouping and "long-distance" relationships

Once we have reconstructed the protolanguage of a family, there are further uses to which we can put the information we have retrieved. This chapter will give a quick overview of some of those further investigations. It will be seen that they vary greatly in feasibility and in the scientific validity of their results.

Subgrouping of languages

When we have reconstructed a significant part of a proto-lexicon and proto-grammar from a set of attested languages by rigorous phonological reconstruction, we can be certain that those languages are related, because we have recovered part of the structure of their common ancestor. But that is only a small part of the languages' prehistory. We would also like to recover as much information as possible about the *descent* of each language (as defined at the beginning of Chapter 10). It will often turn out that a subset of the attested languages shared a line of descent before beginning to diversify; that is, they were still a single language for some time after the initial diversification of the language family. In that case we should be able to reconstruct from them a protolanguage which is a daughter of the protolanguage of the whole family. If we represent linguistic diversification by the diverging lines, or "edges," of a tree diagram, with each protolanguage as a node from which diversifying daughters radiate, we have the familiar "family tree," or *Stammbaum*, representing descent relationships among the daughter languages (though not other aspects of their history and relationships).

But establishing such "subgroups" is not always easy; there are plenty of known cases in which expert judgments disagree. We need criteria for subgrouping languages that are as rigorous as the comparative method is for phonological reconstruction.

The most basic criterion is a matter of simple logic: shared history can be established only by demonstrating shared innovations; moreover, the innovations in question must be unusual enough that they are not likely to have occurred more than once independently. Shared retentions are useless for subgrouping, since any daughter might happen to preserve a trait of the protolanguage unchanged.

We illustrate the importance of *significant* shared innovations with a number of examples.

A large majority of known sound changes are phonetically natural, with the result that they have occurred independently in numerous languages. A good example from western Europe is the change [w] > [β] or [v]. In Latin this change occurred in the early centuries CE (Allen 1978: 40–2); imperial inscriptions in the eastern half of the Empire demonstrate that by the change in the Greek transcription of the Latin name *Valerius* from ΟΥΑΛΕΡΙΟΣ (where ΟΥ is an attempt to represent [w]) to ΒΑΛΕΡΙΟΣ (where Β is an attempt to represent [β] or [v]). The Romance languages therefore inherited a labial fricative rather than a round semivowel. In Norse the same change occurred in the thirteenth century (Noreen 1923: 184–5). In High German it probably occurred still later, toward the end of the Middle Ages. None of those historical changes were connected in any way. Clearly a single shared natural sound change cannot demonstrate shared history.

Somewhat surprisingly, the same is true of some sequences of sound changes (see Ringe *et al.* 2002: 66–7). What is usually summarized as [ti] > [si] is most unlikely to have been a single change; a plausible sequence of natural changes eventuating in [si] would be [ti] > [tʲi] > [tɕi] > [tsi] > [si]. Yet the entire sequence of changes (or similar sequences leading to the same result) has occurred repeatedly in languages widely separated in time and space:

(1)   Proto-Greek (PGk.) *t(ʰ)i > South Greek *si* σι under unclear conditions. (The "South Greek" dialect group includes Mycenaean (written in the Linear B syllabary), Arkadian, Cypriote, and the Attic-Ionic group; the artificial Homeric dialect is based on archaic East Ionic.)

   a. PGk. *dído:ti '(s)he is giving' (Doric [Dor.] /dídɔ:ti/ δίδωτι) > Attic, Ionic [Att., Ion.] /dídɔ:si/ δίδωσι

   b. PGk. *pʰéronti 'they carry' (Dor. /pʰéronti/ φέροντι) > *pʰéronsi (Arkadian [Ark.] /pʰéronsi/ φέρονσι) > Att., Ion. /pʰéro:si/ φέρουσι

   c. PGk. *tria:kátioi '300' (Dor. /tria:kátioi/ τριᾱκάτιοι) > *tria:kásioi (Ark. /tria:kásioi/ τριᾱκάσιοι) → Att., Ion. /tria:kósioi/ τριᾱκόσιοι > (/o/ by lexical analogy with the decad suffix /-konta/ -κοντα)

   d. PGk. *pla:tíon 'near' (Dor. /pla:tíon/ πλᾱτίον) > Att., Ion. /plɛ:síon/ πλησίον

   e. PGk. *eniáutios 'yearly' (Dor. /eniáutios/ ἐνιαύτιος) > Att., Ion. /eniáusios/ ἐνιαύσιος

   f. PGk. *korínthios 'of Corinth' > Mycenaean (*)korínsios *ko-ri-si-jo;* base restored in Attic /Korínthios/ Κορίνθιος, but cf. /Probalí:sios/ Προβαλίσιος 'of *Probalinthos*' (Προβάλινθος, name of a deme on the northeast coast of Attica)

(2)   Proto-Indo-European (PIE) *dʰ > pre-Tocharian *tʰ; then word-final postvocalic *-t(ʰ)i > *-si (> Proto-Tocharian (PToch.) *-sə; Jasanoff 1987: 108–12, Ringe 1996b: 47–8, 80, 88).[†]

[†] Tocharian ṣ was a postalveolar sibilant, perhaps retroflex.

a. PIE act. 1ary 3sg. *-ti (Sanskrit [Skt.], Avestan, Palaic -ti, West Greek /-ti/ -τι, Hittite -zzi, and see further below) > *-si > PToch. *-ṣə, e.g. PIE *gʷémeti '(s)he will step' (aor. subj., Skt. gámat '(s)he will go'; Goth. qimiþ '(s)he comes') > PToch. *śə́məṣə '(s)he will come' > Toch. A śmäṣ

b. PIE ablative *-ti (Hittite -z(zi-), Luvian -ti; Melchert 1994: 60, 183, Melchert and Oettinger 2009: 57–9) ?> *-si > PToch. *-ṣə, e.g. in Toch. A riyäṣ 'from the city', waṣtäṣ 'from the house'

c. PIE iptv. 2sg. *h₁dʰí 'go!' > *itʰí > *isí > → PToch. *pə-yəṣə́ > Toch. A piṣ, B paṣ

(3)   Proto-Finnic (PF) *ti > Proto-Baltic Finnic *si (Fromm and Sadeniemi 1956: 26–7, 39–40, Hakulinen 1961: 34–5, Laanest 1982: 22–3, 102–3, Sammallahti 1988).[†]

a. PF *käti 'hand' (Mari kit, Saami giettâ) > *käsi > Finnish (Finn.), Estonian (Est.) käsi

b. PF *weti 'water' (Mari βyt) > *wesi > Finn., Est. vesi

c. PF *kakte 'two' (Mari kok, koktə, Saami guok'te) > *kakti > *kaksi > Finn. kaksi, Est. kaks

d. PF *wi:ti 'five' (Mari βiťť, Saami vit'tâ) > *wi:si > Finn. viisi, Est. viis

(4)   Proto-Polynesian (PPN) *ti > Tongan (To.) si (Biggs 1978: 703).

a. PPN *tipa 'to turn aside' (Maori [Mao.] tipa, Hawaiian [Haw.] kipa; Rapanui [Rap.] tipatipa 'to shake') > To. sipa 'to stagger'

b. PPN *tiro 'to look at' (Mao. tiro; Haw. kilo 'to watch closely', Samoan [Sam.] tilotilo 'to spy') > To. sio

c. PPN *fati 'to break' (Sam. fati, Haw. haki, Rap. hatihati; Mao. whati 'to be broken off') > To. fasi

d. PPN *ʔoti 'to finish' (Sam., Rap. oti, Haw. oki; Mao. oti 'to be finished') > To. ʔosi 'to be finished'

In addition, the same change has occurred in many other Oceanic languages independently of Tongan and of each other (Malcolm Ross, p.c. July 2009).

Nor do we get better results if we rely on mergers rather than on phonetic changes. One might not expect the merger of short e and i in a system of four or five short vowels to recur in independent lineages, but it does:

(5)   Proto-Germanic (PGmc.) *e, *i > Gothic (Goth.) aí (= [ε]) before r, h, hv; elsewhere i.

a. PGmc. *witaną 'to know' (Old English [OE] witan, Old Norse [ON] vita) > Goth. witan

b. PGmc. *metaną 'to measure' (OE metan; ON meta 'to evaluate') > Goth. mitan

c. PGmc. *silubrą 'silver' (OE siolfor, ON silfr) > Goth. silubr

d. PGmc. *meluk- 'milk' (OE meoloc, ON mjǫlk) > Goth. miluks

e. PGmc. *wiþr- 'against' (ON viðr; OE prefix wiðer-) > Goth. wiþra

---

[†] In the conventional spelling of Finnic languages ä is [æ]; long vowels are written double.

    f. PGmc. *weþruz 'yearling' (OE *weðer*, ON *veðr*, both 'wether') > Goth. *wiþrus* 'lamb'

    g. PGmc. *widuwōn- 'widow' (OE *widuwe*) > Goth. *widuwo*

    h. PGmc. *medumō '(the) middle' (ON *mjǫðm*; OE deriv. *medeme* 'moderate, average') > Goth. *miduma*

    i. PGmc. adj. *midjaz 'middle' (OE *midd*, ON *miðr*) > Goth. *midis → midjis*

    j. PGmc. *fiskaz 'fish' (OE *fisc*, ON *fiskr*) > Goth. *fisks*

    k. PGmc. *þreskaną 'to thresh' (OE *þerscan*) > Goth. *þriskan*

    l. PGmc. *hirdijaz 'herdsman' (OE *hierde*, ON *hirðir*) > Goth. *haírdeis*

    m. PGmc. *herdō 'herd' (OE *heord*, ON *hjǫrð*) > Goth. *haírda*

    n. PGmc. *wihtiz '(living) thing, being' (OE *wiht*) > Goth. *waíhts* 'thing'

    o. PGmc. *fehu 'livestock' (OE *feoh*) > Goth. *faíhu* 'wealth' – etc., etc.

(6)   PIE *e, *i > PToch. word-initial *yə; elsewhere *ə with palatalization (Ringe 1996b: 125–6).

    a. PIE aor. subj. *légʰeti '(s)he will lie down' (cf. aor. indic. Homeric /lékto/ λέκτο; pres. *légʰyeti in Old Church Slavonic *ležetŭ*, OE inf. *licgan*) > PToch. pres. *lyə́śəṣə ~ *lyə́śə > Toch. B *lyaśä-m̥* (with ptcl. *-n, added to all Toch. B primary act. 3sg. forms)

    b. PIE *léymon- ~ *limn-´ 'lake' (Greek /leimɔ́:n/ λειμών 'meadow', /limé:n/ λιμήν 'harbor', /límnɛ:/ λίμνη 'pool, (marshy) lake') > → *límn̥ > PToch. *lyə́mə > Toch. A *lyäm*, Toch. B *lyam*

    c. PIE aor. subj. *gʷémeti '(s)he will step' (see above) > *gʷémesi ~ *gʷéme > PToch. *śə́məṣə ~ *śə́mə '(s)he will come' > Toch. A *śmäs*, > → Toch. B *śman(-ne)* 'it will come (to him)'

    d. PIE collective *h₁itór 'goings' (cf. Lat. *iter* 'way') > *itór > PToch. *yətár- 'path, road' > Toch. A *ytār*, Toch. B *ytārye*

    e. PIE *éḱwos 'horse' (Skt. *áśvas*, Lat. *equos*, etc.) > PToch. *yə́kwë > Toch. A *yuk*, Toch. B *yakwe*

(7)   Proto-Algonkian (PA) *e, *i > Cree *i* (Bloomfield 1946).

    a. PA *po:nime:wa 'he stops talking to him' (Fox *po:nime:wa*) > Cree *po:nime:w*

    b. PA *po:ne:leme:wa 'he stops thinking about him' (Fox *po:ne:neme:wa*) > Cree *po:ne:yime:w*

    c. PA *wa:pimini 'maize' (Fox *wa:pimini*) > Cree *wa:pimin* 'white bead'

    d. PA *aʔsenyali 'stones' (Fox *asenye:ni*) > Cree *asiniya*

    e. PA *po:siko 'embark! (pl.)' (Fox *po:siko*) > Cree *po:sik*

    f. PA *meʔtekwi 'stick' (Fox *mehtekwi*) > Cree *mistik*

It seems clear that, unless they are very unusual, shared single sound changes are not plausible evidence for shared history.

However, *sequences* of unrelated sound changes can be used as evidence of shared history if they are long enough, since the probability that two languages have undergone the same sound changes in the same order decreases rapidly with the length of the sequence. Here is a well-known example from Germanic.

All the Germanic languages show evidence, direct or indirect, for the following sequence of sound changes, which must have occurred in the order discussed.

(a)   "Grimm's Law," part 1 (see e.g. Ringe 2006: 93–8):

stops *p *t *k *kʷ > fricatives *f *þ *h *hʷ respectively, unless an obstruent immediately preceded;

(b)   "Grimm's Law," part 2 (ibid. pp. 98–100):

*b *d *g *gʷ > *p *t *k *kʷ respectively; this must have followed or occurred concurrently with (a), since if this devoicing preceded (a) the two series of stops would have merged as voiceless fricatives;

(c)   "Grimm's Law," part 3 (ibid. pp. 100–2):

*bʰ *dʰ *gʰ *gʷʰ > *β *ð *ɣ *ɣʷ respectively (fricatives, thus not ordered with respect to the above changes[1]);

(d)   "Verner's Law" (ibid. pp. 102–4):

*f *þ *s *h *hʷ > (fricative) *β *ð *z *ɣ *ɣʷ if not word-initial *and* not adjacent to a voiceless sound *and* the last preceding syllable nucleus was unaccented; this must have followed (a), which fed it;

(e)   fricatives *β *ð *ɣ *ɣʷ > stops *b *d *g *gʷ after homorganic nasals, and *ð > *d also after *l and *z (at least); this must have followed both (c) and (d), which fed it, and (b) which it counterfed; also word-initial *β *ð > *b *d, which must have followed (b);

(f)   stress was shifted to the initial syllable of the word; this must have followed (d), because it destroyed triggering environments for (d);

(g)   unstressed *e > *i unless *r followed immediately (see e.g. Ringe 2006: 122–6); this must have followed (f), which both fed it and bled it.

What is the probability that *each* of these changes would occur in a given line of descent? We don't (yet) have enough systematic information about the incidence of particular sound changes to estimate those probabilities, but even informed guesses will be useful (as the reader will see below). A change similar to (a) occurred also in Armenian, another one of the ten uncontroversial subgroups of Indo-European (IE); therefore let us assign a probability of .2 to (a). (b) occurred also in Tocharian, where it caused mergers, and in Armenian, where it did not; let us therefore assign it a probability of .3. (c) might have occurred in Proto-Italic (Meiser 1986: 38); we therefore assign it a probability of .2. (d) is less familiar, but a very similar sound change actually occurred in fifteenth-century English (Jespersen 1909: 199–208 with references); we might reasonably assign it a probability of .1. (e) makes so much phonetic sense that we should assign it a relatively high probability, say .5. (f) also occurred in Proto-Italic and Proto-Celtic; let us assign it a probability of .3. (g) is a very common and repeatable change; we assign it a probability of .5. Now to the point: the probability that *all seven* sound changes would occur in a single line of descent *by sheer chance* is the product of the probabilities that each would occur. All we need to do is multiply:

$$.2 \times .3 \times .2 \times .1 \times .5 \times .3 \times .5 = .00009, \text{ or about one in } 11,111;$$

this already suggests that if such a pattern appears in one language, the probability that it will appear in another by chance is so small that we can take this sequence of changes shared as evidence of shared history. But we are not yet finished with our calculation. The pairwise ordering relations that we can establish between these seven changes yields a chronological sequence

$$a \rightarrow d \rightarrow f \rightarrow g,$$

in addition to (b) following (a), and (e) following (b), (c), and (d). Leaving aside (b), (c), and (e), let us ask what the probability is that the other four changes would have occurred in the observed order by chance. The number of possible orders is obviously $4 \times 3 \times 2 \times 1 = 24$, since we can put any of the four first, we will then have three to choose from for the second slot, and so on. So the probability of the observed order is 1/24, or .0416̄; multiplying this by .00009 yields .00000375, or about one in 266,667. Thus the probability of all seven changes occurring by chance, with (a), (d), (f), and (g) in that order, is so small that this sequence of changes alone validates Germanic as a subgroup of IE. (In fact the number of partially ordered sound changes validating Germanic is much greater; see Ringe 2006: 152 for a graphic summary.)

This is a satisfying result, but we should not be blind to two of its less encouraging implications. In the first place, we are doubly lucky in dealing with Germanic, because we happen to have such a wealth of information about that subgroup and because PGmc. happens to have undergone a large number of precisely identifiable sound changes whose chronology is partly recoverable. For many subgroups of many language families we have far less information, and/or the phonological development of the languages in question offers us far less to work with. Secondly, if we must use ordered sequences of sound changes to validate subgroups, we will "use up" much of our evidence in a single demonstration, since if we reuse some of the same information for a different validation of the same subgroup the arguments will not be independent. What if we attempt a statistical validation using the bulk of the phonological evidence and still come up short?

For all these reasons morphological innovations should also be used for subgrouping. To continue with our Germanic example, at least the following morphological innovations validate the subgroup:

the "weak" past tense formation, characterized by a suffix beginning with a coronal obstruent;
the double paradigm of adjectives, with a suffix in -*n*- characterizing the "weak" paradigm.

We are certain that those two traits are innovations because other IE languages exhibit no formations that match these in detail. Note that both innovations are stated in a way that includes phonological information. This is necessary because it is usually only the phonological shapes of words and affixes that are idiosyncratic enough to provide evidence for common history; abstract morphosyntactic categories are too few, and most are too easily shared by chance, to tell us anything about historical connections between languages. In other words, we need evidence that is arbitrary in the Saussurean sense, and most abstract properties of languages are not arbitrary enough.

But the use of morphological innovations for subgrouping encounters difficulties complementary to those encountered in using phonology. We can often be certain that phonological traits are innovations (because mergers are irreversible), but very many phonological innovations are natural and repeatable. By contrast, many morphological details are so idiosyncratic that we do not need to worry about parallel innovations, but we are often uncertain whether they are innovations at all.

We would not expect syntactic innovations to be useful in subgrouping for the reason noted above in our discussion of morphological innovations: possible syntactic rules are too few and are too easily shared by chance; they are perhaps the least arbitrary part of the grammar.

Finally, there is a "real-world" situation that often stymies attempts to subgroup the languages of a family. If the diversifying dialects of a parent language lose contact fairly quickly, the end result can be a family of languages in which the daughters do not share significant innovations; if those daughters in turn diversify and give rise to subfamilies, it can be easy to assign the resulting languages to the correct subfamilies, since the members of each subfamily will share significant innovations, but there will be no significant innovations that cut across the subfamilies. But languages do not always diversify in such a "clean" fashion; at least as often dialects remain in contact for many generations as they diversify, trading linguistic innovations in an overlapping pattern so that no clear subgrouping is possible. The resulting relationships cannot be realistically represented by a tree; only a network diagram or a dialect map can do justice to the linguistic situation.

Many traditional historical linguists appear to believe that clean speciation of languages virtually never occurs, so that a *Stammbaum* is never a justifiable representation of linguistic relationships. Such an extreme position is certainly incorrect. Populations do migrate (though probably not as often as nineteenth-century linguists imagined) and clean speciations do occur. Moreover, even network-like diversifications can give rise to a clean *Stammbaum* if no two dialects which were originally close neighbors survive, because distant dialects are less likely to share innovations that diffused through the dialect network. It is highly likely that the ten clear subgroups of the IE family are a case in point; while Tocharian, for instance, probably did separate from its relatives by means of an abrupt migration to the east, most of the more centrally located subgroups are probably the surviving remnants of what was once a dialect network, sharply distinct from one another only because they had not been close neighbors in that network. (For a discussion of this topic in depth see especially Ross 1997, conveniently illustrated in Ross 1998.) Finally, the *Stammbaum* hypothesis is always preferable *as a first hypothesis* because it is falsifiable; it is easy to see where it doesn't work and easy to formulate alternatives (either alternative *Stammbäume* or networks). It is much easier to fit recalcitrant data into a network model; for exactly that reason a hypothesis of non-treelike diversification is less useful and should be preferred only when reasonable alternatives have proved untenable.

In the past thirty years numerous teams of linguists and computer scientists have attempted to circumvent these difficulties by computational means. The chief advantage of this approach is that a computer can assess how well each of a large number of linguistic traits fits each of a wide range of plausible trees, even if we do not know whether the traits are innovations, or whether they are parallel innovations. (There are ways to constrain these methods to respect the fact that phonological mergers are always innovations.) Once the "best" tree has been found, according to an explicit mathematical criterion, we not only have a probable *Stammbaum*, we can also examine the distribution of each linguistic trait on the tree to recover information about its probable development in the family in question.

By now the subfield of computational cladistics is too large to be discussed seriously here. Interested readers should consult the following references. An up-to-date summary of relevant work can be found in Nichols and Warnow 2008. The best summary and critique of early work is Embleton 1986. Most computational phylogenetic work still uses only wordlists, and some is still distance-based (in spite of the fact that reducing linguistic differences to a single measure of "distance" between the languages loses most of the information in the comparison). Ringe *et al.* 2002 attempts to remedy those shortcomings in a subgrouping of the IE family; Nakhleh *et al.* 2005a attempts to broaden a standard phylogenetic method to deal with network-like diversification; Nakhleh *et al.* 2005b compares the results of a range of phylogenetic methods applied to a single dataset. Longobardi and Guardiano 2009 attempts to recover a cladogram from a dataset of syntactic parameter settings using a distance-based method. None of these studies has been an unqualified success (nor has any of the numerous other studies to which they refer), but it seems clear that continued refinement of computational techniques can extend our investigation of subgrouping well beyond what traditional methods are capable of.

Inferences from proto-lexica

It is generally agreed that culture and grammar have nothing whatever to do with one another, but the culture and ecology of a speech community are certainly represented in its lexicon, at least to some extent. Since comparative reconstruction yields fragmentary proto-lexica, it seems reasonable to expect that we can recover at least some information about the speech communities that used them. If enough terms for plants, animals, and weather phenomena of restricted distribution can be reconstructed, it might be possible to demarcate an area of the world within which a protolanguage must have been spoken; in that case connections with the archaeological record might be pursued.

The preceding paragraph may strike the reader as completely straightforward, but hard experience shows that it is actually very optimistic. The next few paragraphs will illustrate the difficulties encountered in work of this kind.

To begin with, consider the fact that a word *paaškesikani 'gun' and several related verbs meaning 'shoot with a gun' are reconstructable for Proto-Algonkian (PA; Bloomfield 1946: 106, 108, 114) because the terms in several daughter languages match perfectly: cf. e.g. Fox *paaškesikani*, Cree *paaskisikan*, Ojibwa *paaškisikan*, all 'gun'. But since PA was spoken at least two millennia ago, more or less, it cannot have had any word with that referent in its lexicon; even the Chinese did not have firearms at that date. In fact the reconstruction is a mirage: what is genuinely reconstructable are the pieces *paašk- 'burst' (Bloomfield 1946: 120), *-es- 'by heat' (ibid. p. 114), a suffix *-kee- which makes intransitive verbs from transitive verbs that take inanimate objects (p. 108), and a noun-forming suffix *-n- which combines irregularly with the preceding suffix to form the suffix complex *-ka-n- (p. 106; the *-i- before this complex is a productive "linking vowel," and all inanimate nouns ended in *-i). Once one of the daughter languages had coined the term it could be, and evidently was, translated into the others morpheme by morpheme according to the productive rules of word formation, which are extensive and mostly regular in Algonkian languages. A further detail confirms that that is exactly what happened: the Menomini form *paaskečisekan* includes an extra element *-ečyee- 'whole body, round body, belly' (ibid. p. 117), added when the word was borrowed, apparently to express the lethal potential of firearms (see Bloomfield 1962: 409–10 and 1975 passim). Clearly we should not reconstruct for a protolanguage terms which could have been created, either independently or by a process of dialect borrowing, by completely regular derivational rules in the daughters.

Gaps in a reconstructable lexicon present pitfalls of a different kind. We are not surprised to find that no word for 'iron' is reconstructable for PIE, because several well-differentiated daughters are already attested at a time when the cultures of the eastern Mediterranean were still in the Bronze Age.[2] But no PIE word for 'finger' can be reconstructed either. There must have been one; evidently it has been lost in all the daughters (or all but one). It seems clear that we should not attempt to base arguments about palaeocultures from gaps in reconstructed lexica, because there are too many factors that can create those gaps.

A third type of difficulty arises from failure to pay attention to the cladistic structure of a language family. Frank Siebert used cognate terms for plants and animals to try to determine the area within which PA was spoken (Siebert 1967) and was able to pinpoint southern Ontario as the one area in which all the reconstructable terms could have been used (ibid. p. 35). But Siebert's comparative material includes no cognates from Blackfoot, which probably separated from the other Algonkian dialects while they were still more or less a single language (see the discussion of Goddard 1994b: 187–9). It follows that while Siebert's conclusions can be accepted for the last common ancestor of the non-Blackfoot languages, they do not necessarily hold for "real" PA. Other studies suffer from this shortcoming to a much greater degree; for instance, Friedrich 1970 is far too inclusive, attempting to use doubtfully reconstructable tree names attested in only a few branches of the IE family to determine the PIE "homeland."

Still another problem is posed by semantic change, which is driven by contingent events to such a degree that we often cannot be certain what the referent of a reconstructed word was in the protolanguage. The most notorious example involves the attempt to use cognates meaning 'beech' to locate the "homeland" of PIE in Europe, given that beech trees do not grow east of a line running roughly northwest to southeast through eastern Europe (see the map in Friedrich 1970: 113). Though Latin *fāgus* and the Germanic words (Old High German *buohha*, etc.) do mean 'beech', the Greek cognate φηγός /pʰɛ:gós/ names a species of oak with edible acorns – not surprisingly, since beech trees do not grow in southern Greece. But in that case how do we know that the protoform referred specifically to beeches, and not to some other member of the Fagaceae whose nuts can be eaten? Interested readers can consult the discussion (extensive, but not rigorous) of Friedrich 1970: 106–15 with references; but for those who believe in methodological rigor even the little that has been said in this paragraph fatally undermines the "beech tree argument."[3]

But when all these difficulties and constraints are taken into account, it is still possible to reconstruct some aspects of the culture of a population that spoke a particular protolanguage. Of course, since virtually every statement rests on non-mathematical inferences (as well as on the mathematics of the comparative method), one must be prepared to encounter disagreements between specialists on numerous points. For instance, Mallory and Adams 2006 offers a wealth of information, with copious references, on what is believed about speakers of PIE, but virtually any Indo-Europeanist will object to various details in the book (not always the same details, of course). Fortson 2009 is much more selective, but it still includes controversial statements because on some points any statement at all is controversial.

"Long-distance" language comparison

Using the comparative method we can reconstruct the protolanguages of obvious families, such as Germanic and Slavic, with no difficulty.[†] We can

---

[†] The topics of this section are treated at much greater length and in much greater detail in Campbell and Poser 2008, which we recommend to interested readers.

then use those first-order protolanguages to help reconstruct their common parent, PIE; that is more difficult, but it is still well within the capacity of the comparative method. It is reasonable to ask how much further back we can carry comparative reconstruction. For instance, the protolanguage reconstructed for the Uralic family shows some notable resemblances to PIE, such as first-person pronouns beginning with *m-, second-person pronouns beginning with *t-, an accusative ending *-m, and a handful of basic words that resemble their IE counterparts, such as *nimi 'name' and *weti 'water'. Can we reconstruct "Proto-Indo-Uralic" in the same way we have reconstructed Proto-Uralic and PIE?

The short answer is *no*, for a simple and ineluctable reason. In addition to undergoing regular sound changes and changes in their rule systems, all languages steadily replace their lexical items with new, etymologically different words, often borrowed from different languages. Even inflectional markers are lost or replaced in the long run; for instance, English has lost nearly all the endings marking the person and number of the subjects of verbs, and its regular past tense suffix is a Germanic innovation, not inherited from PIE. When two languages have been diverging for enough time, the inherited items that they still share become so small a proportion of their lexemes and affixes that *they cannot be distinguished from chance resemblances*. At that point we can no longer prove that the languages are related.

It is easy to observe how the loss of inherited vocabulary reduces the material with which relationships might be proved by rough comparison of a basic wordlist in closely related and more distantly related languages – say, English, German, French, and Toch. B. Table 11.1 is such a list of 115 words (a version of the Swadesh 100-word list, plus more numerals and some kinship terms). The following points regarding individual words seem worth noting.

20. French *chien* < Latin *canis* is not a reflex of PIE *ḱwṓ, *ḱwón - ∼ *ḱun-.
26. The English word was borrowed from ON and is therefore not strictly cognate (though the Norse word is cognate with the others).
63. The English word was borrowed from Old French.
77. The English word was borrowed from ON (though the Norse word is a root-cognate with the others).
78. Both the English and the German words were borrowed from Old French.
96. This is the only item with two different cognate sets.
102. The Toch. B form has undergone metathesis of its stop consonants (see the discussion of metathesis in Chapter 6); French *langue* < Latin *lingua* was altered by lexical analogy with *lingere* 'to lick' (the Old Latin form, preserved by grammarians, was the fully cognate *dingua*).

As can be seen even on first inspection, English and German share far more words than any other pair of these languages (eighty-two by our count); that is not surprising, since they have been diverging for at most two millennia or so. (Of course if we allow some semantic leeway in matching lexemes, they share even more; but see below on the consequences of such a decision.) By

Table 11.1 *Comparative wordlist of some Indo-European languages*

	English	German	French	Toch. B
1. all	ɔl	alə	tu	poñc
2. ashes	æːʃɔz	aʃə	sãdrə	taur
3. bark	bɑrk	rɪndə	ekɔrs	enmetre
4. belly	bɛli	baʊx	vãtrə	kātso
5. big	bɪg	groːs	grã	orotstse
6. bird	bərd	foːgəl	uazo	salamo luwo
7. bite	baɪt	baɪsən	mɔrdrə	
8. black	blæk	ʃvarc	nuar	erkent [obl.]
9. blood	blʌd	bluːt	sã	yasar
10. bone	boʊn	knɔxən	ɔs	āy
11. breast	brɛst	buːzən	sɛ̃	pāścane [du.]
12. brother	brʌðər	bruːdər	frɛr	procer
13. burn	bərn	brɛnən	bryle	tsketsi
14. claw	klɔ	klaʊə	grif	
15. cloud	klaʊd	vɔlkə	nyaʒ	tarkär
16. cold	koʊld	kalt	frua	krośce
17. come	kʌm	kɔmən	vənir	śamtsi
18. daughter	dɔtər	tɔxtər	fij	tkācer
19. die	daɪ	ʃtɛrbon	muri	srukatsi
20. dog	dɔg	hʊnd	ʃɛ̃	ku
21. drink	drɪŋk	trɪŋkən	buar	yoktsi
22. dry	draɪ	trɔkən	sɛk	asāre
23. ear	iːr	oːr	ɔrɛy	klautso
24. earth	ərθ	eːrdə	tɛr	kem̩
25. eat	iːt	ɛsən	mãʒe	śwātsi
26. egg	ɛg	aɪ	œf	
27. eight	eɪt	axt	yit	okt
28. eye	aɪ	aʊgə	œj	ek
29. fat	fæt	fɛt	grɛs	ṣalype
30. father	faðər	faːtər	pɛr	pācer
31. feather	fɛðər	feːdər	plym	paruwa [pl.]
32. fire	faɪər	fɔyər	fø	puwar
33. fish	fɪʃ	fɪʃ	puasɔ̃	laks
34. five	faɪv	fʏnf	sɛ̃k	piś
35. fly	flaɪ	fliːgən	vɔle	plu-
36. foot	fʊt	fuːs	pie	paiyye
37. four	fɔr	fiːr	katrə	śtwer
38. full	fʊl	fɔl	plɛ̃	ite
39. give	gɪv	geːbən	dɔne	aitsi
40. good	gʊd	guːt	bɔ̃	kartse
41. green	griːn	gryːn	vɛr	motartstse
42. hair	heɪr	haːr	ʃɔvø	matsi
43. hand	hæːnd	hand	mɛ̃	ṣar

(cont.)

Table 11.1 (*cont.*)

	English	German	French	Toch. B
44. head	hɛd	kɔpᶠ	tɛt	āśce
45. hear	hi:r	hø:rən	ătādrə	klyauṣtsi
46. heart	hɑrt	hɛrc	kœr	arañce
47. horn	hɔrn	hɔrn	kɔrn	krorīyai [obl.]
48. hundred	hʌndrəd	hʊndərt	sã	kante
49. I	ɑɪ	ɪx	ʒə	ñaś
50. kill	kɪl	tø:tən	tye	kautsi
51. knee	ni:	kni:	ʒənu	keni [du.]
52. know	noʊ	vɪsən	savuar	aiśtsi
53. leaf	li:f	blɑt	fœj	pilta
54. lie	lɑɪ	li:gən	ɛtrə kuʃe	lyaśtsi
55. liver	lɪvər	le:bər	fua	wästarye
56. long	lɔŋ	lɑŋ	lɔ̃	pärkare
57. louse	lɑʊs	lɑʊz	pu	pärśeriñ [pl.]
58. man	mæ:n	mɑn	ɔm	eṅkwe
59. many	mɛni	fi:lə	boku də	māka
60. meat	mi:t	flaɪʃ	viãd	misa
61. moon	mu:n	mo:nd	lyn	meñe
62. mother	mʌðər	mʊtər	mɛr	mācer
63. mountain	mɑʊntən	bɛrg	mɔ̃tañ	ṣale
64. mouth	mɑʊθ	mʊnd	buʃ	koyṃ
65. name	neɪm	nɑ:mə	nɔ̃	ñem
66. neck	nɛk	hɑlz	ku	
67. new	nu:	nɔʏ	nuvo	ñuwe
68. night	nɑɪt	nɑxt	nyi	yṣiye
69. nine	nɑɪn	nɔʏn	nœf	ñu
70. nose	noʊz	nɑ:zə	ne	meli
71. not	nɑt	nɪxt	pa	mā
72. one	wʌn	ɑɪns	œ̃	ṣe
73. person	pərsən	mɛnʃ	ɔm	śaumo
74. rain	reɪn	re:gən	plyi	swese
75. red	rɛd	ro:t	ruʒ	ratre
76. road	roʊd	ʃtrɑ:sə	rut	ytārye
77. root	ru:t	vʊrcəl	rasin	witsako
78. round	rɑʊnd	rʊnd	rɔ̃	
79. sand	sæ:nd	zɑnd	sablə	warañc [obl.]
80. say	seɪ	zɑ:gən	dir	wentsi
81. see	si:	ze:ən	vuar	lkātsi
82. seed	si:d	zɑ:mə	grɛn	sārm
83. seven	sɛvən	zi:bən	sɛt	ṣukt
84. sister	sɪstər	ʃvɛstər	sœr	ṣer
85. sit	sɪt	zɪcən	ɛtr asi	lamatsi
86. six	sɪks	zɛks	sis	ṣkas
87. skin	skɪn	hɑʊt	po	yetse

Table 11.1 (*cont.*)

	English	German	French	Toch. B
88. sleep	sliːp	ʃlaːfən	dɔrmir	klantsatsi
89. small	smɔl	klaɪn	pəti	lykaśke
90. smoke	smoʊk	raʊx	fyme	
91. son	sʌn	zoːn	fis	<u>soy</u>
92. stand	<u>stæːnd</u>	ʃteːən	ɛtrə dəbu	stamatsi
93. star	<u>star</u>	ʃtɛrn	etual	ścirye
94. stone	rak	ʃtaɪn	pɪɛr	kärweñe
95. sun	sʌn	zɔnə	<u>sɔlɛj</u>	kauṃ
96. swim	swɪm[1]	ʃvɪmən[1]	naʒe[2]	nāṣtsi[2]
97. tail	teɪl	ʃvanc	kø	
98. ten	tɛn	ceːn	dis	śak
99. that	ðæt	das	səsi	<u>tu</u>
100. this	<u>ðɪs</u>	<u>diːzəs</u>	səla	<u>te</u>
101. three	θriː	draɪ	trua	trai
102. tongue	tʌŋ	<u>cʊŋə</u>	<u>lãg</u>	kantwo
103. tooth	tuːθ	caːn	dã	keme
104. tree	triː	baʊm	arbrə	stäm
105. two	<u>tuː</u>	cvaɪ	dø	<u>wi</u>
106. walk	wɔk	laʊfən	ale	yatsi
107. warm	<u>warm</u>	<u>varm</u>	ʃo	emalle
108. water	<u>wɔtər</u>	<u>vasər</u>	o	<u>war</u>
109. we	<u>wiː</u>	<u>viːr</u>	nu	<u>wes</u>
110. what	<u>wʌt</u>	<u>vas</u>	kua	<u>kuse</u>
111. white	waɪt	vaɪs	blã	ārkwi
112. who	<u>huː</u>	<u>veːr</u>	ki	<u>kuse</u>
113. woman	wʊmən	fraʊ	fam	klyiye
114. yellow	yɛlo	gɛlb	ʒon	tute
115. you (sg.)	<u>yuː</u>	<u>duː</u>	ty	twe

Words of each of the modern languages are given in an appropriate phonemic transcription; Toch. B words are cited in the conventional transliteration, which is close to phonemic. Cognates are underlined; if only the root is shared, the underlining is dotted, but the cognates are still counted in the calculations below. Different cognate sets are distinguished by superscript numerals. (Different decisions could of course have been made in some cases, but the overall result would be about the same.)

contrast, French shares only forty-two cognates with German and thirty-eight with English (the difference is not significant, though it shows that English has been a little less conservative than German in replacing basic words); that is also not surprising, since when English and German were still dialects of West Germanic that language had been diverging from Latin (the contemporary parent of French) for at least two and possibly as much as three millennia. Somewhat surprisingly, Toch. B shows almost as many agreements with the Germanic languages – thirty-six with English, thirty-seven with German – in spite of the gaps in its attested vocabulary. But that could be partly a result of the fact that our attested Toch. B documents were written a millennium or so ago, so that the language had not had as much time to lose inherited words before it became extinct. In any case, it shares even fewer cognates with French – only twenty-seven – presumably because the parent dialects of all three groups had begun to diverge by the time Tocharian lost contact with the others, and pre-Tocharian was near the eastern edge of the dialect continuum whereas pre-Italic was near the western edge. We would expect an Anatolian language – Hittite, for example (the best-attested Anatolian language) – to share even fewer cognates with any of these languages, though the greater gaps in its lexical attestation make that difficult to judge (most numerals, for instance, are written only with abstract symbols and are therefore effectively unattested). It is clear that if divergent development goes on long enough the proportion of cognates will become so small that we will not be able to identify them with confidence because they will not be distinguishable from chance resemblances.[4] The steady loss of inherited lexical and morphological material, combined with the prevalence of chance similarities between unrelated words, effectively imposes a limit on how far back we can reconstruct and what degrees of relationship we can prove.

These straightforward facts are so unwelcome to some researchers that they simply deny that there is anything problematic about "long-distance" reconstruction, or assert that there is an easy way around the problems. The following paragraphs will examine and critique a variety of attempts to pursue long-range comparison.

Probably the oldest response to the problem of chance resemblances is to deny that words and affixes of different languages resemble one another both in sound and in meaning *by chance* with any appreciable frequency; that is the de facto response of the older "Nostraticists" (Vladimir Illich-Svitych, Vitalij Shevoroshkin, Igor Diakonoff, Sergei Starostin, etc.), since they have conspicuously avoided addressing the problem. But in fact it is easy to find chance resemblances between languages whose histories are well enough known to *prove* that the resemblances are fortuitous. For instance, Spanish *mucho* and English *much*, which both resemble and translate each other, are historically unconnected; the former is the regular sound-change outcome of Latin *multum*, which shares a root *mel- with Latin *melior* 'better', while *much* is an abbreviated form of southern Middle English *muchel* 'big' < OE *miċel* < PGmc. *mikilaz (cf. Goth. *mik-ils*), a suffixed derivative of Proto-Indo-European *meǵ- 'big' (cf. Greek μέγας /mégas/). It can be seen that the ancestors of these two words resemble each other less in form and in meaning than the modern words do; *mucho* and *much* are an example of convergent evolution. Nor is that all. In the same way it can be shown that Spanish *haber* (the auxiliary verb) has nothing to do historically with English *have*; that *día* has nothing to do with *day*; that *bola* has nothing to do with *ball*; and so on. Convergent evolution is in fact quite common, and the result is that chance resemblances between words appear wherever we look.[5]

Table 11.2 *The six words in which English initial /f/ matches Toch. B /p/*

	English	Toch. B
30. father	faðər	pācer
31. feather	feðər	paruwa [pl.]
32. fire	faɪər	puwar
34. five	faɪv	piś
35. fly	flaɪ	plu-
36. foot	fʊt	paiyye

To move beyond these general considerations we need to find a way to estimate, at least roughly, the probability of chance resemblances between specific pairs of words. Let us look again at the comparative list given above. Suppose we want to compare the initial consonants of the English and Toch. B words, hoping to find a greater-than-chance similarity. Though the list is 115 items long, we can only compare 108 of the words because of the gaps in the Toch. B list. As it happens, none of the missing Toch. B words would match an English word beginning with /f/. If we choose a word at random in the comparable part of the list, the odds that it would begin with /f/ in English are 10/108, or .0926, because 10 of the words in the English list begin with /f/; the odds that it would begin with /p/ in Toch. B are 12/108, or .1111, because 12 of the words in the Toch. B list begin with /p/. If the initial consonants are distributed randomly, the odds of finding a word that begins with /f/ in English and with /p/ in Toch. B should be .0926 × .1111, or about .0103. Since 1/108 is about .0093, we might expect to find one or at most two such words in the list. In fact we find six, as in Table 11.2. This certainly looks like a greater-than-chance correlation, but how much greater than chance is it? If the words of the lists were randomly arranged, the distribution of outcomes would be "hypergeometric," for the following reason. The word-pairs are sampled "without replacement": when we have matched a word in either list, we have "used it up" and are not allowed to use it for another matching. Under those constraints, for each sound correspondence $a = b$ the distribution of numbers of matches *by chance*, if the wordlists are randomized and compared repeatedly, is determined by the equation

$$h = \frac{\binom{R}{r}\binom{N-R}{n-r}}{\binom{N}{n}}$$

where N is the number of meanings in the lists, n is the number of occurrences of sound a in wordlist A, R is the number of occurrences of sound b in wordlist B, and r is the number of tokens of the correpondence.[6] Solving for all values of r gives what is called the hypergeometric distribution. In this case N is 108,

Table 11.3 *Distribution of chance matches of 10 x and 12 y in a list of 108*

No. of $/f/ = /p/$	Proportion	Cumulative proportion
0	.291299	.291299
1	.401792	.693091
2	.226008	.919009
3	.067718	.986817
4	.011851	.998668
5	.001250	.999918

n is 10, and *R* is 12; the distribution is given in Table 11.3. So if the lists were randomly arranged we would expect to find *5 or fewer* items with English initial /f/ matching Toch. B initial /p/ in 999,918 out of every 1,000,000 repetitions of this experiment, and therefore *6 or more* such items in 82 cases out of every 1,000,000 – fewer than one out of every 100,000. The relevant number here is "6 or more," since more than six would demonstrate a greater-than-chance correlation just as well, or rather better. (This illustrates a general principle of working with probabilities: we must calculate the probability not of the single outcome that we have (or desire), but of all relevant outcomes of equal or less probability, or of equal or greater probability, depending on what we are trying to prove; that will complicate our work substantially in due course.) It would be reasonable to accept this correlation by itself as proof that English and Toch. B are related.

But of course in really interesting cases the evidence is not so overwhelming; we might find three or four sound correspondences that seemed to be a bit more common than we might expect but didn't clear any recognized statistical threshold. How are such "borderline" cases to be handled?

The intuitive response to this problem is to "get more evidence," but that intuition is counterproductive. What matters is the *proportion* of regular sound correspondences in a list comparison, not the absolute number; and we are looking for regular correspondences in the hope that many of the items which exhibit them will turn out to be real cognates rather than chance resemblances. But experience shows that as wordlists are lengthened and more and more "less basic" words are included, the proportion of true cognates declines; if a greater proportion of regularly corresponding items begins to appear, they will almost certainly reflect lexical borrowing from one language into the other. We might instead consider relaxing our standards for sound correspondences; for instance, we might accept not only a match of English /f/ with Toch. B /p/, but also a match of English /b/ or /p/ with Toch. B /p/, as examples of a single sound correspondence. But if we do that, the probability of finding a random match will be more than twice as great (since the combined incidence of /f/, /b/, and /p/ in the English list is

Table 11.4 *Distribution of chance matches of 4 x and 5 y in a list of 35*

No. of /f/ = /p/	Proportion	Cumulative proportion
0	.523396	.523396
1	.387701	.911097
2	.083079	.994176
3	.005730	.999906

21 – subtracting the word beginning with /b/ for which the Toch. B translation is unknown – whereas there are only 10 /f/'s), and it will be that much harder to "beat the odds" with any given number of tokens of the correspondence; in this case we add 11 word-pairs but only 2 new examples of the correspondence, namely 'breast' and 'brother'. Allowing equations between words which do not translate each other (such as Toch. B *ku* and English *hound* rather than *dog*) has a similar effect: for example, if a given word of list A is allowed to be matched with any of 5 different words of list B, then a fair calculation of the probabilities will involve multiplying the probability of a match by 5. All these failed strategies have one thing in common: they raise the threshold which must be cleared to demonstrate a greater-than-chance resemblance between wordlists *without* adequately increasing the resources with which such a demonstration must be made. Almost all attempts at "long-range" comparison exemplify at least one of these basic errors, and most exemplify all three.

A better response is to *decrease* the amount of evidence used – specifically, to shorten the length of the wordlists so that they include only those items believed to be replaced at the lowest rate over many millennia. But it turns out that decreasing N in the equation given above actually makes it harder to cross a given threshold of significance. For instance, suppose we decrease the length of the wordlist from 108 words to 35. In the longer list the 10 English /f/'s amounted to a little over 9% of the list, the 12 Toch. B /p/'s amounted to 11% of the list, and the 6 examples of the correspondence /f/ : /p/ amounted to 5.5% of the word-pairs. In a pair of lists 35 words long the same proportions would be about 3 English /f/'s, between 3 and 4 Toch. B /p/'s, and about 2 examples of the correspondence between them. Since the shorter list is supposed to retain more cognates, let us suppose that we have 4 English /f/'s, 5 Toch. B /p/'s, and 3 examples of the correspondence – a greater proportion than in the longer list. The hypergeometric distribution of random outcomes is given in Table 11.4. We would thus expect to find 3 *or more* examples of the correspondence, if the lists were randomized, in 1 – .994176 = .005824 of repetitions of the list-comparison, or somewhat more often than once in every 200 repetitions of randomized list-comparisons. This is still respectable, but it is nothing like the tiny chance probability we found for a *smaller* proportion of correspondences in the longer list.

Table 11.5 *Distribution of chance matches of 7 x and 8 y in a list of 102*

No. of /m/ = /m/	Proportion	Cumulative proportion
0	.554280	.554280
1	.352724	.907004
2	.029724	.936728
3	.009247	.945975

How, then, can we extract more information from a finite list? To begin with, we might try to calculate the chance probability of occurrence not of just one recurrent correspondence in a given phonotactic position (say, word-initially), but of a whole set of recurrent correspondences in that position. Unfortunately for us, the correspondences of a finite list are not independent: they must add up to the total number of word-pairs in the list. Calculating how many examples of how many correspondences in a single phonotactic position would be necessary to prove a greater-than-chance resemblance *in every case* is too complex to be feasible (though in principle it should be possible). We could instead proceed case by case as follows, continuing with our English-and-Toch. B example. Let us subtract the words exhibiting the correspondence /f/ = /p/ from the list, so that its length is now 102 word-pairs, and examine another recurrent correspondence. A promising candidate is /m/ = /m/, since there are 7 word-initial /m/'s in the English list, 8 in the Tocharian, and 4 examples of the correspondence. The hypergeometric distribution, with $N = 102$, $R = 8$, and $n = 7$ is given in Table 11.5. We expect four or more examples of this correspondence in about .054 of repetitions of the experiment – once in every 18 or 19 repetitions. This is a modest result. But since we excluded the examples of the correspondence /f/ = /p/ from the data before attempting this calculation, this result is effectively independent, and we can multiply the probabilities: $.054025 \times .000082 = .00000443$; that is, numbers of examples of these two correspondences at least as great as what we have found should occur only once in more than 225 thousand list-comparisons – i.e., about 5 times per million – if the lists were truly random.

Alternatively – or additionally – we can examine correspondences in different phonotactic positions. For instance, it is striking that in 3 of the word-pairs exhibiting the /f/ = /p/ initial correspondence there is also a postvocalic /r/ in both languages later in the word. There are 10 other word-pairs in which both words exhibit a postvocalic /r/, namely 'brother', 'daughter', 'four', 'heart', 'horn', 'liver', 'mother', 'sister', 'star', and 'water'. Given 6 word-initial /f/ = /p/ and 13 postvocalic /r/ = /r/, we can calculate how many words should exhibit both correspondences if their distribution was random; since we expect recurrent sound correspondences to "cluster" in true cognates, a greater-than-chance proportion of words exhibiting both correspondences can be taken as further evidence of a historical relationship.

All these methods require a great deal of calculation. Not surprisingly, linguists have looked for easier ways to find greater-than-chance similarities between languages; also not surprisingly, some of those methods work and some do not.

The most notorious failure of long-range comparison is the late Joseph Greenberg's method of "mass comparison," or "multilateral comparison." Greenberg reasoned that whatever the probability of a given sound correspondence between words of two languages might be, it would be much smaller if a third language was added, smaller still if a fourth was added, and so on. From there he jumped to the conclusion that comparison of a very large number of languages simultaneously should be a powerful tool for finding cognates and establishing relationships. Greenberg apparently did not understand that the probability of an n-ary match continues to fall only so long as *every* language compared exhibits a cognate. For instance, if we are looking for cognates for a particular word and find that the probability of a match in any other language averages .05, then if the first nine languages we examine each offer a potential cognate, the probability of that event occurring by chance is indeed $.05^9 = .000,000,000,001,953,125$ (taking the language that we started with as given). But if we find only three potential cognates among those nine languages, the probability is $.05^3 \times C(9, 3) = .000125 \times 84 = .0105$ – just shy of a reasonable statistical threshold. Since Greenberg also used very lax phonological and semantic criteria in identifying "cognates" (see above) and displayed astonishing carelessness with data (apparently in the belief that the heuristic power of his method would override almost any amount of factual error), his comparative work and that of his followers is useless even as a rough indication of what to look for (see e.g. Campbell 1988, Matisoff 1990, Poser 1992, Ringe 1996a, 1999, 2002).

It has been customary to object that since Greenberg produced a "correct" classification of the languages of Africa (Greenberg 1963) using his method, there must be at least something right about it. But that claim too appears to be seriously overblown. Greenberg's classification incorporated the work of predecessors who used the traditional comparative method, with the result that nonspecialists often credited him and his method with successes achieved by others with more reliable methods. Of Greenberg's original suggestions some have proved correct (such as the inclusion of Chadic within Afro-Asiatic and of some Kordofanian languages within Niger-Congo) while others have not (such as his "Khoisan" family and a number of additions to Niger-Congo); his most ambitious construct, a "Nilo-Saharan" phylum, remains unproved and controversial. That is about what one would expect of prescientific work. For specialist assessments, not hostile to Greenberg but in fact rejecting several of his hypotheses, see now Dimmendaal 2008, Sands 2009a, b.

The most workable approach to probabilistic assessment of wordlist comparisons has proved to be the "Monte Carlo" method. In this method a pair of

wordlists is compared, a detailed record is made of the similarities in sound
between them (according to some objective criterion, not necessarily exact sound
correspondences), and an overall "similarity score" is calculated on the basis
of the phonological similarities. The lists are then randomized repeatedly (or,
in a simpler version, one of the lists is repeatedly moved up or down one line,
the stranded line reentering at the bottom or the top) and after each alteration
the similarity score is computed again. After a large number of repetitions the
similarity score of the observed real correspondences is plotted against the curve
representing the random scores. If the real score lies far out to one side of the
random curve, or beyond it, it is evidence of a greater-than-chance relationship,
and the statistical significance of the set of real correspondences can be estimated
by observing where in the curve the real score falls. This method was pioneered
by Robert Oswalt (Oswalt 1970, 1991); a more sophisticated version was devised
and tested by Brett Kessler (Kessler 2001: 181–97). Kessler has even be able to
modify the method to handle multiple languages simultaneously, thus finally constructing a method of "multilateral comparison" that is statistically respectable
(Kessler and Lehtonen 2006); application of the method to "Indo-Uralic" found
that similarities between languages of those two families fell right in the middle
of the expected chance range (ibid. pp. 39–40)! All versions of this approach
require even more computation than the "brute force" calculation of probabilities, but the computation itself is comparatively simple – it is the randomization
and repetition that necessitate the use of computers – and the method yields
statistically robust results.

A quite different approach which gives reliable results is much simpler to
implement, namely exploitation of Johanna Nichols' concept of an "individual-
identifying threshold" (Nichols 1996: 48–56, 60–7; Nichols 2010). Nichols
reasons as follows. Given that there are approximately seven thousand human
languages still spoken or recorded, linguistic phenomena with a probability of
occurrence of 1 in 7,000, or about .000,143, can be expected to appear in one
language by sheer chance *on the average* – some will of course appear more often
than that by chance, some less. But linguistic phenomena less probable by two
orders of magnitude – that is, with a probability of about .000,001,43, or one in
700,000 – are most unlikely to appear in more than one language by chance. If
we find that they do appear in more than one, it is very likely that those languages
acquired that peculiarity from a single source – possibly by borrowing, if the
phenomenon is a lexical item, but overwhelmingly probably by descent from a
common ancestor, if the phenomenon is grammatical. Therefore, if we can find
shared grammatical phenomena whose probability of occurrence is at least that
low, we can use those phenomena as evidence of linguistic relationship.

How can we identify grammatical phenomena of very low probability of
occurrence? Two points are crucial. First, the actual phonological material that
expresses the grammatical functions must be taken into account, because abstract
grammatical categories are usually not idiosyncratic enough to be low-probability
items. Secondly, entire paradigms of grammatical markers should be considered,

because individual markers are almost always too short to be low-probability items. In Nichols' words:

> Paradigmaticity imposes co-occurrences and an ordering on a set of forms each of which, if taken individually, would be much too short for its consonantal segments to reach the individual-identifying threshold. The co-occurrences and ordering allow a probability level for the whole subsystem to be computed as the product of the probabilities of the individual forms and categories.   (Nichols 1996: 52)

A simple illustration will show how this can be done. All the Algonkian languages have a set of person-marking prefixes which are used to express possession of nouns and to express subject or object in some (but not all) verb paradigms. The system has four members; the protoforms are the following:

1st person	*ne-
2nd person	*ke-
3nd person	*we-
indefinite	*me-

Let us begin by calculating the probability of such a paradigm appearing; complications will be dealt with subsequently. Algonkian languages typically have nine or ten consonants that are permitted in word-initial position, and vowel-initial words are common; thus the average probability of each consonant (or zero) appearing in one of these prefixes is about 1/10, or .1. (The vowel *e is the default Algonkian vowel; one would expect it in grammatical morphemes of this kind, so its probability is close to 1 and should be disregarded.) But since it is most unlikely that the same consonant would appear in more than one of these contrastive prefixes, each occurrence "uses up" that consonant for the purposes of our calculation; the probability of the whole set (in any order) is thus $1/10 \times 1/9 \times 1/8 \times 1/7 = .1 \times .1\bar{1} \times .125 \times .1429 = .000,198$, or a bit less than one in 5,000. But the same four consonants could occur in any order; in fact they occur in the same order (if the order of listing of functions is constant; i.e. 1st person is always listed first, and so on). Since there are 24 possible orderings of 4 items, we need to divide the figure already calculated by 24; that yields .000,008,25, or about one in 121,212. This is already close to the individual-identifying threshold; some further quirks of the paradigm put it over the threshold, as follows. In the first place, Algonkian languages are heavily suffixing; these four prefixes are the *only* four prefixes. (There is also a limited system of ablaut called "initial change," as well as some fossilized examples of reduplication, but no other prefixes.) In Haspelmath *et al.* 2005 (hereafter *WALS*) 382 of the 894 languages sampled, or 43%, are heavily suffixing (see http://wals.info/feature/26); the proportion of those languages that exhibit prefixes marking person is not recorded, but it must be fairly small.[7] Those considerations together might reduce the probability of this paradigm to .000,001, putting it over the threshold. If they do not, the following additional peculiarities certainly will. Algonkian nouns are divided into two possession-oriented classes, those (relatively few) that are inalienably possessed and the vast majority that are not. Inalienably possessed nouns include kinship terms, body part terms, and a few other nouns; they must occur with an affix (in these languages a prefix) indicating possession. This is a fairly common distinction; *WALS* (feature 59) shows that about 39 percent of languages sampled have two possessive classes, and these two are by far the commonest. But in Algonkian languages this unremarkable semantic distinction coincides with a purely formal one: when the prefixes are added to inalienably possessed nouns whose stems begin with vowels, the vowel of the prefix is elided, but when they are added to other nouns that begin with vowels, *-t- is inserted between the prefix and the noun stem. Moreover, the indefinite possessor *me- is used only with those inalienably possessed nouns that are *not* kinship terms. These highly specific details reduce the chance probability of the system still further and make it individual-identifying because in principle they are independent of each other; thus for each further peculiarity adduced we must multiply the probability already calculated by some number between zero and one, and at some point the individual-identifying threshold is crossed. (And we haven't even discussed the use of these prefixes in verb forms.)

It seems clear that Nichols' approach is both comparatively easy and a surprisingly powerful tool for demonstrating greater-than-chance similarity between languages. In fact virtually all demonstrations of "long-distance" relationships that have proved to be statistically valid are of this type. For instance, Wiyot and Yurok, two languages of the north California coast, were shown to be distantly related to Algonkian by analysis of a set of pronominal prefixes that matches the Algonkian set point for point (Goddard 1975), though lexical cognates were eventually identified as well; Tlingit was first shown to be related to Athabaskan-Eyak by analysis of a set of verb prefixes called "classifiers" that mark transitivity, passive, and other types of valence (Krauss 1969), though lexical cognates were also eventually identified (Leer 1990, 2010); most recently the Yeniseian family of Siberia, of which Ket is the only surviving member, has (probably) been shown to be related to Na-Dene (the family that includes Tlingit, Eyak, and Athabaskan) by analysis of a different set of verb prefixes (Vajda 2010).

Of course this method is not equally useful in every case; in particular, it will be harder to use on languages which do not exhibit complex inflectional paradigms (though analysis of numerals or systems of kinship terms can also work; see Nichols 1996: 52).[†] Moreover, occasional false positives could still be a problem, as is clear from the discussion of Callaghan 1986. Central Sierra Miwok has a system of subject person-and-number markers that is eerily reminiscent of a system well attested in conservative IE languages, as the comparison in Table 11.6 demonstrates. But while a similar system is reconstructable for Proto-Eastern Miwok, "neither Western Miwok nor the closely related Costanoan family shows personal verbal inflections except for the imperative. So the system cannot

---

[†] For further discussion (and further cautions about the individual-identifying approach and about the use of morphology in general) see Campbell and Poser 2008: 184–93.

Table 11.6 *Subject person-and-number markers in Central Sierra Miwok and PIE*

		Central Sierra Miwok	PIE 2ary	PIE 1ary
sg.	1	-m	*-m	*-m-i
	2	-ş	*-s	*-s-i
	3	∅	*-t	*-t-i
pl.	1	-maş	*-mé	*-mó-s
	2	-toş	*-té	*-té
	3	-p	*-ént	*-ént-i

be reconstructed for Proto-Miwok" (Callaghan 1986: 187). Callaghan points out that the longer forms of the Proto-Eastern Miwok person markers (used when followed by other suffixes) actually resemble the IE forms less, so it is clear that this is a case of convergent evolution; she suggests that "this system arose in pre-Eastern-Miwok through the suffixation of weakened pronouns and analogical extensions of other suffixes" (1986: 187, with reference to Callaghan 1979). Of course it is true (as the reader can see from Table 11.6) that only four of the six Miwok suffixes resemble IE counterparts; further, that two resemble IE "secondary" endings closely while a third resembles the corresponding "primary" ending more closely, and the resemblance of the 2pl. ending to its IE counterpart is less exact (it actually exhibits a greater resemblance to the innovative Latin ending *-tis*); so it seems likely that this case would not clear the individual-identifying threshold in any case. But it needs to be remembered that in any endeavor that must make use of probabilistic reasoning, such as linguistic reconstruction, absolute certainty is not attainable; and because the answers are necessarily probabilistic, both false positives and false negatives must occasionally be expected.

Notes

1 Ringe 2006: 100 suggests that Verner's Law might have been inserted before the end of a preexisting sequence of rules that already included (5), but recent work by Jonathan Gress-Wright raises serious doubts about such a scenario; see the end of Chapter 5 for further discussion.

2 Celtic and Germanic do share a word for 'iron', reconstructable as *īsarnom; it was probably borrowed from Celtic into Proto-Germanic (Cowgill 1986: 68, fn. 10). But Latin *ferrum*, Greek σίδηρος /sídɛ:ros/, etc. have nothing to do with the Celtic word or with each other; Sanskrit *áyas*, Avestan *aiiō* is actually the inherited word for 'bronze' (probably originally 'copper') applied to the new metal.

3 A further weakness of the "beech tree argument" is the fact that many of the supposed cognates meaning 'beech' do not exhibit the usual regular sound correspondences between the languages in which they occur, and so are not likely to have been inherited from the protolanguage; see Friedrich 1970: 106–15 for details.

4 In one way our illustration of lexical loss is actually too optimistic: it reckons as cognates all pairs whose cognation can be established with all the information at our disposal, instead of only those that could be discovered by an inspection of these wordlists. For instance, it is not likely that the Germanic cognates of 'four' or the French cognate of 'five' could be identified from the information given here. In various other passages below we will make such arguments *a fortiori* for the sake of simplicity.

5 Readers who want to check the etymologies of the pairs of English and Spanish words adduced can do the following. Etymologies of the English words can be found in the *Oxford English Dictionary* (widely available online). Etymologies of the Spanish words can be found through Meyer-Lübke 1935 if they are inherited from Latin or have cognates in other Romance languages; the etymologies of their Latin ancestors can be found in one of the standard etymological dictionaries of Latin (de Vaan 2008, Ernout and Meillet 1939, or Walde and Hofmann 1938). Words not inherited from Latin cannot be cognate with the English words; they might conceivably be borrowed from English, in which case an etymological dictionary of Spanish should be consulted.

6 The function $\binom{x}{y}$, also written C(x, y), is called the "choose function" and is read "*x* choose *y*"; it gives the number of *different* ways of constructing a set of size *y* from a larger set of size *x*. It is equal to $\frac{x!}{y!(x-y)!}$; the terms of dividend and divisor cancel in such a way that $\binom{10}{4}$, for example, is equal to $(10 \times 9 \times 8 \times 7) / (1 \times 2 \times 3 \times 4)$, i.e. the product of the *y* largest integers in *x* divided by the product of the integers up to and including *y*.

7 Oddly enough Menomini and Cree, the only Algonkian languages in the *WALS* database for this feature, are characterized as "equal prefixing and suffixing"; that seems to us somewhat inaccurate, unless initial change is considered a prefix and the incidence of the prefixes in running text is taken into account (they are very common).

Appendix: Recovering the pronunciation of dead languages: types of evidence

The subject of this appendix is one aspect of "philology" in the narrowest and most old-fashioned sense, i.e. the analysis of texts from past centuries. From the point of view of a modern descriptive linguist it can be thought of as "salvage linguistics." While text philology is too far removed from the concerns of linguistics proper to be part of a course in historical linguistics, linguists who use the data of recorded documents do need to master the philological details of the specific corpus they are dealing with. This appendix is intended as general orientation for one aspect of that type of study.

The pronunciation of any language of the past can be recovered only approximately; the task of the philologist is to make the approximations as close as possible. For instance, if we are trying to reconstruct the pronunciation of Classical Latin, we should be satisfied if the result is something Cicero would have understood without difficulty, even if he would have noticed a foreign "accent" in our Latin.

Here is a concrete example. We know from the testimony of ancient grammarians and from verse (see below) that Classical Latin had two vowels written with the letter ⟨a⟩, conventionally marked *a* (or *ă*) and *ā*; we also know that the second of those vowels took longer to say than the first, but there is no evidence of any other difference between them. From other evidence (of the types listed below) we can also say the following:

(a)   the Latin a-vowels were low vowels;
(b)   they might have been pronounced as far forward as [a], or as far back as [ɑ], or anywhere in between;
(c)   they were almost certainly not pronounced as far forward as [æ];
(d)   they were almost certainly not pronounced with lip rounding;
(e)   they were certainly nasalized when followed by word-final ⟨m⟩ and before certain consonant clusters beginning with ⟨n⟩;
(f)   they certainly did not resemble [eɪ] (as in English *take*); Latin did have such a diphthong but wrote it ⟨ei⟩.

In other words, we can approximate the pronunciation of the Classical Latin a-vowels very closely, though a small degree of uncertainty remains (especially point (b) above).

The types of evidence we can use to reconstruct the pronunciation of languages before the invention of modern sound recording are discussed in the sections which follow. The reader will soon see that *individual* pieces of evidence for *particular* pronunciations are seldom absolutely clinching; but when half a dozen *independent* pieces of evidence converge on the same conclusion, and there is no evidence to the contrary, that conclusion will be so secure that for all practical purposes it is certain. Of course that also means that every scrap of available evidence must be found and exploited.

The first two types of evidence are provided by a straightforward application of the uniformitarian principle.

1   Phonetics

The structure of the human vocal apparatus imposes tight constraints on what speech sounds are possible, and the limits of human perception impose further constraints; obviously these constraints apply to the languages of past centuries as well as to languages still spoken. In addition, an interesting pattern emerges from the two or three thousand competent descriptions of the sounds of languages and dialects still spoken: a relative handful of speech sounds are extremely common, appearing in language after language, while most of the (very wide) range of attested speech sounds appear in fairly few languages. (Maddieson 1984 gives a good picture of the situation.) This has a probabilistic effect on our reconstructions: evidence that some ancient language used a common sound, typical of human languages in general, can be accepted at face value, while apparent evidence that an ancient language possessed an unusual sound has to be examined much more carefully, since the general probability of such a sound appearing in a language chosen at random is low.

The use of phonetics is illustrated by the discussion of Latin a-vowels above; and in fact the height, frontness, rounding, length, and nasalization of Latin vowels can all be recovered within reasonably precise limits.

2   Phonological structure

Just as the range of sounds used in human language is constrained, both absolutely and probabilistically, so also the patterns in which the sounds appear, and the ways that they interact in specific utterances, are subject to general constraints which can be discovered by examining a large number of the languages still spoken. In other words, there are more or less typical contrasts, phonemic inventories, and phonological rules that reappear in language after language. Practically all the constraints on languages' phonologies are probabilistic, because languages use typical sounds in peculiar ways more often than they use peculiar sounds.

But some patterns are so pervasive that they can be used without hesitation. For example, the ancient grammarians tell us that Latin ⟨b⟩ was pronounced like ⟨p⟩ when followed immediately by ⟨s⟩ or ⟨t⟩, and some Latin inscriptions corroborate that by actually writing ⟨ps⟩, ⟨pt⟩ for usual ⟨bs⟩, ⟨bt⟩ (and, conversely ⟨bs⟩, ⟨bt⟩ for usual ⟨ps⟩, ⟨pt⟩, showing that there was absolutely no difference – see further below). From that pattern of facts any competent linguist should be able to conclude, without further discussion, that the crucial difference between Latin ⟨p⟩ and ⟨b⟩ in other positions was that ⟨p⟩ was voiceless and ⟨b⟩ was voiced. (There could conceivably have been other differences too, but there is no evidence for that.)

3   Surviving statements of native speakers of past languages

The most important of these statements are the systematic treatises of ancient and medieval grammarians. These include, for example, the treatises on the pronunciation of Sanskrit produced in ancient India, the books of the ancient Greek and Roman grammarians (which together fill several sizeable volumes), the *Donatz Proensals* of Uc Faiditz, the famous description of the phonetics of Old Icelandic by the "First Grammarian" of that language (whose real name is unknown), the Middle Chinese *Qièyùn* of Lù Fǎyán and the rhyme tables based on it, and so on – there is far more material of this sort than the general public (or, perhaps, the average linguist) realizes. For English there is very little until the middle of the sixteenth century, but from that point forward there is a continuous tradition of grammatical description (see, for example, the citations in Otto Jespersen's grammar). This systematic literature can occasionally be supplemented with casual remarks made by individual authors.

The quality of these native-speaker observations varies enormously. The grammatical tradition of ancient India that culminated with Pāṇini's work two and a half millennia ago was fully scientific and spectacularly precise – so good that Western phonetics, and linguistics generally, did not catch up with it until the twentieth century. The First Grammarian of Iceland is nearly as good. At the other end of the scale, Uc Faiditz attempts to force Old Provençal grammar into a Latin framework – with disappointing results – and many of the early English grammarians were ludicrously confused by the fact that different English vowels are spelled the same way. (There are exceptions, though; John Hart's sixteenth-century work got measurably better as he learned to hear his vowels more precisely – we know because he published several books between 1550 and 1570 – and Samuel Cooper's English grammar of 1685 [written in Latin] gives descriptions of vowels that are surprisingly easy to interpret in modern terms.) Most of the evidence, of course, falls somewhere in between these extremes, and all of it must be interpreted in the scientific terms of phonetics and phonology (see sections 1 and 2 above). Sometimes a grammarian's unsuccessful attempt to analyze a phenomenon is elucidated by other evidence. For instance, the statement of Quintilian that Latin final ⟨m⟩, "even though it is written, is nevertheless barely pronounced" and the statement of Priscian that "*m* sounds muffled at the end of words" are corroborated by the facts that in Latin verse words ending in ⟨m⟩ are treated as vowel-final, while in some inscriptions word-final ⟨m⟩ is sometimes omitted; and it is a reasonable inference from that constellation of facts that word-final ⟨m⟩ had been reduced to nasalization of the preceding vowel.

Native speakers of the past also provide indirect evidence for their pronunciations, as the following sections will show.

4   Meter

The structure of ancient and medieval verse – partly described by native theorists and partly recoverable by internal analysis of the poetry – provides a great deal of information about the pronunciation of some languages of the past. For example, much of our information about long and short vowels in Latin comes from exhaustive analysis of the thousands of pages of Latin poetry that survive, because the structure of Latin verse was principally governed by rigorous patterns of long and short syllables. (A large proportion of the surviving material is not worth reading as literature; it includes, for example, verses flattering powerful people, a collection of pornographic verse that is almost all disgusting rather than erotic, several very long and tedious epic poems by inferior imitators of Vergil, and so on. But all of it is useful to the linguist. Again, there is far more material than the average educated person is aware of.)

5   Rhyme and other sound-patterns

The significance of rhymes is obvious: they tell us which words had identical sounds in (some) identical positions. For example, *green* and *clean* rhyme in modern English, and so do *white* and *knight*; but in Chaucer we hardly ever find the first pair as a rhyme and we never find the second pair as a rhyme – and (crucially) we have enough of Chaucer's verse, and all four words are common enough as rhymes, to give us confidence that those are not accidental gaps. We have to conclude that in Chaucer's time the vowels of *green* and *clean* were not yet identical, and neither were the vowels of *white* and *knight*. (The modern differences in spelling also suggest that there were originally differences in pronunciation; but modern spelling is *not* fully reliable. For example, in Chaucer *seen* sometimes rhymes with *lean* or *clean* and sometimes with *green* or *keen*.

Evidently the pronunciation of *seen* was variable in his generation – something which could never have been guessed from the modern spelling.)

Caution is necessary, however, because in some traditions (though not in all) "imperfect" rhymes are acceptable. For instance, at the beginning of Book V of *Troilus and Criseyde* Chaucer rhymes both *green* and *clean* with *queen* (which was variably pronounced, like *seen* – see above), thus bringing *green* and *clean* into rhyme with each other even though they had different vowels in the London English of his time. The same reservations apply even more to puns and similar phenomena (including the "etymologies" of ancient grammarians). These are most useful when they corroborate evidence of other types. For example, Cicero's story that Marcus Crassus (who was superstitious) interpreted a street-vendor's cry *Cauneās* '(figs) from Caunus!' as an omen *cavē nē eās* 'don't go!' suggests that in rapid speech Latin word-final vowels were shortened and dropped in certain circumstances, and further that the consonant we write *v* was identical with the second half of the diphthong *au* – that is, it was really [w]; and all those inferences can be corroborated by other evidence. (See immediately below for further evidence bearing on the last one.)

6   Graphemics

Writing systems can differ from one another a good deal, and the principles which underlie them are complex, but one principle is simple enough and general enough to be used for our purposes. When an *alphabetic* writing system is first invented or adapted to write a particular language, the speakers of that language will tend to use a single letter for each surface-contrastive phoneme of their language, *other things being equal*. Of course other things are often not equal; the most common difficulty occurs when a foreign alphabet is adapted and speakers discover that there are not enough letters available for the phonemes of their language. But even then we can learn something about their pronunciation by the ways they try to get around the problem.

For example, when the early Romans acquired the alphabet (probably from the Etruscans, who had got it from the Greeks) they found that they had only five letters to represent vowels, namely ⟨I E A O V⟩; but we know that they had ten vowels, five long and five short (see above). Not surprisingly, they used each of the symbols to represent a pair of vowels, one long and one short. But it follows that, *at the time the alphabet was acquired*, the members of each long-and-short pair must have been very similar in pronunciation in everything but length – not necessarily identical, of course, but very similar. (They did not stay that way.)

But in this case there's a further wrinkle: the two symbols ⟨I V⟩ were also used to write a pair of consonants for which there were no available symbols. (⟨F⟩, the Greek digamma, should have represented [w], but instead it wound up representing [f]; the details are not important here.) Since the high vowels [i] and

[u] are similar to the nonsyllabics [j] and [w] in every respect except syllabicity, we can infer that [j] and [w] were the pronunciations of consonantal ⟨I⟩ and ⟨V⟩ respectively in Latin *at the time the alphabet was acquired*. Other pieces of evidence point in the same direction; for example, the story about Crassus reported in section 5 shows that consonantal ⟨V⟩ was still being pronounced [w] in the first century BCE. (Again, things did not stay this way; by the time the Roman Empire fell apart, consonantal ⟨V⟩ had shifted its pronunciation to [β] or [v] even in upper-class urban Latin. See further below.)

7   Variation in spelling

In the history of writing, fixed standard spelling systems are by no means universal; usually there is some spelling variation in the documents of a language, and often there is a great deal of variation. This is useful for an obvious reason: if a particular sound in a particular position can be spelled with either of two letters, we can infer that those letters represented similar (but not necessarily identical) sounds in other positions too. A concrete example is given in section 2 above.

Even more interesting are the cases in which a standard spelling system, established by long tradition, begins to break down, with writers making systematic errors; that shows that the actual sounds have changed, so that the traditional system is no longer a good representation of the sounds. Modern English spelling, which is more than 500 years out of date, provides numerous examples – in spite of the fact that much of the educational system is designed to enforce the archaic spelling rules. For instance, the American spelling *plow* for inherited *plough*, and the substandard spelling *nite* for *night*, would show that the sound originally represented by *gh* no longer exists in English even if English were a dead language accessible only through its written documents.

8   Representation of animal sounds

This is rarely useful, because animal sounds are usually very different from human speech sounds, so that the representation of one by the other is to a large extent governed by arbitrary convention; but once in a while it gives us valuable evidence. The classic case is the representation of the sound a sheep makes by βῆ βῆ [bɛ̂ː bɛ̂ː] in ancient Greek comedy. For a while in the Renaissance (and, surprisingly, even later) there were some scholars who insisted that ancient Greek *must* have been pronounced like modern Greek; but the modern Greek pronunciation of those letters would be [vi vi] – and it is literally impossible that anyone would have used those sounds to represent what a sheep says! At the very least the vowel must have been much lower – and, of course, this establishes the more general point that modern Greek pronunciation is not a good guide to ancient Greek pronunciation.

We also obtain some information about the pronunciation of particular languages of the past from speakers of other languages contemporary with them, as follows.

9   Direct cross-linguistic evidence

Occasionally words of one language are written in the spelling system of another for pedagogical purposes, and that provides information about the pronunciation of both languages by showing what in language A was equivalent to what in language B. For example, in the middle of the eighteenth century Jacob de Castro, a native speaker of Portuguese, wrote down a list of English words in Portuguese spelling, and he transcribed *nature* as ⟨neitar⟩. That's interesting for the following reason. Though the first vowel of this word is phonetically a diphthong in standard modern English, there is plenty of evidence that it had not been one at least as late as the middle of the sixteenth century. Evidently it had become a diphthong by the middle of the eighteenth century.

Notice how this piece of evidence is used. By itself it shows only that there was an equivalence between, for example, English "long" ⟨a⟩ and Portuguese ⟨ei⟩ at a particular point in time; the rest of the inference is possible only because we know from modern work in phonetics that both those sounds are now diphthongs, and because we know a good deal about their earlier history from other sources. The equivalence is merely one piece of a larger picture, though it does impose a significant constraint on which analyses could conceivably be correct.

10   Loanwords

These can be used in much the same way as the transcriptions noted in section 9, but they have to be used with much greater caution, because the pronunciations of loanwords are often adjusted to fit the phonology of the borrowing language.

For example, it is clear that the more southerly of the early Germanic dialects borrowed the Latin word *vīnum* 'wine' together with the trade article, and it is clear that that occurred well within the imperial period (at the latest), because the word already appears in mid-fourth-century Gothic; and there is good evidence that the word was borrowed with an initial [w]. (In English it still has an initial [w], though in German, for example, the sound has since shifted to [v].) If that were our only piece of evidence for the pronunciation of Latin consonantal ⟨V⟩, it wouldn't mean much; we would only be able to conclude that at the time the word was borrowed, [w] was the Germanic sound most similar to the Latin sound. But of course this piece of evidence and the ones cited above converge on the same conclusion, and that *is* useful.

Finally, there are three types of evidence that involve extrapolations from the present into the past, not only in general terms (as in sections 1 and 2 above), but sometimes very specifically.

11   Phonetic change

For the past fifty years William Labov and his co-workers and students have been recording phonetic changes in progress, and by now an immense amount of information is available; we know what kinds of changes are most likely, how they occur, and in some cases even why they occur. Recent work by experimental phoneticians, especially at Haskins Laboratories in New Haven and at Berkeley and UCLA, has also shed light on how and why phonetic changes occur. Precisely the same kinds of phonetic changes are recoverable from a comparison of historical documents from different periods – but of course we have to work them out indirectly, by evidence of all the kinds discussed above.

Once the phonetic history of a particular language or dialect of the past has been sketched out, we can compare what we think we know about it with actually observed examples of change in progress. As one would expect, it turns out that some changes (such as "chain shifts" of long front vowels) are very common, both among recorded changes in progress and in the historical record, while others are rare; and we can exploit these statistical facts in much the same way as we do the general facts about the phonetics and phonology of human language (see sections 1 and 2 above). However, on the average inferences of this sort are more uncertain than general inferences about the phonetics and phonology of human languages, simply because at the present time less is known about phonetic change.

12   Phonemic change

Here there is only one principle, but it is watertight: *mergers*, in which a phonemic contrast is lost, *are irreversible*. This follows directly from the nature of first-language acquisition: children must work out the grammar of their native language from the data they hear, and if all the evidence for a contrast has disappeared, it can no longer be learned. It follows that apparent reversals of mergers in the historical record (which are rare in any case) must be something else: possibly no merger really occurred, but for some reason the writing system was inadequate to express the contrast that did persist; possibly a merger did occur in one dialect, but later records are actually from a closely related dialect in which the merger had not occurred – etc., etc.

13   Tradition

Finally, in various cultures there are religious and academic traditions about the pronunciations of dead languages that have remained culturally important – about the pronunciation of Sanskrit in India, for example, and about the pronunciation of Latin in western Europe. These traditions have some value, but in detail they are actually the least trustworthy of the thirteen kinds of evidence listed here, simply because human traditions change over time (far more than traditionalists appear to believe). For example, Latin ⟨s⟩ is pronounced as an alveolar sibilant in all the European "school pronunciations"; but in some it is voiced [z] between vowels, whereas there is good ancient evidence that it was actually voiceless [s] in that position.

Further reading

Books about the pronunciation of ancient or medieval languages generally focus on particular languages; the following are some accessible examples known to us, which deal (naturally enough) with languages we work with and/or teach about.

Allen 1978, 1987 are now the standard reference works for the pronunciation of Latin and Ancient Greek respectively. Allen 1953 is a good introduction to the pronunciation of Sanskrit, but it is much more difficult for a non-linguist to use.

For those who can read Latin or Greek, Sturtevant 1940 is still useful, especially because it quotes statements of ancient grammarians at length.

For the development of English pronunciation since the Middle English period, Jespersen 1909 is still probably the best introduction. For earlier periods of English a good sketch of the main points can be found in Moore 1957. Kökeritz 1953 is useful not only for those who want to recover the actual sound of Shakespeare's plays, but also as a reasonable reconstruction of London English c. 1600.

Wright 1907 is a good introduction to the development of German pronunciation; Wright 1910 is likewise a good introduction to Gothic (the earliest reasonably well-attested Germanic language, which has left no modern descendants). Gordon 1957 includes a sketch of the phonetics of Old Norse.

For many ancient and medieval languages one has to consult the standard reference grammars, which presuppose considerable knowledge of linguistics; a typical example is Thurneysen 1946. For still others there is nothing reliable written in English, and a reading knowledge of French and/or German is essential if you want to work on them. Sometimes the most important works have been translated into English; for example, Valentin Kiparsky's indispensible *Russische historische Grammatik* has been translated (V. Kiparsky 1979).

References

Adams, Douglas Q. 1999. *A dictionary of Tocharian B*. Amsterdam: Rodopi.

Aissen, Judith. 1987. *Tzotzil clause structure*. Dordrecht: Reidel.

Alexandris, Alexis. 1999. "The Greek census of Anatolia and Thrace (1910–1912): a contribution to Ottoman historical demography." In Gondicas and Issawi (eds.), pp. 45–76.

Allen, Cynthia. 2008. *Genitives in early English: typology and evidence*. Oxford University Press.

Allen, Shanley, and Martha Crago. 1989. "Acquisition of noun incorporation in Inuktitut." *Papers and Reports on Child Language Development* 28: 49–56.

Allen, W. Sidney. 1953. *Phonetics in ancient India*. Cambridge University Press.

    1978. *Vox latina*. 2nd edn. Cambridge University Press.

    1987. *Vox graeca*. 3rd edn. Cambridge University Press.

Anderson, Stephen. 1982. "Where's morphology?" *Linguistic Inquiry* 13: 571–612.

Appel, René, and Pieter Muysken. 1987. *Language contact and bilingualism*. London: Edward Arnold.

Aronoff, Mark. 1976. *Word formation in generative grammar*. Cambridge, MA: MIT Press.

    1994. *Morphology by itself: stems and inflectional classes*. Cambridge, MA: MIT Press.

Babbitt, E. H. 1896. "The English of the lower classes in New York City and vicinity." *Dialect Notes* 1: 457–64.

Bagemihl, Bruce. 1991. "Syllable structure in Bella Coola." *Linguistic Inquiry* 22: 589–646.

    1998. "Maximality in Bella Coola (Nuxalk)." In Ewa Czaykowska-Higgins and M. Dale Kincade (eds.), *Salish languages and linguistics: theoretical and descriptive perspectives*. Berlin: Mouton de Gruyter, pp. 71–98.

Baker, Mark. 1985. "The Mirror Principle and morphosyntactic explanation." *Linguistic Inquiry* 16: 373–416.

    1988a. *Incorporation: a theory of grammatical function changing*. University of Chicago Press.

    1988b. "Theta theory and the syntax of applicatives in Chichewa." *Natural Language and Linguistic Theory* 6: 353–89.

Baranowski, Maciej. 2006. "Phonological variation and change in the dialect of Charleston, SC." Dissertation, University of Pennsylvania.

Bauer, Brigitte. 2010. "Forerunners of Romance -*mente* adverbs in Latin prose and poetry." In Eleanor Dickey and Anna Chahoud (eds.), *Colloquial and literary Latin*. Cambridge University Press, pp. 339–53.

Baylis, Jeffrey R. 1982. "Avian vocal mimicry: its function and evolution." In Kroodsma, Miller, and Ouellet (eds.), vol. II, pp. 51–83.

Becker, Peter H. 1982. "The coding of species-specific characteristics in bird sounds." In Kroodsma, Miller, and Ouellet (eds.), vol. I, pp. 213–52.

Bellugi, Ursula. 1988. "The acquisition of a spatial language." In Frank S. Kessel (ed.), *The development of language and language researchers: essays in honor of Roger Brown*. Hillsdale, NJ: Erlbaum, pp. 153–85.

Bennett, J. A. W., and G. V. Smithers. 1968. *Early Middle English verse and prose*. 2nd edn. Oxford: Clarendon Press.

Bentley, Mayrene, and Andrew Kulemeka. 2001. *Chichewa*. Munich: Lincom Europa.

Bertoncini, Josiane, and Jacques Mehler. 1981. "Syllables as units in infant speech perception." *Infant Behavior and Development* 4: 247–60.

Besch, Werner. 1967. *Sprachlandschaften und Sprachausgleich im 15. Jahrhundert*. Munich: Francke.

Bhatia, Tej K., and William C. Ritchie. 1999. "The bilingual child: some issues and perspectives." In Ritchie and Bhatia (eds.), pp. 569–643.

Bickerton, Derek. 1977. "Pidginization and creolization: language acquisition and language universals." In Albert Valdman (ed.), *Pidgin and creole linguistics*. Bloomington: Indiana University Press, pp. 49–69.

  1981. *Roots of language*. Ann Arbor: Karoma.

  1995. "Creoles and the bankruptcy of current acquisition theory." In Wekker (ed.), pp. 33–43.

Biggs, Bruce. 1978. "The history of Polynesian phonology." In Stephen Wurm and Lois Carrington (eds.), *Second International Conference on Austronesian Linguistics: Proceedings*, Fascicle 2. Canberra: Australian National University, pp. 691–716.

Björkman, Erik. 1900–2. *Scandinavian loan-words in Middle English*. Halle: Niemeyer.

Blevins, Juliette. 1995. "The syllable in phonological theory." In John A. Goldsmith (ed.), *The handbook of phonological theory*. Oxford: Blackwell, pp. 206–44.

  2003. "The independent nature of phonotactic constraints." In Caroline Féry and Ruben van de Vijver (eds.), *The syllable in optimality theory*. Cambridge University Press, pp. 375–403.

  2004. *Evolutionary phonology*. Cambridge University Press.

Blevins, Juliette, and Andrew Garrett. 1998. "The origins of consonant–vowel metathesis." *Language* 74: 508–56.

  2004. "The evolution of metathesis." In Bruce Hayes, Robert Kirchner, and Donca Steriade (eds.), *Phonetically based phonology*. Cambridge University Press, pp. 117–56.

Bloomfield, Leonard. 1925. "Notes on the Fox language." *International Journal of American Linguistics* 3: 219–32.

  1933. *Language*. New York: Holt.

  1946. "Algonquian." In Cornelius Osgood (ed.), *Linguistic structures of Native America*. New York: Viking Fund, pp. 85–129.

  1962. *The Menominee language*. New Haven: Yale University Press.

  1975. *Menomini lexicon*. Milwaukee: Milwaukee Public Museum.

Blumstein, Sheila E., and Kenneth N. Stevens. 1979. "Acoustic invariance in speech production: evidence from measurements of the spectral characteristics of stop consonants." *Journal of the Acoustical Society of America* 66: 1001–17.

Bobalijk, Jonathon D., and Höskuldur Thráinsson. 1998. "Two heads aren't always better than one." *Syntax* 1: 37–71.

Bouchard, Denis. 1982. "Les constructions relatives en français vernaculaire et en français standard: étude d'un paramètre." In Claire Lefebvre (ed.), *La syntaxe comparée du français standard et populaire: approches formelle et fonctionelle*, vol. I. Québec: Office de la Langue Française, pp. 103–33.

Brandl, Alois, and O. Zippel. 1949. *Middle English literature*. 2nd edn. New York: Chelsea.

Braune, Wilhelm, and Ingo Reiffenstein. 2004. *Althochdeutsche Grammatik*. Vol. I, 15th edn. Tübingen: Niemeyer.

Breatnach, Liam. 1977. "The suffixed pronouns in Early Irish." *Celtica* 12: 75–107.

Bresnan, Joan, and Sam A. Mchombo. 1987. "Topic, pronoun, and agreement in Chicheŵa." *Language* 63: 741–82.

Browman, Catherine, and Louis Goldstein. 1991. "Gestural structures: distinctiveness, phonological processes, and historical change." In Ignatius G. Mattingly and Michael Studdert-Kennedy (eds.), *Modularity and the motor theory of speech perception*. Hillside, NJ: Lawrence Erlbaum, pp. 313–38.
    1992. "Articulatory phonology: an overview." *Phonetica* 49: 155–80.

Brunner, Karl. 1948. *Abriß der mittelenglischen Grammatik*. 2nd edn. Halle: Niemeyer.
    1965. *Altenglische Grammatik*. 3rd edn. Tübingen: Niemeyer.

Buck, Carl. 1928. *A grammar of Oscan and Umbrian*. 2nd edn. Boston: Ginn & Co.
    1933. *Comparative grammar of Greek and Latin*. University of Chicago Press.

Buckley, Eugene. 2000. "On the naturalness of unnatural rules." *Proceedings from the Second Workshop on American Indigenous Languages, UCSB working papers in linguistics* 9: 16–29.
    2009. "Phonetics and phonology in Gallo-Romance palatalisation." *Transactions of the Philological Society* 107: 31–65.

Buckley, Eugene, and Amanda Seidl. 2005. "On the learning of arbitrary phonological rules." *Language Learning and Development* 1: 289–316.

Bynon, Theodora. 1977. *Historical linguistics*. Cambridge University Press.

Callaghan, Catherine. 1979. "An 'Indo-European' type paradigm in Proto Eastern Miwok." In Kathryn Klar *et al.* (eds.), *American Indian and Indoeuropean studies: papers in honor of Madison S. Beeler*. The Hague: Mouton, pp. 31–41.
    1986. "A comment on 'Protolinguistics'." *International Journal of American Linguistics* 52: 186–8.

Callary, Robert E. 1975. "Phonological change and the development of an urban dialect in Illinois." *Language in Society* 4: 155–69.

Campbell, Alistair. 1962. *Old English grammar*. Revised edn. Oxford University Press.

Campbell, Lyle. 1988. Review of Greenberg 1987. *Language* 64: 591–615.

Campbell, Lyle, and Alice C. Harris. 2002. "Syntactic reconstruction and demythologizing 'Myths and the prehistories of grammars.'" *Journal of Linguistics* 38: 599–618.

Campbell, Lyle, and William Poser. 2008. *Language classification: history and method.* Cambridge University Press.

Carroll, John B., Peter Davies, and Barry Richman. 1971. *The American Heritage word frequency book.* Boston: Houghton Mifflin.

Carstairs, Andrew. 1987. *Allomorphy in inflection.* London: Croom Helm.

Chantraine, Pierre. 1925. "Les verbes grecs en *-θω." In *Mélanges linguistiques offerts à M. J. Vendryes.* Paris: Champion, pp. 93–108.

1927. *L'histoire du parfait grec.* Paris: Champion.

Chomsky, Noam. 1970. "Remarks on nominalization." In Roderick Jacobs and Peter Rosenbaum (eds.), *Readings in English transformational grammar.* Waltham, MA: Ginn and Co., pp. 184–221.

1981. *Lectures on government and binding.* Dordrecht: Foris.

Christmann, Ernst. 1964. "Kleine Beiträge zur deutschen Wortkunde." *Zeitschrift für Mundartforschung* 31: 187–98.

Clark, Cecily. 1958. *The Peterborough Chronicle 1070–1154.* Oxford University Press.

Clogg, Richard. 1999. "A millet within a millet: the Karamanlides." In Gondicas and Issawi (eds.), pp. 115–42.

Coetsem, Frans van. 1988. *Loan phonology and the two transfer types in language contact.* Dordrecht: Foris.

Cook, Eung-Do. 1994. "Against moraic licensing in Bella Coola." *Linguistic Inquiry* 25: 309–26.

Cook, V. J., and Mark Newson. 1996. *Chomsky's Universal Grammar: an introduction.* 2nd edn. Oxford: Blackwell.

Corbett, Greville. 1991. *Gender.* Cambridge University Press.

Cowgill, Warren. 1965. "The Old English present indicative ending -*e*." In Jan Safarewicz (ed.), *Symbolae linguisticae in honorem Georgii Kuryłowicz.* Wrocław: Polska Akademia Nauk, pp. 44–50.

1975. "The origin of the Insular Celtic conjunct and absolute verbal inflexions." In Helmut Rix (ed.), *Flexion und Wortbildung.* Wiesbaden: Reichert, pp. 40–70.

1986. "Einleitung." In Cowgill and Mayrhofer, pp. 9–71.

1987. "The distribution of infixed and suffixed pronouns in Old Irish." *Cambridge Medieval Celtic Studies* 13: 1–5.

Cowgill, Warren, and Manfred Mayrhofer. 1986. *Indogermanische Grammatik*, vol. I. Heidelberg: Winter.

Crisma, Paola, and Giuseppe Longobardi (eds.). 2009. *Historical syntax and linguistic theory.* Oxford University Press.

Cutler, Anne, Jacques Mehler, Dennis Norris, and Juan Segul. 1989. "Limits on bilingualism." *Nature* 340: 229–30.

Dąbrowska, Ewa. 2001. "Learning a morphological system without a default: the Polish genitive." *Journal of Child Language* 28: 545–74.

Dailey-O'Cain, Jennifer. 1997. "Canadian raising in a midwestern U.S. city." *Language Variation and Change* 9: 107–20.

Daniloff, Raymond, Gordon Schuckers, and Lawrence Feth. 1980. *The physiology of speech and hearing.* Englewood Cliffs, NJ: Prentice Hall.

Dawkins, R. M. 1910. "Modern Greek in Asia Minor." *Journal of Hellenic Studies* 30: 109–32, 267–91.

1916. *Modern Greek in Asia Minor.* Cambridge University Press.

Delbrück, Berthold. 1888. *Altindische Syntax*. Halle: Verlag der Waisen Hauses.
    1893–1900. *Vergleichende Syntax der indogermanischen Sprachen*. Strassburg: Trübner.
De Simone, Carlo. 1980. "L'aspetto linguistico." In Conrad Stibbe, Giovanni Colonna, Carlo de Simone, and H. S. Versnel, *Lapis Satricanus*. The Hague: Staatsuitgeverij, pp. 71–94.
Devine, Andrew. 1970. *The Latin thematic genitive singular*. Stanford University Committee on Linguistics.
Dimmendaal, Gerrit. 2008. "Language ecology and linguistic diversity on the African continent." *Language and Linguistics Compass* 2: 840–58.
Dorian, Nancy. 1981. *Language death: the life cycle of a Scottish Gaelic dialect*. Philadelphia: University of Pennsylvania Press.
Dresher, B. Elan. 1999. "Child phonology, learnability, and phonological theory." In Ritchie and Bhatia (eds.), pp. 299–346.
Drosdowski, Günther (ed.). 1984. *Duden Grammatik der deutschen Gegenwartssprache*. 4th edn. Mannheim: Dudenverlag.
Eckert, Penelope. 1991. "Social polarization and the choice of linguistic variants." In Eckert (ed.), pp. 213–32.
Eckert, Penelope (ed.). 1991. *New ways of analyzing sound change*. San Diego: Academic Press.
Eijk, Jan van. 1997. *The Lillooet language*. Vancouver: University of British Columbia Press.
Ekwall, Eilert. 1930. "How long did the Scandinavian language survive in England?" In N. Bøgholm, Aage Brusendorff, and C. A. Bodelsen (eds.), *A grammatical miscellany offered to Otto Jespersen on his seventieth birthday*. Copenhagen: Levin & Munksgaard, pp. 17–30.
    1936. "The Scandinavian settlement." In H. C. Darby (ed.), *An historical geography of England before A. D. 1800*. Cambridge University Press, pp. 133–64.
Ellegård, Alvar. 1953. *The auxiliary* do*: the establishment and regulation of its use in English*. Stockholm: Almqvist & Wiksell.
Embick, David. 1997. "Voice and the interfaces of syntax." Dissertation, University of Pennsylvania.
    2008. "Variation and morphosyntactic theory: competition fractionated." *Language and Linguistics Compass* 2: 41–60.
Embick, David, and Morris Halle. 2003. "Latin inflections." Paper presented at Nijmegen, Nov. 21, 2003.
Embick, David, and Rolf Noyer. 2007. "Distributed morphology and the syntax–morphology interface." In Gillian Ramchand and Charles Reiss (eds.), *The Oxford handbook of linguistic interfaces*. Oxford University Press, pp. 289–324.
Embleton, Sheila. 1986. *Statistics in historical linguistics*. Bochum: Brockmeyer.
Enderlin, Fritz. 1913. *Die Mundart von Kesswil im Oberthurgau*. Frauenfeld: Huber.
Engel, Ralph, and Mary Allhiser de Engel. 1987. *Diccionario zoque de Francisco León*. Mexico: Instituto Lingüístico de Verano.
Ernout, Thomas, and Antoine Meillet. 1939. *Dictionnaire étymologique de la langue latine*. 4th edn. Paris: Klincksieck.

Eska, Joseph. 2003. "The distribution of the Old Irish personal object affixes and forward reconstruction." In Karlene Jones-Bley, Martin E. Huld, Angela Della Volpe, and Miriam Robbins Dexter (eds.), *Proceedings of the Fourteenth Annual UCLA Indo-European Conference (Los Angeles, November 8–9, 2002)*. Washington, DC: Institute for the Study of Man, pp. 25–36.

2009–10. "Where have all the object pronouns gone? The growth of object agreement in earlier Celtic." *Zeitschrift für celtische Philologie* 57: 25–47.

Fantini, Alvino E. 1985. *Language acquisition of a bilingual child: a sociolinguistic perspective (to age ten)*. San Diego: College-Hill Press.

Ferraresi, Gisella, and Maria Goldbach (eds.). 2008. *Principles of syntactic reconstruction*. Amsterdam: Benjamins.

Filppula, Markku. 1999. *The grammar of Irish English: language in Hibernian style*. London: Routledge.

Fletcher, Richard. 1997. *The barbarian conversion*. New York: Holt.

Fortescue, Michael, and Lise Lennert Olsen. 1992. "The acquisition of West Greenlandic." In Slobin (ed.), pp. 111–219.

Fortson, Benjamin W. IV. 2009. *Indo-European language and culture: an introduction*. 2nd edn. Oxford: Blackwell.

Franck, Johannes. 1910. *Mittelniederländische Grammatik*. 2nd edn. Leipzig: Tauchnitz.

Friedrich, Paul. 1970. *Proto-Indo-European trees*. University of Chicago Press.

1975. *Proto-Indo-European syntax: the order of meaningful elements*. Butte, MT: Journal of Indo-European Studies.

Fromm, Hans, and Matti Sadeniemi. 1956. *Finnisches Elementarbuch*. Vol. I: *Grammatik*. Heidelberg: Winter.

Gallée, Johan Hendrik. 1993. *Altsächsische Grammatik*. Halle: Niemeyer.

Gleitman, Lila. 1990. "The structural sources of verb meanings." *Language Acquisition* 1: 3–55.

Goddard, Ives. 1974. "An outline of the historical phonology of Arapaho and Atsina." *International Journal of American Linguistics* 40: 102–16.

1975. "Algonquian, Wiyot, and Yurok: proving a distant genetic relationship." In M. Dale Kinkade, Kenneth Hale, and Oswald Werner (eds.), *Linguistics and anthropology in honor of C. F. Voegelin*. Lisse: Peter de Ridder, pp. 249–62.

1988. "Stylistic dialects in Fox linguistic change." In Jacek Fisiak (ed.), *Historical dialectology*. Berlin: Mouton de Gruyter, pp. 193–209.

1994a. *Leonard Bloomfield's Fox lexicon. Critical edition*. Winnipeg: Algonquian and Iroquoian Linguistics. (= Memoir 12.)

1994b. "The west-to-east cline in Algonquian dialectology." In William Cowan (ed.), *Actes du Vingt-Cinquième Congrès des Algonquinistes*. Ottawa: Carleton University, pp. 187–211.

2007. "Phonetically unmotivated sound change." In Alan Nussbaum (ed.), *Verba Docenti: Studies... presented to Jay H. Jasanoff*. Ann Arbor: Beech Stave Press, pp. 115–30.

Goldsmith, John A. 1990. *Autosegmental and metrical phonology*. Oxford: Blackwell.

Gondicas, Dimitri, and Charles Issawi (eds.). 1999. *Ottoman Greeks in the age of nationalism*. Princeton: Darwin Press.

Goossens, Jan. 1977. "De tweede nederlandse auslautverscherping." *Tijdschrift voor Nederlandse Taal- en Letterkunde* 93: 3–23.

Gordon, Eric Valentine. 1957. *Introduction to Old Norse.* 2nd edn., revised by A. R. Taylor. Oxford: Clarendon Press.

Grant, Michael. 1990. *The fall of the Roman empire.* Revised edn. New York: Macmillan.

Greenberg, Joseph. 1963. *The languages of Africa. IJAL* Supplement 29(1), Part 2.

1987. *Language in the Americas.* Stanford University Press.

2000. *Indo-European and its closest relatives: the Eurasiatic language family.* Vol. I: *Grammar.* Stanford University Press.

Gress-Wright, Jonathan. 2010. "Opacity and transparency in phonological change." Dissertation, University of Pennsylvania.

Griffith, Aaron. 2011. "Old Irish pronouns: agreement affixes vs. clitic arguments." In Andrew Carnie (ed.), *Formal approaches to Celtic linguistics.* Cambridge: Cambridge Scholars Press, pp. 65–93.

Grimm, Jakob, and Wilhelm Grimm. 1860. *Deutsches Wörterbuch.* Berlin: Deutsche Akademie der Wissenschaften.

Gumperz, John J., and Robert Wilson. 1971. "Convergence and creolization: a case from the Indo-Aryan/Dravidian border in India." In Dell Hymes (ed.), *Pidginization and creolization of languages.* Cambridge University Press, pp. 151–67.

Habick, Timothy. 1991. "Burnouts versus rednecks: effects of group membership on the phonemic system." In Eckert (ed.), pp. 185–212.

Hackstein, Olav. 1995. *Untersuchungen zu den sigmatischen Präsensstammbildungen des Tocharischen.* Göttingen: Vandenhoeck & Ruprecht.

Haeri, Niloofar. 1997. *The sociolinguistic market of Cairo: gender, class, and education.* London: Kegan Paul International.

Haiman, John. 1991. "From V/2 to subject clitics: evidence from Northern Italian." In Elizabeth Closs Traugott and Bernd Heine (eds.), *Approaches to grammaticalization.* Vol. II: *Focus on types of grammatical markers.* Amsterdam: Benjamins, pp. 135–57.

Hakulinen, Lauri. 1961. *The structure and development of the Finnish language.* Tr. by John Atkinson. Bloomington: Indiana University.

Hale, Kenneth. 1973. "Deep-surface canonical disparities in relation to analysis and change: an Australian example." In Thomas Sebeok, Henry Hoenigswald, and Robert Longacre (eds.), *Current trends in linguistics.* Vol. 11: *Diachronic, areal, and typological linguistics.* The Hague. Mouton, pp. 401–58.

Hale, Mark. 1998. "Diachronic syntax." *Syntax* 1: 1–18.

2007. *Historical linguistics: theory and method.* Oxford: Blackwell.

Hall, Nancy. 2006. "Cross-linguistic patterns of vowel intrusion." *Phonology* 23: 387–429.

Halle, Morris. 1962. "Phonology in generative grammar." *Word* 18: 54–72.

1973. "Prolegomena to a theory of word formation." *Linguistic Inquiry* 4: 3–16.

1997. "Distributed morphology: impoverishment and fission." *MIT Working Papers in Linguistics* 30: 425–49.

Hamp, Eric P. 1984. "Notes on the Early Irish suffixed pronouns." *Études celtiques* 21: 139–40.

Harley, Heidi, and Rolf Noyer. 1999. "State-of-the-article: Distributed Morphology." *Glot International* 4/4: 3–9.

Harris, Alice C. 2008. "Reconstruction in syntax: reconstruction of patterns." In Ferraresi and Goldbach (eds.), pp. 73–95.

Harris, Alice C., and Lyle Campell. 1995. *Historical syntax in cross-linguistic perspective.* Cambridge University Press.

Haspelmath, Martin, *et al.* (eds.). 2005. *The world atlas of language structures.* Oxford: Oxford University Press. (Available online at http://wals.info/index.)

Helten, W. L. van. 1890. *Altostfriesische Grammatik.* Leeuwarden: Meijer.

Herold, Ruth. 1990. "Mechanisms of merger: the implementation and distribution of the low back merger in eastern Pennsylvania." Dissertation, University of Pennsylvania.

Hinds, John. 1986. *Japanese.* London: Croom Helm.

Hock, Hans Henrich. 1991. *Principles of historical linguistics.* 2nd edn. Berlin: Mouton de Gruyter.

Hockett, Charles. 1981. "The phonological history of Menominee." *Anthropological Linguistics* 23: 51–87.

Hoenigswald, Henry. 1960. *Language change and linguistic reconstruction.* University of Chicago Press.

Hoffmann, Karl, and Bernhard Forssman. 2004. *Avestische Laut- und Flexionslehre.* 2nd edn. Innsbruck: Institut für Sprachwissenschaft der Universität.

Hohepa, Patrick. 1967. *A profile generative grammar of Maori.* Baltimore: Linguistic Society of America.

Honti, László. 1975. *System der paradigmatischen Suffixmorpheme des wogulischen Dialektes an der Tawda.* The Hague: Mouton.

  1988. "Die ob-ugrischen Sprachen I: Die wogulische Sprache." In Denis Sinor (ed.), *The Uralic languages.* Leiden: Brill, pp. 147–71.

Householder, Fred, Kostas Kazazis, and Andreas Koutsoudas. 1964. *Reference grammar of literary Dhimotiki.* The Hague: Mouton.

Hyltenstam, Kenneth, & Loraine K. Obler (eds.). 1989. *Bilingualism across the lifespan.* Cambridge University Press.

Imedadze, Natela, and Kevin Tuite. 1992. "The acquisition of Georgian." In Slobin (ed.), pp. 39–109.

Jackendoff, Ray. 1975. "Morphological and semantic regularities in the lexicon." *Language* 51: 639–71.

Jacobs, Neil G. 2005. *Yiddish: a linguistic introduction.* Cambridge University Press.

Janse, Mark. 2009. "Greek–Turkish language contact in Asia Minor." *Études helléniques / Hellenic Studies* (Montréal) 17: 37–54.

Jasanoff, Jay. 1976. "Gr. ἄμφω, lat. *ambō* et le mot indo-européen pour 'l'un et l'autre'." *Bulletin de la Société de Linguistique de Paris* 71: 123–31.

  1987. "Some irregular imperatives in Tocharian." In Calvert Watkins (ed.), *Studies in memory of Warren Cowgill.* Berlin: de Gruyter, pp. 92–112.

  2009. "**-bhi, *-bhis, *-ōis*: following the trail of the PIE instrumental plural." In Jens Elmegård Rasmussen and Thomas Olander (eds.), *Internal reconstruction in Indo-European.* Copenhagen: Museum Tusculanum, pp. 137–49.

Jespersen, Otto. 1909. *A Modern English grammar on historical principles.* Part I: *Sounds and spellings.* Revised edn. London: Allen & Unwin.

  1914. —. Part II: *Syntax.* Vol. I. Heidelberg: Winter.

  1954. —. Part VI: *Morphology.* London: Allen & Unwin.

Johnson, Jacqueline S., and Elissa L. Newport. 1989. "Critical period effects in second language learning: the influence of maturational state on the acquisition of English as a second language." *Cognitive Psychology* 21: 60–99.

Johnson, Keith. 2003. *Acoustic and auditory phonetics*. 2nd edn. Oxford: Blackwell.

Jonasson, Jan. 1972. "Perceptual factors in phonology." In André Rigault and René Charbonneau (eds.), *Proceedings of the Seventh International Congress of Phonetic Sciences*. The Hague: Mouton, pp. 1127–30.

Jones, Charles (ed.). 1993. *Historical linguistics: problems and perspectives*. London: Longman.

Joseph, Brian D., and Richard D. Janda (eds.). 2003. *The handbook of historical linguistics*. Oxford: Blackwell.

Jutz, Leo. 1931. *Die alemannischen Mundarten*. Halle: Niemeyer.

Kálmán, Béla. 1964. *Vogul chrestomathy*. Bloomington: Indiana University.

Karatsareas, Petros. 2009. "The loss of grammatical gender in Cappadocian Greek." *Transactions of the Philological Society* 107: 196–230.

Kari, James. 1976. *Navajo verb prefix phonology*. New York: Garland.

Kari, James, and Ben Potter (eds.). 2010. *The Dene–Yeniseian connection* (= Anthropological Papers of the University of Alaska, New Series, vol. 5 [1–2].) Department of Anthropology, University of Alaska at Fairbanks.

Kayne, Richard S. 1991. "Romance clitics, verb movement and PRO." *Linguistic Inquiry* 22: 647–86.

1994. *The antisymmetry of syntax*. Cambridge, MA: MIT Press.

Keenan, Edward L. 2003. "An historical explanation of some binding theoretic facts in English." In John Moore and Maria Polinsky (eds.), *The nature of explanation in linguistic theory*. Stanford: CSLI, pp. 153–89.

Keller, Madeleine. 1985. "Latin *escit, escunt* a-t-il des correspondants?" *Revue de Philologie* 59: 27–44.

Keller, Rudolf. 1961. *German dialects*. Manchester University Press.

Kenstowicz, Michael. 1994. *Phonology in generative grammar*. Oxford: Blackwell.

Kessler, Brett. 2001. *The significance of word lists*. Stanford: CSLI.

Kessler, Brett, and Annukka Lehtonen. 2006. "Multilateral comparison and significance testing of the Indo-Uralic question." In Peter Forster and Colin Renfrew (eds.), *Phylogenetic methods and the prehistory of languages*. Cambridge: McDonald Institute, pp. 33–42.

King, Andrew P., and Meredith J. West. 1977. "Species identification in the North American cowbird: appropriate responses to abnormal song." *Science* 195: 1002–4.

King, Robert D. 1967. "Functional load and sound change." *Language* 43: 831–52.

King, Ruth. 2000. *The lexical basis of grammatical borrowing*. Amsterdam: Benjamins.

Kiparsky, Paul. 1982a. *Explanation in phonology*. Dordrecht: Foris.

1982b. "From cyclic phonology to lexical phonology." In Harry van der Hulst and Norval Smith (eds.), *The structure of phonological representations*, vol. I. Dordrecht: Foris, pp. 131–75.

1982c. "Productivity in phonology." In Kiparsky 1982a, pp. 165–73.

Kiparsky, Valentin. 1979. *Russian historical grammar*. Revised edn., translated by J. I. Press. Ann Arbor: Ardis.

Klatt, Dennis H. 1989. "Review of selected models of speech perception." In William Marslen-Wilson (ed.), *Lexical representation and process.* Cambridge, MA: MIT Press, pp. 169–226.

Kleiner, Yuri. 2006. Review of Jacobs 2005. *Diachronica* 23: 417–25.

Kluge, Friedrich. 1995. *Etymologisches Wörterbuch der deutschen Sprache.* 23rd edn., revised by Elmar Seebold. Berlin: de Gruyter.

Kökeritz, Helge. 1953. *Shakespeare's pronunciation.* New Haven: Yale University Press.

König, Werner. 2001. *dtv-Atlas Deutsche Sprache.* 13th edn. Munich: Deutscher Taschenbuch Verlag.

Kranzmayer, Eberhard. 1956. *Historische Lautgeographie des gesamtbairischen Dialektraumes.* Vienna: Böhlau.

Krause, Wolfgang. 1971. *Die Sprache der urnordischen Runeninschriften.* Heidelberg: Winter.

Krauss, Michael. 1969. "On the classification [*sic; read* classifiers] in the Athapaskan, Eyak, and Tlingit verb." *Supplement to IJAL* 35(4): 49–83.

Kroch, Anthony S. 1989. "Reflexes of grammar in patterns of language change." *Language Variation and Change* 1: 199–244.

    1994. "Morphosyntactic variation." In Katharine Beals *et al.* (eds.), *Papers from the 30th Regional Meeting of the Chicago Linguistic Society: Parasession on Variation and Linguistic Theory.* Chicago Linguistic Society, pp.180–201.

    1996. "Dialect and style in the speech of upper class Philadelphia." In Gregory Guy *et al.* (eds.), *Towards a social science of language.* Vol. I: *Variation and change in language and society.* Amsterdam: Benjamins, pp. 23–45.

    2001. "Syntactic change." In Mark Baltin and Chris Collins (eds.), *The handbook of contemporary syntactic theory.* Oxford: Blackwell, pp. 699–729.

Kroch, Anthony, Ann Taylor, and Don Ringe. 2000. "The Middle English verb-second constraint: a case study in language contact and language change." In Susan Herring, Pieter van Reenen, and Lele Schøsler (eds.), *Textual parameters in older languages.* Amsterdam: Benjamins, pp. 353–91.

Kroodsma, Donald E. 1977. "A re-evaluation of song development in the song sparrow." *Animal Behavior* 25: 390–9.

    1982. "Learning and the ontogeny of sound signals in birds." In Kroodsma, Miller, and Ouellet (eds.), vol. II, pp. 1–23.

Kroodsma, Donald E., Edward H. Miller, and Henri Ouellet (eds.). 1982. *Acoustic communication in birds.* New York: Academic Press.

Kümmel, Martin Joachim. 2007. *Konsonantenwandel. Bausteine zu einer Typologie des Lautwandels und ihre Konsequenzen für vergleichende Rekonstruktion.* Wiesbaden: Reichert.

Kuryłowicz, Jerzy. 1949. "La nature des procès dits 'analogiques'." *Acta Linguistica Hafniensia* 5: 15–37.

Laanest, Arvo. 1982. *Einführung in die ostseefinnischen Sprachen.* Translated by Hans-Hermann Bartens. Hamburg: Buske.

Labov, William. 1963. "The social motivation of a sound change." *Word* 19: 273–309.

    1966. *The social stratification of English in New York City.* Washington, DC: Center for Applied Linguistics.

    1972. "Some principles of linguistic methodology." *Language in Society* 1: 97–120.

    1994. *Principles of linguistic change.* Vol. I: *Internal factors.* Oxford: Blackwell.

2001. *Priniciples of linguistic change*. Vol. II: *Social factors*. Oxford: Blackwell.

2007. "Transmission and diffusion." *Language* 83: 344–87.

Labov, William, Sharon Ash, and Charles Boberg. 2006. *Atlas of North American English*. Berlin: Mouton de Gruyter.

Labov, William, Mark Karen, and Corey Miller. 1991. "Near-mergers and the suspension of phonemic contrast." *Language Variation and Change* 3: 33–74.

Labov, William, Malcah Yaeger, and Richard Steiner. 1972. *A quantitative study of sound change in progress*. Philadelphia: National Science Foundation.

Ladefoged, Peter. 1962. *Elements of acoustic phonetics*. University of Chicago Press.

1975. *A course in phonetics*. New York: Harcourt Brace Jovanovich.

Ladefoged, Peter, and Ian Maddieson. 1996. *The sounds of the world's languages*. Oxford: Blackwell.

Landau, Barbara, and Lila Gleitman. 1985. *Language and experience: evidence from the blind child*. Cambridge, MA: Harvard University Press.

Lanza, Elizabeth. 2000. "Concluding remarks: language contact – a dilemma for the bilingual child or for the linguist?" In Susanne Döpke (ed.), *Cross-linguistic structures in simultaneous bilingualism*. Amsterdam: Benjamins, pp. 227–45.

Laughlin, Robert M. 1975. *The great Tzotzil dictionary of San Lorenzo Zinacantán*. Washington: Smithsonian Institution Press.

Leer, Jeff. 1990. "Tlingit: a portmanteau language family?" In Philip Baldi (ed.), *Linguistic change and reconstruction methodology*. Berlin: Mouton de Gruyter, pp. 73–98.

2010. "The palatal series in Athabaskan-Eyak-Tlingit, with an overview of the basic sound correspondences." In Kari and Potter (eds.), pp. 168–93.

Lefebvre, Claire. 1984. "Grammaires en contact: définition et perspectives de recherche." *Revue Québécoise de Linguistique* 14: 11–47.

Lehmann, Winfred. 1974. *Proto-Indo-European syntax*. Austin: University of Texas Press.

Lenneberg, Eric H. 1967. *Biological foundations of language*. New York: Wiley & Sons.

Lennig, Matthew. 1978. "Acoustic measurement of linguistic change: the modern Paris vowel system." Dissertation, University of Pennsylvania.

Lessen Kloeke, Wus van. 1982. *Deutsche Phonologie und Morphologie: Merkmale und Markiertheit*. Tübingen: Niemeyer.

Lessiak, Primus. 1933. *Beiträge zur Geschichte des deutschen Konsonantismus*. Brünn: Rohrer.

Liberman, Alvin M., and Ignatius G. Mattingly. 1985. "The motor theory of speech perception revised." *Cognition* 21: 1–36.

Lightfoot, David W. 1999. *The development of language: acquistion, change, and evolution*. Oxford: Blackwell.

Longobardi, Giuseppe. 2001. "Formal syntax, diachronic minimalism, and etymology: the history of French *chez*." *Linguistic Inquiry* 32: 275–302.

2003. "Methods in parametric linguistics and cognitive history." *Language Variation Yearbook* 3: 101–38.

Longobardi, Giuseppe, and Cristina Guardiano. 2009. "Evidence for syntax as a signal of historical relatedness." *Lingua* 119: 1679–1706.

Luick, Karl. 1914–40. *Historische Grammatik der englischen Sprache*. Vol. I. Leipzig: Tauchnitz.

Lust, Barbara. 1999. "Universal grammar: the strong continuity hypothesis in first language acquisition." In Ritchie and Bhatia (eds.), pp. 111–55.

Maddieson, Ian. 1984. *Patterns of sounds*. Cambridge University Press.

Mallory, J. P., and Douglas Q. Adams. 2006. *The Oxford introduction to Proto-Indo-European and the Proto-Indo-European world*. Oxford University Press.

Malmberg, Bertil. 1955. "The phonetic basis for syllable division." *Studia linguistica* 9: 80–7.

Mańczak, Witold. 1958. "Tendences générales des changements analogiques." *Lingua* 7: 298–325, 387–420.

Martinet, André. 1955. *Économie des changements phonétiques*. Bern: Francke.

Matisoff, James. 1990. "On megalocomparison." *Language* 66: 106–20.

Matras, Yaron. 1998. "Utterance modifiers and universals of grammatical borrowing." *Linguistics* 36: 281–331.

Mayrhofer, Manfred. 1986. "Lautlehre (segmentale Phonologie des Indogermanischen)." In Cowgill and Mayrhofer 1986, pp. 73–216.

McCarthy, John. 1988. "Feature geometry and dependency: a review." *Phonetica* 43: 84–108.

McCone, Kim. 1985. "Varia II. 2. OIr. *olc, luch-* and IE *w[̥kwos, *lúkwos* 'wolf'." *Ériu* 36: 171–6.

McMahon, April. 2000. *Change, chance, and optimality*. Oxford University Press.

Meid, Wolfgang. 1967. *Germanische Sprachwissenschaft*. Vol. III: *Wortbildungslehre*. Berlin: de Gruyter.

Meisel, Jürgen M. 1989. "Early differentiation of languages in bilingual children." In Hyltenstam and Obler (eds.), pp. 13–40.

Meiser, Gerhard. 1986. *Lautgeschichte der umbrischen Sprache*. Innsbruck: Institut für Sprachwissenschaft der Universität.

Melchert, H. Craig. 1994. *Anatolian historical phonology*. Amsterdam: Rodopi.

1997. "Traces of a PIE aspectual contrast in Anatolian?" *Incontri Linguistici* 20: 83–92.

Melchert, H. Craig, and Norbert Oettinger. 2009. "Ablativ und Instrumental im Hethitischen und Indogermanischen." *Incontri Linguistici* 32: 53–73.

Meyer-Lübke, Wilhelm. 1895. *Grammaire des langues romanes*. Vol. II: *Morphologie*. Translated by Auguste and Georges Doutrepont. Paris: Welter.

1935. *Romanisches etymologisches Wörterbuch*. 3rd edn. Heidelberg: Winter.

Miller, D. Gary. 1975. "Indo-European: VSO, SOV, SVO or all three?" *Lingua* 37: 31–52.

2010. *Language change and linguistic theory*. Oxford University Press.

Mills, Anne E. 1985. "The acquisition of German." In Slobin (ed.), pp. 141–254.

Milroy, James, and John Harris. 1980. "When is a merger not a merger? The MEAT/MATE problem in a present-day English vernacular." *English World Wide* 1: 199–210.

Mitchell, Bruce. 1985. *Old English syntax*. Vol. I. Oxford: Clarendon Press.

Mithun, Marianne. 1989. "The acquisition of polysynthesis." *Journal of Child Language* 16: 285–312.

Mondon, Jean-François. 2009. "The nature of homophony and its effects on diachrony and synchrony." Dissertation, University of Pennsylvania.

Moore, Samuel. 1927. "Loss of final *n* in inflectional syllables of Middle English." *Language* 3: 232–59.

1957. *Historical outlines of English sounds and inflections*. 2nd edn., revised by Albert Marckwardt. Ann Arbor: Wahr.

Moore, Samuel, and Thomas A. Knott. 1955. *The elements of Old English*. Ann Arbor: Wahr.

Morse-Gagné, Elise E. 2003. "Viking pronouns in England: charting the course of THEY, THEIR, and THEM." Dissertation, University of Pennsylvania.

Mossé, Fernand. 1952. *A handbook of Middle English*. Translated by James Walker. Baltimore: Johns Hopkins University Press.

Mundinger, Paul C. 1982. "Microgeographic and macrogeographic variation in the acquired vocalizations of birds." In Kroodsma, Miller, and Ouellet (eds.), vol. II, pp. 147–208.

Munkácsi, Bernát, and Béla Kálmán. 1986. *Wogulisches Wörterbuch*. Budapest: Akadémiai Kiadó.

Murphy, Lawrence. 1968. "Sosva Vogul grammar." Dissertation, Indiana University.

Nakhleh, Luay, Don Ringe, and Tandy Warnow. 2005a. "Perfect phylogenetic networks: a new methodology for reconstructing the evolutionary history of natural languages." *Language* 81: 382–420.

Nakhleh, Luay, Tandy Warnow, Don Ringe, and Steven N. Evans. 2005b. "A comparison of phylogenetic reconstruction methods on an Indo-European dataset." *Transactions of the Philological Society* 103: 171–92.

Nater, H. F. 1984. *The Bella Coola language*. Ottawa: National Museums of Canada.

Newton, Glenda. 2008. "Motivating the loss of V-to-C movement in Old Irish." Paper presented at the Tenth Diachronic Generative Syntax Conference, Cornell University.

Ní Chasaide, Ailbhe. 1989. "Sonorization and spirantization: a single phonetic process?" In Tamás Szende (ed.), *Proceedings of the Speech Research '89 International Conference*. Budapest: Linguistics Institute of the Hungarian Academy of Sciences, pp. 108–11.

Nichols, Johanna. 1990. "Linguistic diversity and the first settlement of the New World." *Language* 66: 475–521.

1996. "The comparative method as heuristic." In Mark Durie and Malcolm Ross (eds.), *The comparative method reviewed*. Oxford University Press, pp. 39–71.

2010. "Proving Dene – Yeniseian genealogical relatedness." In Kari and Potter (eds.), pp. 299–309.

Nichols, Johanna, and Tandy Warnow. 2008. "Tutorial on computational linguistic phylogeny." *Language and Linguistic Compass* 2: 760–820.

Noreen, Adolf. 1923. *Altnordische Grammatik*. Vol. I: *Altisländische und altnorwegische Grammatik*. 4th edn. Halle: Niemeyer.

Noyer, R. Rolf. 1997. *Features, positions, and affixes in autonomous morphological structure*. New York: Garland.

Nussbaum, Alan. 1975. "-ī- in Latin denominative derivation." In Calvert Watkins (ed.), *Indo-European Studies II*. Cambridge, MA: Harvard Department of Linguistics, pp. 116–61.

Odlin, Terence. 1997. "Bilingualism and substrate influence: a look at clefts and reflexives." In Jeffrey Kallen (ed.), *Focus on Ireland*. Amsterdam: Benjamins, pp. 35–50.

Ohala, John. 1981. "The listener as a source of sound change." In Carrie Masek, Roberta Hendrick, and Mary Frances Miller (eds.), *Papers from the parasession on language and behavior*. Chicago Linguistic Society, pp. 178–203.

1993. "The phonetics of sound change." In Jones (ed.), pp. 237–78.

2003. "Phonetics and historical phonology." In Joseph and Janda (eds.), pp. 669–86.

Osthoff, Hermann, and Karl Brugmann. 1878. "Vorwort." *Morphologische Untersuchungen auf dem Gebiete der indogermanischen Sprachen* 1: iii–xx.

Oswalt, Robert. 1970. "The detection of remote linguistic relationships." *Computer Studies in the Humanities and Verbal Behavior* 3: 117–29.

1991. "A method for assessing distant linguistic relationships." In Sydney Lamb and E. Douglas Mitchell (eds.), *Sprung from some common source*. Stanford University Press, pp. 389–404.

Paul, Hermann. 1960. *Prinzipien der Sprachgeschichte*. 6th edn., unaltered from the 5th edn. of 1920. Tübingen: Niemeyer.

Paul, Hermann, Hugo Moser, and Ingeborg Schröbler. 1969. *Mittelhochdeutsche Grammatik*. 24th edn. Halle: Niemeyer.

Perlmutter, David M. 1991. "The language of the deaf." *The New York Review*, March 28, pp. 65–72.

Peters, F. E. 1970. *The harvest of Hellenism*. New York: Simon & Schuster.

Peters, Martin. 1991. "Ein tocharisches Auslautproblem." *Die Sprache* 34: 242–4.

Pinker, Steven. 1989. *Learnability and cognition: the acquisition of argument structure*. Cambridge, MA: MIT Press.

1994. *The language instinct*. New York: William Morrow.

Pinkster, Harm. 1990. *Latin syntax and semantics*. London: Routledge.

Pintzuk, Susan. 2003. "Variationist approaches to syntactic change." In Joseph and Janda (eds.), pp. 509–28.

Pintzuk, Susan, and Anthony S. Kroch. 1989. "The rightward movement of complements and adjuncts in Old English." *Language Variation and Change* 1: 115–43.

Poletto, Cecilia. 1995. "The diachronic development of subject clitics in North Eastern Italian dialects." In Adrian Battye and Ian Roberts (eds.), *Clause structure and language change*. Oxford University Press, pp. 295–324.

Poplack, Shana, and Marjory Meechan. 1995. "Patterns of language mixture: nominal structure in Wolof-French and Fongbe-French bilingual discourse." In Lesley Milroy and Pieter Muysken (eds.), *One speaker, two languages: cross-disciplinary perspectives on code-switching*. Cambridge University Press, pp. 199–232.

Poplack, Shana, Susan Wheeler, and Anneli Westwood. 1989. "Distinguishing language contact phenomena: evidence from Finnish-English bilingualism." In Hyltenstam and Obler (eds.), pp. 132–54.

Poser, William J. 1992. "The Salinan and Yurumanguí data in *Language in the Americas*." *International Journal of American Linguistics* 58: 202–29.

Prince, Ellen F., and Pintzuk, Susan. 2000. "Bilingual code-switching and the open/closed class distinction." *University of Pennsylvania Working Papers in Linguistics* 6(3): 237–57.

Quin, E. G. 1975. *Old-Irish workbook*. Dublin: Royal Irish Academy.

Ramsey, S. Robert. 1987. *The languages of China*. Princeton University Press.

Richards, Julian D. 2000. *Viking age England*. Revised edn. Stroud: Tempus.

Ridouane, Rachid. 2008. "Syllables without vowels: phonetic and phonological evidence from Tashlhiyt Berber." *Phonology* 25: 321–59.

Ringe, Don. 1995. "Nominative–accusative syncretism and syntactic case." *University of Pennsylvania Working Papers in Linguistics* 2: 45–81.

1996a. "The mathematics of 'Amerind'." *Diachronica* 13: 135–54.

1996b. *On the chronology of sound changes in Tocharian.* Vol. I. New Haven: American Oriental Society.

1999. "How hard is it to match CVC roots?" *Transactions of the Philological Society* 97: 213–44.

2002. Review of Greenberg 2000. *Journal of Linguistics* 38: 415–20.

2006. *From Proto-Indo-European to Proto-Germanic.* Vol. I of *A linguistic history of English.* Oxford University Press.

Ringe, Don, Tandy Warnow, and Ann Taylor. 2002. "Indo-European and computational cladistics." *Transactions of the Philological Society* 100: 59–129.

Risch, Ernst. 1974. *Wortbildung der homerischen Sprache.* 2nd edn. Berlin: de Gruyter.

Ritchie, William C., and Tej K. Bhatia (eds.). 1996. *Handbook of second language acquisition.* San Diego: Academic Press.

1999. *Handbook of child language acquisition.* San Diego: Academic Press.

Rix, Helmut. 1992. "Zur Entstehung des lateinischen Perfektparadigmas." In Oswald Panagl and Thomas Krisch (eds.), *Latein und Indogermanisch.* Innsbruck: Institut für Sprachwissenschaft der Universität, pp. 221–40.

Rizzi, Luigi. 1997. "The fine structure of the left periphery." In Liliane Haegeman (ed.), *Elements of grammar: handbook in generative syntax.* Dordrecht: Kluwer, pp. 281–337.

Roberts, Ian. 2007. *Diachronic syntax.* Oxford University Press.

Roeper, Thomas. 1995. "Comments on Bickerton's paper." In Wekker (ed.), pp. 45–9.

Ross, Malcolm. 1997. "Social networks and kinds of speech-community event." In Roger Blench and Matthew Spriggs (eds.), *Archaeology and language.* Vol. I: *Theoretical and methodological orientations.* London: Routledge, pp. 209–61.

1998. "Sequencing and dating linguistic events in Oceania: the linguistics / archaeology interface." In Roger Blench and Matthew Spriggs (eds.), *Archaeology and language.* Vol. II: *Archaeological data and linguistic hypotheses.* London: Routledge, pp. 141–73.

Sammallahti, Pekka. 1988. "Historical phonology of the Uralic languages." In Denis Sinor (ed.), *The Uralic languages.* Leiden: Brill, pp. 478–554.

Sands, Bonny. 2009a. "Africa's linguistic diversity." *Language and Linguistics Compass* 3: 559–80.

2009b. "Teaching and learning guide for: Africa's linguistic diversity." *Language and Linguistics Compass* 3: 1357–65.

Sankoff, Gillian. 2002. "Linguistic outcomes of language contact." In J. K. Chambers, Peter Trudgill, and Natalie Schilling-Estes (eds.), *The handbook of language variation and change.* Oxford: Blackwell, pp. 638–68.

Santorini, Beatrice. 1993. "The rate of phrase structure change in the history of Yiddish." *Language Variation and Change* 5: 257–83.

Schachter, Jacquelyn. 1996. "Maturation and the issue of universal grammar in second language acquisition." In Ritchie and Bhatia (eds.), pp. 159–93.

Schein, Barry, and Donca Steriade. 1986. "On geminates." *Linguistic Inquiry* 17: 691–744.

Schrijver, Peter. 1994. "The Celtic adverbs for 'against' and 'with' and the early apocope of *-i.*" *Ériu* 45: 151–89.

Schumacher, Stefan. 2004. *Die keltischen Primärverben: ein vergleichendes, etymologisches und morphologisches Lexikon.* Innsbruck: Institut für Sprachwissenschaft der Universität.

Seebold, Elmar. 1966. "Die ae. schwundstufigen Präsentien (Aoristpräsentien) der *ei*-Reihe." *Anglia* 84: 1–26.

  1970. *Vergleichendes und etymologisches Wörterbuch der germanischen starken Verben.* The Hague: Mouton.

Seidenberg, M., and Laura Petitto. 1979. "Signing behavior in apes: a critical review." *Cognition* 7: 177–215.

Siddiqi, Daniel. 2009. *Syntax within the word.* Amsterdam: Benjamins.

Siebert, Frank. 1967. "The original home of the Proto-Algonquian people." In *Contributions to Anthropology: Linguistics I (Algonquian).* Ottawa: National Museum of Canada, pp. 13–47.

Sihler, Andrew. 1995. *New comparative grammar of Greek and Latin.* Oxford University Press.

Sims-Williams, Patrick. 1984. "The double system of verbal inflexion in Old Irish." *Transactions of the Philological Society* 82: 138–201.

Singleton, Jenny L., and Elissa L. Newport. 2004. "When learners surpass their models: the acquisition of American Sign Language from inconsistent input." *Cognitive Psychology* 49: 370–407.

Slobin, Dan Isaac (ed.). 1985. *The crosslinguistic study of language acquisition.* Vol. I: *The data.* Hillsdale, NJ: Lawrence Erlbaum.

  (ed.). 1992. *The crosslinguistic study of language acquisition.* Vol. III. Hillsdale, NJ: Lawrence Erlbaum.

Smyth, Herbert Weir. 1956. *Greek grammar.* Revised edn. Cambridge, MA: Harvard University Press.

Sommer, Ferdinand. 1948. *Handbuch der lateinischen Laut- und Formenlehre.* 2nd and 3rd edns. Heidelberg: Winter.

Sommerstein, Alan. 1973. *The sound pattern of Ancient Greek* (= Publications of the Philological Society 23). Oxford: Blackwell.

Spencer, Andrew. 1991. *Morphological theory.* Oxford: Blackwell.

Speyer, Augustin. 2008. "Topicalization and clash avoidance: on the interaction of prosody and syntax in English with a few spotlights on German." Dissertation, University of Pennsylvania.

Steinitz, Wolfgang. 1955. *Geschichte des wogulischen Vokalismus.* Berlin: Akademie-Verlag.

Steriade, Donca. 1982. "Greek prosodies and the nature of syllabification." Dissertation, MIT.

Stetson, R. H. 1951. *Motor phonetics.* Amsterdam: North-Holland.

Stiles, Patrick. 1985. "The fate of the numeral '4' in Germanic (1)." *North-Western European Language Evolution* 6: 81–104.

Stockall, Linnaea, and Alec Marantz. 2006. "A single route, full decomposition model of morphological complexity." *The Mental Lexicon* 1: 85–123.

Streitberg, Wilhelm. 1920. *Gotisches Elementarbuch*. Heidelberg: Winter.

Studdert-Kennedy, Michael, and Louis Goldstein. 2003. "Launching language: the gestural origin of discrete infinity." In Morten Christiansen and Simon Kirby (eds.), *Language evolution*. Oxford University Press, pp. 235–54.

Sturtevant, Edgar. 1940. *The pronunciation of Greek and Latin*. Philadelphia: Linguistic Society of America.

Surendran, Dinoj, and Partha Niyogi. 2006. "Quantifying the functional load of phonemic oppositions, distinctive features, and suprasegmentals." In Ole Nedergaard Thomsen (ed.), *Competing models of linguistic change: evolution and beyond*. Amsterdam: Benjamins, pp. 43–58.

Taylor, Ann. 1994. "The change from SOV to SVO in Ancient Greek." *Language Variation and Change* 6: 1–37.

    1996. "A prosodic account of clitic position in Ancient Greek." In Aaron L. Halpern and Arnold M. Zwicky (eds.), *Approaching second*. Stanford: Center for the Study of Language and Information, pp. 477–503.

Terrace, Herbert S., Laura A. Petitto, R. J. Sanders, and Thomas G. Bever. 1980. "On the grammatical capacity of apes." In Keith E. Nelson (ed.), *Children's language*, vol. II. New York: Gardner, pp. 371–495.

Thomas, Alan R. 1997. "The Welshness of Welsh English: a survey paper." In Hildegard L. C. Tristram (ed.), *The Celtic Englishes*. Heidelberg: Winter, pp. 55–85.

Thomason, Sarah Grey, and Terrence Kaufman. 1988. *Language contact, creolization, and genetic linguistics*. Berkeley: University of California Press.

Þórhallsdóttir, Guðrún. 1993. "The development of intervocalic *j in Proto-Germanic." Dissertation, Cornell University.

Threatte, Leslie. 1996. *The grammar of Attic inscriptions*. Vol. II: *Morphology*. Berlin: de Gruyter.

Thurneysen, Rudolf. 1946. *A grammar of Old Irish*. Revised and translated by D. A. Binchy and Osborn Bergin. Dublin: Institute for Advanced Studies.

Trager, George L. 1930. "The pronunciation of 'short *a*' in American Standard English." *American Speech* 5: 396–400.

    1940. "One phonemic entity becomes two: the case of 'short a'." *American Speech* 15: 255–8.

Trask, R. Lawrence. 1997. *The history of Basque*. London: Routledge.

Trudgill, Peter. 1983. *On dialect: social and geographical perspectives*. New York University Press.

Vaan, Michiel de. 2008. *Etymological dictionary of Latin and the other Italic languages*. Leiden: Brill.

Vajda, Edward. 2010. "A Siberian link with Na-Dene languages." In Kari and Potter (eds.), pp. 33–99.

Veselinović, Elvira. 2003. *Suppletion im irischen Verb*. Hamburg: Dr. Kovač.

Villar, Francisco. 1997. "The Celtiberian language." *Zeitschrift für celtische Philologie* 49–50: 898–949.

Wackernagel, Jacob. 1920. *Vorlesungen über Syntax, mit besonderer Berücksichtigung von Griechisch, Lateinisch und Deutsch*. Basel: E. Birkhäuser.

Walde, Alois, and J. B. Hofmann. 1938. *Lateinisches etymologisches Wörterbuch*. 3rd edn. Heidelberg: Winter.

Wang, William S.-Y., and Chinfa Lien. 1993. "Bidirectional diffusion in sound change." In Jones (ed.), pp. 345–400.

Wanner, Georg. 1941. *Die Mundarten des Kantons Schaffhausen*. Frauenfeld: Huber.

Wanner, Hans, *et al.* 1973. *Schweizerisches Idiotikon: Wörterbuch der schweizerdeutschen Sprache*. Vol. XIII. Frauenfeld: Huber.

Warner, Anthony. 1997. "The structure of parametric change and V-movement in the history of English." In Ans van Kemenade and Nigel Vincent (eds.), *Parameters of morphosyntactic change*. Cambridge University Press, pp. 380–93.

    2006. "Variation and the interpretation of change in periphrastic *do*." In Ans van Kemenade and Bettelou Los (eds.), *The handbook of the history of English*. Oxford: Blackwell, pp. 45–67.

Watkins, Calvert. 1963. "Preliminaries to a historical and comparative analysis of the syntax of the Old Irish verb." *Celtica* 6: 1–49.

    1976. "Towards Proto-Indo-European syntax." In Sanford B. Steever, Carol A. Walker, and Salikoko S. Mufwene (eds.), *Papers from the Parasession on Diachronic Syntax*. Chicago Linguistic Society, pp. 305–26.

Wegener, Heide. 1999. "Die Pluralbildung im Deutschen: ein Versuch im Rahmen der Optimalitätstheorie." *Linguistik online* 4(3). (Accessible at www.linguistik-online.de/3_99/wegener.html.)

Weinreich, Uriel, William Labov, and Marvin Herzog. 1968. "A theory of language change." In Winfred Lehmann and Yakov Malkiel (eds.), *Directions for historical linguistics*. Austin, TX: University of Texas Press, pp. 97–195.

Wekker, Herman (ed.). 1995. *Creole languages and language acquisition*. Berlin: Mouton de Gruyter.

Wełna, Jerzy. 1980. "On gender change in linguistic borrowing (Old English)." In Jacek Fisiak (ed.), *Historical morphology*. The Hague: Mouton, pp. 399–420.

Wexler, Kenneth. 1999. "Maturation and growth of grammar." In Ritchie and Bhatia (eds.), pp. 55–109.

Williams, Edwin. 1981. "On the notions 'lexically related' and 'head of a word'." *Linguistic Inquiry* 12: 245–74.

Wonderly, William L. 1946. "Phonemic acculturation in Zoque." *International Journal of American linguistics* 12: 92–5.

Wright, Joseph. 1907. *Historical German grammar*. Vol. I. Oxford University Press.

    1910. *Grammar of the Gothic language*. Oxford: Clarendon Press.

Xu, Fei, and Steven Pinker. 1995. "Weird past tense forms." *Journal of Child Language* 22: 531–56.

Yang, Charles. 2002. *Knowledge and learning in natural language*. Oxford University Press.

    2006. *The infinite gift*. New York: Scribner.

Zerdin, Jason. 2000. "Studies in the Ancient Greek verbs in *-skō*." Dissertation, University of Oxford.

Zribi-Hertz, Anne. 1984. "Prépositions orphelines et pronoms nuls." *Recherches linguistiques* 12: 46–91.

General index

Index of languages and families

Names for earlier stages of languages (Old English, etc.) and for reconstructed languages (Proto-Algonkian, etc.) will be found under the distinctive part of the name.

27189028R00182

Printed in Great Britain
by Amazon